Perception, Causation, and Objectivity

Consciousness and Self-Consciousness

This series arises from the activities of the Consciousness and Self-Consciousness Research Centre at Warwick University. The present volume is one of three interdisciplinary volumes growing out of an AHRC Project hosted by the Centre between 2004 and 2008, on 'Causal Understanding: Empirical and Theoretical Foundations for a New Approach'. Much of the thought behind the project on causal understanding was informed by the idea that making progress on questions regarding consciousness and self-consciousness requires, amongst other things, getting clearer about the extent to which causal understanding is implicated in our awareness of and interaction with our environment, as well as in our grasp of our own place in it. This in turn, however, also requires getting clearer about what exactly causal understanding consists in, and what its distinctive features are. The three volumes explore these issues by integrating philosophical work with experimental and theoretical work in developmental psychology, cognitive psychology, and neuropsychology.

Also published in the series:

Time and Memory, edited by Christoph Hoerl and Teresa McCormack

Agency and Self-Awareness, edited by Johannes Roessler and Naomi Eilan

Joint Attention: Communication and Other Minds, edited by Naomi Eilan, Christoph Hoerl, Teresa McCormack, and Johannes Roessler

Perception, Causation, and Objectivity, edited by Johannes Roessler, Hemdat Lerman, and Naomi Eilan

Understanding Counterfactuals, Understanding Causation, edited by Christoph Hoerl, Teresa McCormack, and Sarah Beck

Tool Use and Causal Cognition, edited by Christoph Hoerl, Teresa McCormack, and Stephen Butterfill

Perception, Causation, and Objectivity

EDITED BY
Johannes Roessler
Hemdat Lerman
and Naomi Eilan

OXFORD
UNIVERSITY PRESS

OXFORD
UNIVERSITY PRESS

Great Clarendon Street, Oxford OX2 6DP

Oxford University Press is a department of the University of Oxford.
It furthers the University's objective of excellence in research, scholarship,
and education by publishing worldwide in

Oxford New York

Auckland Cape Town Dar es Salaam Hong Kong Karachi
Kuala Lumpur Madrid Melbourne Mexico City Nairobi
New Delhi Shanghai Taipei Toronto

With offices in

Argentina Austria Brazil Chile Czech Republic France Greece
Guatemala Hungary Italy Japan Poland Portugal Singapore
South Korea Switzerland Thailand Turkey Ukraine Vietnam

Oxford is a registered trade mark of Oxford University Press
in the UK and in certain other countries

Published in the United States
by Oxford University Press Inc., New York

© The several contributors 2011

British Library Cataloguing in Publication Data

Data available

Library of Congress Cataloging in Publication Data

Data available

Typeset by SPI Publisher Services, Pondicherry, India
Printed in Great Britain
on acid-free paper by
MPG Books Group, Bodmin and King's Lynn

ISBN 978-0-19-969204-0 (Hbk)
ISBN 978-0-19-969205-7 (Pbk)

1 3 5 7 9 10 8 6 4 2

Contents

List of Contributors   vii

1. Introduction: Perception, Causation, and Objectivity   1
    Johannes Roessler

2. Tackling Berkeley's Puzzle   18
    Quassim Cassam

3. Relational vs Kantian Responses to Berkeley's Puzzle   35
    John Campbell

4. Experiential Objectivity   51
    Naomi Eilan

5. Realism and Explanation in Perception   68
    Bill Brewer

6. Epistemic Humility and Causal Structuralism   82
    James Van Cleve

7. Seeing What Is So   92
    Barry Stroud

8. Causation in Commonsense Realism   103
    Johannes Roessler

9. Perceptual Concepts as Non-causal Concepts   121
    Paul Snowdon

10. Perception and the Ontology of Causation   139
    Helen Steward

11. Vision and Causal Understanding   161
    William Child

12. The Perception of Absence, Space, and Time   181
    Matthew Soteriou

13. Perception, Causal Understanding, and Locality   207
    Christoph Hoerl

14. Causal Perception and Causal Cognition   229
    James Woodward

15. Children's Understanding of Perceptual Appearances   264
    Matthew Nudds

16. Perspective-Taking and its Foundation in Joint Attention   286
    Henrike Moll and Andrew N. Meltzoff

17. A Two-Systems Theory of Social Cognition: Engagement
    and Theory of Mind   305
    Martin Doherty

18. Development of Understanding of the Causal Connection
    between Perceptual Access and Knowledge State   324
    Elizabeth J. Robinson

19. Social and Physical Reasoning in Human-reared Chimpanzees:
    Preliminary Studies   342
    Jennifer Vonk and Daniel J. Povinelli

    Index   369

Contributors

BILL BREWER, University of Warwick

JOHN CAMPBELL, University of California, Berkeley

QUASSIM CASSAM, University of Warwick

WILLIAM CHILD, University College, Oxford

JAMES VAN CLEVE, University of Southern California

MARTIN DOHERTY, University of Stirling

NAOMI EILAN, University of Warwick

CHRISTOPH HOERL, University of Warwick

HEMDAT LERMAN, University of Warwick

ANDREW N. MELTZOFF, University of Washington

HENRIKE MOLL, Max Planck Institute for Evolutionary Anthropology, Leipzig

MATTHEW NUDDS, University of Edinburgh

DANIEL J. POVINELLI, University of Louisiana

ELIZABETH J. ROBINSON, University of Warwick

JOHANNES ROESSLER, University of Warwick

PAUL SNOWDON, University College London

MATTHEW SOTERIOU, University of Warwick

HELEN STEWARD, University of Leeds

BARRY STROUD, University of California, Berkeley

JENNIFER VONK, University of Southern Mississippi

JAMES WOODWARD, University of Pittsburgh

1

Introduction
Perception, Causation, and Objectivity

Johannes Roessler

Perceptual experience, that paradigm of subjectivity, constitutes our most immediate and fundamental access to the objective world. At least, this would seem to be so if commonsense realism is correct—if perceptual experience is (in general) an immediate awareness of mind-independent objects, and a source of direct knowledge of what such objects are like. Commonsense realism raises many questions. First, can we be more precise about its commitments? Does it entail any particular conception of the nature of perceptual experience and its relation to perceived objects, or any particular view of the way perception yields knowledge? Second, what explains the apparent intuitive appeal of commonsense realism? Should we think of it as a kind of folk theory held by most human adults or is there a sense in which we are pre-theoretically committed to it—in virtue of the experience we enjoy or in virtue of the concepts we use or in virtue of the explanations we give? Third, is commonsense realism defensible, in the face of formidable challenges from epistemology, metaphysics, and cognitive science? The project of the present volume is to advance our understanding of these issues and thus to shed light on the commitments and credentials of common-sense realism. As you may have guessed from the title, the volume also aims to highlight the pivotal role the concept of causation plays in these debates. Central issues to be addressed include the status and nature of causal requirements on perception, the causal role of perceptual experience, and the relation between objective perception and causal thinking—issues that, as many chapters in the volume bring out, are inseparable from concerns with the very nature of causation.

The chapters in this volume explore commonsense realism from a range of perspectives. The psychological essays are concerned with the development, phylogenetic and ontogenetic, of the human adult conception of perception. Some of the philosophical essays are mainly concerned with the explanatory role of perceptual experience—its role in explaining our possession of knowledge, and concepts, of mind-independent objects, and our grasp of the very idea of objectivity. Others focus on issues concerning the causal conditions for objective perception and the nature of causation. My aim here is not to summarize the chapters. Rather, I want to bring out some interconnections among their respective concerns, taking as my central theme an argument John Campbell put forward in his paper 'Berkeley's Puzzle'. The argument forms the background to his exchange, in this volume, with Quassim Cassam. It also provides a springboard for introducing the volume as a whole.

1   Berkeley's Puzzle

According to commonsense realism, perception provides *immediate* access to the *mind-independent* world. Berkeley took the two highlighted elements of this outlook to be mutually incompatible. His reaction was to retain its naïve view of our cognitive contact with the world, but to discard its realism. Campbell deplores this. Yet he maintains that Berkeley reached his rejection of realism by pressing a principle that we have every reason to respect. Campbell calls the principle

The explanatory role of experience: Concepts of individual physical objects and their observable characteristics are made available by our experience of the world. (Campbell 2002a, p. 128)

Berkeley's point was that, given a causal analysis of objective perception—such as Locke's—experience is unable to make concepts of mind-independent objects available to us. He concluded that our concepts of physical objects are not concepts of mind-independent objects. In Campbell's view, Berkeley was perfectly right about the implications of a Lockean causal analysis of objective perception. If experience of physical objects is a matter of being aware of ideas that are signs of their regular causes, experience cannot provide us with a conception of what physical objects are like. Campbell's recommendation is that we should therefore reject the Lockean causal analysis. Instead we should embrace what he calls the relational view of experience. For only the relational view makes it possible to respect both realism and the explanatory role of experience. Focusing on the case of vision, the view can be summarized as follows:

The relational view of visual experience: to see a mind-independent object O is to have a visual experience of which O is a constituent, with the character of the experience being determined partly by the features of O visible from the perceiver's point of view.

The relational view stands opposed to what is sometimes called a 'factorizing' account of object perception. Seeing an object, on the relational view, is a primitive cognitive phenomenon, with a distinctive explanatory role. The notion of seeing an object is not open to a reductive analysis in terms of some 'purely mental ingredient'—visual experience—plus certain external conditions, including perhaps some causal condition. No such 'purely mental ingredient', even in combination with further conditions, could play the distinctive explanatory role of seeing an object. Importantly, the relational view also makes a claim about the nature of the character of perceptual experience. It holds that the character of the experience you have in seeing O is partly determined or constituted by the visible features of O (and, as Campbell elaborates in his chapter, partly by the point of view from which the thing is perceived). Thus Campbell is in agreement with the 'disjunctivist' view that a perception of O and a hallucination as of O have no 'experiential factor' in common (2002a, p. 133). I think that, as Campbell sees things, the two aspects of the relational view—its rejection of a factorizing account and its commitment to disjunctivism—are closely connected.[1] They both arise from the explanatory significance of the character of experience, as constituted by the layout and characteristics of perceived external objects. (See 2002b, p. 116.)

Campbell's argument for the relational view (and against an extended family of alternative theories of perception, from Locke through Burge to McDowell) turns on a specific claim as to what it takes to respect the explanatory role of experience. If experience is to make concepts of mind-independent objects available to us, it has to *explain and justify* our use of such concepts—specifically, our use of them in patterns of reasoning that manifest our understanding of the mind-independence of their reference. An example might be the sort of reasoning that can be involved in working out whether the tree now before you is the same as the tree you encountered at a certain time in the past (2002a, p. 137).

This is not the place for a detailed analysis of Campbell's argument. Of the numerous issues raised by it, I select three that represent major themes of the volume as a whole:

1. What does it mean to conceive of the world as objective?
2. What is the status of causal requirements for the perception of mind-independent objects?
3. What role, explanatory and/or justificatory, does perceptual experience play in making objective thought possible?

2 Conceiving the world as objective

Given that physical objects are in fact mind-independent, why does the explanatory role of experience pose a problem, let alone a puzzle? Does it not follow trivially from the mind-independence of physical objects that anyone who has concepts of physical objects has concepts of mind-independent objects? One response to this question would be to draw a distinction between, on the one hand, particular concepts of what are in fact mind-independent objects and properties and, on the other hand, the abstract, general concept of a mind-independent object. Then perhaps there is a puzzle over the role of experience in making this latter abstract concept available to us. In chapter 2, Quassim Cassam argues that the key to a solution, or dissolution, of this puzzle is to realize that the concept of a mind-independent object is a theoretical

---

[1] See Martin 2004 for an illuminating discussion of these matters.

concept, albeit one that is instantiated in experience. I'll return to Cassam's discussion in section 4 below. Campbell's interest is primarily in particular empirical concepts, such as 'that knife'. He thinks that grasp of such concepts involves more than representing objects that are in fact mind-independent. It involves a conception of objects *as* mind-independent, in the minimal sense that it requires the ability to understand certain *modal* and *tensed* propositions: 'propositions to the effect that the object could have existed even though I had not, or that the object exists even at times at which I am not experiencing it' (2002a, p. 137). If this is right, there is a minimal sense in which anyone who uses concepts of physical objects and their properties conceives of the physical world as mind-independent.

On one view, objective thought, in this sense, can only be attributed to subjects who have some understanding of the notion of a point of view. Gareth Evans argued that grasping the idea of an objective world requires the ability to think of the course of one's perceptual experience as jointly determined by where one is and what is there to be perceived (plus further enabling conditions of perception in a given modality). It is possession of this 'primitive theory of perception' that allows us to 'make sense of' the idea of existence unperceived: 'to understand why what is perceivable should sometimes be, and sometimes not be, perceived' (Evans 1985, p. 263). This view of the *status* of the primitive theory may be disputed. Objective thought, it may be argued, is a more basic achievement than a reflective understanding of perception and its enabling conditions. Admittedly, Campbell's illustration of a tensed proposition of the kind that manifests objective thought is that 'the object exists even at times at which *I am not experiencing it*'. But it is not obvious that thought about one's own experience is essential here. What matters, it might be said, is the ability to think of objects as numerically the same over time, including over periods of time during which, as a matter of fact, they are not perceived. Campbell's account, as elaborated in chapter 3, is congenial to this view. On his account, causal thinking is a prerequisite of objective thought. But the causal thinking he regards as critical is not a reflective understanding of the enabling conditions of perception but a grasp of physical objects as a mechanism by which causal influence is transmitted (e.g. of the fact that sharpening a knife at t_1 affects the behaviour of the knife when it is used to chop tomatoes at t_2). Of course it is a further question whether one can think of objects in this way without being able to reflect on the course of one's experience. Still, it is not obvious that the primitive theory is constitutive of objective thought, though it may of course be required to make the realist commitments of objective thought explicit. (For a more detailed discussion of different conceptions of objective thought, and their bearing on debates about the intentionality of perception, see Naomi Eilan's chapter in this volume.)

I want to raise two further questions about the primitive theory: one to do with its content, the other with what is involved in grasping it. An illuminating way to approach these issues is to ask a seemingly simple question: at what point in development do children acquire a primitive theory of perception in Evans's sense? Part of the philosophical interest of developmental work in this area is that it forces us to elaborate and refine this question, and in this way helps to shed light on what it means, and takes, to possess a primitive theory. It will be useful to highlight two distinctions that have structured the developmental debate in recent years. First, a large body of evidence suggests, or appears to suggest, that children have some understanding of the enabling conditions of perceiving *objects* in the various modalities several years before they are able to perform well on tasks requiring them to compare and contrast the way an object looks from the way it is, or the way it looks from one perspective from the way it looks from another. The point is often put in terms of Flavell's distinction between level-1 and level-2 perspective taking. (See Flavell 2004.) A fundamental question raised by this work is what kind of understanding is critical for success on level-2 perspective taking tasks. On one view, success on such tasks requires a conception of perceptual experience as a state with representational content: children need to appreciate that their visual experience may, for example, represent a sponge *as* a rock. In chapter 15, Matthew Nudds presents an alternative view. To pass standard appearance-reality tests, he suggests, children have to master a relatively sophisticated way of talking about a certain aspect of *perceived objects*, viz. their looks. He argues that this involves no representational conception of experience, and furthermore questions whether young children's poor performance indicates a conceptual deficit, as opposed to difficulties with a particular conversational format.

A second central distinction is between two sources of relevant evidence: direct vs indirect tests.[2] Direct tests probe children's understanding in some area simply by asking them a question the correct answer to which would make the kind of understanding we're interested in explicit. Indirect tests include (a) looking time studies, (b) evidence concerning looking in expectation, and (c) evidence concerning children's interpretation of referential gestures.

An interesting finding of type (c) is discussed by Henrike Moll and Andrew N. Meltzoff in chapter 16. When an adult ambiguously expresses interest in, and makes a request for, one of three objects, children as young as 12 months tend to accede to her request by handing her the object she has not seen before. Moll and Meltzoff dub the ability manifested in this task 'level-1 *experiential* perspective-taking', as it seems to involve an understanding of what someone has experienced or is familiar with or 'knows', in the 'objectual' sense of knowing. This ability apparently precedes level-1 visual perspective taking by almost a year. Indirect tests, of course, are also used in experiments with non-human primates. A striking result, discussed by Martin Doherty, is that when presented with two pieces of food in the presence of a dominant chimpanzee, subordinates are more likely to go for the piece that is hidden from the dominant by an opaque barrier than for the one visible to him (Hare *et al.* 2000).

Indirect tests have generated intense and occasionally heated debate. In the case of chimpanzees, one influential position has it that 'although chimpanzees almost

---

[2] See Perner and Roessler 2010, appendix 1, for further discussion of the distinction between direct and indirect tests.

certainly do not understand other minds in the same way that humans do (e.g. they apparently do not understand beliefs) they do understand some psychological processes (e.g. seeing)' (Tomasello *et al.* 2003, p. 239). In opposition to this, other (equally influential) primatologists have argued that not only does the current evidence not license the attribution of psychological understanding to chimpanzees, but extant research paradigms are *in principle* unable to provide the evidence that would be needed to justify such an attribution (Povinelli and Vonk 2004). In their chapter, Vonk and Povinelli continue this debate, focusing on the specific question of the effect of enculturation on chimpanzees' mind-reading abilities.

Martin Doherty proposes a general framework for integrating discrepant evidence concerning children's understanding of gaze. While indirect tests reveal sensitivity to gaze from an early age, children's explicit judgements of eye direction do not become accurate until about the age at which they start to pass explicit theory of mind tasks (about 4 years). Doherty argues that young children have some understanding of the causal role of a state he labels 'engagement'—something like attentional contact with objects. But he cautions against the assumption that this amounts to an early grasp of *seeing*, or perception. Young children's conception of 'engagement', he argues, is not 'mentalistic' or 'representational'. While children treat someone's 'engagement' with an object as an enabling condition of appropriate action on the object, they do not think of it as a cause of belief, knowledge, or desire. And while they have some grip on the enabling conditions of 'engagement' itself, these are somewhat less stringent than those of visual experience. For example, once 'engagement' has been established, it is not possible to disrupt it by inserting a barrier between subject and object. This picture contrasts with the more continuous approach favoured by Moll and Meltzoff. On their view, even one-year-olds' capacity for level-1 'experiential perspective taking' manifests an understanding of what it means to *see* an object, though that understanding is limited, for example by one-year-olds' tendency to 'overestimate another person's perceptual access in communicative situations' (this volume p. 295).

Doherty's account aims to make sense of the developmental evidence in terms of a distinction in the *content* of children's understanding (their understanding of 'engagement' vs perception). Elizabeth Robinson is interested in a distinction regarding the *nature* of children's understanding. In chapter 18 she reviews work on the development of children's understanding of the role of perception as a source of knowledge. She considers the hypothesis that an explicit grasp of the epistemic role of experience, as probed in direct tests, is preceded by an implicit understanding, informing various kinds of 'finding out behaviour'. Some support for this hypothesis is provided by evidence that even younger children—who find it difficult to *report* on the source of their knowledge—sometimes manifest an appreciation of the relevance of particular sources of knowledge in the way they go about answering questions; for example, in their spontaneous use of a particular sensory modality (looking vs touching) in answering questions about particular kinds of features of an object (what colour it is vs whether it is soft).

In summary, the developmental debate raises, and sheds light on, at least two kinds of questions. First, what is the essential content of the primitive theory of perception? What do we need to know about perception, and perspective, to 'make sense' of existence unperceived? Is it enough to have some grasp of the conditions of object perception, or is it essential to be able to reason about perceptual appearances? Is it enough to think of perception as an enabling condition of appropriate action, or is it essential to understand the epistemic role of perception? Second, what is the nature of the understanding that's required for possession of a primitive theory? Is it possible to grasp the primitive theory through a practical or implicit understanding of the conditions for sharing attention with others in communicative situations, or is it essential to have a detached grasp of the explanatory role of perception?[3]

An issue that is relevant to both kinds of questions is in what sense, if any, the primitive theory is a *causal* theory; and in what sense, if any, the concept of perception is a *causal* concept. I now turn to a set of chapters that address this issue.

3 Causal requirements on perception

The main target of Campbell's argument in 'Berkeley's Puzzle' is the idea that 'experience is *only* caused by the object it is of' (2002b, p. 129, emphasis added). The word 'only' here is obviously significant. It ensures that the idea is inconsistent with the relational view, on which perceived objects are *constituents* of experience. If the lemon before me is a constituent of the visual experience I enjoy in seeing it, there is evidently more to the relation between the lemon and my experience than that the former is the cause of the latter. The relationship would not be *only* causal. Still, this leaves open whether the relationship is *also* causal.

It is often taken to be obvious and undeniable that a causal element is part and parcel of the concept of perception. And it used to be thought to be relatively easy to say what this means. As Grice presents it, the 'causal theory of perception' identifies necessary and jointly sufficient conditions of its being the case that someone perceives a material object (1989). According to Strawson, 'the idea of the presence of the thing as accounting for, or being responsible for, our perceptual awareness of it is implicit in the pre-theoretical scheme [of commonsense realism] from the very start' (1988, p. 103). Clearly a 'causal theorist' of perception wants to credit the causal condition with a distinctive status. The idea is that it is not just an empirical truth that perceived objects figure in the causal explanation of our perceptions of them. But how should we understand the special status of the causal condition? And how is the causal condition to be formulated? What are its relata? Should the condition refer to a certain kind of causal *process*? Or should it be couched in terms of the object *making a difference* to the experience? Finally, how is the causal analysis to be supported?

---

[3] See Eilan 2005 for illuminating discussion of this last point.

In what is sometimes called the golden age of conceptual analysis, philosophers tended to be confident both that they knew what counted as support for the causal analysis, and that such support was indeed available. If this confidence has recently been waning somewhat, this is probably due, in part, to a general decline in the respect commanded by the project of conceptual analysis; but also, in particular, to a series of well-known papers by Paul Snowdon, in which he identified a serious weakness in traditional arguments for the causal analysis (1980–81, 1990). Briefly, Snowdon's point was that the traditional route to the causal analysis—reflection on intuitions elicited by certain sorts of examples, e.g. by cases of 'veridical hallucinations'—is predicated on a particular conception of the nature of perceptual experience. It is assumed that a veridical experience and a subjectively indistinguishable hallucination are events 'the intrinsic natures of which are independent of anything outside the subject' (1990, p. 123). He then pointed out that there is a rival, disjunctivist conception of experience, according to which veridical and hallucinatory experiences do not share a common intrinsic nature. The mere coherence of this alternative conception, he argued, is sufficient to undermine the traditional case for the causal analysis.

Several chapters in this volume are engaged in a debate provoked by William Child's response to Snowdon (Child 1994). Child made two key points. First, he claimed the causal analysis is in fact compatible with disjunctivism (and with the relational view of experience that underpins disjunctivism). Second, he argued that the causal analysis can be supported in a way that is quite independent of the kind of consideration Snowdon took issue with, by offering an account of the conditions for mastery of perceptual concepts. The following quote illustrates this alternative route to the causal analysis:

> For example, if one has the concept of vision, one must know that S will stop seeing something if she shuts her eyes, or if we interpose something opaque between her and the object, and if the object is moved away; and to know that is to know that something cannot be seen if it is prevented from, or cannot be, causally affecting S. (Child 1994, p. 165)

It is instructive to compare this line of argument with a similar, but in some important respects weaker suggestion. Suppose it is agreed that mastery of perceptual concepts requires an understanding of some of the enabling and disabling conditions of perception in the given modality, i.e. grasp of a 'primitive theory of perception'. And suppose it is accepted, further, that possession of a primitive theory amounts to, or at least comprises, the capacity to give causal explanations of facts as to what someone sees or hears etc., or is in a position to see or hear etc. One small but nevertheless significant difference between this proposal and Child's is that where Child appeals to knowledge of *truths* ('one must know that. . .'), the Evans-inspired proposal invokes a capacity for engaging in a certain pattern of explanation. A second, more tangible difference is that the current proposal merely insists that explanations of perception in terms of enabling conditions are or at least include causal explanations; it does not mention the idea of perception as a causal process, as a matter of objects *'causally affecting'* the perceiver.

Would the weaker proposal be sufficient to encourage a version of a causal analysis of perception? This depends on two background questions:

(1) Is the causal theorist committed to the existence of truths that anyone possessing the concept of vision has to accept?

(2) Is the causal theorist committed to the idea that the concept of vision represents vision as a causal process?

Child's original discussion appears to endorse an affirmative answer to (1). Snowdon responds to this (in chapter 9) by voicing scepticism about the idea that 'anyone with the concept of vision must acknowledge those relatively specific things' (that we can be disabled from seeing an object by shutting the eyes, interposing an opaque barrier, or moving the object away). He thinks 'it would hardly discredit someone as a possessor of the concept if he should think that some people can see through their eyelids' (this volume p. 135). And he suggests that young children may be 'relatively uninformed about factors affecting visibility', yet can surely be credited with knowledge of what vision is. Now, on this latter point, current practice in developmental psychology may be said to support Child's stance. As we have seen, Doherty is inclined to deny that young children's performance on gaze understanding shows a grasp of seeing (as opposed to 'engagement'), precisely because they seem unable to appreciate that someone's seeing an object, once established, can be interrupted by inserting an opaque barrier. Be that as it may, in chapter 11 Child explicitly dissociates himself from the idea of truths that anyone grasping the concept of vision has to accept. He now recommends that the causal theorist should defend a more modest claim: 'our ordinary thought about vision is a form of causal thinking' (this volume p. 169). Child spells this out in terms of ordinary explanatory practice, along the lines of Evans's 'primitive theory'.

But would this modest claim be enough to show that seeing is a *causal* concept in any interesting sense? Consider the suggestion that possession of the concept of being asleep requires a primitive theory of the typical enabling conditions of being asleep (e.g. being tired, adopting a recumbent position). On the face of it, this would not lead one to conclude that the concept of being asleep is a causal concept; that the causal requirements for being asleep are somehow part of the very concept of being asleep. We can distinguish two ways a causal theorist of perception may react to this point, corresponding to two kinds of response to (2), the issue of whether the causal theorist is committed to the idea of vision as a causal *process*. We can call them liberal vs orthodox causalism. An orthodox causalist thinks a commitment to vision as a causal process is integral to causalism. A liberal causalist denies this.

Helen Steward advocates a liberal form of causalism. She argues that traditional formulations of the causal theory of perception are wedded to an implausible view of the ontology of causation. On the traditional picture, it is part of the concept of vision that vision involves a *causal chain*, a sequence of causally related events, where events are construed as particulars. Now, as a completely general matter, Steward denies that 'all causation need involve chain-like phenomena' (this volume p. 156). There are notable parallels between her rejection of 'causal particularism' and James Woodward's rejection of 'geometrical/mechanical' theories of causation in favour of 'difference-making' theories. The former regard causation as a relation between events linked by a 'connecting causal process', where this is often spelled out in terms of a 'spatio-temporally continuous process that transmits a conserved quantity such as energy and/or momentum' (Woodward this volume p. 236). Difference-making theories, on the other hand, start from the idea that causes must make a difference to their effects, where, in Woodward's own version of the difference-making approach, this is spelled out by reference to 'intervention' counterfactuals—counterfactuals concerning what would happen to an effect under selective external manipulations of its cause. (See also Christoph Hoerl's chapter for discussion of the contrast between 'difference-making' and 'causal process' theories of causation).

To return to Steward's liberal causalism, her central claim is that the causal theory of perception should be formulated in terms of causal-explanatory relations among *facts*, not in terms of any 'transactional relationships between particulars' (this volume p. 157). Part of the significance of this move, in her view, is that it allows us to defend Child's compatibilist view of the relation between the causal theory of perception and disjunctivism. Strawson's causalist slogan, she suggests, is exactly right so long as it is read as follows: 'the idea of the presence of the thing (= the fact that it is present) as accounting for our perceptual awareness of it (= for the fact that we can see it) is implicit in the pre-theoretical scheme [of commonsense realism] from the very start'.

Of course, there remains the question of whether this is enough to make the concept of vision a causal concept. But it is not obvious that the liberal causalist is without resources here. For one thing, she might simply appeal to Strawson's slogan. There is no analogous slogan about being asleep—there is no single essential causal factor responsible for being asleep remotely comparable to the fundamental role of the spatial enabling conditions of vision. Anyone with the concept of vision, it might be suggested, has to be disposed to engage in patterns of explanation that manifest an appreciation that vision causally depends on (amongst other things) the presence of the seen object. Perhaps this would suffice to make the concept of vision a causal concept, at least in the weakest of the three senses distinguished by Snowdon: 'a causal concept₃' is a concept such that 'by and large any relatively mature person with the concept takes it that it applies only if a (sort of) causal link obtains' (this volume p. 125).

Orthodox causalists insist that the enabling and disabling conditions of perception must be conceived not just as conditions that causally explain someone's seeing or hearing something, but as conditions that permit or disrupt the unfolding of a causal process. Of course, orthodox causalists do not pretend that having the concept of vision requires any knowledge of vision science. Instead they may adopt Grice's suggestion: 'I see nothing absurd in the idea that a nonspecialist concept should contain, so to speak, a blank space to be filled in by the specialist' (Grice 1989, p. 240). But what grounds are there for thinking that the idea of a causal *process*, originating with the seen object and terminating in a visual experience, is integral to the concept of vision?

One way to answer this question would be to cite phenomenological considerations. It is often regarded as a truism that perceptual experience involves a distinctive kind of *passivity*. Historically, the idea has tended to be articulated in causalist terms, the most influential example being Kant's account of receptivity. In chapter 12 Matthew Soteriou argues that the passivity of perceptual experience is partly a matter of the way 'the temporal location of a perception is determined by the temporal location of its object'. This analysis of the phenomenology of perceptual experience, he suggests, encourages a causal conception of experience 'as the passive effects on us of the objects we perceive' (this volume p. 186).

An alternative tack would be to put pressure on the liberal causalist's conception of the enabling and disabling conditions for perception. One way to do so would be to argue that the idea that ordinary reasoning about the enabling conditions of vision involves causal explanation is inseparable from the idea (in Child's words) that 'pre-theoretical thought about vision represents it as a causal process' (this volume p. 172). There would then be a kind of incoherence at the heart of liberal causalism. I want to end this section by sketching one way of understanding the issue here, drawing on a contrast Campbell makes between two 'dimensions' to our ordinary causal thinking. According to a liberal causalist, there are a variety of ways in which we may obstruct someone's visual experience of an object. We may intervene on the distance between object and subject, we may interpose something non-transparent, or we may shut the perceiver's eyes. There are reliable and robust counterfactual connections here. This, on the liberal conception, is simply what the primitive theory of perception is about: it is about grasping causal factors that make it possible to explain and manipulate the course of our own and others' experience. The orthodox causalist finds this an implausibly shallow representation of the primitive theory. What disturbs him is the complete absence in it of what Campbell describes as a 'second dimension to our ordinary thinking about causation', viz. our tendency to 'think in terms of mechanisms by means of which the counterfactual connections exist' (this volume p. 37). For the orthodox causalist, an indispensable element of the primitive theory of perception is the idea of a mechanism in virtue of which the various counterfactual connections obtain: we think of vision as a causal process that constitutes the *reason why* interventions on certain variables—distance, interposed objects, and so forth—make a difference to someone's visual experience of an object.

4 The explanatory role of perceptual experience

Campbell's argument for the relational view of experience proceeds in two steps. The first step articulates what Campbell regards as a commitment of commonsense realism: if commonsense realism is correct, it must be possible to explain and justify our use of concepts of physical objects by appeal to our experience of the world. The second step argues that this demand can be satisfied only if the relational view of the nature of experience is correct. I will focus here on the notion of justification at work in the first step of the argument. What does Campbell's demand for justification involve, and how is it motivated? I want to pursue this question by asking how the kind of justification that Campbell claims is demanded by realism, and can (only) be provided by experience as conceived on the relational view, is related to another kind of justification, which Barry Stroud, in chapter 7, argues should *not* be demanded and, in any case, can *not* be provided by experience (however conceived). For ease of reference, I will call the former C-justification and the latter S-justification. I begin by setting out the case for compatibilism, i.e. for the idea that the availability of C-justification is compatible with the unavailability of S-justification.

Stroud is in agreement with Campbell on the importance of *object perception*. They both regard the concepts of perceiving physical objects in particular modalities as fundamental for explaining our ability to have thoughts about, and knowledge of, such objects. For Stroud, object perception matters, in part, because, in conjunction with recognitional conceptual capacities, it enables us to perceive immediately *that* a particular object falls under a certain concept. (See this volume p. 95.) That you see *a* can help to account for your ability to see that *a* is *F*, and thus help to explain how you *know* that *a* is *F* (given that seeing that *a* is *F* is a way of knowing that *a* is *F*). What Stroud denies is that this sort of explanation involves identifying 'a reason or ground or justification for the knowledge-claim in question', or 'something on the basis of which the believer justifiably accepts or believes what he does' (this volume p. 97).

This suggests that S-justification and C-justification are quite different matters. S-justification pertains to *beliefs*. To be S-justified in believing that *p* is to hold the belief on the basis of what one takes to be good reason for believing that *p*. C-justification, in contrast, applies to our *use of concepts* of physical objects in certain patterns of reasoning. Moreover, Campbell's account does not encourage the thought that C-justification is something ordinary reasoners should be able to articulate. (He sees a parallel between the way perceptual experience justifies our use of patterns of reasoning about mind-independent objects and the way truth-tables justify the rules of inference for the propositional constants.) The obvious conclusion is that there is no disagreement between Stroud and Campbell. Campbell claims it is a demand of realism that experience of objects justify certain patterns of reasoning. Stroud denies that experience of objects can justify non-inferential perceptual beliefs. The claim and the denial are mutually consistent.

It is possible, though, that this superficial analysis conceals a genuine and profound disagreement. For one thing, one might wonder whether C-justification and S-justification are independent of each other. If your experience justifies your use of concepts in reasoning, should it not also be expected to justify your use of such concepts in perceptual judgements? But the real issue, I think, lies in the dialectical role of scepticism. It is often said that there is an intimate relationship between realism and scepticism. As Thomas Nagel puts it, realism makes scepticism intelligible (Nagel 1986). There is more than one thing this may be taken to mean, some of them stronger, and more contentious, than others. I think it is in this area that there may be an interesting disagreement between Campbell and Stroud.

We can distinguish three readings of the slogan that realism makes scepticism intelligible:

(a) Realism makes scepticism intelligible in the basic sense that it implies the coherence of certain sceptical possibilities. Given that the world is the way it is independently of how we take it to be, and how it appears to us in perceptual experience, it is logically possible that the world is quite unlike the way we take it to be.

(b) Realism makes scepticism intelligible in the stronger sense that it implies that the sceptic has identified a real and pressing *question*, a defining feature of which is its complete generality. We have to confront the question of how it is possible for perceptual experience to provide a basis for knowing, or justifiably believing, *anything at all* about the mind-independent world, in the face of the sceptical challenge.

(c) Realism makes scepticism intelligible in the sense that it lends some plausibility to the sceptic's *answer*, viz. the denial that experience can be an adequate basis for knowledge of or justified belief about physical objects. For a genuinely realist view of physical objects is really incompatible with the naïve idea that in perceptual experience we can be directly presented with such objects.

If (c) were correct, part of the philosophical significance of scepticism would be that it undermines commonsense realism: it is unlikely that any philosophical refutation of scepticism could reinstate the commonsense realist view that experience immediately reveals what the world is like. In Stroud's terms, the likely outcome would be a 'stepwise explanation' of perceptual knowledge, on which knowledge of mind-independent objects can never be obtained by perception alone but results from a combination of knowledge of perceptual appearances with something we know from other sources. Stroud takes a dim view of the prospects for the 'stepwise' conception. Campbell takes a similarly dim view of the prospects for solving Berkeley's Puzzle once we have been cajoled into endorsing (c). They are agreed in rejecting (c). Nor is there any dispute about (a), which both accept.

As for (b), things are less clear. There is some reason to think that Campbell accepts (b). For a certain sceptical possibility seems to play a significant role in motivating the first step of Campbell's argument for the relational view (viz. the claim that it is a commitment of commonsense realism that our use of concepts of physical objects can be explained and justified by appeal to our experience of the world). He characterizes the sceptical possibility he is interested in as follows:

Suppose you think that the world we are in is fundamentally quite unlike anything we encounter in experience. You might be encouraged in this view, on which the external world is alien, by your reading of physics, or by your reading of Kant. In that case, our possession and use of the concepts we ordinarily use on the basis of perception, concepts relating to the medium-sized world, cannot be explained or justified by appeal to facts about our environment (this volume p. 35).

By a happy coincidence, the two sources of the conception of the world as alien mentioned here receive full-length treatment in the chapters by Bill Brewer and James Van Cleve. Brewer considers the physicalist challenge that ordinary explanations of perceptual experience in terms of experienced objects and features are falsified by the correct scientific account of the causes of experience in terms of fundamental physics. Van Cleve examines Rae Langton's reconstruction of an argument for 'Kantian humility', the doctrine that perceptual experience yields no knowledge of the intrinsic properties of things. Both challenges to commonsense realism turn on substantive claims about the nature of causal explanation and causation. Brewer argues that the physicalist challenge relies on a certain kind of explanatory reductionism, which denies what he calls the 'robustness' of commonsense explanations of perceptual experience in terms of perceived objects and features. Van Cleve argues that the Kantian challenge depends on a hidden premise to the effect, roughly, that there is no causation without necessitation. Suppose both challenges can be defused, as Brewer and Van Cleve offer reason to think they can. Still, we can ask what the putative upshot of these challenges, that the world is fundamentally unlike anything we encounter in experience, would take away from us. Campbell suggests it would take away our right to use concepts of mind-independent objects the way we use them. Reflection on the sceptical view of the world as alien is used here to identify a commitment of ordinary objective thought—that we do in fact have the right of which the sceptic would deprive us. In other words, it is a commitment of objective thought that there is a justifiable affirmative answer to be given to the sceptic's completely general question. It does look, then, as if (b) may be doing some important work in Campbell's argument. It seems to provide us with the question to which the relational view of experience is held to be the answer.

The importance of this point is nicely illustrated in Campbell's exchange with Cassam. Cassam's proposed solution to Berkeley's Puzzle exhibits some structural analogies with Kant's account of the categories. Cassam argues that while the abstract concept of a mind-independent object cannot be 'extracted' from experience, it is 'sensibly realized', or 'instantiated in experience' (this volume p. 32). Importantly, he thinks that his more modest conception of the explanatory role of experience subverts Campbell's case for the relational view of experience. Suppose we deny that perceived objects are constituents of perceptual experience. Suppose that instead we think of perceptual experience as a state with non-conceptual representational content. This view, Cassam contends, would not disable us from acknowledging the role of experience in 'sensibly realizing' the abstract concept of a mind-independent object.

Campbell's central line of response to this picture is to question its realist credentials. What justifies our use of concepts of mind-independent objects? Within the Kantian framework, Campbell claims, the answer has to take the form of what Kant called a transcendental deduction, deriving our right to use certain concepts from 'facts relating to the inner architecture of the mind' (this volume p. 35). The trouble with this account, in Campbell's view, is that it is incompatible with commonsense realism. The Kantian validation of our use of concepts of mind-independent objects is underpinned by the Kantian view of the world as alien. On the Kantian conception, 'our patterns of reasoning and their validation come first, and they are projected onto an alien underlying reality' (this volume p. 47). Our use of concepts of mind-independent objects is explained and justified by facts about us, not facts about the experienced mind-independent world.

This line of response assumes that the task of 'validating' or justifying our use of concepts of mind-independent objects is in a certain way inescapable. If you resist a validation in terms of experienced objects, this leaves you with a choice between unmitigated scepticism and transcendental idealism. I think it is here that we may locate a genuine disagreement between Campbell and Stroud. Stroud sketches a line of argument that aims to undermine (c) by showing that the capacity to recognize that it *looks as if* (say) some object is red requires the capacity to recognize directly, in appropriate circumstances, that an object *is* red (this volume p. 97). If this sort of connective analysis can be defended, it would in a certain way defuse the sceptical challenge. Crucially, though, in Stroud's view, it would not do so by securing an affirmative answer to the completely general question the sceptic is pressing, but by giving us grounds for repudiating the very project of engaging with that question. It would expose as illusory the sceptic's assumption that the coherence of certain sceptical possibilities implies that they represent a *threat* to our perceptual knowledge of the mind-independent world. Being in a position to gain direct knowledge of the mind-independent world would turn out to be a necessary condition of an ability the sceptic takes for granted, that of gaining direct knowledge of sensory appearances. (See Stroud 2000 for discussion of this 'modest' type of transcendental argument.)

Stroud's denial that perceptual beliefs are S-justified, then, is motivated in part by his *scepticism* concerning (b), whereas Campbell's insistence that our use of concepts of mind-independent objects stands in need of C-justification seems to reflect his *affirmation* of (b). The 'modest' transcendental argument that leads Stroud to question (b) is of course a descendant of Kant's 'transcendental' investigation of human knowledge. Yet there can be no doubt that the historical Kant would have endorsed (b). He considered the sceptic a 'benefactor of human reason', precisely because the sceptic compels us to confront the question of whether our putative right to use concepts of external objects is a 'well-earned possession'. (Kant 2007, A 377–78) On this crucial point, it seems to be Campbell who sides with Kant.

I should stress that this anti-compatibilist analysis is not intended to be the last word on the matter. Closer scrutiny may reveal that the demand for C-justification is not in fact wedded to the philosophical project that Stroud's 'modest' transcendental argument aims to deconstruct. In any case, note that it is a further question how the debate I have been reviewing bears on the credentials of the relational view of experience; in particular, on the success or otherwise of arguments that aim to derive that view from the explanatory role of experience. Such arguments *may* take the form of invoking the relational view as part of an affirmative, reassuring answer to some version of the traditional philosophical question over the role of experience in grounding our conception of the objective world (the very question which scepticism answers in the negative). But it is not clear that they have to take that form. Instead, it may be argued that the relational view articulates a commitment of our ordinary explanatory practice, of making our possession of knowledge intelligible in terms of experienced objects, a practice that may not be open to the kind of philosophical understanding demanded by the traditional question. (I examine this suggestion in more detail in chapter 8.)

References

Campbell, John 2002a: 'Berkeley's Puzzle', in T. Gendler and J. Hawthorne (eds.), *Conceivability and Possibility*. Oxford: Oxford University Press.

——2002b: *Reference and Consciousness*. Oxford: Oxford University Press.

Child, William 1994: *Causality, Interpretation, and the Mind*. Oxford: Clarendon Press.

Eilan, Naomi 2005: 'Joint Attention, Communication, and Mind', in N. Eilan, C. Hoerl, T. McCormack, and J. Roessler (eds.), *Joint Attention: Communication and Other Minds*. Oxford: Clarendon Press.

Evans, Gareth 1985: 'Things Without the Mind—A Commentary upon Chapter Two of Strawson's *Individuals*', in his *Collected Papers*. Oxford: Clarendon Press.

Flavell, John 2004: 'Development of Knowledge about Vision', in D. Levin (ed.), *Thinking and Seeing*. Cambridge, Mass.: MIT Press.

Grice, Paul. 1989: 'The Causal Theory of Perception', in his *Studies in the Way of Words*. Cambridge, Mass.: Harvard University Press.

Hare, B., Call, J., Agnetta, M., and Tomasello, M. 2000: 'Chimpanzees know what conspecifics do and do not see', *Animal Behaviour* 59, 771–778.

Kant, Immanuel 2007: *Critique of Pure Reason*. Translated by M. Weigelt and M. Müller. London: Penguin.

Martin, Michael 2004: 'The Limits of Self-Awareness' *Philosophical Studies* 120, 37–89.

Nagel, Thomas 1986: *The View from Nowhere*. Oxford: Oxford University Press.

Perner, Josef and Roessler, Johannes 2010: 'Teleology and Causal Understanding in Children's Theory of Mind', in J. Aguilar and A. Buckareff (eds.), *Causing Human Action: New Perspectives on the Causal Theory of Action*. Cambridge, Mass: MIT Press.

Povinelli, Daniel and Vonk, Jennifer 2004: 'We don't need a microscope to explore the Chimpanzee mind', *Mind and Language* 19, 1–28.

Snowdon, Paul 1980–81: 'Perception, Vision, and Causation', *Proceedings of the Aristotelian Society* 81, 175–192.

——1990: 'The Objects of Perceptual Experience', *Proceedings of the Aristotelian Society Supp. Vol.* 64, 121–150.

Strawson, Peter F. 1988: 'Perception and its Objects', in G. McDonald (ed.), *Perception and Identity: Essays presented to A. J. Ayer*. London: Macmillan, pp. 41–60 (1979). Reprinted in J. Dancy (ed.), *Perceptual Knowledge*. Oxford: Oxford University Press.

Stroud, Barry 2000: *Understanding Human Knowledge*. Oxford: Oxford University Press.

Tomasello, M., Call, J., and Hare, B. 2003: 'Chimpanzees versus humans: it's not that simple', *Trends in Cognitive Science* 7, 239–40.

2

Tackling Berkeley's Puzzle

Quassim Cassam★

1 Introducing the Puzzle

Among the various concepts that we employ in our thinking are concepts of objects. To judge that apples grow on trees or that the suitcase one is carrying is heavy is to employ concepts of objects in one's thinking because *apple*, *tree*, and *suitcase* are examples of such concepts. Indeed, they are not just concepts of objects but concepts of *mind-independent* objects. Objects in this sense are individuals that can be perceived and exist unperceived. Apples, trees, and suitcases are mind-independent objects, and it is natural to assume that the possibility of existence unperceived is somehow built into our grasp of concepts of such objects.

One prominent form of scepticism focuses on whether it is possible for us to know that there are mind-independent objects. Berkeley asks a more basic question: how is it possible for us even to have concepts of mind-independent objects? He raises this question because he has a view of the relation between concepts and experience that appears to make it impossible for us to grasp concepts of mind-independent objects. He does not deny that we have concepts like apple, suitcase, and tree but he concludes that these are concepts of mind-dependent objects, objects whose *esse* is their *percipi*.

This is how John Campbell describes Berkeley's reasoning in support of this surprising conclusion:

Berkeley is trying to respect a principle about the relation between experience and concepts that is both important and difficult to keep in place. This is what I will call the *explanatory role of experience*. The principle is that concepts of individual physical objects, and concepts of the observable characteristics of such objects, are made available by our experience of the world. It is experience of the world that explains our grasp of these concepts. The puzzle that Berkeley is addressing is that it is hard to see how our concepts of mind-independent objects could have been made available by experience of them. The resolution he finds is to acknowledge that we do not have concepts of mind-independent objects. (2002a: 128)

★ Thanks to John Campbell for stimulating discussions of the topic of this paper and to Ciara Fairley for helpful comments on an earlier draft.

Why is it hard to see how our concepts of mind-independent objects could have been made available by our experience of mind-independent objects? Because we do not have such concepts unless we have the conception of objects as mind-independent, as capable of existing unperceived.[1] If we have this conception then experience of objects has to explain how we have it. But experience of objects cannot explain how we have the conception of objects as mind-independent. So we do not have this conception, and therefore do not have concepts of mind-independent objects. We have concept of objects but they are concepts of concepts of mind-dependent objects.

This complex argument can be summarized as follows:

1. We have concepts of objects.
2. Concepts of objects are made available to us by experience; it is experience of the world that explains our grasp of concepts of objects.[2]
3. We cannot have concepts of mind-independent objects unless we have the conception of objects as mind-independent.
4. We can only have the conception of objects as mind-independent if experience makes it available to us; experience of objects has to explain how it is that we have the conception of objects as mind-independent.
5. Experience of objects cannot make available to us the conception of objects as mind-independent; it cannot explain how we have the conception of objects as mind-independent.
6. We do not have the conception of objects as mind-independent.
7. We do not have concepts of mind-independent objects.
8. Our concepts of objects must be concepts of mind-dependent objects.

We can call premise 3 the *Possession Premise* since it states a condition on possession of concepts of mind-independent objects. Premise 4 Berkeley's is *Explanatory Requirement* and premise 5 is the *Experience Premise*.

The conclusion of Berkeley's argument is unacceptable. We have the conception of objects as mind-independent and concepts of mind-independent objects so it is false that our concepts of objects must be concepts of mind-dependent objects. The case for thinking that we have the conception of objects as capable of existing unperceived is this: to have this conception is to be able to think or reason in certain ways.[3] So, for example, someone who thinks that the table in his study exists even though no one is perceiving it, or who reasons that the table he can now see is the same as the one he saw

---

[1] This is the key to Berkeley's Puzzle. As Campbell writes:

Our topic is the role of experience in providing the conception of objects as mind-independent. How can experience of an object provide you with a grasp of the idea that the object can continue in existence through gaps in observation. How can perceptual experience of objects be what provides you with a grasp of the possibility of existence unperceived? This is Berkeley's Puzzle (2002a: 137).

[2] The formulations before and after the semicolon are Campbell's. One might wonder whether they are equivalent. This is an issue taken up below.

[3] Cf. Campbell (2002a: 137).

last week, is manifesting his grasp of the conception of objects like tables as mind-independent. To say that someone thinks and reasons in these ways is not to say that he is *justified* in doing so or that he has a *right* to conceive of objects as mind-independent. The point is rather that someone who thinks and reasons in these ways *is* conceiving of objects as mind-independent. Since we actually think and reason in these ways it follows that we do conceive of objects as mind-independent.

Berkeley would be unconvinced by this line of argument because, for reasons we do not need to go into here, he would think that thinking and reasoning in these ways is not sufficient for grasp of the possibility of existence unperceived.[4] For the purposes of the present discussion I am going to assume that Berkeley is wrong about this and that there is at least a strong *prima facie* case against 6. However, 6 follows from 4 and 5 so if we want to reject 6 then we must show what is wrong with the Explanatory Requirement or with the Experience Premise. If we accept 6 we can still avoid 7 by denying the Possession Premise but it makes more sense to start with 6 and the premises from which it follows. So the first question is this: what is the motivation for the Explanatory Requirement?

Someone who has the conception of objects as mind-independent is someone who has the concept of a mind-independent object.[5] Berkeley is adamant that experience has to explain how it is that we have this concept because he has an empiricist conception of the relation between concepts and experience. On this conception, the explanatory role of experience is not limited to concepts of objects and their observable characteristics. The empiricist principle about the relation between experience and concepts is assumed to apply to all our concepts. There are no exemptions from the Explanatory Requirement. If we have the concept of a mind-independent object then experience of objects has to be able to explain how we have it.

Why accept the Experience Premise? On one reading, to think that experience of objects 'makes available' the conception of objects as mind-independent is to think that it is possible for us to *extract* or *acquire* this conception from experience of objects.[6] So the question is whether it is possible for us to extract from experience of objects the idea that the objects of experience can exist unperceived. Here is one reason for thinking that this is not possible: experience of objects only gives us conscious images of objects. These images are mind-dependent; that is, they depend for their existence on being experienced. So 'if your conception of the object was provided by your experience of the object, you would presumably end by concluding that the object

---

[4] As Ayers points out, Berkeley thinks that the content of my thought that the table in my study exists unperceived is that it *would* exist (i.e. be perceived) if someone were looking at it. Unperceived, the table does not actually exist. See Ayers (1975: xii).

[5] There are purposes for which it might be important to distinguish between concepts and conceptions. I am taking it that 'S has the conception of objects as mind-independent' and 'S has the concept of a mind-independent object' are equivalent.

[6] This is sometimes what Campbell appears to have in mind. See his (2002a: 135).

would not have existed had you not existed, and that the object exists only when you are experiencing it' (Campbell 2000b: 121).

As Campbell sees things, this argument for the Experience Premise relies on what he calls a Representational View of experience. He claims that this premise can be resisted on a Relational View of experience.[7] This says that experience of an object involves the mind-independent thing itself as a constituent. This undermines the Experience Premise since it seems that 'it ought to be possible to extract the conception of a mind-independent world from an experience which has a mind-independent object as a constituent' (2002b: 121). The Representational View has to accept the Experience Premise because it cannot allow that experience of objects has mind-independent objects as constituents.

Are Campbell's arguments in support of the claim that the Representational View is stuck with the Experience Premise good ones? I will argue in part 2 that they are not. There *are* good reasons for thinking that the Representational View fails to explain how the concept of a mind-independent object can be extracted from experience but they are different from the ones that Campbell gives. Does the Relational View fare any better in this regard than the Representational View? I will argue that it does not. Even if perceptual experiences of mind-independent objects have such objects as constituents this does not explain how we can acquire the concept of a mind-independent object from experience. The right thing to think is that this is a concept that cannot be extracted from experience. If this is the point of the Experience Premise then we should endorse this premise.

One concern about arguing in this way is that it raises a question about the possibility of extracting concepts of mind-independent objects—concepts like *tree*—from experience. If the Possession Premise is correct, how can concepts of mind-independent things be extracted from experience if the concept of a mind-independent thing cannot be extracted from experience?[8] I will address this question in section 3. In section 4, I will focus on a different issue: if the concept of a mind-independent object cannot be extracted from experience then it would appear that we must either conclude that we do not have this concept or that we have at least one *bona fide* concept that cannot be extracted from experience. The former is Berkeley's conclusion, the latter is Kant's. In Kant's terminology, legitimate concepts that cannot be acquired from experience are

---

[7] The core commitments on the Relational View are that (a) when one sees an object the object itself is a constituent of one's experience, (b) experience of objects is more primitive than, and in fact explains, the ability to think about objects, and (c) there is nothing intrinsic in common between the case in which one perceives, say, a dagger and the case in which one is having a vivid hallucination of the dagger. Campbell represents the Representational View as denying all three claims. I argue below that there are versions of the Representational View that can endorse (b).

[8] Strictly speaking the Possession Premise says that we cannot have concepts of mind-independent objects unless we have the conception of objects as mind-independent. I am taking this as equivalent to the claim that we cannot have concepts of mind-independent objects unless we have the concept of a mind-independent object. The worry is that if one needs the concept of a mind-independent object in order to have any concepts of mind-independent objects then the latter can be derived from experience only if the former can be so derived. See section 3 below for more on this.

non-empirical or *a priori* concepts.[9] If Kant is right that the concept of a mind-indepen-dent object is *a priori* then it would seem that the Explanatory Requirement has to be given up. However, Berkeley's point is that this requirement is non-negotiable, so we are back to square one: either the concept of a mind-independent object is one that we do not possess or experience has to be capable of making it available to us.

The key to resolving this stand-off, and to solving Berkeley's Puzzle, is to recognize that the Explanatory Requirement and the Experience Premise can both be read in different ways. On one interpretation, the Explanatory Requirement is concerned with the *acquisition* of concepts. It says that:

(ER$_a$)   If we have the concept of a mind-independent object it must have been acquired from experience.

On a different reading, the Explanatory Requirement focuses on what it is to *grasp* the concept of a mind-independent object. The claim is that:

(ER$_g$)   If we have the concept of a mind-independent object then experience must have a role to play in explaining our grasp of this concept.

The non-negotiable version of the Explanatory Requirement is (ER$_g$). (ER$_a$) is far more contentious. I will suggest that we can and should endorse (ER$_g$) without endorsing (ER$_a$).[10]

The two versions of the Experience Premise are:

(EP$_a$)   The concept of a mind-independent object cannot be acquired from experi-ence of objects.

(EP$_g$)   Experience of objects can play no role in explaining our grasp of the concept of a mind-independent object.

One can think that (EP$_a$) is true without thinking that (EP$_g$) is true. Given (ER$_a$), (EP$_a$) puts pressure on the idea that we have the concept of a mind-independent object but we should not endorse (ER$_a$). (ER$_g$) commits us to denying (EP$_g$), but we should reject this version of the Experience Premise.

We now have the outlines of a response to Berkeley's Puzzle: Berkeley is wrong to deny that we have the concept of a mind-independent object but right to claim that this is not a concept that can be acquired from experience. Nevertheless, experience of objects can and must play a role in explaining our grasp of this concept, and this means that there is no conflict with the non-negotiable version of the Explanatory Require-ment. The challenge is to identify the precise explanatory role of experience in relation to the concept of a mind-independent object given that this concept cannot be

---

[9] In the terminology of Cassam (2003) *bona fide* concepts that cannot be derived from experience are 'derivationally *a priori*'.

[10] Campbell tends to run the two versions of the Explanatory Requirement together in his discussion.

extracted from experience. I will return to this issue below. In the meantime, it is worth noting that the right thing to say about the concept of a mind-independent object is exactly what Kant says about his categories: it is an *a priori* concept our grasp of which nevertheless has a basis in experience.[11]

2 The Experience Premise

The idea that the Representational View of experience is stuck with the acquisition version of the Experience Premise is, on the face of it, implausible.[12] The Representational View says that many of our perceptual experiences are not just experiences of what are in fact mind-independent objects but experiences *as of* mind-independent objects.[13] Experiences as of mind-independent objects are experiences with a certain representational or intentional content: they represent mind-independent objects as such and thereby make it possible for us to acquire the concept of a mind-independent object from experience.[14] Or so it would seem. The Representational View insists that the representational content of an experience of a mind-independent object may be the same as that of a matching vivid hallucination of a mind-independent object but this is not a reason for thinking that this view precludes the acquisition of the concept of a mind-independent object from experience. It is only a reason for thinking that one could just as well acquire the concept of a mind-independent object from hallucinations of such objects.

What should we make of the concern that, on the Representational View, experience only gives us mind-dependent images of objects, and that 'we cannot extract the conception of a mind-independent world from a mind-dependent image' (Campbell 2002b: 121)? This account of the Representational View might be disputed by representationalists who do not use the terminology of conscious images. Even representationalists who are prepared to speak in these terms should insist that what is important for their purposes is the *content* of the images rather than the nature of the images themselves. Mental images are mind-dependent but proponents of the Representational View who think that the concept of an object can be extracted from experience of objects do not need to suppose that the content of this concept is fixed by the ontological status of conscious images as such. What matters is the *content* of the images. The proposal is that the concept of a non-mental object can be acquired from experience as long as objects of experience are represented in experience as mind-independent. The mind-dependence of the bearers of this content is neither here nor there.

---

[11] In Kant's terminology experience is what provides the categories—concepts like *substance* and *cause*—with 'objective reality'.

[12] As Mohan Matthen also notes. See Matthen (2006) and compare Campbell (2002b: 121).

[13] Cf. Susanna Siegel's remark that 'the objects we seem to see are presented to us as subject-independent' (2006: 356).

[14] To be more precise, such experiences make it possible for us to acquire the concept of a mind-independent object *because* they represent their objects as mind-independent.

A potentially serious objection to this proposal is this: it is only possible for one to have experiences as of mind-independent objects if one already has the concept of a mind-independent object, and this means that this concept cannot be extracted from such experiences. Why not? Because the experiences from which a concept F is extracted must, on pain of circularity, not presuppose one's possession of F. It is the fact that one has experiences as of mind-independent objects that is supposed to make it possible for one to get hold of the concept of a mind-independent object so it had better not turn out that one's grasp of this concept is what makes it possible for one to have experiences as of mind-independent objects in the first place.

The claim that a concept F cannot be acquired from experiences that presuppose it is not beyond dispute but let that pass.[15] A more pressing question is whether it is true that one cannot have experiences as of mind-independent objects if one lacks the concept of a mind-independent object. The underlying issue here is whether the Representational View has to regard the representational content of such experiences as conceptual. Campbell thinks that it does. He claims that the Representational View takes the intentionality of experience for granted, and that taking this for granted is equivalent to taking it for granted that 'experience of the world is a way of grasping thoughts about the world' (2000b: 121). The implication is that the Representational View regards the representational content of experience as conceptual, and this is the basis of Campbell's allegation that it cannot account for the explanatory role of experience: if experience of objects is a way of grasping thoughts then how can it explain how it is that we are able to think about the world around us?

It is true that the Representational View takes the intentionality of experience for granted but it is not committed to the conception of intentionality that Campbell attributes to it. Many proponents of this view characterize the representational content of experience as at least partly non-conceptual.[16] They do not think that experience of objects is a way of grasping thoughts and are happy to accept that someone who, say, lacks the concept *sphere* can still have an experience as of a sphere. Why, then, should they not think that one can have an experience as of a mind-independent object even if one lacks the corresponding concept? Perhaps the worry is that only relatively basic contents can be non-conceptual. A person who lacks the concept *sphere* might be able to have an experience as of a sphere but it is much less plausible that someone who lacks the concept of a Geiger counter can have an experience as of a Geiger counter. *Some* representational contents can only be conceptual. However, the important question for present purposes is whether the content of experiences as of mind-independent objects must be conceptual. Given that even babies and some animals can have such experiences despite their lack of conceptual sophistication the obvious thing to think is that such experiences need *not* presuppose the concept of a mind-independent object.

---

[15] See Cassam (1999) for further discussion.

[16] See, for example, Peacocke (2001). Campbell claims that 'the move to thinking in terms of "non-conceptual" content does not help' (2002b). It is not clear why Campbell thinks that this move does not help.

So it appears that the Representational View can avoid (EP$_a$) as long as it takes seriously the possibility of non-conceptual representational content.

The problem with this argument is that the considerations that make it plausible that experiences as of mind-independent objects need not be conceptual make it correspondingly difficult to see how the concept of a mind-independent object could be extracted from such experiences. For what makes it plausible that experiences as of mind-independent objects need not be conceptual is the suggestion that more intellectual sophistication is required for grasp of the concept of a mind-independent object than can reasonably be attributed to the many creatures that are capable of having experiences as of mind-independent objects. The more demanding our idea of what it is to grasp the concept of a mind-independent object the stronger the case for denying that possession of this concept is necessary for one to have experiences as of mind-independent objects. At the same time, however, the more demanding our idea of what it is to grasp the concept of a mind-independent object the harder it becomes to see how this concept could be extracted from experience.

Consider what is involved in having the concept of a mind-independent object. The concept of such an object is the concept of something that can exist unperceived and that possesses mind-independent properties such as shape. We can, of course, find out the shape of an object, and some of our ways of discovering an object's mind-independent properties are canonical. For example, perceiving the shape of an object from different perspectives is a canonical method for establishing its shape. However, as Peacocke observes:

For someone who has at least a rudimentary conception of objectivity, an object's having a certain property is not something constituted by a certain method's having a particular outcome. It is rather something that may potentially be investigated by new means, in need of discovery, new means whose detailed nature cannot be circumscribed in advance. New means are possible because the canonical methods are conceived as latching on to independently existing objects and properties.... For the thinker with some conception of objectivity, the methods that are canonical need not be exhaustive. (2001: 614–15)

Perceptual states can exist in the absence of the ability to conceive of canonical methods as latching on to independently existing objects and properties, and this strengthens the case for regarding the content of such states as non-conceptual. Yet given how much is built into even a rudimentary conception of objectivity there is little prospect of this conception being one that can be acquired from experience. It is not possible to read off from experience the idea that an object's having a certain property is not constituted by a certain method's having a particular outcome. Intuitively, this is too sophisticated an idea to be built into the content of a non-conceptual representational state, and therefore too sophisticated an idea to be extracted from such a state.[17]

---

[17] This is not to deny that there is some sense in which creatures that lack the concept of a mind-independent object can perceptually represent 'object permanence'. See, for example, Baillargeon (1999) for more on this.

A closely related consideration is that to think of a perceivable object as capable of existing unperceived is to think of it as a space-occupier. I think of the table in my study as existing unperceived by thinking of it as occupying a region of space at which no perceiver is present. To think of the table as a space-occupier is to think of it as possessing *primary properties*, and a grasp of such properties relies on implicit knowledge of the propositions of a primitive mechanics. These propositions, which specify the ways in which bodies can and cannot behave, are incapable of being, as Evans puts it, 'woven out of materials given in experience' (1980: 97). This has a bearing on (EP$_a$) because it is only a short step from the claim that the principles of primitive mechanics cannot be woven out of the materials given in experience to the conclusion that the concept of a mind-independent object cannot be extracted from experience.[18]

On this account of the case for (EP$_a$) a Relational View of experience does not make this version of the Experience Premise any less plausible. Suppose that, as the Relational View claims, experiences of objects have objects as constituents. Campbell suggests that it should be possible to extract the concept of a mind-independent object from an experience which has a mind-independent object as a constituent but it is not clear that this is right. To get a sense of the problem consider the following analogy: gold has the atomic number 79, and lumps of gold are things that we can perceive. But even if experiences of lumps of gold have those lumps as constituents it does not follow that it is possible to extract the concept of an atomic number from such experiences. Lumps of gold do not give us the *concept* of an atomic number just because they *have* an atomic number, and the fact that an experience has a lump of gold as a constituent does not explain how the concept of an atomic number can be derived from experience. By the same token, mind-independent objects do not give us the *concept* of mind-independence just because they *are* mind-independent, and the fact that an experience has a mind-independent object as a constituent does not explain how the concept of a mind-independent object can be extracted from the experience.

It might be objected that this is not a good analogy. The fact that gold has an atomic number does not show up in our experience of gold, and that is why the concept of *atomic number* cannot be derived from experience. In contrast, the mind-independence of an object of experience does show up in an experience of that object that has it as a constituent. The experience *registers* the object's mind-independence and that is what allows us to derive the concept of a mind-independent object from experience. But what is it for an experience of a mind-independent object to register the object's mind-independence? An obvious thought is that for an experience of a mind-independent object to do this kind of registering is for it to *represent* the object as mind-independent. One question, therefore, is whether the Relational View can allow that experiences

---

[18] Readers who are familiar with Evans (1980) will recognize the argument of this paragraph as one of Evans' arguments in that wonderful paper. Although Evans is not entirely explicit about this he seems to think that the primitive mechanics is innate.

are, in this sense, representational.[19] If not, then it is still a mystery how an experience is supposed to give one the concept of a mind-independent object just because it has a mind-independent object as a constituent. If, on the other hand, the Relational View allows that experiences have representational content and sees this as the key to explaining how the concept of a mind-independent object can be acquired from experience then it faces the same difficulties in this regard as the Representational View.[20] So whether or not we think of experiences as having objects as constituents, there is still a strong case for (EP$_a$).

None of this commits us to (EP$_g$). Even if the concept of a mind-independent object cannot be extracted or acquired from experience it could still be the case that experience has a role in explaining our grasp of this concept, whether we have a Representational or a Relational View of experience. One might think, for example, that in order to have the concept of a mind-independent object one must have some concepts of mind-independent objects. *Mind-independent object* is a formal concept. Concepts of objects—concepts like *apple*, *suitcase*, and *tree*—are sortal concepts.[21] On the plausible assumption that experience plays a direct role in explaining our grasp of sortal and other empirical concepts it follows that it plays at least an indirect role in explaining our grasp of the concept of a mind-independent object. To endorse (EP$_g$) would be to think, in effect, that one can have the *a priori* concept of a mind-independent object even if one has *no* empirical concepts, and this is not a sensible thing to think. Indeed, the role of experience in relation to the concept of a mind-independent object might be even more direct than the discussion so far suggests. To imagine someone who has no experience of mind-independent objects is to imagine someone whose grasp of the concept of a mind-independent object is empty and formal. Concepts without intuitions are empty, and this puts further pressure on (EP$_g$).[22] This version of the Experience Premise is both implausible and unmotivated. There is no reason to think that experience of objects can play *no* role in explaining our grasp of the concept of a mind-independent object, despite the range of powerful arguments in support of (EP$_a$).

---

[19] From the claim that there is nothing intrinsic in common between perceptual experiences and matching hallucinations it does not follow that the former lack representational content. However, Campbell talks about perceptual experiences having 'phenomenal character' rather than representational content.

[20] Notice that if the Relational View regards experiences as representational then it would open itself up to the *ad hominem* objection that it takes the intentionality of experience for granted and so cannot allow that experience of objects explains our ability to think about objects. To deal with this objection it would need to avail itself of the idea that the representational content of experience is non-conceptual. Perhaps it would be better, in that case, for the Relational View to ally itself with those who think that experience does not have a representational content. See Travis (2004).

[21] For the distinction between formal and sortal concepts see Wiggins (1980: 63–4).

[22] On the idea that concepts without intuitions or experiences in some way corresponding to them are 'empty' see Kant (1932), especially the opening paragraphs of the Transcendental Logic and the Schematism of the Pure Concepts of Understanding.

3 The Possession Premise

Although the acquisition version of the Experience Premise has a lot going for it we might still be reluctant to endorse it. One reason is this: the Possession Premise says that in order to have concepts of mind-independent objects one must have the concept of a mind-independent object. But if the latter cannot be derived from experience then how can the former still be derived from experience? The problem is that concepts like *apple*, *tree*, and *suitcase* are empirical concepts, that is, ones that *are* derived from experience. If they come from experience then it seems either that (EP$_a$) is false or that the Possession Premise is false: either the concept of a mind-independent object originates in experience or one does not need this concept in order to have concepts of mind-independent objects.

This argument turns on the following *Parity Thesis*:

(PT)   If possession of the concept of a mind-independent object is necessary for possession of concepts of mind-independent objects then the latter can be derived from experience only if the former can be derived from experience.

Why should one accept (PT)? That depends on why the Possession Premise—the antecedent of (PT)—is thought to be correct. One way of motivating this premise would be to appeal to the Containment Model of concepts. According to this model, most concepts are structured complexes of other concepts.[23] One concept is a structured complex of other concepts just if it has those other concepts as proper parts. If the concept F has the concepts G and H as proper parts then it is plausible that one cannot have F unless one has both G and H, and that F cannot be derived from experience unless G and H can be so derived. So if we assume that concepts of mind-independent objects are complex concepts that have the concept of a mind-independent object as a proper part then the Possession Premise and the Parity Thesis follow straightforwardly: if concepts like *apple*, *tree* and *suitcase* embed the concept of a mind-independent object then one cannot have the former unless one has the latter, and concepts like *apple*, *tree* and *suitcase* cannot be derived from experience unless the concept of a mind-independent object can be derived from experience.

Strictly speaking this argument only shows that sortal concepts cannot be entirely or exclusively derived from experience, but the idea that even supposedly empirical concepts have an *a priori* component is not incoherent. One might, in any case, be sceptical about the Containment Model and the suggestion that the Possession Premise is committed to this model. It is worth remembering how the concept of a mind-independent object was first introduced into the discussion. The initial thought was that in order to have concepts of mind-independent objects one must have the conception of objects *as* mind-independent or, as Campbell puts it, 'the conception of a mind-independent world' (2002b: 121). It was then stipulated that someone who has the

---

[23] This is the account of the Containment Model given in Margolis and Laurence (1999).

conception of objects as mind-independent is someone who has the concept of a mind-independent object. To say that someone has the latter concept is simply a way of making the point that they have the conception of a mind-independent world. If they do not have this conception they can hardly be said to have concepts of mind-independent objects, but this has little to do with the idea that concepts of mind-independent objects *contain* the concept of a mind-independent thing. If F and G are distinct concepts one can coherently think one must have G in order to have F without thinking that F contains G.

Even if F does not contain G, one might think that there is still something odd about combining the following claims:

(a) In order to have F one must have G.

(b) F is an empirical concept.

(c) G is a non-empirical concept.

The coherence, or otherwise, of combining these claims is an issue that Kant takes up in his account of the relationship between empirical concepts and the categories. He claims that the concept *tree* is an empirical concept that is acquired from experience by means of various operations of the understanding, and that these operations presuppose the prior synthesis of experiential input by means of categorial concepts like *substance* and *object*.[24] The categories are themselves non-empirical. They cannot be acquired from experience but they make it possible for us to acquire empirical concepts from experience and thereby make it possible for us to possess empirical concepts: in order to have the concept *tree* one must have one or more of the categories, *tree* is an empirical concept but the categories are non-empirical. This is how Kant combines (a), (b), and (c). His idea is that the enabling conditions for the acquisition or possession of empirical concepts do not themselves have to be empirical.[25]

The role of the concept of a mind-independent object in relation to sortal concepts is analogous to the supposed role of the Kantian categories in relation to sortal or other empirical concepts. To have the concept of a mind-independent object or conception of a mind-independent world is to be able to think or reason in certain ways. Being able to think or reason in the relevant ways is an enabling condition for grasp of empirical concepts but this does not imply that concepts like *apple*, *tree*, and *suitcase* are not really empirical or that the concept of a mind-independent object is really just another empirical concept. Without the Containment Model hovering in the background there is no reason to believe the Parity Thesis. But the Possession Premise remains in good shape: someone who lacks the concept of a mind-independent object, and all that this concept brings with it, is either someone who lacks concepts like *apple*,

---

[24] The operations of the understanding by means of which empirical concepts are acquired from experience are comparison, reflection and abstraction. See Longuenesse (1998) for further discussion and references.

[25] For an account of Kant's conception of the relationship between empirical and categorial concepts see Longuenesse (1998) and Cassam (2007: chapter 4).

tree, and *suitcase* or someone for whom these concepts can only be concepts of mind-dependent objects.

4 The Explanatory Requirement

Suppose that (EP_a) is right and that the concept of a mind-independent object cannot be derived from experience. What follows, according to Berkeley, is that we do not have the concept of a mind-independent object.[26] He thinks this follows because he is committed to the acquisition version of the Explanatory Requirement (ER_a), which says that if we have the concept of a mind-independent object it must be acquired from experience. If (EP_a) is right and the concept of a mind-independent object cannot be derived from experience then we do not have this concept. Kant's reaction to the success of (EP_a) is different. His idea is that since we clearly do have the concept of a mind-independent object, and since this concept cannot be acquired from experience, (ER_a) has got to be false. Indeed, he views the impossibility of deriving any of his categorial concepts—concepts like *substance* and *cause*—from experience as the single most powerful argument against the concept empiricism to which (ER_a) gives expression.

The proposal that the acquisition version of the Experience Premise casts doubt on the acquisition version of the Explanatory Requirement is one that Georges Rey takes up in his response to Campbell's discussion of Berkeley's Puzzle. Commenting on the concern that experience of objects could not be what explains our having the conception of objects as mind-independent Rey protests:

But who besides the Classical Empiricists is even tempted by the view that experience alone could 'be what provides us with our concepts' of mind-independent objects—or, for that matter, with any other of our fundamental concepts? It seems to me that Berkeley's idealism was a superb *reductio* of that idea, but, if that was not good enough, the failure of classic phenomenalistic reductions and the substantial evidence for nativism have surely been nails in the coffin. (2005: 140)

Campbell's response to Rey is instructive. He denies that Berkeley's Puzzle rests on the idea that experience alone must be what provides us with our concepts of mind-independent objects. On Campbell's reading of Berkeley, 'the point is only that perceptual experience has some role to play in explaining our grasp of concepts, not that it is the only thing that has a role to play' (2005: 162). If this very modest Explanatory Requirement is sufficient to generate the Puzzle then Rey's response misses the point since it consists in disputing a quite different Explanatory Requirement.

What is striking about the exchange between Rey and Campbell is, in my terms, that while (ER_a) is Rey's target Campbell does not defend (ER_a). What he does instead is to insist on (ER_g). (ER_g) and (ER_a) are not equivalent, and defending (ER_g) is not a

---

[26] The explicit target of Berkeley's attack is the notion of matter. He says that this notion 'involves a contradiction in it' (1975: 79) because it is the concept of something that can exist unperceived.

way of defending (ER$_a$). So Campbell and Rey are, to some extent, arguing at cross purposes. Be that as it may, the philosophically significant questions raised by their exchange are these:

(i) Should we accept (ER$_a$)?
(ii) Does (ER$_a$) make it hard to see how we could have the concept of a mind-independent object or concepts of mind-independent objects?
(iii) Should we accept (ER$_g$)?
(iv) Does (ER$_g$) make it hard to see how we could have the concept of a mind-independent object or concepts of mind-independent objects?

The answer to (i) is 'no'. There is little to be said in favour of (ER$_a$) and one major thing to be said against it: we have plenty of concepts, including the concept of a mind-independent object, that cannot be extracted from experience. The answer to (ii) is, as argued above, 'yes'. However, the empiricism to which (ER$_a$) gives expression is far from irresistible so the fact that the concept of a mind-independent object cannot be extracted from experience does not show that this concept is not available to us.

Turning to (iii) and (iv), (ER$_g$) says that experience must have a role in explaining our grasp of the concept of a mind-independent object. Whether this is something we should accept depends on what specifically the explanatory role of experience is supposed to be. There are some concepts in relation to which the explanatory role of experience is substantial. For example, colour experience plays an important role in our grasp of colour concepts.[27] In the absence of colour experience one might be able to talk about particular colours but one would not really know what it is for something to be, say red. One's grasp of the concept *red* would be deficient because it would lack any experiential underpinning and so would be purely theoretical. In the case of other concepts, like *black hole* or *quark*, it would be bizarre to think that one needs to be able to experience their instances in order to count as having a proper grasp of the concept. A physicist's grasp of such concepts is not deficient for being 'purely theoretical' since these are theoretical rather than observational concepts. The explanatory role of experience in relation to concepts that are incapable of being instantiated or realized in experience is bound to be even less direct and substantial than its explanatory role in relation to concepts that can be instantiated in experience.

The concept of a mind-independent object is both theoretical and observational. While grasp of this concept requires grasp of a surrounding theory it is integral to a proper grasp of it that we can perceive its instances.[28] The specific role that experience must play in relation to the concept of a mind-independent object is to present us with instances of it. Experience is what gives the concept what Kant would call its 'objective reality', and that is why we must be able to perceive mind-independent objects, and

---

[27] See Campbell (2006) for much more on this.
[28] See Evans (1980) for the idea that the concept of a mind-independent object cannot stand on its own, without grasp of a surrounding theory.

perceive them *as* mind-independent objects, if we are to count as grasping the concept. There is more to grasping the concept than being able to perceive its instances but *mind-independent object* is not a purely theoretical concept.[29] If this is the point of (ER$_g$) then we should accept this version of the Explanatory Requirement. The answer to (iii) is 'yes'.

It should now be clear that the answer to (iv) is 'no': we can and do perceive mind-independent things as such so (ER$_g$) does not make it hard to see how we could have the concept of a mind-independent object or concepts of mind-independent objects. To think that (ER$_g$) states a requirement that cannot be satisfied would be to agree with Berkeley and Hume that the senses are incapable of presenting their objects as mind-independent. Both representationalists and relationalists about experience can agree that Berkeley and Hume were wrong about this, and this means that there is no longer a puzzle about our possession of concepts of mind-independent objects. The version of the Explanatory Requirement that cannot be satisfied is (ER$_a$) rather than (ER$_g$). The version of this requirement that we should accept is (ER$_g$) rather than (ER$_a$). So there is no puzzle: even on a Representational View of experience there is no Explanatory Requirement on our grasp of the concept of a mind-independent object that is both compelling and incapable of being fulfilled.

The question that Berkeley raises is a how-possible question, a question of the form 'How is X possible?'. Such questions are obstacle-dependent. They get their bite from the factors that make X look impossible.[30] So Berkeley's question is: how is it possible for us to have concepts of mind-independent objects given the factors that make it look impossible for us to have such concepts? Suppose that the factor that makes X look impossible and that prompts the how-possible question is some requirement R that looks like it cannot be fulfilled. One response to the how-possible question would be to accept that R is a genuine requirement but argue that this requirement can be fulfilled. This is what might be called an *obstacle-overcoming* response to the question. An *obstacle-dissipating* response would be to argue that while R cannot be fulfilled it does not represent a genuine requirement on X. X is possible regardless of whether R can be fulfilled.

Berkeley thinks that the Explanatory Requirement is fundamentally what makes it impossible for us to have concepts of mind-independent objects. He asks: how, given this requirement, is it possible for us to have such concepts? And his answer is: it is not possible. I have been recommending a response to Berkeley's how-possible question that is neither exclusively obstacle-dissipating nor exclusively obstacle-overcoming. It can be described as an obstacle-dissipating response to the extent that it questions the

---

[29] In this respect the concept of mind-independent object is similar to Kant's categories. It is worth remembering that Kant describes his categories as 'concepts of an object in general, and argues that if they are not sensibly realized—instantiated in experience—then they are merely functions of the understanding that represent no object. My account of the role of perceptual experience in providing the concept of a mind-independent object with objective reality is self-consciously Kantian.

[30] This is the account of how-possible questions given in Cassam (2007).

legitimacy of (ER$_a$). It can also be described as an obstacle-overcoming response to the extent that it accepts (ER$_g$) and tries to show that this requirement can be fulfilled. As with all the best how-possible questions in philosophy there is a genuine insight that underlies Berkeley's question. What Berkeley recognizes is that there is a sense in which our concepts are made available by our experience of the world. There are, however, also some serious mistakes at the heart of his thinking. One is to think that all concepts are empirical. The other is his failure to see that experience can present its objects as mind-independent. Kant's discussion of these issues is so much better than Berkeley's because he makes neither mistake. He sees that there must be some *a priori* concepts and also that the content of perceptual experience is not nearly as limited as Berkeley supposes. In tackling Berkeley's Puzzle, it is Kant's lead that we should follow.

References

Ayers, M. R. (1975), 'Introduction' to Berkeley 1975.

Baillargeon, R. (1999), 'The Object Concept Revisited: New Directions in the Investigation of Infants' Physical Knowledge', in Margolis and Laurence 1999.

Berkeley, G. (1975), *Philosophical Works, including the works on vision*, ed. M. R. Ayers (London and Melbourne: J. M. Dent & Sons Ltd).

Campbell, J. (2002a), 'Berkeley's Puzzle', in T. Gendler and J. Hawthorne (eds.) *Conceivability and Possibility* (Oxford: Oxford University Press).

Campbell, J. (2002b), *Reference and Consciousness* (Oxford: Clarendon Press).

Campbell, J. (2005), 'Reply to Rey', *Philosophical Studies*, 126.

Campbell, J. (2006), 'Manipulating Colour: Pounding and Almond', in T. Gendler and J. Hawthorne (eds.) *Perceptual Experience* (Oxford: Oxford University Press).

Cassam, Q. (1999), 'Self-Directed Transcendental Arguments', in R. Stern (ed.) *Transcendental Arguments: Problems and Prospects* (Oxford: Oxford University Press).

Cassam, Q. (2003), '*A Priori* Concepts', in Hans-Johann Glock (ed.) *Strawson and Kant* (Oxford: Oxford University Press).

Cassam, Q. (2007), *The Possibility of Knowledge* (Oxford: Oxford University Press).

Evans, G. (1980), 'Things Without the Mind—A Commentary upon Chapter Two of Strawson's *Individuals*', in Z. Van Straaten (ed.) *Philosophical Subjects: Essays Presented to P. F. Strawson* (Oxford: Clarendon Press).

Kant, I. (1932), *Critique of Pure Reason*, trans. N. Kemp Smith (London: Macmillan).

Longuenesse, B. (1998), *Kant and the Capacity to Judge: Sensibility and Discursivity in the Transcendental Analytic of the Critique of Pure Reason*, trans. C. T. Wolfe (Princeton: Princeton University Press).

Margolis, E. and Laurence, S. eds. (1999), *Concepts: Core Readings* (Cambridge, Mass.: The MIT Press).

Matthen, M. (2006), 'On Visual Experience of Objects: Comments on John Campbell's *Reference and Consciousness*', *Philosophical Studies*, 127.

Peacocke, C. (2001), 'Phenomenology and Nonconceptual Content', *Philosophy and Phenomenological Research*, 62.

Rey, G. (2005), 'Explanation, Not Experience: Commentary on John Campbell's *Reference and Consciousness*', *Philosophical Studies*, 126.

Siegel, S. (2006), 'Subject and Object in the Content of Visual Experience', *Philosophical Review*, 115.

Travis, C. (2004), 'The Silence of the Senses', *Mind*, 113.

Wiggins, D. (1980), *Sameness and Substance* (Oxford: Blackwell).

3

Relational vs Kantian Responses to Berkeley's Puzzle

John Campbell

In earlier work (Campbell 2002), I argued that Berkeley's Puzzle requires that we take a Relational View of experience. Quassim Cassam says that Berkeley's Puzzle is better addressed by Kant's analysis of experience in terms of intuition and concept. This issue has a lot of reverberation for what we say about our relation to our surroundings.

I begin by saying something about what Berkeley's Puzzle is (sections 1 and 2). Then I look at Cassam's distinction between a role for experience in the acquisition of concepts and a role for experience in the possession of concepts (section 3). I then formulate the issue between Relational and Kantian responses to Berkeley's Puzzle (section 4). Finally, I elaborate somewhat on the Relational response (section 5).

My main point is that the issue has to do with the explanation and justification of our reasoning about the objects around us. Suppose you think that the world we are in is fundamentally quite unlike anything we encounter in experience. You might be encouraged in this view, on which the external world is alien, by your reading of physics, or by your reading of Kant. In that case, our possession and use of the concepts we ordinarily use on the basis of perception, concepts relating to the medium-sized world, cannot be explained or justified by appeal to facts about our environment. We have to look rather at facts relating to the inner architecture of the mind, just as Kant supposes in setting out the doctrine of intuition and concept.

On the other hand, suppose that the world we are in is fundamentally the way we think it is. Perhaps physics merely describes a fine level of grain, or operates at a level of description orthogonal to the medium-sized world that interests us. So suppose ordinary perceptual experience does indeed acquaint us with what the world is like. Then our possession and use of concepts of the medium-sized world can be explained and justified by appealing to perceptual acquaintance with our environment. Perceptual experience can be thought of as a relation to our surroundings that explains and justifies our patterns of reasoning about the medium-sized world, just as the Relational View supposes.

I begin with some remarks on Berkeley's Puzzle.

1 Counterfactuals involving concrete objects

As a preliminary, notice that when we consider the counterfactuals about experience that figure in our ordinary thinking about the perceived world, we need a distinction between "backtracking" counterfactuals and "intervention" counterfactuals. To illustrate, suppose I say, "Had I not been fired, the company would not have gone bankrupt." For if I had not been fired, that could only have been because the company was doing well; and if the company was doing well it would not have been bankrupt. That's a backtracking counterfactual. In contrast, suppose I say: "If something had come from outside the usual nexus of factors affecting our company, to bring it about selectively that I was not fired, then the company would not have gone bankrupt." That is an intervention counterfactual. On natural assumptions, in this case the backtracking counterfactual is true and the intervention counterfactual is false. (For more on these notions see Lewis 1979 and Woodward 2003.)

Even from a Berkeleyan standpoint, you might argue that there are the resources available to make sense of our ordinary understanding of objects as existing independently of us. After all, Berkeley claimed the right to speak with the vulgar. Berkeley says:

The table I write on, I say, exists, that is, I see and feel it; and if I were out of my study I should say it existed, meaning thereby that if I was in my study I might perceive it, or that some other spirit actually does perceive it. (*Principles of Human Knowledge*, §3)

As Cassam notes, there is a subtle issue here: is Berkeley saying that if he were in his study to experience it, the table would exist? Or is Berkeley saying that the table exists whether or not he is in study, but what its existence comes to is this: that if he were in his study to perceive it, the table would exist? The first reading is arguably what Berkeley meant (Ayers 1975, p. xi). The second reading, though, gives a way of explaining what it is to have the concept of objects as existing unperceived. It can be extended to cover further aspects of our ordinary conception of physical objects as mind-independent. We suppose that different people can all see one and the same tree, that it can be the same tree that I saw yesterday that now, after an interval, I see again today. And so on. We can explain what this comes to in terms of counterfactual reasoning about perceptual qualia. For example, we say that you and I are currently seeing the same thing. It is not just that we are having similar qualia, we see one and the same external object. What this comes to, the phenomenalist says, is that there are counterfactuals correlating your experience with mine. Had your color qualia been different, mine would have been different. Had you had an experience of green, I would have had an experience of green. Had you had an experience of red, I would have had an experience of red. Similarly, consider the idea that it is one and the same object that I saw yesterday as I see today. You might try to interpret this in terms of counterfactuals about sensations. Had I had a different experience yesterday, I would be having a different experience today.

This approach does not recognize the distinctions we ordinarily make between different kinds of counterfactual relating to ordinary physical objects. In particular, insofar as these counterfactuals about sensations can be interpreted so as to come out true, they are backtracking counterfactuals. If you had a different color sensation on looking at the object, that would have been because the object was a different color, and consequently I would have had a different color sensation. If I had had a different color sensation yesterday, that would have been because the object was a different color, so it would have had the same color today, and I would have a different color sensation today. The fact that the counterfactuals are backtracking shows up when we consider what would happen if some external force had intervened on your sensation. If something had come from entirely outside the system of the usual causes and effects, and selectively made a difference just to your experience, there would have been no difference in my experience. If something had come from outside the system of the usual causes and effects, and made a difference selectively to my earlier experience, there would have been no difference in the experience I am having now.

It is when we consider these intervention counterfactuals (counterfactuals about what would happen within the system were there an external intervention selectively on one or another aspect of it) that we see how our ordinary thinking about physical objects goes beyond counterfactual relations between patterns of experiences. The mind-independence of ordinary physical objects shows up when we reflect:

(a) It is possible for something to come from outside the system and selectively change e.g. the color or shape of an object, without doing so by affecting anyone's perceptual experiences.

(b) If something does selectively intervene on e.g. the color of an object at one time, that will make a difference to the experiences people have of that object later.

Here is one way to put Berkeley's Puzzle: merely appealing to the idea of experience as sensations caused in us by the world will not explain how it is that we have the idea of physical objects as the subjects of such external interventions. We do have and use the idea of physical objects as the potential subjects of external interventions that would make a difference to our perceptual experiences. And on the view I am recommending, it is perceptual experience itself that makes it possible for us to think of material objects in this way. It is in perceptual experience that we encounter those objects. That is what gives us the right to reason in terms of these loci of potential interventions. But that means that we cannot be thinking of perception as merely a matter of sensations being produced in us. So we have to find another analysis of perceptual experience. That is what the Relational View provides. Cassam suggests a Kantian alternative. I will look at these options in sections 4 and 5. For now I want to look further at how to characterize the way of thinking about objects as mind-independent that experience gives us the right to. I will propose that the analysis in terms of objects as the loci of intervention counterfactuals ultimately gives way to thinking of objects as causal mechanisms, their movements transmitting causal influence from place to place. That is the way of thinking of objects that perception makes available to us.

2 Objects as causal mechanisms

Let me go back over the kind of reasoning that seems to demand justification here. I have in mind reasoning that reflects the conception of objects as mind-independent. It is fairly easy to see that Berkeley conceives of objects as mind-dependent. On his view the identity of an object just is the identity of a perception, and two people cannot share the same perception, the same perception cannot be encountered in different sense-modalities or at different times. Yet obviously we do ordinarily talk in terms of one and the same object being encountered by different people, through different sense-modalities and at different times. How is it that we have the conception of it being one and the same object here? How is it that we can conceive of the unity of an object without conceiving of it in terms of its relation to a mind?

The suggestion that has been considered by most theorists working on the subject is that our conception of the unity of an ordinary concrete object is the conception of a causal unity. To have the conception of concrete objects as mind-independent is to have some understanding of their identity-conditions; and those identity-conditions have to do with the causal dependence of the way the object is later on the way the object was earlier. When we characterize the identity of the object in this way, we do not need to bring in its relation to a mind. That is how we have the conception of the object as mind-independent.

When I put it like this, however, it also looks as though we could give a comprehensive characterization of how one has the conception of objects as mind-independent without bringing in one's experience of objects at all. For you could give a theoretical characterization of the causal dependencies here, and how the subject grasps them, without mentioning the subject's experience of objects. So this way of explaining what it is to have the conception of objects as mind-independent seems to lose any role for the subject's experience of objects.

In its own terms, this objection seems to me correct. To put the point in perspective, I want to remark that in general, we think of causal connections in two ways. First, we think in terms of causation as a matter of there being a counterfactual connection between two variables, Y and X. For Y to be counterfactually dependent on X is for it to be the case that the value of Y would have been different, had the value of X been different. The kinds of variables that matter for questions of the identity of objects are variables such as "whether saw Y cut through the wood easily at t2," and "whether saw X had been oiled at t1," where t2 is later than t1. If saw Y and saw X are different saws, then there will in general be no counterfactual dependence of the first variable on the second. That is, how easily saw Y is cutting through the wood would not have been any different whether or not you had oiled saw X. However, if the value of variables such as that first variable is counterfactually dependent on the value of the second variable, then that is the kind of causal connection that it takes for saw Y at t2 to be identical to saw X at t1. A grasp of this kind of counterfactual connection between variables relating to how the object is later and variables relating to how the object was earlier does not seem to exploit the subject's experience of the object.

Of course, it is a familiar point that the counterfactuals here must not be "back-tracking" counterfactuals. We have to be considering counterfactuals relating to what would happen to the value of one variable were there to have been an intervention on the value of the other variable. But I will not pursue these points here.

There is a second dimension to our ordinary thinking about causation. We do not think merely in terms of counterfactual connections between variables; we think in terms of mechanisms by means of which the counterfactual connections exist. Suppose we consider any finding established by a randomized controlled trial, such as a role for vitamin E in the prevention of heart disease. The trial might establish that interventions on the level of vitamin E in a patient will make a difference to the risk of heart disease. But there is a further, compelling question: What is the mechanism by which vitamin E affects the risk of heart disease? The answer: "There is no mechanism" would seem barely intelligible to most researchers. The truth of the intervention counterfactuals is one thing, and the mechanism implicated in the causation here is something else.

The notion of a mechanism here is notoriously difficult to characterize, and I am not going to attempt a general characterization of it, beyond remarking on its importance. I do want to suggest that a prototypical case of a mechanism is provided by our ordinary conception of an ordinary medium sized object transmitting causal influence from place to place. This is one of the prototypical examples of a mechanism, it provides us with one of the basic pictures of what a mechanism is that we bring to more difficult cases.

Let me give a simple example. Suppose I have two knives, knife A and knife B. And I have a knife-sharpener. Knife B is over at the cutting-board, with tomatoes ready to be chopped. Knife A is at the other end of the room, beside the knife-sharpener. Here are two cases:

Case 1.   I sharpen knife A, and put it down beside the sharpener. I go to the other side of the room and use knife B to chop tomatoes. The chopping goes faster and better than it would have done if I had not sharpened knife A. Let us suppose that this is established by extensive experiment.

Case 2.   I sharpen knife A. I take it over to the chopping board and use it to chop tomatoes. The chopping goes faster and better than it would have done if I had not sharpened the knife.

Case 1 is an unusual and puzzling case. How does it happen that the intervention at the sharpener is making a difference to what happens over at the cutting board? The natural question is, "What's the mechanism?". Surely this must be some kind of conjuring trick. There must be some kind of machinery linking the two places, at the sharpener and at the cutting board, that we have not yet described. Case 2 seems quite different. What has happened at the sharpener is making a difference to what happens at the cutting board. But there is no puzzle about how this is happening. It is not that there is no mechanism here for transmitting causal influence from place to place. There is a mechanism. It is the movement of knife A. The movement of knife A from one place to another is the mechanism by which causal influence has been transmitted from one place to the other. This point is evidently quite general. The movements of concrete objects from place to place are the mechanisms by which causal influence is transmitted from place to place. This point is so familiar that it is easy to miss. But once you point it out, it is obviously basic to our thinking about causation in the immediate environment. That is what I mean by saying that concrete objects here are prototypical mechanisms by which causal influence is transmitted.

You might say that this is just a matter of what we are familiar with as opposed to what we are not familiar with. We are not familiar with Case 1 interventions whereas we are familiar with Case 2 interventions. But that response understates the contrast. Suppose Case 1 interventions did become commonplace. We would still look for a mechanism explaining why they happened. Similarly we look for mechanisms explaining why light switches turn on lights, no matter how familiar we are with the phenomenon. It is not that there is some a priori guarantee that we will always find what we are looking for. It is just there is some looking to be done. In a Case 2 intervention, however, it is not just that the thing is familiar. The mechanism linking intervention and upshot is palpably there. Ordinary perception confronts us with the mechanism.

One reason it is easy to miss this point is that when we are looking for mechanisms we are often looking for something hidden. For example, it might take a lot of work to find the mechanism linking vitamin E with heart disease. But in this case the mechanism in play is perfectly obvious. You might point out that there is a hidden structure here, the molecular composition of the knife being transported from place to place. But this is not an alternative to thinking of the movement of the knife itself as the mechanism for the transmission of influence. All it provides us with is an equation: the movement of the knife is the movement of a collection of molecules. That identity may be true, but it is still the movement of the knife from place to place that is the mechanism for the transmission of causal influence.

To sum up. A grasp of the identity of knife A over time may consist partly in a grasp of intervention counterfactuals. You know that an intervention on A earlier will make a difference to how it is later. But grasp of the identity of A provides more than this. Your grasp of the identity of A means that you know the mechanism linking what happens at the earlier place to what happens at the later place. In contrast, you could know that an intervention on A is going to make a difference to how B is later. But you might still not know the mechanism involved. Knowledge of the mechanism involved is something over and above knowledge of the intervention counterfactual. This understanding of the physical object as mechanism is not a matter merely of knowing, explicitly or implicitly, various counterfactuals about what would happen under interventions. In the absence of experience of objects, it is difficult to see how we could have such a conception at all.

Suppose we do have this conception of physical objects as the prototypical mechanisms for transmitting causal influence from place to place. This is a conception of the concrete object as mind-independent: you think of the mechanism as having a unity that has nothing to do with its relation to any mind. Grasp of this idea cannot be explained as a matter of, for example, understanding in practice that your actions on the object earlier will make a difference to how it is later. You could grasp that there was this fact about the upshot of your actions without having any idea what mechanisms are involved. Our ordinary conception of a concrete physical object does provide us with understanding of mechanism, that must go beyond a mere practical grasp of intervention counterfactuals. So in virtue of what do we have this conception of the object as a mind-independent unity? The great merit of the Relational View of experience is that it lets us understand how experience of the object could provide us with this conception. However, Cassam argues at length that it is not possible to "extract" or "acquire" a concept on the basis of experience, so I will review this argument in section 3. I will fill out the way in which experience of the object, on the Relational View, makes it possible for us to operate with the conception of object as mechanism in sections 4 and 5.

3 Justifying the conception of objects as mind-independent

In general, when there is some pattern of reasoning that we engage in, we can ask: with what right or justification do we do so? In some ways the most elementary case is provided by the classical propositional constants. We engage in patterns of reasoning such as and-introduction and and-elimination, modus ponens and conditional proof. And we can ask: with what right or justification do we reason in this way? The classical answer, that every introductory class learns, is that the justification for our reasoning in this way is provided by the classical truth tables.

Berkeley's Puzzle arises because we take experience of ordinary objects to be what explains and justifies our use of concepts of ordinary objects; but if "experience" is merely a matter of having sensations produced by an alien world, it is hard to see how any explanation or justification of our talk of mind-independent objects is provided by experience. Berkeley's own conclusion is that we do not have the right to think in terms of mind-independent objects.

Cassam says that the concept of a mind-independent object cannot be "extracted" from experience, or "acquired on the basis of" experience. One way to put his point here is to say that the pattern of reasoning that constitutes grasp of the concept of a mind-dependent object cannot, in general, be derived from scratch, merely using a perceptual encounter with the object. Justifying the pattern of use of a term is notoriously something that cannot always be done from scratch; that is, without making use of the very pattern of reasoning you are trying to justify. Yet that does not mean that the exercise is pointless. The case of the propositional constants provides a helpful model. If you are not allowed to make use of any rules of logical inference, then you have no way of deriving the correctness of the classical rules of inference from the truth tables. Nonetheless, if you are simply given a collection of inference rules for various signs, it is not a trivial exercise to find truth tables for those signs. For some coherently statable inference rules, it will simply be impossible to find a truth-table that validates them. And when you do have a sign for whose inference rules you can find a truth table, it is your grasp of the truth-table that provides you with your knowledge of what is being said when someone uses the sign; your knowledge of the truth-conditions of utterances involving it. Inference rules without truth tables are empty; truth tables without inference rules are blind.

Cassam says that the key to solving Berkeley's Puzzle is to distinguish two different theses:

(EP$_a$)   The concept of a mind-independent object cannot be acquired from experience of objects, and:

(EP$_g$)   Experience of objects can play no role in explaining our grasp of the concept of a mind-independent object. (This volume pp. 22–23.)

Cassam's strategy is to acknowledge that the concept of a mind-independent object cannot be acquired from experience of objects, but to argue that nonetheless, experience of objects does still play a role in explaining our grasp of the concept of a mind-independent object. That is, he accepts (EP$_a$) but rejects (EP$_g$). The implication is that Berkeley saw that (EP$_a$) was correct, but was mistaken in concluding that we do not have the conception of mind-independent objects. For we can have the right to use a concept without having acquired it on the basis of experience. What makes Berkeley's argument seem powerful, Cassam suggests, is that there is a role for experience in an account of what it is to have the concept of a mind-independent object. I will review Cassam's argument for (EP$_a$), then look at his resistance to (EP$_g$) and the positive account he gives of the role of experience in our understanding of the idea of a mind-independent object.

Consider again the situation of someone who has no grasp of logical reasoning at all, no capacity for deductive inference, who is presented with the truth table for a logical constant. Obviously if this person is just left to get on with it they have no hope of deriving the correctness of any particular rules of inference. In that sense, the concepts of the propositional connectives cannot be "extracted" or "acquired" from the truth tables. It remains possible, however, that there is a role for grasp of the truth tables in an account of what it is to have the concepts of the propositional constants. That is, it may be, for example, that to understand a logical constant one must (a) be able to reason in accordance with the relevant rules of inference, and (b) grasp that those rules of inference are validated by the relevant truth table. So even though the concepts of the propositional connectives cannot be "extracted" from the truth tables, there may still be a role for the truth tables in an account of what it is to grasp the propositional connectives.

Similarly, consider the situation of someone who does not grasp any of the principles of reasoning governing our thinking about mind-independent objects. This person cannot reason in a way that exploits the persistence over time of an object, or that exploits the fact that one and the same object can be perceived through different sense-modalities or at different times. This person cannot reason using the distinction between the case in which sameness of object functions as a mechanism transmitting causal influence from place to place, and the case in which there is no persisting object to function as a mechanism for the transmission of causal influence, and some other mechanism must be sought. If we have such a subject as this, mere sensory confrontation with a concrete object will not enable them to derive the correctness of those principles of reasoning.

Much of Cassam's argument can be seen as elaborating on this point, in the context of one or another model of what it is to have a sensory encounter with an object. As he says, on one Representationalist analysis, to have a sensory encounter with an object is just to have a perception that has as its propositional content a representation of that very object. But on this way of thinking of it, a "sensory encounter" with the object requires that one already has the relevant principles of reasoning in place, so there is no way in which the encounter could be regarded as providing a basis from which the correctness of those principles of reasoning could be derived. Alternatively, the Representationalist might say that the content of the perceptual experience is non-conceptual; here there is no circularity, but just because the basis is weaker than full grasp of the concept, it is hard to see how this could be a basis sufficient to enable the subject to derive the correctness of the usual styles of reasoning that reflect one's grasp of the idea of the object as mind-independent (this volume pp. 24–25).

Cassam also considers whether any help is provided by the Relational View of experience, on which the mind-independent object is itself a constituent of the experience. It is, he writes, "a mystery how an experience is supposed to give one the concept of a mind-independent object just because it has a mind-independent object as a constituent" (this volume p. 27). The only way to bypass this mystery is to suppose that in a characterization of the perceptual encounter, we say something about, as it were, what the subject makes of the concrete object. But that, Cassam says, is tantamount to supposing that the experience has representational content; there is some concept embedded in the experience itself. But that is, he thinks, just to fall back on the Representational View, and now this line of thought "faces the same difficulties in this regard as the Representational View" (this volume p. 27). That is, in order to say what the subject is making of the object that is a constituent of the experience, we have to say what principles of inference the subject regards as applicable to the experience; and now there is no way of appealing to the experience itself to explain how the subject has derived or extracted the correctness of these principles of inference.

I think it is indeed compelling that we cannot regard experience of concrete objects as allowing the subject to derive from scratch the correctness of principles of reasoning that reflect the mind-independence of the object. You could nonetheless argue that for someone who already has mastered those principles of reasoning, including their causal component, experience of the object in effect provides a semantic justification for those principles. I will elaborate on this line of thought in the next section. Similarly, for someone who has already mastered the rules of inference for a propositional connective, knowledge of the truth table may provide a semantic justification for those rules of inference.

4 Relational vs Kantian analyses

I think we can see in outline what Cassam's Kantian analysis is of the right reaction to Berkeley's Puzzle. The idea is that there are two types of concept, empirical concepts such as "knife" and formal concepts such as "mind-independent object." So there are two different levels at which the question of justification can be raised. You can ask: "How is it that we have the right to use empirical concepts as we do?", and you can ask, "How is it that we have the right to use formal concepts such as 'mind-independent object' as we do?" Now a Relationalist need not question that there are these two different kinds of concept, or that there are these different levels at which the question of justification can be raised. I think the key issue is how we see the connection between the two levels of justification.

For the Relationalist, the fundamental level of justification is our use of empirical concepts, and here justification is provided by perceptual experience. You have the right to use demonstratives such as "that knife" because of your perception of the thing. Any justification you have for the use of formal concepts such as "mind-independent object" is derivative on this more basic level. You have the right to use the empirical concepts as you do whether or not you even possess such abstract concepts as "mind-independent object." Given that this foundation is in place, you may derivatively have the right to use such abstract concepts as "mind-independent object." Now if perceptual experience is to take this massive justificatory weight, it is hard to see how its phenomenal content can be anything short of the external objects and properties themselves. If we suppose, for example, that the phenomenal content of experience is merely some representational content or other, the question of justification is simply shoved back: how is it that we have the right to use those representational contents as we do? On the Relational analysis, when we are talking about perceptual experience we are talking about a kind of engagement with the world that does not fundamentally involve representations at all, and which is therefore capable of providing the basis of our right to use representations as we do, to use the patterns of reasoning we actually use.

Now some of what Cassam says actually seems to suggest a picture like this. Cassam does argue, as we saw above, that you can maintain (EP$_a$) but reject (EP$_g$); that you can still find a role for experience in an account of what it is to grasp the concepts of mind-independent objects. Cassam's Kant takes it that there are two types of concept, empirical concepts such as "tree" and formal concepts such as "mind-independent object." And there is a connection between them:

> One might think, for example, that in order to have the concept of a mind-independent object one must have some concepts of mind-independent objects. *Mind-independent object* is a formal concept. Concepts of objects—concepts like *apple*, *suitcase*, and *tree*—are sortal concepts. On the plausible assumption that experience plays a direct role in explaining our grasp of sortal and other empirical concepts it follows that it plays at least an indirect role in explaining our grasp of the concept of a mind-independent object. (This volume p. 27.)

Strictly speaking, this remark is consistent with what the Relationalist says about the role of experience in justifying our patterns of reasoning about material objects. In order to have the right to use an empirical concept like "that tree," one must have experience of the tree. It is experience of the tree that justifies one's use of the demonstrative. An account of how we have the right to use the demonstrative as we do might be expected to have some bearing on how we have the right to use more abstract concepts such as "mind-independent object" as we do.

Is Cassam offering an alternative to the interpretation of Kant as a Relationalist? Cassam says, "experience plays a direct role in explaining our grasp of sortal and other empirical concepts," but what role is that? Does he think that experience plays the role of providing us with a semantic validation for the patterns of reasoning that we engage in concerning physical things? If so, then it is difficult to see what alternative there is to Relationalism; for how could any other analysis of perceptual experience explain how it can provide us with a semantic validation for the patterns of reasoning we use? What Cassam actually says is this:

> The specific role that experience must play in relation to the concept of a mind-independent object is to present us with instances of it. Experience is what would give the concept what Kant would call its "objective reality," and that is why we must be able to perceive mind-independent objects, and perceive them *as* mind-independent objects, if we are to count as grasping the concept. There is more to grasping the concept than being able to perceive its instances but *mind-independent object* is not purely a theoretical concept. (This volume p. 31.)

Why does it matter that experience "presents us with instances" of a concept? On the analysis I have been proposing, it matters because experience provides us with the semantic basis we have for using the concept as we do; for using it in the patterns of inference we do. Only the Relationalist analysis explains how perceptual experience could be playing this fundamental justificatory role.

There is an instructive footnote in Cassam's discussion. He writes:

> [T]he concept of mind-independent object is similar to Kant's categories. It is worth remembering that Kant describes his categories as "concepts of an object in general," and argues that if they are not sensibly realized—instantiated in experience—then they are merely functions of the

understanding that represent no object. My account of the role of perceptual experience in providing the concept of a mind-independent object with objective reality is self-consciously Kantian. (This volume, p. 32 n. 29.)

This does suggest a non-Relationalist line one might take on the validation of our use of empirical concepts. Though Cassam does not explicitly mention it, there is after a Transcendental Deduction of the Categories in Kant's work that might be thought to do some work in validating our use of concepts of the mind-independent world. And a properly Kantian approach here might be thought to challenge the order of justification I suggested. I said that a Relationalist will regard the justification of our use of ordinary empirical concepts such as "that knife" as fundamental, and hold that the justification of one's use of more abstract concepts such as "mind-independent object," is optional and derivative. However, a Kantian response holds that justification of the use of an empirical concept such as "that knife" already depends on the justification afforded by the Transcendental Deduction of the use of concepts such as "mind-independent object." There may be a perceptual component to the justification of a concept such as "that knife," but the work of establishing that we have a right to use concepts such as "that knife," which relate to mind-independent objects, will already have been accomplished by the Transcendental Deduction.

It is possible to wonder whether, within a Kantian framework, anything as strong as exemplification of an empirical concept is actually needed. Consider a subject who has nothing but hallucinations, a subject who, let us suppose, has conscious experiences but is not actually perceiving any concrete objects. It is hard to see why, on a Kantian view, such a subject could not be said to be grasping empirical concepts, and the experiences of this subject could give their concepts what Kant calls "objective reality." After all, in this subject the operations of synthesis upon the raw manifold of intuition may be proceeding in full accordance with the demands of the Transcendental Deduction. Of course, the experiences of this subject would not provide anything like a semantic justification for the rule of inference they employ in thinking about mind-independent objects. For these hallucinatory experiences do not constitute encounters with the "intended model" of the thought and talk; for this subject, there is no "intended model," nothing about which they are thinking and talking.

Your reading of Kant, or your reading of physics, may have convinced you that our own situation is not so very different from the situation of this subject. You may hold that the mind-independent reality in our world, the world of noumena, or the world of physics, is so alien to ordinary thought that it cannot be said to provide the intended model of our everyday thought and talk. And you may hold that this alien landscape is the only external reality there is. In that case, there really is no way of taking our ordinary experience to provide a semantic justification for our patterns of reasoning concerning mind-independent objects. There would be no threat here, on a Kantian account, to the "objective reality" of our concepts, for they are still correctly related to the manifold of raw intuition. In fact, what we have here is an idealist or projectivist analysis of the objects about which we ordinarily think and talk. Our patterns of reasoning and their validation come first, and they are projected onto an alien underlying reality. Once it is properly grasped, this Kantian picture is hard to believe. Certainly, it does not constitute an unequivocal defense of common-sense realism again Berkeley's critique. It reads more like a kind of idealism. It is a kind of idealism. For that reason, I would myself have some reservations about Cassam's claim that "In tackling Berkeley's Puzzle it is Kant's lead that we should follow" (this volume p. 33).

5 The Relational View of experience

Suppose we step back from the Kantian approach, and try supposing that the mind-independent world of concrete objects is there, just as we think it is. We can then view our ordinary perceptual experience as being a relation to those objects and properties, just as we ordinarily suppose it is. When you see a mountain and a tree, your experience is a relation between you and that scene. The objects, properties, and relations of that world provide the intended model for ordinary thought and talk: they are the objects, properties, and relations that we ordinarily think and talk about. And our experience of them provides us with the justification for our ordinary patterns of reasoning about mind-independent objects. Nothing like a transcendental deduction is needed; our experience of the world itself supplies all the justification required for those patterns of reasoning.

I pointed out that we think of ordinary concrete objects as the mechanisms by which causal influence is transmitted from place to place. We operate, in our ordinary dealings with concrete objects, with an "intuitive physics," that includes a grasp of the counterfactual dependencies between the state of an object at one time and its state later, perhaps after interactions with other objects. We use our grasp of these dependencies in acting on objects and predicting their behavior. This happens many times a day. You know how cooking an animal will affect its flavor, you know how damping a log will affect the way it burns, you know how whittling a stick will allow it to be used as cutlery. This is a matter of grasping counterfactual dependencies: you know it would not taste like that if you did not cook it, it would not burn so slowly if you had not damped it, it would not spear the meat so well if it had not been honed to a point. I am not suggesting that a mere glance at a thing would allow you to derive such counterfactual dependencies if you did not know them already. Perception of itself will no more allow the derivation than mere knowledge of a truth-table will allow you to derive rules of inference if you did not know any already. Nonetheless, if you do know the counterfactual dependencies and can reason in accord with them, there is a sense in which your reasoning may yet be empty; you may not have knowledge of the categorical object on which you are acting.

Suppose you are working with a machine that has a surface say only a little smaller than the room it occupies, and suppose this surface is translucent, so that light gets through, but you cannot see any of the objects below the surface. Suppose the controls of the machine allow objects to be moved about beneath the surface of the machine. You can push a button to set fire to an object that is underneath the surface, at the leftmost end of the machine. And you can move the object around underneath the surface, and can tell when a lit object is at the rightmost end of the machine by the glow through the surface. In this kind of case, you can grasp the counterfactual dependencies between what you observe at the right and what you did at the left. If you had not set fire to the object on the left, there would not now be that glow on the right. But you do not know the mechanism by which your intervention at the leftmost end of the machine is having its influence transmitted to the new place. So this kind of case sharply contrasts with our ordinary manipulations of objects. In our ordinary manipulations of objects we do not know only the counterfactual dependencies, we are also aware of the categorical objects themselves, the mechanisms by which causal influence is transmitted from one place to another. When you finally look underneath the surface and see the stick being moved around, you learn something about why those counterfactuals were true; you learn about the mechanism by which causal influence was being transmitted. It is in that sense that experience can supply you with a justification for the patterns of reasoning you ordinarily use; it confronts you with the explanation of their correctness.

I said that this way of thinking of it requires a Relational View of experience. If the experience were thought to have a representational content, the experience itself would merely be an exercise in using the relevant concepts of objects, and it could not explain why our pattern of use of those concepts is correct. No more would be provided by perception than an application of the concept; and merely an application of a concept cannot of itself explain anything about why it is right to use it in one way rather than another.

The Relational View needs a lot of elaboration, however. Notice first that to specify the phenomenal content of an experience, it is not enough merely to say what it is that is being experienced and by whom. Experience, on the Relational View, is not a two-place relation between the perceiver and the scene perceived: it is a three-place relation between the perceiver, the scene perceived, and the point of view from which it is being perceived (Campbell 2009). If we had only the two-place relation between the perceiver and the scene, that would not allow us to differentiate an object being touched from an object being seen, or an object being viewed from one angle from the same object being viewed from another angle. We will need to elaborate on this to give a full account of what it is to be encountering the categorical ground of the possibility of transmission of causal influence from place to place. For the moment, the important point is that this kind of elaboration will not of itself bring back in the notion of the perception as representational. An appeal to the idea of the "concept" by means of which the object is presented in experience looks like a quick fix—the object is being perceived under one conceptual "mode of presentation" rather than another— but that only seems like an answer because an account of the notion of a perceptual "mode of presentation" will in the end have to do the work of specifying the object, the perceiver, and the point of view from which the object is being perceived.

Cassam asks whether the Relational View is in any better position than a Representational View to say how experience grounds our use of concepts. He gives the following example:

Gold has the atomic number 79, and lumps of gold are things that we can perceive. But even if experiences of lumps of gold have those lumps as constituents it does not follow that it is possible to extract the concept of an atomic number from those experiences. . . .By the same token. . .the fact that an experience has a mind-independent object as a constituent does not explain how the concept of a mind-independent object can be extracted from experience. . . .(This volume p. 26.)

It is a good question, Cassam goes on to say, how we can draw the distinctions we need here without appealing to the idea that perception does not represent the atomic number of the gold, whereas perception does represent the mind-independence of the object. Well, it is a good question, but we do have to explain the difference between your perceptual relation to an object's molecular structure and your relation to the object's color, if we are to say that you do not experience the molecular structure but you experience the color. To appeal to the idea that your perception does not exercise a concept of molecular structure but does exercise a concept of color only postpones the difficult questions, for now we would have to ask in virtue of what it is that your experience does not exercise the concept of molecular structure but does exercise the concept of color. And whatever answer we give here could be used instead to give a direct account of how it is that you are not experiencing the molecular structure but you are experiencing the color; that is, an account that does not appeal to the idea of concepts in perception. Similarly, we would plan to give a direct account of the sense in which you are experiencing the object as categorical, as a mechanism by which causal influence is transmitted from place to place.

The way of doing this that I am sketching is to appeal to the three-place nature of the perceptual relation between the perceiver, the scene observed, and the point of view from which the scene is being observed. Characterizing the "point of view" will not be a trivial matter. Our entry point is the idea that it involves the physical location from which the scene is being viewed and the sensory modality or modalities in play. Consideration of the dynamic aspects of perception will bring a lot of further factors into play: the focus of the subject's attention, the context of the subject's perceptions before the current moment, and so on. But there is no very evident reason to suppose that any of this will bring into play the concepts possessed by the subject. And if we can in this way fill out the Relational View of the subject's experience, then we should be able to fill out the absolutely intuitive idea that in ordinary experience:

(1) We are presented with substantial, categorical objects;
(2) Our encounters with those objects cause and justify our use of patterns of reasoning that reflect their status as mind-independent;

(3) Our encounters with those objects cause and justify, in particular, our grasp of various counterfactual dependencies, of the type I discussed above.

Our encounters with those objects "cause" our use of the relevant patterns of inference not by generating those patterns of inference from scratch, but by sustaining them: if we could not, on a particular occasion, encounter the object in experience, we would abandon the use of that kind of reasoning, unless some auxiliary cause came into play. This is an alternative to the Kantian approach to justifying our conception of objects as mind-independent. Unlike the Kantian approach, it does find significant theoretical work for experience to do in justifying the patterns of inference that reflect our conception of objects as mind-independent. The Relational response thus acknowledges the force of Berkeley's Puzzle, but unlike the Kantian approach, it relies on the structure of the world in showing that our ordinary patterns of reasoning are after all legitimate.

References

Ayers, Michael R. "Introduction." M. R. Ayers (ed.), *Berkeley: Philosophical Works* (London: Everyman 1975), vi–xxiv.

Berkeley, George. 1734/1975. *A Treatise Concerning the Principles of Human Knowledge*. Reprinted in M. R. Ayers (ed.), *Berkeley: Philosophical Works* (London: Everyman 1975), 62–127.

Campbell, John. 2002. "Berkeley's Puzzle." In Tamar Szabo Gendler and John O'Leary Hawthorne (eds.), *Conceivability and Possibility* (Oxford: Oxford University Press), 127–143.

Campbell, John. 2009. "Consciousness and Reference." In Brian McLaughlin and Ansgar Beckermann (eds.), *Oxford Handbook of Philosophy of Mind* (Oxford: Oxford University Press).

Cassam, Quassim. 2011. "Tackling Berkeley's Puzzle." In this volume pp. 18–34.

Kant, Immanuel. 1932. *Critique of Pure Reason*, trans. N. Kemp Smith (London: Macmillan).

Lewis, David. 1979. "Counterfactual Dependence and Time's Arrow." *Noûs* 13, 455–476.

Woodward, James. 2003. *Making Things Happen: A Theory of Causal Explanation*. Oxford: Oxford University Press.

4

Experiential Objectivity

Naomi Eilan

I Introduction

The world around us 'contains objects, variously propertied, located in a common space and continuing in their existence independently of our interrupted and relatively primitive perceptions of them'. Thus Strawson, in 'Perception and its Objects', on what he calls the 'commonsense view' of the world, a conception of the world around us that delivers what he calls our 'commonsense realism' about it. Strawson holds that it is part and parcel of our commonsense realism that we take our perceptions to be causally explained by the way things are in the world and our own position in it, though he concedes this aspect of the theory is available only on reflection (Strawson, 1979).

One set of questions one might direct at Strawson concerns the details of his account of our commonsense conception of the world—and I return to some of these in the last section. However, the issues I am mainly concerned with, which are actually Strawson's own main concern in this paper, can be approached, at least initially, in abstraction from such questions. Assuming, in rough outline, his sketch of the content of our commonsense conception, and assuming we are commonsense realists: how should we account for what perception itself delivers? This is Strawson's chief interest, and his chief claim is that, contra the sense datum theory, our perceptions themselves are not neutral or silent relative to the existence of the various located mind independent objects. Perceptions have something I will call 'objective import', where it is in virtue of such import that they put us in touch with the world of physical objects.

Suppose perceptions have objective import. How should their possession of such import be explained? Strawson's own answer is that the contents of our commonsense conception of the world are embedded in the very contents of perception. The account he sketches of what such embedding consists in is intended to acknowledge the depth of the link between experience and our conception of the world as containing objects variously located in space, without resorting to a Kantian appeal to transcendental idealism to explain the inseparability of this conception and experience, without, that is, explaining the link by appeal to space being 'in us' in a way that loses us the realist element in our commonsense realism.

I return to Strawson's motivation for his account of objective import in the last section of the paper. To get there, I will focus on two of the many dimensions along which we may distinguish answers to the question 'How should objective import be explained?' both of which emerge from thinking about Strawson's own position here. I will call the first, the 'Division of Labour Question' (DL). This is an issue highlighted by Tyler Burge in his recent critique of Strawson's account of perceptual objectivity. The particular form it takes in this context rests on two distinct questions. (a) How much, if any, of the full content of our commonsense realism, the idea that objects we perceive are independent of us, should be thought of as part of the actual content of perception itself? (b) If (contra Strawson) it is not all part of the content, how, and to what end, should the philosopher deploy commonsense realism in explaining the objective import of perceptions?

I will call the second question the 'Consciousness Question'. When explaining the objective import of perception, is the basic explanandum *conscious* perception, or is objectivity to be explained independently of how we explain consciousness? Someone who adopts what I will call the *Experiential Objectivity Claim* (EO) insists on the primitiveness of conscious objectivity, on the impossibility of deriving explanations of conscious objectivity from explanations of what it is for non-conscious perceptions to have objective import; someone who rejects it holds that consciousness and objectivity require independent explanations.

Burge explicitly endorses a division of labour strategy in explaining perceptual objectivity and implicitly rejects EO. Strawson (strongly) implicitly endorses EO and (weakly) implicitly rejects division of labour. One aim of this paper is simply to draw out these commitments in the writings of each and to examine the role they play in their respective account of objective import. Doing so helps, I will suggest, to show why some recent debates about perceptual content talk past each other. It also serves to show up the possibility of endorsing, with Strawson and contra Burge, the Experiential Objectivity Claim; and endorsing, with Burge and probably contra Strawson, a version of a division of labour strategy. This is the position I think we should ultimately end up with: and, for what it is worth, it does not seem to me that either philosopher has any good arguments against it. But my aim in this paper is not to argue for this position but to put centre stage in discussions of perceptual objectivity the kinds of questions thrown up by juxtaposing debates about the DL and EO claims.

In the next section I lay out particular aspects of the Division of Labour Question, as it emerges in Burge's critique of Strawson, where the complaint is that Strawson over-intellectualizes the contents of perception. As we shall see, a full account of one of the dimensions of difference here ultimately requires addressing the Consciousness Question. With the main issues under the latter heading in place, I then turn to a discussion of debates between relational and representational theories, as these get formulated once the Experiential Objectivity Claim has been spelled out. In the last section I come back to the relation between realism, the Division of Labour Question and the Experiential Objectivity Claim, and to different ways of doing justice to Strawson's main intuition about the deep embeddedness of commonsense realism in the very fabric of what perception itself delivers.

II Division of labour

Strawson's paper is an extended critique of A. J. Ayer's sophisticated version of a sense datum theory, on which (a) perceptions deliver sensations, mental items with no objective import, that is, items the intrinsic nature of which does not 'point at', in any sense, external physical objects, (b) our commonsense view of the world is the upshot of a theory we form about what we take to be the causes of these sensations. Strawson rejects both ingredients in the theory. Perceptions themselves have objective import in the sense that they 'point at' the external world in virtue of their representational, truth conditional content; and our commonsense view does not have the status of a theory relative to the data provided by sensations.

In his recent paper 'Perceptual Objectivity', Tyler Burge too rejects the sense datum theory in favour of the idea that perceptions have objective import, and would agree with Strawson, as his view has so far been stated. But one of his main targets is Strawson's own positive account of the way in which perceptions have such import. He holds that Strawson delivers a far too intellectualized account, one that, correlatively, 'leaves it doubtful that animals and human infants perceptually represent (or represent as of) bodies or any other element in the physical environment.' (Burge, 2009). Strawson is a prime example of someone who endorses a position Burge calls 'Individual Representationalism' (IR), according to which some constitutive conditions on objective representation must be *represented* by the *individual* if the individual is to engage in objective representation. This is the general position Burge is arguing against, Strawson's version being one of the main ones he discusses.

A good example of the kind of account he is rejecting is to be found in the paper we are discussing, though it is not one Burge himself discusses. In countering Ayer's sense datum theory, Strawson says that our experiences themselves are soaked or infused with the concepts, grasp of which is necessary for being a commonsense realist. More specifically, he claims (a) that commonsense realism is 'embodied' in our perceptual judgements; and (b) that such realism is already present in our experiences, the latter being soaked or infused with the concepts we use in our perceptual judgements. These concepts will include not only the concept of physical objects, causation, and space, but also concepts required for grasping the idea that one's perceptions are explained jointly by the way the world is and one's own position in it.

Recall, the Division of Labour Question has two components. (a) How much, if any, of the full content of our commonsense realism, the idea that objects we perceive are independent of us, should be thought of as part of the actual content of perception itself? (b) If (contra Strawson) it is not all part of the content, how, and to what end, should the philosopher deploy it in explaining the objective import of perceptions? Call the first the 'how much' question, and the second the 'where to' question. The 'over-intellectualization' criticism is initially presented as a response to the first, and it will be the focus of this section. I come back to the 'where to' question in the last section.

There is no doubt that the accounts do indeed differ radically in response to the 'how much' question. Crudely, Strawson says it is all there, some of it albeit implicitly; Burge says almost none of it is there. Strawson's and Burge's positions lie at polar extremes. One immediate question that occurs, given the vast distance is: what are the intermediate positions one might hold here? This depends in part on whether you think they are answering the same question, the main issue we return to. But, by way of an initial rough descriptive classification of positions philosophers have taken here, the following may help.

Consider a perception-based judgement such as: 'This table is square'. Recall, Strawson makes two claims. First, commonsense realism is embedded in the content of the judgement; second, the perception is infused with the concepts that go into the judgement. One ongoing debate about the 'how much' question is concerned specifically with content of perceptual judgements. In order to be credited with a demonstrative thought about what is in fact a physical object must one (a) have the general concept of a physical object; and (b) a reflective grasp of mind independence? Gareth Evans (1982), and Strawson say yes to (a) and to (b); many recent theories of demonstrative thought, including Burge's, say no to both; an intermediate position might be ascribed to those who hold that in thinking a demonstrative thought a subject must be credited with grasp of an intuitive physics (yes to (a)) but need not have reflective grasp of the perception-independence of physical objects (no to (b)) (Peacocke, 1986; Campbell, this volume).

Turning now to the contents of perception: if you think perceptions have conceptual contents, then the same variation of claims is available to you, where what gets added is the possibility that you assign one level down of sophistication to perceptions in contrast to judgements. For example you might hold that perceptions have demonstrative contents, the correct ascription of which to a perception requires simultaneous ascription to the subject of a grasp of an intuitive physics, but not a full grasp of mind-independence which comes in only with judgement, and so forth. Or you might hold that the contents are non-conceptual in which case, on the face of it, many of the questions about richness and sophistication of the content re-open, applied here to non-conceptual content.

There are, then, many choices one makes in undertaking the journey from Strawson to Burge, many answers one gives to many different questions under the 'how much' heading. Given the proliferation of possible moves here we must ask: are there more general issues we can appeal to which fix the rules of the game and provide constraints for assessing these moves? It is the burden of this paper to suggest that two such organizing issues are (a) one's answer to the 'where to' part of the Division of Labour

Question, to which we return in the last section; and (b) one's attitude to the Experiential Objectivity Claim. By way of introducing the latter, consider the following major difference between Strawson and Burge.

According to Strawson, what we are aiming to do is get right the nature of those states we ordinarily refer to in response to questions such as 'Give us a description of your current visual experience' or 'How is it with you visually at the moment?'. In response we will find locutions such as 'I see the red light of the setting sun'. When alerted to the fact that what is required is a description of the experience itself, without commitment to the external world, our interlocutor will, according to Strawson, put the previous report in inverted commas or oratio obliqua and say something like: 'I had a visual experience such that it would have been natural to describe it by saying that I saw a red deer' (Strawson, 1979: 43–44).

Having fixed the datum to be explained, the experiences we refer to when asked such questions, the second issue is: what is the correct philosophical account of the contents of experiences thus referred to? This is where Strawson's rich theory comes in: our experiences themselves contain the full contents of our commonsense realism. Commonsense realism does not have the status of a falsifiable theory about the causes of our sensations—the contents of our commonsense realist conception of the world can be read off the contents of the experience itself. Or, to put it less strongly: having such experiences presupposes a background grasp of the concepts that go into being a commonsense realist.

In responding to Strawson, then, there are at least two potential sources of disagreement. The first turns on whether the everyday descriptions of experiences pinpoint the datum that our theory of perceptual objectivity should aim to explain. The second turns on whether Strawson gives a correct account of the datum we are trying to account for, supposing he is right about what the datum is.

Turning now to Burge: on his account, the datum that needs explaining is delivered by scientific theories of perception. We need an account of the kind of objectivity we should ascribe to perceptual input, given the account of such input we find in these theories. His theory of constancies is his interpretation of what psychological theories deliver.

Here, too, there is the question of whether he gives a correct account of the contents of perceptions, given the work done so far in psychological theories of perception. But there is also the more general question of whether he is right in his appeal to the psychological theory to deliver the datum to be explained when we are interested in perceptual objectivity, where an initial contrast is with our introspection-based everyday descriptions of experience.

This is not a question Burge addresses directly in this paper. That being so, various options are left open. On one reading, Burge is implicitly denying that our everyday descriptions of our experiences have any constraining role at all to play in a philosophical account of perceptual objectivity. We should simply bypass these, and move on to account for the content of perceptions, as delivered by scientific psychology. Note, if this is his position, this leaves open the possibility that Strawson is quite right about how to do justice to our ordinary everyday account of what perception provides us with. It is just that it is neither here nor there where accounts of the objectivity of perception are concerned. Alternatively, he may hold that Strawson is exactly right about the datum to be explained, but wrong in his philosophical explanation of the datum, where the correct account will appeal to scientific psychology.

We do not yet have enough material before us to spell out what the difference is between these responses, let alone tell which Burge would opt for. To move on, note the following feature of the discussion so far. In laying out the Division of Labour Question I have, throughout, oscillated between referring to perceptions and to experiences. I have done this to keep both Burge and Strawson in play. Experiences are conscious perceptions. A sure mark that one is talking about our commonsense conception of perception and what it delivers is that one takes it that the datum to be explained is conscious perceptions. (It is worth remembering that only thirty years ago philosophers were still having arguments about whether the very idea of subliminal perception so much as made sense.) Consciousness and experience do not get a mention in Burge's account of perceptual objectivity, whereas there is no talk of perception in Strawson that is not about the question of what makes experiences have objective import. This is the most important difference between them, and the one we move on to under the heading of the Consciousness Question. As we shall see, Burge's answer to this question delivers, implicitly, answers to some, but not all, of the questions left hanging in response to the datum question.

III The Consciousness Question

The Consciousness Question in general is: what, if any, is the relation between explanations of perceptual consciousness and explanations of objective import? To get going I will focus, initially, exclusively on the problem of how we explain perceptual consciousness, bracketing questions about objective import, beginning, as many do, with the phenomenon of blindsight.

As the phenomenon of blindsight is appealed to in discussions of consciousness, it is said to show the possibility of the following combination of states of affairs.

1. The subject has perceptual information about the environment (inferred from his capacity to guess, when so instructed by the experimenter, some of the properties in the 'functionally blind' area of the visual field, and, when similarly instructed, to direct appropriate movements towards them).
2. The subject is in a generally undisturbed state of being awake.
3. The perception is not in the stream of consciousness, not 'in mind'. (There is no 'intransitive consciousness'.)
4. There is no phenomenal consciousness, no experience.

5. There is no 'monitoring consciousness'—there is no immediate or automatic representation of the occurrence plus contents of the perception.
6. The perceptions do not provide the basis for rational judgements and rationally guided action. (The subject merely guesses, the perception information provides him with no idea why what he says is true, if it is.) There is no 'access consciousness'.
7. There is no presence of the world to the subject; the world represented by the informational state is not present to the subject in the way it is in normal cases of perception.

One thing that all people agree on is that blindsight shows that being awake and being in possession of something we would count as perceptually acquired information with respect to a property, say the orientation of a line, is not sufficient for any other aspects of consciousness. From our perspective, the key question is: what implications does this have for the way we should explain the kind of consciousness referred to in (7), to be labelled henceforth 'perceptual presence'? That is, how should we explain the sense in which perceptions make the world present to the subject?

Now one radical claim might be that in the case of blindsight the world is as present as it ever is in perception, in virtue of the contents of the information produced by the 'blind' perception. I take it few would find this appealing. Most would hold that in the blindsight case the world is not present to the subject in the same way it is in normal cases. Something more is needed.

One claim might be that what is lacking in blindsight, as far as connectedness to the world is concerned, is access consciousness, where such consciousness is defined roughly as Ned Block does. As he defines it, a state is access conscious if its contents are (a) 'Inferentially promiscuous', that is, poised for use as a premise in reasoning; (b) Poised for rational control of action; (c) Poised for the rational control of speech (Block, 1997).

To accept this suggestion is to say that the imagined cases Block calls cases of 'superblindsight' give us everything we normally have as far as the way in which the world is present to the normal subject. In more detail: suppose a blindseer could be trained to guess at will what is in the functionally blind areas of his visual field, that is, without being prompted to do so. In such a case, says Block, visual information will simply 'pop into mind' in the way solutions to problems do. He would describe himself as 'simply knowing' the answer to the question, say about the orientation of a line. Critically, he would contrast these kinds of case with his normal perceptual experiences, in which there is something it is like, a phenomenal feel. On the view we are currently considering the claim would be that the sense in which ordinary perceptions put us in touch with the world is that they are access conscious, thereby becoming hooked up to our thought system and our capacity to form beliefs about the world. This is, as far as I can tell, a view many philosophers either hold explicitly, or would be forced into, if asked, given their approach to phenomenal consciousness, to which I now turn.

Block himself uses the case of superblindsight to demonstrate the separateness of access consciousness from what he calls 'phenomenal consciousness'. As he defines it, (phenomenal)-consciousness is:

(a) Experiential consciousness, it is consciousness of the kind that yields a 'something it is like' to be in the state that has such consciousness. This is the kind of consciousness which people find metaphysically problematic.

(b) It is the kind of consciousness we ascribe primarily though not exclusively to experiences (Block, 1997).

Now, suppose we accept that the conceivability of superblindsight does show that phenomenal consciousness is distinct from access consciousness, the debate I am interested in turns on the question of whether and how the absence of phenomenal consciousness can and should be linked to the sense in which the world is present to subject, in normal cases of perception.

Again, a radical claim would deny outright that there is anything relevant to the way perceptions put us in touch with the world which is lacking when there is no phenomenal consciousness. A less radical claim would concede that we ordinarily suppose that something is lacking, but maintain that our notion of perceptual presence is actually a hybrid concept, which can be analysed into an access component and a phenomenal component in such a way that, on analysis, we see that only the access component is actually doing work in putting the subject in touch with the world. On such a bifurcationary approach, then, we explain the missing presence of the world thus: as far as access to the *world* is concerned, everything is supplied by access consciousness. However, what is lacking is phenomenal consciousness, constituted, say, by the presence of sensations. When both of these are in play we feel or say that the world itself is present to us, but strictly speaking, only access consciousness gives us the world.

This bifurcationary approach is deflationary in that it proposes that, strictly speaking, it is not the world that is phenomenally present, but, rather, sensations. Our talk of 'presence of the world' should, in a sense, be understood metaphorically. The kind of availability of the world to the subject that we get in normal perception can and should be explained wholly in access-consciousness terms. The opposing approach proposes to take presence of the world as a basic unanalysable type of phenomenal consciousness. The claim that it is 'unanalysable' should be understood as the claim that we cannot account for perceptual presence of the world to the subject by saying it consists in presence of something other than the world (a sensation), coupled with a non-phenomenal account of what it is for the world to be available to the subject in perception, for example by appeal to access consciousness. To take this line is to endorse something I will call 'the primitiveness claim'.

Let us now turn to the second question, that of the relation between explanations of perceptual consciousness and accounts of objective perceptual import, which brings us back to the dispute between Strawson and Burge. As I noted, Strawson nowhere contemplates the possibility that in explaining the kind of objectivity perceptions have we might be talking about anything but the sense in which conscious perceptions, experiences, make the world present. Although the question of the primitiveness or otherwise of perceptual consciousness is never addressed by him, I shall take him to be implicitly committed to it. As he puts it: 'mature sensible experience (in general) presents itself as, in the Kantian phrase, an immediate consciousness of the existence of things outside us' (Strawson, 1979: 47).

To take this line is, as I will be interpreting it, to assume that the basic explanandum we are concerned with when explaining perceptual objectivity just is this presence of the world to the subject. For Strawson, explaining perceptual objectivity and explaining presence of the world to us come to the same thing. To adopt this line is to adopt what I am calling the Experiential Objectivity Claim (EO).

In direct contrast, Burge is more or less explicit about rejecting EO, though not under that description. He holds that explanations of phenomenal consciousness, on the one hand, and explanations of perceptual representational content, including its objectivity, on the other, are two distinct enterprises. (Burge, 1997, 2009). On his account, phenomenal consciousness in perception should be explained by appeal to an 'act-object' account of the presence of sensations to the subject. If he were pressed on the subject of what kind of consciousness explains the sense in which the world is present to the subject in normal perception, it is likely he would appeal to his own account of access consciousness, and, perhaps to the bifurcationary account sketched above. To do so is to reject, if implicitly, the primitiveness claim, which means that the Experiential Objectivity Claim, as I have defined it, does not get a look in.

I think it is obvious that there is this difference between Burge and Strawson. What is less obvious is what role if any endorsing EO has in generating Strawson's particular account of the relation between the deliverances of perception and commonsense realism. This applies both to his very formulation of what commonsense realism consists in, and to the reflective way he introduces it into the contents of perception. This is the issue I return to in the last section.

Before that, in the next section, I want to say something about the role that (implicit) adoption of EO by some, but not all, recent participants in debates about the nature of perceptual content has in structuring that debate, specifically with respect to radically different explanations we find of objective import.

IV Objective perceptual import

On the sense datum theory, the deliverances of perception have no objective import at all. The most familiar corrective to this is to insist that perceptions themselves have a kind of intentionality, representational directedness, in virtue of which they 'point' to the world beyond the perception itself. More specifically, the claim is that perceptions point to the world in the same way propositional attitudes point to the world, in virtue, that is, of their representational content. Perceptions represent objects as having certain properties: the link with the world is via the veridicality conditions, reference to which is needed for specifying the content of the representations.

One difference among representationalists turns on whether they hold that the representational contents are wholly conceptual, wholly non conceptual or a combination of both. Another difference turns on the singular component. When the content of a perception is made true or false by the state of a particular object, is this in virtue of the perceptual content containing an identifying description of the object, or in virtue of the object being the de facto cause of the occurrence of the perception. However, one of the most important initial differences, I suggest, is between those who invoke representational content in order to explain the directedness of conscious perception, that is, who accept the Experiential Objectivity Claim, implicitly or explicitly, and those who, again implicitly or explicitly, reject it.

If the only alternative to representational theories is one on which perceptions deliver sensations with properties that have no objective import, then the only way of claiming that perceptions themselves have objective import is by letting representational contents do the job. As this idea was originally introduced, in the analytic tradition at least, for instance by Anscombe in 'The Intentionality of Sensation', there was no question but that one was talking about conscious perceptions. In more recent discussions of representational content this has not been so. One mark of whether or not one is, at least implicitly, being guided by the Experiential Objectivity Claim is that one is trying to do justice to phenomenology, to how things are from the experiencing subject's perspective in explaining the representational contents of perception. But this is not enough. Michael Tye, for example, when appealing to the non-conceptual contents of perceptions to capture phenomenology does not count as endorsing the Claim, because for him it is a further question whether a state with such contents yields presence of the world to the subject. States can have such contents in the absence of such presence: what delivers the latter is, essentially, access consciousness. As I shall understand it, to adopt the Experiential Objectivity Claim is to insist that presence to the subject of the world is entailed by the phenomenal character of the state. If one holds that this is delivered by the representational contents of the state, then we must introduce a kind of contents that has this result. I will call this kind of theory the 'special content' theory.

The most plausible, in my view, such account was sketched by John McDowell and developed by Bill Brewer: the special contents of perceptions are demonstrative contents. On Brewer's version the special contents of perception come down to something like 'this is thus'. Intuitive support for this idea comes from the idea that it would be wrong to ascribe demonstrative contents to the judgements made by blindseers about the entities about which they hazard guesses. (Brewer, 1999; McDowell, 1994.)

From the perspective of issues I am interested in, the most decisive objection to this suggestion was made by John Campbell. It seems a legitimate question to ask: why is it wrong to credit blindseers with demonstrative contents? This does not seem like a brute inexplicable fact. And the intuitive answer is that they cannot think demonstrative thoughts because they are not conscious of the objects about which they issue judgements. If this is right, phenomenal perceptual consciousness is being given an explanatory role and cannot be defined by appeal to demonstrative contents (Campbell, 2002).

As we have seen, though, there can be two quite different accounts of this role. If you do not accept Experiential Objectivity, you will invoke sensations to explain the absence of phenomenal presence, on the bifurcationary model sketched above. You might then say that when such sensations are lacking, subjects do not feel confident enough to issue in demonstrative thoughts and produce existentially quantified ones instead. In contrast, if you do accept the Experiential Objectivity Claim, and do think phenomenal consciousness has an explanatory role here, you will move on to some version of what has been called in recent years, following Campbell, a 'relational theory of perceptual consciousness'. On such theories, presence of the world to the subject is explained by taking perceptual consciousness to consist not in a representation of the object one is conscious of, but, rather, as a state that puts one in a direct two-term relation with it.

Suppose Jake loves Sally, is disgusted by Sam and sees Saul. Prima facie, his psychological states of loving and being disgusted and seeing are all relational, in that their instantiation, as thus described, requires the existence of the object (accusative) of the relation. How should we explain the 'purely' psychological character of the state the subject is in such cases? On what I will call non relational views, the purely mental character of the loving, the seeing and the being disgusted can all be accounted for wholly by reference to the object-independent representational content of the state, conceptual and/or non conceptual; and/or by reference to the character of sensations. As to the object (accusative): if it is explicitly descriptively identified in the representational contents of the state, then it comes in via de dicto reports of the representational content of the state. If it does not come in this way, it comes in not as internal to the mental character of the state, but, rather, in virtue of being the cause of the state, where reference to the object does presuppose its existence, but such existence is not internal to the psychological mental character of the state.

In contrast, on relational views, the purely mental character of the state can only be specified when we refer to the object (accusative) of the state the subject is in. In philosophy we find such claims made in recent years specifically with respect to exteroceptive perceptual states. Perhaps the easiest way to introduce such claims is to recall 'act-object' views of sensations, on which consciousness of a sensation was said to consist in the instantiation of a two-term relation between subject and sensation which was such that the properties of the sensation determined the subjective character of the subject's state immediately, in virtue of being presented to the subject, rather than in virtue of being represented by the subject. Recent relational theories of perception say the same account should be given of the way in which external perceived objects determine the phenomenal character of perceptual states.

Relationalism only makes sense for conscious perceptions, so someone who adopts relationalism is committed to the Experiential Objectivity Claim. One dispute between relationalist and representationalist theories is a dispute between those who accept the Experiential Objectivity Claim. Another is between relationalists who adopt the Experiential Claim, on the one hand, and representationalists who reject it, on the other. In the latter case, where this rejection is not made explicit, we get arguments and claims that fail to engage with each other. Something like this happens, I think, when Burge takes on disjunctivist theories, which overlap with relational theories in many of their claims. (For an account of disjunctivism which illuminates this overlap, see Martin, 2004.) In his 'Disjunctivism and Perceptual Psychology', Burge says that psychological science shows disjunctivism and/or relationalism is false (Burge, 2005). If what I have been saying is along the right lines, though, it doesn't, at least not directly. To falsify relationalism we need, first, arguments for rejecting Experiential Objectivity and these, to my knowledge, are not forthcoming from Burge. So long as they are not forthcoming, there is a lack of engagement between the motivation for relational theories, and the constraints they operate under, and the kind of considerations Burge brings to bear on explaining perceptual content. This also explains why someone who endorses a relational theory may be quite happy to agree that scientific psychology says perceptions have the kind of content Burge ascribes to them (though there is room for argument here too). I will take it that for someone who adopts the Experiential Objectivity Claim it is a further question how the commonsense datum, conscious experiences, and scientific theories of perceptual input are related to each other. Many options remain open, and a lot more than simply citing the theory is needed for falsifying the relational claim.

V Realism, consciousness, and division of labour

According to Ayer, commonsense realism is a theory we have about the causes of our sense data, a theory that is in fact falsified by science. According to Strawson this must be wrong: commonsense realism is not a theory relative to neutral data. We cannot get rid of commonsense realism so easily. To so much as get experience right we must take it at its own word, so to speak, where to do this is, in effect, to endorse commonsense realism, for experience presents itself as the experience of a mind-independent world.

As Strawson notes, to say commonsense realism is so deeply entrenched in experience is not to say it is true, but it does do away with the combination of senses datum theory and scientific realism as a starting point for talking about experience and the world of which it is an experience. Strawson's own proposal, towards the end of the paper, is that we should treat commonsense realism and the deliverances of science as affording two perspectives on what is actually the same reality. I will not discuss this here. Rather, I want to focus on the way he initially combines the task of getting phenomenology right with that of saving the status of commonsense realism from being a (false) theory about theory-neutral sense data.

A distinctive feature of his commonsense realism, so far not mentioned, is that to be such a realist is to hold that the various located objects that populate our world are phenomenally-propertied, they have 'colours, visual shapes and felt textures' (Strawson, 1979: 54). Ayer agrees with this characterization, and speaks of commonsense realism inhabiting the world with 'visuo-tactile continuants'. But on Ayer's account this is a false theory about the world, one that projects properties of sensations onto the objects we perceive. This is the claim Strawson is arguing against when he speaks of our experiences being permeated with the concepts that go into being a commonsense realist.

'Experience presents itself as the experience of a mind independent reality'. As Strawson interprets this, for experience to have this character, the subject herself must be capable of representing reality as mind independent, and this capacity informs the content of her perceptions. In contrast, according to the relationalist, it is we, as theorists of consciousness, rather than as subjects of experience, who need to assume the truth of commonsense realism in order to give a correct account of the subjective character of perceptual experiences because we need to refer to objects with these properties in giving an account of the nature of any particular conscious perception. Of course, to say that is not to prove or demonstrate the truth of commonsense realism; but it is to say we cannot make a move in describing experiences without assuming its truth, which is the result Strawson wanted to achieve, but without requiring of the subject that she be able to do the theory of her situation.

In effect what the relationalist is doing can be seen as adopting a division of labour strategy between theorist and subject which is similar to the kind of strategy Burge adopts in his answer to the 'where to' question in his account for the actual contents of perceptions; with the critical difference that the assumption of the world out there is applied to the subjective character of the perception. Let us take this more slowly.

A general background force driving Burge's answer to the 'where to' question is his anti-individualism, argued for over years with respect to conceptual content. Ascriptions of content to a subject's representations need not and should not rely on the subject's own capacity to produce individuating correct descriptions of the referents. In some cases, in accounting for the content of an individual's thought we should appeal to a social division of labour, in others, to a division of labour between what the subject can do, on the one hand, and, on the other, what the world delivers in virtue of de facto causal relations between the psychological states the subject is in and the external world, in particular physical objects that cause her to be in those states. For example, the fact that a particular object causes a perception on which a demonstrative thought is based suffices to make that object the referent of the thought, independently of the subject's capacities to individuate it from all others, so long as the subject is in the right functional state to be ascribed a demonstrative way of thinking.

The relationalist adopts the same strategy, with the big exceptions that this is being done in order to get right the subjective character of the experience, and what is appealed to by the theorist are objects with phenomenal properties. I return to this difference in a moment, but first a word about the relationalist move in comparison with Strawson's. As Strawson notes, Kant made the commonsense view of the world indispensable to getting experience right by making it all come from us. Space is 'in us' and it is 'solely from the human standpoint that we can speak of space, of extended things and so on'. What Strawson seeks to do, is retain indispensability for experience, while dropping the transcendental idealist move, on the grounds that it is unnecessary for securing the deep link between experience and such realism. But it is arguable that he leaves a gap that needs filling. If we take Strawson at his word, the link between commonsense realism and experience is a brute fact: experiences represent the world in one way, captured in the claims of commonsense realism, and science represents it in another. There is no explanation of why experience represents the word in this way. This is an explanation Kant seems to provide. In effect, the relationalist is stepping into the breach and providing a radically different explanation, for which he claims priority. We need to assume the truth of commonsense realism in a theoretical account of experience. It is a further question whether we can 'prove' or justify the truths we need to assume. Transcendental idealism is a response to the latter question, but that is a question down the line, one which we may have independent reasons for thinking need not and cannot be addressed.

A final word on the relation between the relationalist use of commonsense realism to explain experiences, and Strawson's embedding of it in the contents of perception. Strawson holds that it is integral to our everyday concept of perception, and to the idea that perceptions inform us about a mind–independent world, that we think of our perceptual experiences as caused by the objects of which they are experiences. He writes: 'it should really be obvious that with the distinction between independently existing objects and perceptual awareness of objects we already have the general notion of causal dependence of the latter on the former, even if this is not a matter to which we give much reflective attention in our pre-theoretical days'. (1979: 51) The relationalist says objects and their properties are part of the experience, as it were, rather than its cause. So this particular formulation of the causal dependence thesis is not something she will accept. But this does not require rejecting the claim that we think that the way the world is causally explains the course of our experiences. It only means that this causal explanation will not invoke a causal relation between the experience and the object. Instead one might think of the causal explanation as holding between the fact that one is having an experience of such and such a kind and fact about one's environment. Other options exist, discussed in particular in Child's and Steward's papers in this volume, the point here being that it does not seem to me that the particular formulation Strawson uses is critical to the connection he wants to emphasize between perception as a source of knowledge, on the one hand, and causal explanation on the other.

Coming back now to Burge: in his account of perceptual objectivity, many features of commonsense realism are taken up into the background assumed by the theorist of perception. Objects located in space cause perceptions, where the perceptual system achieves objectivity in virtue of capturing perceptual constancies, invariant (relative to the perceiver) properties of objects that cause the perception. It is tempting to say that on his account too commonsense realism is assumed by the theorist, but that is not quite right because of the absence of any reference to the phenomenality of the properties of perceived objects. Nor is this surprising, as the experience of them is not taken as the explanandum. But on the face of it this leaves Burge-like accounts of perception vulnerable to the kind of problem that worried Ayer, even when endorsing scientific realism. This was the problem of what gets left over when phenomenal properties are subtracted, and what justification there could be for saying that some but not other properties of the objects as we perceived them are the ones that science will deliver in its account of the world out there.

Now Burge's line on such worries would presumably be that biology and the general ecological approach to perception justify talk of objects and causation. The claim would be, that is, that the concepts needed for describing animals in their environment provide the materials we help ourselves to in speaking of perceptions as being caused by objects in the environment. It is not clear how far this gets one, though. For it is far from clear which properties we need to refer to from this perspective. Gibson thought it was affordances, defined in terms of what they enable animals to do, rather than the properties that science and mathematics assign to the world (and, indeed, rather than shapes and colours as we phenomenally define them— phenomenal properties for him were properties of sensation). This talk of affordances has largely been dropped by the kind of vision science Burge appeals to, the central flavour of which became familiar to philosophers through David Marr's book *Vision*. What has replaced it? In fact, when we look at the properties of objects that such scientists speak of, they seem very like our ordinary everyday phenomenal properties; and the data they seek to explain take experiences of such properties as their starting point. More generally, it is our experiences of properties, on the face of it, that provide the original datum for working out the computational processes involved in perceptual subsystems delivering the kind of objective representation Burge is concerned with. Or so it appears. If this is right there is nothing in their actual practice to suggest that they do not endorse some version of the Experiential Objectivity Claim with respect to the initial datum to be explained. Of course, they do seek to explain *consciousness*, Marr is clear about that, but, rather, the workings of the subsystem which, when things go as they should, deliver conscious perceptions. If this is right, there is nothing, on the face of it, that Burge need object to in EO, once its reflective gloss has been dropped. Or so I would argue. Moreover, on the face of it, given that such theories do not seek to explain consciousness, it is arguable that there is nothing to stop them endorsing a relational version of EO, which is, in effect, to take the opposite line from Burge's own, on which science is said to falsify relational theories.

This is of course far too quick, but it does, in my view, show up the kinds of questions that open up when the Experiential Objectivity is confronted head-on, questions that need to be confronted in explaining the way in which perceptions put us in touch with the world. I end with a brief indication of one such question.

Suppose you agree that one central difference between Burge and Strawson is captured by their positions with respect to the Experiential Objectivity Claim. One question you may ask then is: so what? What substantive difference does it make to the account you give of perceptual objectivity if you do endorse EO? Are there general constraints it imposes on the kind of account we give of perceptual content? And are their reasons intrinsic to adoption of EO that might lead you to adopt a reflective account of perceptual content?

Burge says that there is a cluster of motivations lying behind the pervasive adoption of Individual Representationalism (IR), including vestiges of verificationism, if not outright adoption of it, and vestiges of individualism, if not outright adoption of that. I think he is right, and that there is some of that in some of Strawson's writing. In 'Perception and its Objects' it is probably some implicit commitment to a kind of individualism that leads him to adopt IR. More specifically: although his complaint against sense data theorists is that they get phenomenology wrong, his aim in introducing his correction to their account of phenomenology is actually to save the status of commonsense realism from the 'false theory' status assigned to it by a combination of a sense datum theory and scientific realism. The commonsense-embodying account he gives of phenomenology is intended to achieve that result. But if what I have been saying is right, adopting the division of labour strategy implicit in relationalism can serve that end as well, if not better. And if that is right, EO on its own, as so far formulated, does not provide him with intrinsic reasons to adopt IR.

Does that mean that he has no reason intrinsic to EO itself that generates his commitment to IR? Can there be such reasons? There can, and he does have them, but we do not find them in 'Perceptions and its Objects'. Perhaps the clearest articulation of these reasons, which are the main ones that need to be taken seriously, in my view, is to be found in his discussions of Kant on the unity of experience and objectivity in *The Bounds of Sense*. I end with a brief indication of the kind of issues it raises.

Very roughly, and in very condensed form, the direct route from EO to IR, as we find it in these discussions, begins with the very idea of presence of an item to a subject in experience. The question is: what are the conditions that must be met if it is to be right on any particular occasion to regard a subject as being presented with such an item. On Strawson's rendition of Kant, for this to be true it must also be true that we have in play a subject who is on occasion confronted with items he takes to be part of an objective spatio-temporal order. The reason the objectivity condition must be met, in turn, is that it is only when it is met that it is possible for the 'I think' to accompany experiences, where this in turn is required for there to be conscious perceptions in play in the first place.

I suggest that unpacking these claims, and, more generally, tackling the problem of the connection between unity, objectivity and the 'I' is where we should turn to if we are to understand the substantive difference that adopting EO makes to one's account of perceptual objectivity, and if we are to understand the deep motivation for, and argue convincingly against, adoption of a reflective account of perceptual objectivity. More specifically: I noted earlier that there are many choices one makes in undertaking the journey from Strawson to Burge in addressing the 'how much' question—the question of how much of the content of commonsense realism is embodied in the content of perception. And I raised the question of whether there are general constraints we can appeal to which fix the rules of the game here. What I am suggesting now is that the next step for those who adopt EO, the most profitable place to look for these constraints, and for material we can use to distinguish different ways of meeting them (different answers to the 'how much question') is Kantian-inspired claims about links between having experiences, unity of consciousness and objectivity.

References

Block, Ned, 1997: 'On a Confusion about the Function of Consciousness', in Block, Flanagan and Guzeldere, eds. *The Nature of Consciousness*, Cambridge Mass. MIT Press.

Brewer, Bill, 1999: *Perception and Reason*, Oxford, Oxford University Press.

Burge, Tyler, 1997: 'Two Kinds of Consciousness', in Block, Flanagan and Guzeldere, eds. *The Nature of Consciousness*, Cambridge, Mass. MIT Press.

Burge, Tyler, 2005: 'Disjunctivism and Perceptual Psychology', *Philosophical Topics* 33 (1): 1–78.

Burge, Tyler, 2009: 'Perceptual Objectivity', *Philosophical Review* 118 (3): 285–324.

Campbell, John, 2002: *Reference and Consciousness*, Oxford, Oxford University Press.

Evans, Gareth, 1982: *The Varieties of Reference*, Oxford, Oxford University Press.

McDowell, John, 1994: 'The Content of Perceptual Experience', *Philosophical Quarterly* 44 (175): 190–205.

Marr, David, 1983: *Vision*, Cambridge, Mass. MIT Press.

Martin, Mike, 2004: 'The Limits of Self Awareness', *Philosophical Studies* 120 (1–3): 37–89.

Peacocke, Christopher, 1986: *Thoughts: An Essay on Content*, Oxford, Basil Blackwell.

Strawson, Peter, 1966: *The Bounds of Sense*, London, Methuen.

Strawson, Peter, 1979: 'Perception and its Objects', in G. MacDonald, ed. *Perception and Identity*, London, Macmillan Press.

5

Realism and Explanation in Perception

Bill Brewer★

Suppose that we identify *physical objects*, in the first instance, by extension, as things like stones, tables, trees, people, and other animals: the persisting macroscopic constituents of the world in which we live. Of course, there is a substantive question of what it is to be *like* such things in the way relevant to categorization as a physical object. So this can hardly be the final word on the matter. Still, it is equally clear that this gives us all a perfectly respectable initial conception of what we are talking about; and it is an entirely adequate starting point for what follows.

Reflection on the history of epistemological and metaphysical discussions of perception, especially through the early modern period, shows philosophers struggling in practice to combine two intuitively compelling ideas about physical objects and our relation with them in perception.

1. Physical objects are the very things that we are *presented* with in perceptual experience, in the sense that perceptual experience thereby provides us with at least a rough provisional conception of what physical objects are. I call this basic idea *empiricism*.
2. Physical objects themselves are mind-independent, in the sense that the nature of such things is entirely independent of their appearance, and not in any way a matter of how they do or might appear to anyone. I call this basic idea *realism*.[1]

★ Many thanks to Michael Ayers, Tom Baldwin, Steve Butterfill, Quassim Cassam, James Conant, John Divers, Naomi Eilan, Hannah Ginsborg, Christoph Hoerl, Hemdat Lerman, Guy Longworth, John McDowell, Ian Phillips, Johannes Roessler, Peter Simons, David Smith, Paul Snowdon, Matt Soteriou, Helen Steward, Tom Stoneham, Charles Travis, and Robbie Williams for helpful comments on earlier versions of this material.

[1] I mean by the *nature* of the entities of a given kind here the most fundamental answer to the question what such things are. This is of course a contentious notion. I take it for granted here without argument and without committing myself to any specific philosophical elaboration. The justification I offer for doing so rests on the merits of what follows within this framework. For a helpful and sympathetic historically informed elucidation of this notion of an object's nature, see Wiggins (1995). For a highly influential further

I call the conjunction of the two *empirical realism*.

Locke (1975) notoriously attempts to secure empirical realism *indirectly*. Perceptual experience consists in our direct acquaintance with mind-dependent entities. Still, these sufficiently resemble the distinct mind-independent physical objects that are normally their cause—there is resemblance in *primary qualities* at least—that we may nevertheless acquire a conception of what physical objects are through perception. Berkeley (1975a, 1975b) equally notoriously rejects this purported combination, effectively arguing from empiricism against realism. Crudely, if, as empiricism contends, perception provides us with a conception of what physical objects are, then these must indeed stand in some appropriate resemblance relation with the mind-dependent entities that we are acquainted with directly in such experience; but 'an idea can be like nothing but an idea' (Berkeley, 1975b, § 8); hence physical objects must themselves be likewise mind-dependent.

This line of objection to the Lockean indirect empirical realist combination seems to be confirmed by Rae Langton's (1998) reconstruction of Kant's transcendental idealism (1929), according to which perception in principle fails to afford us knowledge of *any* of the intrinsic properties of mind-independent physical objects themselves. So the idea that we grasp what such things are through perception, since this discloses their nature at least as bearers of *primary qualities* that are both intrinsic and known, is again indefensible. Berkeley's accusation that introducing a domain of mind-independent causes of our experience at best changes the subject from the nature of the genuine physical objects that we all know and love is quite just. For this procedure results in a theoretical postulation of intrinsically unknowable physical objects as the causes we know not what of such and such experiential effects in us. Thus, retaining realism certainly *appears* to be in some tension with empiricism.

Of course there is a great deal going on here; and I certainly do not wish to endorse everything involved in these various considerations against a straightforward combination of realism with empiricism. I offer these familiar moves rather as a historical illustration of a prima facie tension that I take as my starting point.

My plan in what follows is to pursue a specific version of this traditional problem in some detail. This version of the problem centres on the commonsense assumption that we may explain the actual and counterfactual order and nature of our perceptual experience of physical objects by appeal to the prior and independent nature of the physical objects themselves that we perceive. Thinking of physical objects as entities whose nature explains our experience in this way plays a crucial role in securing their status as mind-independent in the sense required for realism. I spell out exactly what I think this status consists in and explain how the commonsense explanatory assumption secures it.

development of his own position, see Wiggins (2001). Charles (2000) elaborates the Aristotelian source of these ideas with great force and illumination. Strawson (1959) contains important motivation for the modern relevance of the notion. Ayers (1991, esp. parts I & III) offers an alternative development to Wiggins that focuses more directly on the idea of the nature of physical objects in general as causally integrated enduring and spatially extended material unities. Although I intend to remain neutral on this here, I am myself more persuaded by Ayers' position. See also Campbell (2002, esp. ch. 4).

On its most familiar interpretation and development, though, this assumption that we explain the order and nature of our perceptual experience of physical objects by appeal to the nature of the physical objects themselves raises a serious problem. For it threatens the basic empiricist idea that we are genuinely presented with those mind-independent physical objects themselves in perceptual experience, that it is through our experience of them that we acquire a rough and provisional conception at least of what mind-independent physical objects are.

I argue that this threat may be avoided by resisting the orthodox development of the realist's explanatory strategy that effectively began with Locke. The assumption that we may explain the actual and counterfactual order and nature of our perceptual experience of physical objects by appeal to the prior and independent nature of the physical objects themselves that we perceive succeeds in securing realism without threatening empiricism provided that we respect the autonomous standing of our everyday commonsense explanations of experience. These are in no need of any fundamental scientific revision in such a way as to undermine empiricism.

The paper has two sections. First, I elaborate the explanatory assumption, explain in detail its role in securing the mind-independence of the physical objects that we perceive, and outline the threat that the orthodox development of this strategy poses to the presentation of those very objects to us in experience. Second, I suggest how this threat should be avoided. I argue that there is a perfectly adequate interpretation of the explanatory assumption that secures the status of physical objects as mind-independent without in any way threatening the idea that these are the very things that are subjectively presented to us in perception.

I

We ordinarily cite the properties of physical objects in explanation of the actual and counterfactual order and nature of our perceptual experience of those very things. In vision, for example, we regularly give explanations along the following lines.

(E1)   The coin looks circular to Janet because it is circular and she is viewing it from head on.

(E2)   The coin looks elliptical to John because it is circular and he is viewing it from an angle.

(E3)   The coin would look elliptical to Janet if she were to change her point of view because it is circular and she would then be viewing it from an angle.

(E4)   The jumper looks red outdoors because it is red and lighting conditions are normal outdoors.

(E5)   It looks mauve in the store because it is red and the lighting conditions are artificially dingy in the store.

(E6)   It would look red if the lights in the store were improved because it is red and it would then look its actual colour.

I contend that our offering and accepting such explanations constitutes a commitment to realism about the physical objects that they cite. For, first, realism consists in a certain priority of the natures of physical objects themselves over the perceptual appearances to which they may give rise; and, second, the explanatory standing of such explanations depends upon this very priority. I elaborate each of these two points in turn.

First, let us begin with the familiar distinction between primary and secondary qualities, for example, between the shapes and colours of physical objects respectively (Locke, 1975). It is hardly uncontroversial how best to draw this distinction. The approach that both seems to me faithful to the key historical arguments in the area and is in any case most useful for my purposes here characterizes this as a distinction between the relation that the relevant properties of physical objects bear to the perceptual appearances to which they may give rise in the two cases. I call this the *standard account*.[2]

Thus, the most basic distinctions concerning secondary qualities are between, say, red-type and green-type *appearances*, and the rest, conceived quite independently of the question of what their worldly correlates, if any, may be. The characterization of such appearances is prior to, and independent of, any characterization of the worldly properties that may in some way be presented or indicated by them. Having given such a characterization, of red-type appearances, say, we may then define a property—*redness*—which applies to mind-independent objects, as that of being disposed to produce those kinds of appearances—red-type ones—or, alternatively, as the property of having whatever underlying physical constitution happens in the actual world to ground that disposition.

In contrast, the most basic distinctions concerning the primary qualities are those between, say, squareness and circularity, and the rest, *as properties of mind-independent things themselves*, conceived quite independently of the question of what appearances, if any, they might produce. Having first identified which property squareness is, we can then identify square-type appearances as those that present something as having *that property*—squareness. So, the relevant appearances are to be characterized only by appeal to a prior, and independent, characterization of the worldly properties that they may present.

Generalizing this basic idea, I claim that the mind-independence of the objects that we perceive consists in the individuative priority of their nature over the various appearance properties that show up in our perception of them. So an account of our perceptual experience of physical objects preserves realism if and only if it offers a characterization of the nature of physical objects themselves as the prior and independent basis on which it goes on to give characterizations of the relevant appearances that such objects may present in perception. As I explain and illustrate in what follows, this

---

[2] I should say that I do not myself endorse the following characterization of secondary qualities and our perceptions of them. See Campbell (1993) for an alternative that I prefer. This will become relevant later with my inclusion of the colour explanations (E4)–(E5) alongside shape explanations (E1)–(E3) throughout.

individuation of appearances proceeds in specific instances on the basis of particular determinate modifications of the general nature of the mind-independent physical objects that we perceive. Skipping ahead to the version of the position that I myself favour, the picture is something like this. Mind-independent physical objects are persisting, unified, extended space occupants. A specific modification of this general nature would be that of being circularly extended, for example; and the corresponding visual appearance is to be individuated precisely as the look of a circular physical object presented from head on in normal lighting conditions, say.

It is natural to object to this whole approach that priority of *characterization* is one thing, *metaphysical status* quite another. The first is a matter of how *we* identify the phenomena in question; the second is a matter of the nature of *those phenomena themselves*. Indeed, the standard account of secondary qualities outlined above surely serves to make just this point. Suppose that we do first of all characterize the red-type appearances, as specific conscious experiential phenomena, conceived quite independently of the question of what their worldly correlates, if any, may be; and suppose that we do then go on derivatively to characterize the redness of physical objects as their possession of whatever underlying physical constitution happens in the actual world to ground the disposition to produce such red-type appearances in normal subjects under normal circumstances. Then an object's possession of *that underlying physical property*, whichever it may be, is a perfectly mind-independent matter. It is entirely independent of the way in which it does or might appear to anyone. Thus, although the redness of physical objects is *characterized* only on the basis of a prior characterization of the experiential appearances to which it gives rise, the property itself is perfectly mind-independent.

In reply I admit entirely that there is *a* mind-independent property here: whichever underlying physical property it is that turns out actually to ground objects' disposition to produce red-type appearances in normal subjects under normal circumstances. The crucial point, though, is that, by the explicit lights of the account under consideration, this is absolutely not the property that such objects are subjectively *presented* as having in our perceptual experience of their colour. For we have no idea whatsoever which property this underlying physical property is on the basis of our perception of it on the standard account of secondary qualities in question. The property presented is rather that of appearances' being a *red-type*, which is in itself quite neutral on what the worldly correlate, if any, of such appearances may be. Thus, the property, if any, that physical objects are presented as having in our colour experience, *on this view*, is *not* mind-independent at all, but rather a mind-dependent one.[3] Suppose that colour appearances were conceived quite differently. Suppose, that is to say, that they were correctly

---

[3] I take this to be the substance of Descartes' (1986) contention—and indeed his argument for it—that the ascription of secondary qualities *as we perceive them* to mind-independent physical objects is not just contingently false but entirely confused and incoherent, presupposing as it does that such objects effectively have sensations.

characterized *as* presentations of specific properties of things not themselves individuated by any reference to their appearances, as appearances of squareness are characterized according to the standard account of primary qualities above as presentations of a specific geometric shape. This is in my view the correct account of colour appearances, although it is of course quite contrary to the standard account currently under consideration here by way of illustration of the notion of mind-dependence in play. In that case the colour properties presented in perception would indeed be mind-independent. But this is precisely what is not the case on the standard account.

I conclude that this standard account of the distinction between primary and secondary qualities in fact serves strongly to confirm my criterion of mind-independence. The mind-independence of the objects that are presented in perception consists in the individuative priority of their nature over the various appearance properties that show up in our perception of them.[4]

Second, the explanatory standing of our ordinary explanations of the order and nature of perceptual experience on the basis of the nature of the physical objects themselves that we perceive depends upon precisely this individuative priority of objects over appearances. For suppose that the individuative priority were the reverse, as in the standard account of secondary qualities given above. In that case, purportedly explanatory ascriptions of properties of physical objects are in reality ascriptions of properties essentially characterized in terms of the disposition to produce such and such appearances in normal subjects under normal circumstances. Thus the resultant explanations of those very appearances are either unsatisfying or mere placeholders for genuine explanations in quite different terms that re-establish the individuative priority with properties of objects independent and prior to any question of their appearances. Simply being told that something appears a certain way because it is disposed to do so gives us no substantive understanding *why* it appears as it does without some indication of what grounds the relevant disposition. Articulating this ground, along with the general law that things that are so constituted normally appear thus and so, does provide an explanation; but only by citing a grounding constitution that is characterized prior to and independently of any question as to what appearances, if any, things so constituted may produce. Thus the genuine explanatory standing of explanations of perceptual appearances depends upon an individuative priority of the explanatory properties of physical objects over the appearances to be explained.

It is sometimes said that the relation between certain perceptible properties of physical objects and the appearances that these present in perception is one of no straightforward priority either way (McDowell, 1985). I find it difficult to articulate the proposal fully; but the essential outline is as follows. On the basis of certain experiences that we have, we are able directly to sort various objects into groups, without, as it

---

[4] The key claims involved in this illustration from the standard account of the primary/secondary quality distinction, and especially the crucial role of empiricism as defined above, return at the heart of the main argument of section II below.

were, paying any heed to the nature of the experiences that provide our cues to do so. We may call the relevant groups of objects 'red', 'green' and so on. Reflecting on this capacity for object categorization, we may go on to sort our experiential cues into groups also, characterizing these in turn as appearances of red, appearances of green, and so on. Thus there is an epistemological priority, on the subject's part at least, from the colour properties of objects to their colour appearances. Still, there is nothing 'in reality' that unifies all the red objects other than their disposition normally to produce appearances of red in us. These appearances are unified *metaphysically* as single kind in virtue of their intrinsic subjective type, entirely independently of the question of what their worldly correlates, if any, may be; and this in turn, and derivatively, imposes a metaphysical unity on the red physical objects, as those disposed to produce such appearances in normal subjects under normal circumstances. Thus there is a metaphysical priority from colour appearances to the colour properties of objects. There is no straightforward single priority either way.

If this really were a view on which there is no individuative priority *of the relevant kind* either way between the perceptible properties of physical objects and the various appearance properties that show up in our perception of them, then my argument above would fail. For I conclude that our explanations of perceptual appearances by their objects depend upon an individuative priority from objects to appearances from the fact that they are incompatible with an individuative priority from appearances to objects. I ignore the possibility of any genuinely no-priority view. Fortunately the position outlined above is categorically not a no-priority view of this threatening kind. For the primary unification is at the level of appearances, in the characterization of which subjective condition is that of something 'looking red', say, only on the basis of which is it then possible to characterize the corresponding property of physical objects themselves: being red. So, regardless of the epistemological claims, about our capacity for sorting coloured objects in advance of sorting their colour appearances, there is a clear *individuative* priority of the relevant kind from appearances to objects. The point is confirmed by the fact that any genuinely mind-independent unity that there may be to the objects sorted as red, say, on this view, is not the unity that those things are subjectively presented as having. For we have no idea whatsoever what this may be on the basis of our perception of them. So this position is definitively an instance of the order of individuative priority characteristic of the standard account of secondary qualities given above.

Indeed it is difficult to see how there possibly could be a genuinely no-priority view of the kind required to block my argument. For what it is to be an appearance of *F*-ness must in general have something to do with what it is to be *F*. I offer two possibilities: being *F* is characterized in terms of appearing *F* (as in the case of the standard account of secondary qualities); or appearing *F* is characterized in terms of being *F* (as in the case of the standard account of primary qualities). A no-priority view must presumably either endorse neither of these claims or endorse both of them. If it endorses neither, then the worry is that appearing *F* and being *F* fail to be related to each other in any way that is adequate to sustain the prima facie impression that '*F*' is being used without equivocation between them. If it endorses both, then the danger is that the resultant circularity will obstruct any attempt to distinguish the two pairs: being *F* and appearing *F*, on the one hand, and being *G* and appearing *G*, on the other, for any *F* and *G* of the same general type—e.g. colours. Thus in the absence of any clearly articulated candidate for a genuinely no-priority view, I contend that my argument goes through.

To reiterate my second key point about explanations of perceptual appearances by appeal to the physical objects that we perceive then, their explanatory standing depends upon the individuative priority of the natures of the physical objects themselves over the perceptual appearances to be explained.

Putting this together with the constitutive account of mind-independence, in terms of precisely such individuative priority, it follows that the explanatory standing of our explanations of the order and nature of our perceptual experience of physical objects on the basis of the nature of the physical objects themselves that we perceive delivers a clear positive verdict on the status of physical objects as mind-independent. Offering and accepting such explanations constitutes a commitment to realism about physical objects. Call this the *Explanatory Strategy* (ES) for vindicating realism. The key claim is that we sustain realism concerning physical objects by thinking of physical objects themselves as the explanatory grounds of our various perceptual experiences of those very things from different points of view and in different circumstances of perception.

(ES) raises a serious problem, though. For it is *prima facie* plausible to accept the best scientific-physical theories as providing essential substantive revisions to our initial commonsense explanations (E1)–(E6) of our perceptual experience by appeal to the physical objects that we perceive. Thus, we may be inclined to appeal ultimately to fundamental scientific-physics for the complete and *correct* articulation of such explanations. Call this the *scientific* implementation of (ES).

On this way of thinking, the correct and genuinely explanatory explanations of the actual and counterfactual order and nature of our perceptual experience of physical objects are to be given only in the language of fundamental scientific-physics. This in turn determines the natures of the objects whose mind-independence is thereby secured by (ES). For these are the entities whose natures are explanatorily relevant in such fundamental scientific-physical explanations. Thus, insofar as their mind-independence is secured by (ES), physical objects *are* mereological sums, over regions of space and time, or perhaps some other kind of composition, of whatever turn out to be the most basic elements of the correct fundamental scientific-physical theory.

The theoretical conception that most of us have of what such things are actually like is no doubt very primitive. Indeed, Lewis (2009) presents a powerful argument for the claim that we are irremediably ignorant of the intrinsic natures of their fundamental scientific-physical components. In any case, it is quite clear that these are not the very things that we are *presented* with in perception. For, as I explicated the notion at the outset, perceptual presentation provides us with at least a rough and provisional conception of what the objects *are* with which we are presented; and we have no conception whatsoever of what the most fundamental scientific-physical primitives are simply on the basis of perception. So we have no conception whatsoever of what any simple mereological sum or composition of such things might be either. The objects whose mind-independence is secured by the current scientific implementation of (ES) are therefore not *subjectively presented* to us in perception. Thus, the scientific implementation of (ES) is incompatible with *empiricism* as defined above.

This consequence should be resisted if at all possible for two reasons. First, as I said at the outset, empiricism is intuitively highly compelling. We come to these issues with the strong conviction that we *are* presented with mind-independent physical objects in perception in just this sense. Second, and more importantly, empiricism plays a fundamental role in setting the domain for the most important and contested philosophical controversy concerning realism as I envisage it from the start. The *physical objects* whose status is at stake here are precisely those things that *are* subjectively presented to us in experience. Preserving realism at the cost of distinguishing mind-independent physical objects from the stones, tables, trees, people, and other animals that we all know and love is a hollow victory indeed for the realist.

At this stage, then, with only the scientific implementation of (ES) in view, it looks rather as though Berkeley (1975a, 1975b) must be right in his contention that the only conceivable form of realism involves changing the subject matter entirely from the physical objects with which we are presented in perception. For those things—the things whose metaphysical status *is* our initial and primary concern—perhaps we really must accept some kind of anti-realism.

II

I shall now argue that this threat may be overcome. (ES) is absolutely the right strategy for securing realism. The unacceptable consequence of undermining empiricism that follows from its *scientific* implementation may, however, be avoided. It is correct to secure metaphysical realism concerning physical objects by thinking of physical objects themselves as the explanatory grounds of our various perceptual experiences of those very things from different points of view and in different circumstances of perception. It is a mistake, though, to look to fundamental scientific-physical explanation to provide and characterize what are therefore phenomenologically mysterious targets of this identification. The key lies, instead, in our initial commonsense-physical explanations themselves, which I claim are in excellent standing absolutely as they are, in no need of any scientific-physical revision.

Thus, the scientific-physical option outlined above, and incompatible with empiricism, is not the only possible implementation of (ES). An alternative *commonsense* implementation is available that preserves empiricism and is also in my view a perfectly stable and adequate defence of realism. The truth and explanatory standing of our initial commonsense-physical explanations of perceptual appearances *as they stand* is sufficient to secure realism for the physical objects that are presented to us in perception. Furthermore these commonsense-physical explanations are in absolutely no need of any substantive revision and correction by anything from scientific-physics. For they have features that any purported scientific-physical explanations of perceptual appearances lack that are crucially relevant to precisely this project of securing empirical realism. These features simultaneously establish the autonomous explanatory standing of commonsense-physical explanations and avoid the unacceptable anti-empiricist consequences that come with the move to scientific-physics in defence of realism.[5]

To begin with, then, recall that commonsense-physical explanations of the actual and counterfactual order and nature of our perceptual experience of physical by appeal to the familiar perceptible natures of those very things, along with our point of view and other relevant circumstances of perception, depend upon the individuative priority of the natures of the physical objects presented in perception themselves relative to their various appearances. For the latter appearances are explicitly individuated *in terms of* the prior natures of the physical objects that they present. Thus, in my toy examples, the explananda visual appearances are individuated explicitly in terms of the shape and colour properties they (apparently) present: as the coin's looking *circular* or *elliptical*, and the jumper's looking *red* or *mauve*. As we saw above in connection with the standard account of secondary qualities, if the order of individuative priority were the reverse, then insofar as the offered explanations point to anything genuinely explanatory this would inevitably proceed in terms of imperceptible grounding properties of the physical objects in question. The definitive feature of *commonsense*-physical explanations, that these appeal precisely to the familiar *perceptible* natures of physical objects in explaining their perceptual appearances, would be lost entirely.

Most importantly at this stage of the argument, commonsense-physical explanations of the order and nature of perceptual experience by appeal to the perceptible properties of physical objects have two distinctive features that make them far superior for the purpose of vindicating empirical realism to anything available at the level of scientific-physical explanation. What I call their explanatory *robustness* avoids the purported *need* for any scientific-physical revision of commonsense-physical explanations in connection with securing *realism* on the basis of (ES). The particular priority relation between the natures of the physical objects that constitute the explanantia of such explanations and the appearances that are their explananda ensure in contrast with the scientific implementation of (ES) considered above that *empiricism* is preserved. I take these two points in turn.

---

[5] Note that it is entirely compatible with this fundamental role for commonsense-physical explanations that these may be elaborated and refined to some extent on the basis of research in the psychology of vision, say. This holds no threat along the lines of that elaborated above in connection with the scientific-physical implementation of (ES). For the commonsense nature of the world of mind-independent physical objects that we perceive is simply taken for granted in advancing and testing the relevant explanatory hypotheses.

First, in comparison with any candidate scientific-physical explanations of perceptual appearances, commonsense-physical explanations are *robust*. That is to say, they maximize modal correlation with the perceptual appearances they explain in the following sense. All other things being equal, objects with quite different scientific-physical properties that share the same commonsense-physical properties will appear in the same way; and what unifies the various respects in which their scientific-physical properties might differ in such a way as to alter these appearances is precisely that these are just those scientific-physical variations that significantly alter the commonsense explanatory properties in question.

By way of illustration from a related area independent of perceptual appearances, compare Putnam's (1978) famous observation that the best explanation of the fact that a given one inch square peg passes through a one inch square hole and not through a one inch round hole is given by citing its size and shape. All other things being equal, it is precisely this property—one inch squareness—whose presence facilitates, and absence obstructs, its passage. Any proposed move in the direction of scientific-physical explanation by appeal to lattices of elementary particles and the like reduces this robust modal generality. For one inch square pegs of quite different materials equally pass through a one inch square hole and not through a one inch round hole, regardless of the fact that the scientific-physical properties involved in explanation of their motion and interaction are quite different; and whatever their scientific-physical differences may be—within reason[6]—appropriately sized pegs that are not square will not pass through a one inch square hole, and square pegs greater than one inch in size will not do so either. Thus, all other things being equal, the scientific-physical differences between pegs that do, and pegs that do not, pass through a one inch square hole but not through a one inch round hole, are explanatorily unified as those in which the peg is one inch square versus those in which it is not. This is what I mean by the explanatory virtue of robustness.

Similarly, in connection with the explanations of our perceptual experience of physical objects that are central to (ES), commonsense-physical explanations are robust in comparison with scientific-physical explanations. The most robust explanation of why a coin looks circular to Janet viewing it head on and elliptical to John viewing it from a specific angle is given by citing its stable circular shape and not by appeal to the way in which its fundamental scientific-physical properties affect the scientific-physical properties of their respective perceptual systems. For, other things being equal, similarly circular objects of quite different materials look equally circular and elliptical respectively, to them and to other observers, from these same points of view, regardless of the fact that what is going on in scientific-physical terms may be quite different; and the scientific-physical changes to such objects that would alter these appearances are precisely those that significantly affect the commonsense-physical explanatory shape. This, rather than anything specific

---

[6] Excluding, for example, pegs made of material that dissolves the sides of the hole and so on.

at the scientific-physical level is what unifies the objects that look circular and elliptical from these respective points of view as against those that do not. Thus, commonsense-physical explanations of such appearances have the explanatory virtue of robustness.

Again, I contend, the most robust explanation of why a jumper looks red outdoors and mauve in the store is given by citing its red colour and the relevant variation between normal and artificially dingy lighting conditions, not by appeal to the way in which its fundamental scientific-physical properties affect viewers' perceptual systems in the two conditions. For, other things being equal, similarly red objects of quite different materials look equally red and mauve respectively in these same lighting conditions, regardless of the fact that what is going on in scientific-physical terms may be quite different; and the scientific-physical changes to such objects that would alter these appearances are precisely those that significantly affect the commonsense-physical explanatory colour. This, rather than anything specific at the scientific-physical level is what unifies the objects that look red and mauve in these respective lighting conditions as against those that do not. Thus, commonsense-physical explanations of such appearances again have the explanatory virtue of robustness.[7]

Having said all this, there is no obvious conflict, so far as I can see, between the robustness of commonsense-physical explanations of perceptual appearances of the kind involved in (ES), on the one hand, and the equal robustness of fundamental scientific-physical explanations of closely related but distinct phenomena, on the other. For example, it may well be that the most robust explanation of highly specific retinal or neural phenomena involved in our perception of some red objects in some circumstances are most robustly explained by appeal to the very specific scientific-physical properties of the light arriving at the eye reflected from the surfaces of such objects. That is to say, I see no good reason in what has been said here to deny that commonsense-physics and scientific-physics are two perfectly compatible but quite distinct explanatory projects, running in parallel, in no real competition, with each other. In any case, the key point from this discussion is that commonsense-physical explanations have the virtue of robustness over candidate scientific-physical explanations in connection with the perceptual appearances that figure in (ES).

This provides an illustration of how and why any blanket explanatory *reductionism* is to be rejected, where this is the crude idea that the best explanation of anything going on in the physical world is ultimately to be given in terms of fundamental scientific-physics. It certainly blocks directly any suggestion, however *prima facie* plausible, that the commonsense physical explanations of perceptual appearances that we began with in setting out (ES) are *essentially* subject to substantive revision by scientific-physics, in a way that then threatens empiricism as I understand it here. There *is* no such general

---

[7] Notice that in extending the commonsense-physical explanatory picture in this way to secondary quality appearances, such as those of an object's colour, I am explicitly rejecting the standard model of the primary vs secondary quality distinction set out above. See, again, Campbell (1993) for discussion and defence of this idea. Note, though, that this extension is not essential to the main argument of the current work.

obligation; and thus, so far at least, such commonsense-physical explanations are in perfectly good explanatory standing absolutely as they are.

There may be another worry about their explanatory status, though. For the properties of physical objects that are involved sound very much like the perceptual appearances that they are invoked to explain. How can the fact that something *is* red, or round, say, be a genuine explanation of the fact that it looks red, or round? It is far from obvious what the condition on explanation is supposed to be that is failed by such explanations; and we will see again below that the close individuative relation between the natures of objects and appearances involved here is crucial to the preservation of empiricism. Still, it is worth emphasizing two points about commonsense-physical explanations that should silence this general line of objection. First, an object may clearly be *F* (red, or round, for example) without looking *F*, because it is not seen at all; because although it is seen the subject is attending exclusively to certain other features, and so only has eyes for them, as it were; or because it is seen in misleading perceptual conditions and so looks *G* instead. Second, an object may look *F* and yet not be *F*, again due to any number of variously misleading perceptual circumstances. So insofar as the general worry is that there is insufficient modal independence between explanans and explanandum for commonsense-physical explanations to get any genuine explanatory purchase, then this seems to me to be simply false.

I conclude therefore that the commonsense implementation of (ES) suffices as it stands to secure *realism* as defined at the outset. Physical objects are mind-independent: their nature is entirely independent of their appearance, and not in any way a matter of how they do or might appear to anyone. Furthermore, in avoiding the need for any substantive revision of commonsense-physical explanations by scientific-physics, this version of (ES) avoids the loss of empiricism that I argued above comes with any such move. I end by explaining in a little more detail how exactly this commonsense implementation also positively secures empiricism. This is the second point that I distinguished above: the priority relation between the natures of the physical objects that constitute the explanantia of such explanations and the appearances that are their explananda *ensures* in contrast with the scientific implementation of (ES) considered earlier that empiricism is preserved.

The standard account of primary qualities outlined earlier lies at the heart of the commonsense implementation of (ES). According to the current strategy, this model applies to all the properties of physical objects and their appearances that figure in commonsense explanations of our perceptual experience.[8] That is to say, the natures of the perceptual appearances to be explained are characterized precisely *as* the subjective presentation of certain specific and independently individuated properties of physical

---

[8] Note, again, that my inclusion of secondary quality explanations of perceptual experience such as (E4)–(E5) above, alongside primary quality explanations such as (E1)–(E3), marks a significant departure from orthodoxy by embracing the secondary qualities under the familiar primary quality model. See Campbell (1993) for defence of this 'Simple View'.

objects in the world around the perceiver. Even in illusory cases, in which something that is F looks G, say, the appearance in question transparently presents the object as being a specific way that such things may be, although this one is in fact not. In the normal veridical case, something's looking F makes absolutely evident which way that very thing out there is. The explanatory ground of that very appearance in its mind-independent object's F-ness itself is entirely transparent to the subject in that very experience. Hence physical objects really are the very things that we are presented with in experience—our perception of them provides us with at least a rough provisional conception of what such physical objects are. Thus the commonsense implementation of (ES) also secures empiricism as defined above.

So the *mind-independent* physical world *is* the world of the *familiar* macroscopic objects that we all know and love; and those very things are subjectively *presented* to us in perception. The physical objects whose mind-independence is secured by the commonsense implementation of (ES) are precisely those that we are genuinely presented with in perception. Commonsense (ES) secures empirical realism.

References

Ayers, M. 1991. *Locke*, vol. ii. London: Routledge.

Berkeley, G. 1975a. *Three Dialogues Between Hylas and Philonous*. In M. Ayers (ed.), *George Berkeley: Philosophical Works*. London: Everyman.

——1975b. *A Treatise Concerning the Principles of Human Knowledge*. In M. Ayers (ed.), *George Berkeley: Philosophical Works*. London: Everyman.

Campbell, J. 1993. 'A Simple View of Colour'. In J. Haldane and C. Wright (eds.), *Reality, Representation, and Projection*. Oxford: Oxford University Press.

——2002. *Reference and Consciousness*. Oxford: Oxford University Press.

Charles, D. 2000. *Aristotle on Meaning and Essence*. Oxford: Oxford University Press.

Descartes, R. 1986. *Meditations on First Philosophy*, trans. J. Cottingham. Cambridge: Cambridge University Press.

Kant, I. 1929. *Critique of Pure Reason*, trans. N. Kemp Smith. London: Macmillan.

Langton, R. 1998. *Kantian Humility*. Oxford: Oxford University Press.

Lewis, D. 2009. 'Ramseyan Humility'. In R. Nola and D. Braddon-Mitchell (eds.), *Conceptual Analysis and Philosophical Naturalism*. Cambridge, Mass.: MIT Press.

Locke, J. 1975. *An Essay Concerning Human Understanding*, ed. P. H. Nidditch. Oxford: Oxford University Press.

McDowell, J. 1985. 'Values and Secondary Qualities'. In T. Honderich (ed.), *Morality and Objectivity*. London: Routledge.

Putnam, H. 1978. *Meaning and the Moral Sciences*. London: Routledge.

Strawson, P. F. 1959. *Individuals*. London: Methuen.

Wiggins, D. 1995. 'Substance'. In A. C. Grayling (ed.), *Philosophy: A Guide through the Subject*. Oxford: Oxford University Press.

——2001. *Sameness and Substance Renewed*. Cambridge: Cambridge University Press.

6

Epistemic Humility and Causal Structuralism

James Van Cleve

Rae Langton's book *Kantian Humility* offers a provocative interpretation of one of Kant's central theses and one of the arguments for it.[1] The thesis is that *we have no knowledge of things in themselves*, which Langton interprets as meaning *we have no knowledge of the intrinsic properties of things*. We have knowledge of mind-independent things, not just of appearances, but what we know about these things is only how they are related to other things and to us, not what they are like in nonrelational respects or "in themselves." This is the doctrine Langton calls Humility. Kant's argument for the doctrine is based on the premise that human sensory knowledge is Receptive—that we have knowledge only of those features of things that have some causal impact on our faculty of sensibility. But how does Receptivity imply Humility? Strawson complained that the link between the two is "a fundamental and unargued complex premise of the *Critique*."[2] Langton undertakes to identify the Kantian assumption that must be added to Receptivity to get Humility. However, I believe that her own reconstruction of Kant's argument still leaves a significant gap. In this essay, I try to do for Langton's Kant what Langton did for Strawson's Kant: to identify and assess an unstated premise that is needed to make the argument go through. In my reconstruction, the missing premise is that causal relations hold (when they hold at all) of necessity. When contemporary philosophers maintain this anti-Humean thesis, they generally do so as a consequence of a view about property individuation sometimes known as causal structuralism. I examine the credentials of causal structuralism below.[3]

---

[1] Rae Langton, *Kantian Humility: Our Ignorance of Things in Themselves* (Oxford: Clarendon Press, 1998).

[2] Langton, p. 44, quoting P. F. Strawson, *The Bounds of Sense* (London: Methuen, 1966), p. 250.

[3] In an earlier discussion of Langton's work ("Receptivity and Our Knowledge of Intrinsic Properties," *Philosophy and Phenomenological Research*, 65 (2002), 218–36), I argued that Langton's Kantian argument from Receptivity was invalid as stated, and I considered several proposals for filling the gap. I did not there consider causal structuralism.

1 An argument for Humility

The central contention of Langton's book is that Kant offers us the following argument:

Receptivity: Human knowledge depends on sensibility, and sensibility is receptive: we can have knowledge of an object only in so far as it affects us.

Irreducibility: The relations and relational properties of substances are not reducible to the intrinsic properties of substances. Therefore,

Humility: We have no knowledge of the intrinsic properties of substances.[4]

Langton maintains that Irreducibility is an important tenet of Kant's philosophy both early and late, that it is exactly what we must add to Receptivity to get Humility, and that it is true.

To understand what the Irreducibility premise says and how it bears on Kant's conclusion, we must note two points. First, the relations and relational properties spoken of include *causal* relations and *causal* powers. Second, to say that one class of properties or relations is not reducible to another class is to say (for Langton) that the obtaining of the relations or properties in the second set does not *necessitate* the obtaining of any of those in the first. Furthermore, the necessitation she speaks of is necessitation of the strongest kind—logical or metaphysical necessity as opposed to nomological or physical necessity. Putting these points together, we may restate the essential import of the Irreducibility premise by saying that the causal relations and causal powers of things are not necessitated by any of their intrinsic properties. The argument might therefore be restated as follows:

Receptivity: We have knowledge only of those properties of things in virtue of which they enter into causal relations with us.

Irreducibility: The causal relations between things are not necessitated by their intrinsic properties. Therefore,

Humility: We have no knowledge of the intrinsic properties of things.

I pause to note two different ways of taking the Receptivity premise. When we speak of "knowledge" of some property P of an object O, do we mean knowledge *that* O has P? Or do we mean *acquaintance* with the property P? Either way, the Receptivity premise has contemporary adherents. Some philosophers impose a causal requirement on empirical propositional knowledge;[5] others impose a causal requirement on our being acquainted with a property, or on having that property as part of the content of a

---

[4] I have taken the wording for these propositions from pp. 124–27 in Langton. On p. 126, she seems to be identifying a third premise in the central argument, *Distinction* (=Things in themselves are substances that have intrinsic properties; phenomena are relational properties of substances). But Distinction is not needed to get Humility. Its role is only to allow the restatement of Humility in its more familiar Kantian form—we have no knowledge of things in themselves.

[5] See Alvin Goldman, "A Causal Theory of Knowing," *The Journal of Philosophy*, 64 (1967), 357–72, and "Discrimination and Perceptual Knowledge." *The Journal of Philosophy*, 73, (1976), 771–91.

perception.[6] And either way, the conclusion of the Humility argument would be truly humbling. In the first case, we could not know that O has P, for any intrinsic property P; in the second case, we could not even grasp the proposition that O has P (assuming that acquaintance with the constituents of a proposition is necessary for knowing it).

Whether Receptivity and Humility are concerned with propositional knowledge, acquaintance, or both, the question still arises whether the two-premise argument above is valid. It seems clear to me on inspection that the argument is *not* valid. It would be quite possible to affirm both premises, yet consistently deny the conclusion. The views of Thomas Reid afford an example. Human beings are so constituted, Reid tells us, that they achieve knowledge of the properties of the objects around them only because through those properties the objects affect their sense organs. This is to uphold Receptivity. He also affirms that the laws whereby things with their various intrinsic properties have the effects they do are brutely contingent; we can give no explanation of why they are true but the will of our maker. This is to uphold Irreducibility. Yet for all that, Reid holds that we have knowledge of some of the intrinsic properties of things, the primary qualities being the prime example. When we know, as we sometimes do, that one object is round and another square, we thereby know something about how they are in themselves and not just about their relations.[7] I cannot see any inconsistency in Reid's position, and I must therefore consider Langton's argument for Humility to be invalid as formulated.

If the argument for Humility as stated is incomplete, what further premises are needed to round it out? One premise that would fill the bill is the following:

> *Inertness:*   The intrinsic properties of things are inert; it is never by virtue of them that things enter into any causal relations with us.

Clearly, this premise would combine with Receptivity to yield Humility. But why suppose that it is true? And what work is the Irreducibility premise now doing? We can answer both questions at once if we suppose that the following premise is also part of the argument:

> *Necessitation:*   A causal relation holds between two things in virtue of certain of their properties only if necessarily, any two things with those properties are causally related.

For short, there is no causation without necessitation. The entire argument may now be set forth as follows:

---

[6] In his *From Metaphysics to Ethics: A Defense of Conceptual Analysis* (Oxford: Clarendon Press, 1998), Frank Jackson holds that experience E presents property P only if P causes E. In his *Naturalizing the Mind* (Cambridge, MA: MIT Press, 1995), Fred Dretske holds that a property is represented in an experience only if the experience has the function of indicating that property—a broadly causal or nomic notion.

[7] For Reid's upholding of the premises, see his *An Inquiry into the Human Mind*, edited by Derek Brookes (Edinburgh: Edinburgh University Press, 1997), Ch. 6, Sec. 21 ("Of the process of nature in perception"), pp. 174–76. For his denial of the conclusion, see the *Inquiry*, Ch. 5, Sec. 4, pp. 61–62, and also his *Essays on the Intellectual Powers of Man*, edited by Derek Brookes (University Park, PA: Pennsylvania State University Press, 2002), Essay II, Ch. 17 ("Of the objects of perception; of primary and secondary qualities"), pp. 200–11.

Receptivity: We have knowledge only of those properties of things in virtue of which they enter into causal relations with us.

Irreducibility: The causal relations between things are not necessitated by their intrinsic properties.

Necessitation: There is causation only where there is necessitation. Therefore,

Humility: We have no knowledge of the intrinsic properties of things.

In brief, there is no knowledge without causation, no causation without necessitation, no necessitation by intrinsic properties, and therefore no knowledge of intrinsic properties.[8]

2 Causal structuralism: help or hindrance?

In an influential article, Sidney Shoemaker has advanced the view that properties are individuated by the causal powers they bestow on their bearers.[9] This view, which is an instance of the thesis John Hawthorne has christened causal structuralism,[10] seems custom-made to yield the Necessitation premise.

Here are two of the ways in which Shoemaker formulates his view:

[W]hat makes a property the property it is, what determines its identity, is its potential for contributing to the causal powers of the things that have it. This means, among other things, that if under all possible circumstances properties X and Y make the same contribution to the causal powers of the things that have them, X and Y are the same property.[11]

[P]roperties are identical, whether in the same possible world or in different ones, just in case their coinstantiation with the same properties gives rise to the same powers.[12]

To cite his running illustration of the latter claim, nothing could be the property of being knife-shaped unless its conjunction with the property of being made of steel gave its possessor the power to cut butter.

I shall not be concerned here with the arguments for Shoemaker's view,[13] but only with the consequences of it. Among the consequences Shoemaker notes are these: the

---

[8] I have suppressed one qualification. No one would hold that fire melts wax *solely* in virtue of the intrinsic properties of the two relata; it is required as well that the fire be near enough to the wax. So the Irreducibility premise should really be put this way: the causal relations between things are not necessitated by their intrinsic properties and their proximal relations alone. There should be a similar reference to proximal relations in the other premises; thus, the Receptivity premise should say that we have knowledge only of those properties of things in virtue of which (together with their proximal relations) they enter into causal relations with us, and the Necessitation premise should say that a causal relation holds between two things in virtue of certain of their properties only if necessarily, any two things with those properties and the right proximal relations are causally related.

[9] Sidney Shoemaker, "Causality and Properties," in *Time and Cause*, edited by Peter van Inwagen (Dordrecht, Holland: Reidel, 1980), pp. 109–35; reprinted in Sydney Shoemaker, *Identity, Cause, and Mind* (Cambridge: Cambridge University Press, 1984).

[10] John Hawthorne, "Causal Structuralism," *Philosophical Perspectives*, 15 (2001), 361–78; reprinted in John Hawthorne, *Metaphysical Essays* (Oxford: Oxford University Press,), pp. 211–27.

[11] Shoemaker, *Identity, Cause and* Mind, p. 212.

[12] Shoemaker, p. 221.

[13] Most of his arguments are epistemological, being variations on the theme that if properties were not essentially tied to their effects, we could not know which properties were exemplified in various situations. He also argues that we need his view to distinguish genuine properties from "Cambridge" properties, such as being 50 feet from a barn.

causal potentialities of a property are essential to it; properties having the same causal potentialities are identical; and causal laws hold necessarily when they hold at all.

Shoemaker's view thus implies the Necessitation premise. If there were a possible world in which steel knives did not cut butter, the knives would not really be knives or the steel would not really be steel or the butter would not really be butter. Properties must enter into the causal relations they do to be the properties they are.

Here, then, is an influential view that seems to bolster Langton's Kantian argument. Yet in a critical review of Langton's book, Lucy Allais has cited Shoemaker-style views, in opposition to Langton.[14] Specifically, she has cited causal structuralism in opposition to Langton's case for the Irreducibility premise. So does causal structuralism help or hurt the argument for Humility?

The heart of Langton's case for the Irreducibility premise is a thought experiment and the modal intuition it is meant to elicit:

Many philosophers share Kant's intuition that causal powers are extrinsic properties. What guides this intuition is a thought that things could be just the same as they are with respect to their intrinsic properties, yet different with respect to their powers—in particular, that if the laws of nature were different, things could have the same intrinsic properties but different powers. . . . In a world where the laws of nature were very different, things might not have an attractive power, despite having the very same intrinsic properties that attractive things actually have.[15]

I share the intuition. Langton sometimes puts the point using Locke's language of "superaddition:" once God has bestowed upon things all their intrinsic properties, it must be through a further act of superaddition that he gives things their causal powers.[16]

Allais disputes the intended upshot of the thought experiment. She notes that it depends on the assumption that what is conceivable or intuited as possible really is possible—an assumption that can fail if there are necessary truths that are not discoverable *a priori*, as Kripke has taught us with the famous example of water = H_2O. If *p* is such a necessary truth, its negation (an impossibility) will not be knowable *a priori* to be false, and will in that sense be something we find conceivable. We may even have a clear impression of its possibility.

Moreover, Allais notes that Shoemaker-style views give truths about the causal relations among properties the status of Kripkean necessary truths. The metaphysical natures or identities of various properties make the causal connections among them essential to them, even if it seems to us that those very properties could be instantiated in a world in which those connections are absent.[17]

---

[14] Lucy Allais, "Intrinsic Natures: A Critique of Langton on Kant," *Philosophy and Phenomenological Research,* 73 (2006), 143–69.

[15] Langton, p. 118.

[16] Langton, p. 118; she also cites passages in which Kant uses language remarkably similar to Locke's.

[17] In section 10 of his paper, Shoemaker notes that his view implies that conceivability is not sufficient for possibility.

What, then, is the bearing of causal structuralism on Langton's argument—help or hindrance? The answer, I think, is *both*: it helps by supporting the Necessitation premise, but it hurts by undermining the Irreducibility premise. And that means that, all things considered, it is a hindrance. Someone who patches your left tire but punctures your right still keeps you from going where you want to go.

We could put this as a dilemma: without causal structuralism, the Necessitation premise is unsupported; with it, the Irreducibility premise is false.

There is one more possible bearing of causal structuralism on Humility I would like to explore. On first glance, it may look as though causal structuralism defines each property as a node in a network of relations in such a way as to imply that *there is no such thing* as an intrinsic property. If so, Kantian Humility would be true, though for an unintended reason: we would have no knowledge of intrinsic properties because there would *be* no intrinsic properties. Could that be right?

As a preliminary point, note that we cannot show that colors are not intrinsic merely by pointing out that scarlet entails red and excludes turquoise. Intrinsic properties may stand in complicated webs of necessary connection.

But we need to look closer at the notion of an intrinsic property. Langton gives two criteria for intrinsicality, intending them to be individually necessary and jointly sufficient. The first criterion is *compatibility with loneliness*: an intrinsic property is a property that a thing could have even if it were all alone in the universe—like the property of being square, perhaps, but unlike the property of owning a pig.[18] Does the Shoemaker view make all properties extrinsic by this criterion? As far as I can see, the answer is no, except on one special assumption. The assumption is that Aristotle and Armstrong are right in holding that properties are constituents of laws, but that they exist only when instantiated. We could then argue as follows. Suppose it is essential to the property of being a proton that protons attract electrons (as causal structuralism would have it) and suppose there is a proton. Then there must also be the property of being an electron (since it is a constituent of the attraction law), and if the AA assumption is correct, there must therefore also be an electron. So there could not be a solitary proton, and the property of being a proton would not be intrinsic. If all properties of things are lawfully linked to properties of other things, it would follow by similar reasoning that there are no intrinsic properties.

However, the assumption on which this reasoning rests is not mandatory. As far as I can see, there is no reason why someone with SS views would have to embrace AA views as well.

Langton's second criterion is *compatibility with lawlessness*.[19] Here the idea is that being water-soluble is an extrinsic property of sugar not because its instantiation requires water to exist (it does not), but because it depends on a law about how sugar would

---

[18] Langton, pp. 18-19.   [19] Langton, p. 119.

behave in water if there were any. Intrinsic properties are those a thing might have even in the absence of law.

By this criterion, causal structuralism does rule out the existence of intrinsic properties. (Or perhaps one should say that the criterion, along with the existence of intrinsic properties, rules out causal structuralism—by fiat.) But that is not to say that causal structuralism makes Kantian Humility true. In its intended sense, Kantian Humility is surely the doctrine that there *are* intrinsic properties, and that we are ignorant of them.

3 A dilemma for causal structuralism

John Hawthorne has leveled against causal structuralism the objection that it identifies properties that we should recognize as distinct. To pave the way for this objection, we must first state causal structuralism in Hawthorne's way by reference to Ramsey sentences. Let causal laws be written in the form AnB, meaning that having property A nomologically necessitates having property B. Now take the conjunction of all the laws (the "lawbook") and construct its Ramsey sentence: replace all property constants by variables and form the existential generalization that contains quantifiers for each of these variables.[20] Finally, define each property as the property that satisfies the open sentence that results if you delete "its" quantifier (that is, the quantifier containing the variable that replaced the constant for that property). In effect, this is to define each property as the property that plays a certain causal or nomic role. It is a consequence of this style of definition that each property bears the causal relations it does to all other properties essentially. If A did not nomically necessitate B, A and B would not be the properties they are. The Hawthorne strategy thus delivers the results Shoemaker wants: each property has its causal profile essentially, and causal laws hold with necessity.

Hawthorne's objection may now be stated. Suppose there is a simple world containing just four properties, A, B, C, and D, related by just three laws: AnC, BnC, and (A&B)nD. Here A and B are naturally regarded as distinct properties, for as Hawthorne notes, "Their coinstantiation has different effects (the addition of D to the world) than is produced by either being instantiated alone."[21] But A and B are not distinguished by the Ramseyfied lawbook; they have the same definition in terms of Ramsey sentences. A is defined as the property F such that $\exists G\exists H\exists K[FnH \ \& \ GnH \ \& \ (F\&G)nK]$. B is defined as the property G such that $\exists F\exists H\exists K[FnH \ \& \ GnH \ \& \ (F\&G)nK]$. By rewrite of bound variables, the second definiens is equivalent to "the property F such that $\exists G\exists H\exists K[GnH \ \& \ FnH \ \& \ (G\&F)nK]$," which is equivalent to the first definiens by commutation of conjuncts. So the two definitions define the same property.[22]

---

[20] Hawthorne notes that the lawbook will also contain clauses ensuring that the laws in the conjunction are all the laws that there are; I omit this complication.

[21] Hawthorne, p. 224.

[22] It is not necessary to maintain here that logically equivalent definitions always define the same property, but only that definitions equivalent by rewrite of bound variables and commutation of conjuncts define the same property. "$\exists y(x$ is the parent of y & x is male)" defines the same property of x as "$\exists z(x$ is male & x is the parent of z)"—namely, the property of being a father.

In a postscript to his article, Hawthorne notes that Shoemaker has said in reply that he had not necessarily envisioned defining properties in terms of Ramsey sentences in the manner above. Instead, he proposes defining them in terms of what Hawthorne calls Shoemaker sentences. To construct the Shoemaker-sentence definition of the property A from the lawbook above, do not replace *all* property constants in the lawbook by variables, but only the constant A, the one you wish to define. Then say: A is the property V such that VnC, BnC, and (V&B)nD. This does not merely say that A is the property that necessitates C and, along with some C necessitator, necessitates D; that would be equally true of B. It says that A is the property that necessitates C and, *along with B*, necessitates D. That is not true of B, so the distinction between A and B has been upheld.

Notice, however, what is going on. If we defined B in the same manner, we would say that B is the property V such that AnC, VnC, and (A&V)nD—defining B in terms of A. We are defining A as the property that (among other things) couples with B to produce D, and we are defining B as the property that (among other things) couples with A to produce D. By mentioning the properties in the definientia by name rather than simply referring to them by quantified variables, we are committing a circularity. We are incurring the objection Russell once made when he spoke of theories that make all the things in the world "each other's washing."[23] This is the objection that thoroughly Ramseyfied functional definitions are supposed to avoid, but we incur it again when we go with Ramsey only part of the way.

The view to which we have now been led may be compared to an analogous view about the individuation of individuals. Consider a Max Black-type universe in which there are two billiard balls allegedly alike in every way and individuated (or differentiated) only by this: A is the ball adjacent to B and B is the ball adjacent A. It seems clear to me that two balls cannot be differentiated *only* in this way. Such individuation presupposes that each ball has its own haecceity, one of the balls being A and the other being B, and if so, there is no need to mention the other. The analogous view about properties would be that each property has its own quiddity, an essence not fully capturable by its structural role.[24] But once quiddities have been admitted, why cannot they float free of the nomic net altogether, making their possessors the properties they are independently of their causal relations to other properties?

The dilemma, then, is that causal structuralism either (i) identifies properties that should be distinguished or (ii) individuates properties in a circular fashion, perhaps losing in the bargain the ability to sustain the essentialist consequences Shoemaker wants.

---

[23] Bertrand Russell, *The Analysis of Matter*, p. 325; quoted in Simon Blackburn, "Filling in Space," *Analysis*, 50 (1990), 62–65, where a similar concern is aired. Compare also Keith Campbell's lament about Boscovichian theories of matter, which characterize material points as points that repel other material points: "We seem to be caught in a regress or circle, forever unable to say what these things are which have an effect on each other." (Keith Campbell, *Metaphysics: An Introduction* (Encino, CA: Dickenson, 1976), p. 93).

[24] See Hawthorne for more about quiddities and the analogies between views about them and views about haecceities.

4 Conclusions

The Kantian argument for Humility as initially formulated by Langton is a *non sequitur*. It requires some further premise to be valid, the most obvious candidate being the anti-Humean premise that there is no causation without necessitation.

Causal structuralism, as advocated by Shoemaker and several other contemporary philosophers, would deliver the anti-Humean premise.

However, causal structuralism faces a dilemma. It either identifies properties that are plausibly regarded as distinct, or it commits a circle in individuation.

Moreover, even if causal structuralism were true, it would not rescue the argument for Humility. It would provide support for one of the premises (Necessitation), but it would undercut another (Irreducibility).

I should note in closing that in a reply to Allais, Langton has repudiated causal structuralism—not surprisingly, given her "compatibility with lawlessness" criterion for the intrinsic.[25] She has also made it clear that she does not think (as Allais and I had conjectured she did) that Inertness follows from Irreducibility alone—though she thinks Kant may have believed it did.[26] This is as much as to say that the Kantian argument for Humility is unsound—containing a false premise if we add causal structuralism and remaining invalid if we do not.

But Langton also notes that there is an overall dilemma in support of Humility,[27] since if causal structuralism is *false*, the way is open for another argument for epistemic humility. If properties are *not* defined by their causal roles, then two properties could be switched in our overall scheme of things without our being any the wiser for it; we could not know which property was where or even grasp the difference between them. This is the gist of the argument David Lewis has advanced under the banner "Ramseyan Humility."[28]

Lewis's argument concerns properties that are posited in theories to explain our observations. In Lewis's view, we can characterize such properties only as the properties that play certain causal roles—as properties that interact with each other and with observable properties in a way that makes the Ramsey sentence for our overall theory of the world true.[29] Moreover, Lewis holds that there are various possible permutations

---

[25] Rae Langton, "Kant's Phenomena: Extrinsic or Relational Properties? A Reply to Allais," *Philosophy and Phenomenological Research*, 73 (2006), 170–85.

[26] *Ibid.*, p. 177. Langton here refers to Irreducibility as "the contingency thesis," meaning the thesis that the association between intrinsic properties and causal powers is contingent.

[27] *Kant's Humility*, p. 176, and "Kantian Phenomena," p. 178.

[28] David Lewis, "Ramseyan Humility," in *Conceptual Analysis and Philosophical Naturalism*, edited by David Braddon-Mitchell and Robert Nola (Cambridge, MA: Press, 2009), pp. 203–22. Dustin Locke's "A Partial Defense of Ramseyan Humility," pp. 223–41 in the same volume, gives helpful commentary on Lewis's argument and discussion of some of the critical literature on it.

[29] Confusion can threaten at this point because Lewis says properties denoted by the terms of a theory are "defined" by their roles. He does not mean by this what a causal structuralist à la Shoemaker would mean by it—that the causal role of a property is essential to it. For Lewis, properties "defined" by their roles can nonetheless switch roles; for Shoemaker, properties defined by their roles *cannot* switch roles.

of these properties (with each other or with properties exemplified in other possible worlds) that would make the same Ramsey sentence true. He concludes that our observational evidence could never settle which properties play which roles and that in consequence we do not *know* which properties play which roles. As I put it above, a switch among two or more theoretical properties would leave us none the wiser. Such is Ramseyan Humility.

I shall not undertake here to assess the cogency of Lewis's argument, but only its reach. The argument concerns those properties we know only as the occupants of certain roles; if there are any intrinsic properties that we do not know merely as the occupants of roles, the argument does not apply to them.[30] According to Reid, what is distinctive of the primary qualities (such as shape and hardness) as opposed to the secondary qualities (which are conceived of only as the causes of certain sensations in us) and the tertiary qualities (which are conceived of only as the causes of effects in other physical things) is precisely that we are directly acquainted with the primaries, not merely cognizant of them as the occupants of certain roles. If Reid is right, Ramseyan Humility falls short of Kantian Humility—it does not extend to intrinsic properties across the board.

---

[30] A similar point is made by Dustin Locke when he notes that a "direct realist" could sidestep Lewis's argument. I assume that Reid would count as a direct realist in the relevant sense.

7

Seeing What Is So

Barry Stroud

I think any satisfactory understanding of human perceptual knowledge must make room for the fact that we know things about the world around us by perception alone.[1] What I mean by that is something that many philosophical theories of knowledge have denied. Those theories have said in one way or another that the most we can know by perception alone is something that in itself implies nothing about the way things are in the world around us. This view has not usually been taken by its defenders to imply that therefore we can know nothing about the world. Rather, it has been taken to show that perceptual knowledge of the world is a combination of two separate ingredients: what we know by sense-perception alone plus some things we know in some other ways.

I think this way of understanding our knowledge of the world, when pressed, cannot really explain to those of us who have that knowledge how the knowledge we have is possible. It leaves us vulnerable to what we can recognize as reasons to doubt the grounds for any steps we are said to take beyond what we can know from perception alone. To identify and explain those doubts would be a long story that I will not go into here.[2] So I start here from the need to reject any such conception of our knowledge of the world. I would like to suggest by contraposition that since we can and do know many things about the world around us by perception alone, all views that restrict the range of perceptual knowledge in that way must be rejected. The question is whether we can really understand perceptual knowledge of the world in the way that I think we need.

I will speak only about visual perception: seeing. I think we very often see and thereby know that *p*, where what fills the place of 'p' is something that is so in the world around us and would be so whether anyone perceives it to be so or not. And I think it is possible to get knowledge of that kind that is not based on anything else we

[1] This is the main proposal of my 'Scepticism and the Senses', *European Journal of Philosophy* 2009.

[2] I have tried to elaborate these doubts in my 'Understanding Human Knowledge in General' and 'Scepticism, "Externalism", and the Goal of Epistemology', both in my *Understanding Human Knowledge* (Oxford 2000) and in 'The Epistemological Promise of Externalism', in R. Schantz (ed.), *The Externalist Challenge* (Berlin and New York 2005).

know that we somehow combine with what we get from sense-perception alone to give us knowledge that *p*. We simply see, and in seeing know, that *p*. So I think the idea we need is not just that seeing is believing, but that seeing is, or can be, knowing. I see, and in seeing know, that there is a chair in this room.

Knowledge is knowledge that something or other is so. It involves a propositional thought that is true. So the seeing that *p* that amounts to knowing that *p* involves a propositional thought that is true. The very same thought is involved in both the seeing and the knowing: what you see to be so is what you know to be so. So the seeing I have in mind could be called 'propositional' seeing, or seeing that takes a propositional object. Putting it that way can be misleading if it suggests that what you see is a proposition. No; what I see is that there is a chair in this room. To say that that is a propositional object of seeing is only to say that my seeing is described in a sentence in which the complement of the perceptual verb 'see' is a sentence with a truth-value, not a singular term referring to an object.

Of course, in this case I also see that chair. That is stated in a sentence with a perceptual verb followed by a singular term. This could be called 'objectual' seeing— the seeing of an object.[3] 'Propositional' seeing that *p* typically, but not always, involves seeing objects in this 'objectual' sense. Seeing that the cat is on the mat typically involves seeing the cat and seeing the mat. But when I see only that it is foggy everywhere, for instance, I see and thereby know that that is how things are, but it could be that I do not see any objects at all. And it is also possible to come to know something about an object I do not see by seeing a certain other object. I can see that my neighbour is at home by seeing her car parked in front of her house.

But in the typical case now before us, I know that there is a chair in this room because I see that chair. I might have come to know that there is a chair in this room in some other way, not by seeing that chair. What would explain my knowing what I know in that case would be something other than my seeing that chair. If my seeing that chair is in fact how I come to know that there is a chair in this room, my knowledge is of something 'propositional', but my seeing that chair is not 'propositional' seeing.

I think what I am calling 'objectual' seeing does not require knowing or perhaps even believing anything about the object you see. I might see that chair that is in fact in this room even though I do not know it is a chair or know that it is in this room. Under those conditions, I would still see that chair. A creature—e.g., an ant or a mouse—can see an object that is blocking its way even if the creature has no knowledge of anything beyond having a capacity for moving around in the world. In a sentence of the form 'He sees *x*', any expression that is true of the object that '*x*' stands for can be put in its place without changing the truth-value of the sentence. Many things can be true of the objects I see without my knowing that they are true. I can see something that costs $50

---

[3] This is what Fred Dretske called 'non-epistemic' seeing in his *Seeing and Knowing*, (London 1969).

without knowing that it costs $50, just as a dog standing next to me also sees that thing that costs $50.

But I could not see *that* there is a chair in this room without thinking and knowing that there is a chair in this room. And, as with all knowledge, I could not know it if it were not true—if there were no chair in this room. So I could not see that there is a chair in this room if there were no chair here. In this way, this kind of seeing amounts to knowledge. What I want to suggest is that we must be capable of this kind of seeing and knowing if we know things about the world by visual perception.

Seeing an object in the 'objectual' sense requires certain capacities or expertise on the part of the perceiver. An ability to see objects involves having one's attention visually drawn to the object, or discriminating it from its surroundings in some way, or visually responding to it attentively, perhaps tracking it with your gaze if it is moving. What exactly is involved in visually discriminating and so seeing an object is not easy to say. But many different creatures all have such a capacity; they can see and respond to objects. When I see that chair, and attend to it or find it within my awareness, the chair is available to me for thinking and saying things about. It is therefore available to me to come to know things about. But I do not think I need to know anything about the object I see for it to be available to me in that way. Of course, typically I do believe and know many things about the objects I see. But I do not need to know or believe anything about an object for it to be there and to be the object of my 'objectual' awareness, my seeing.

The possibility of this kind of access makes 'objectual' seeing very important, perhaps essential, to explaining the possibility of thought. It has been argued, for instance, that having *de re* attitudes towards some objects is a necessary condition of having any propositional attitudes at all.[4] That is primarily how human thought is connected to the world, and so can be about something or other. If this general 'priority' of *de re* over *de dicto* attitudes holds in particular for *de re* perceptual attitudes, this would mean that 'objectual' perceiving would be fundamental for thought. *De re* perception would make something available as an object of a possible thought without that thing's having to be thought about in any way in order to be available as the object of that thought.

This is also especially important for language-learning.[5] How could language be learned at all if we were not capable of perceiving things in a way that does not require believing or knowing something about the things we see? Some objects have to be perceptually available both to the conceptually unequipped pupil and to the sophisticated expert speaker if the pupil can learn to apply new predicates correctly to objects that both teacher and pupil can see. If the concepts expressed by those predicates were

---

[4] See, e.g., Tyler Burge, 'Belief *De Re*', and 'Postscript to "Belief *De Re*"', in his *Foundations of Mind* (Oxford 2007).

[5] As Burge has also stressed in the same essay.

needed even for seeing the objects in the first place, there would be no way to get started.

A closely related thought lies behind John Campbell's defence of what he calls a 'relational' view of perception of an object. If experience is the source of thought, as he argues, and perceptual experience of objects is what explains our ability to think about objects at all, there must be within our experience some 'cognitive relation' to objects that is 'more primitive' than having thoughts about them. Conscious attention, he says, 'by bringing the object itself into the subjective life of the thinker, makes it possible to think about that object'.[6] So for Campbell a 'relational', non-conceptual view of the perception of objects is essential to the explanatory potential of perceptual experience.

But even if what I am calling 'objectual' seeing is essential for all thinking about objects, that does not necessarily explain how we can think the things we actually think about the objects we see. Thinking something about the objects you see obviously requires more than just seeing those objects. Seeing objects puts us in a position to have thoughts about them, but a thought, a propositional thought, about an object comes only with the mastery of certain concepts or predicates. That conceptual capacity is a capacity to make judgements involving those concepts: an ability to apply the concept or predicate to items you take it to be true of. Having such thoughts about an object is more than simply attaching a label to the thing, and more than being able to attach that same label to other similar things. Thinking that something is true of an object is also more than simply discriminating one kind of thing from another, or being able to sort things into different groups. It is a matter of having a propositional thought, and of being able to put something forward as true, and of knowing how to do it under the appropriate conditions while understanding what you thereby think or say. And that capacity is not present simply in seeing objects in the 'objectual' or 'relational' sense.

Knowledge requires propositional judgement, and judgement requires predication: the application of a concept to an object. 'Objectual' seeing can make an object available for predication, and so for propositional judgement, but the kind of perceptual knowledge I want to draw attention to requires a capacity to recognize, in the right circumstances, that an item now within your awareness falls, or does not fall, under a concept you are master of and understand. And for some concepts and situations, application of the appropriate concepts must be direct in the sense of not being made on the basis of any feature of the object other than its instantiating the concept in question. When an object is present, the perceiver's recognitional conceptual capacities must enable him to see without further assistance or guidance that the concept applies, or does not apply, to the object. That is possible, of course, only for perceivers who have the appropriate conceptual and recognitional capacities.

Someone who has such concepts and can recognize that an object present to him is a chair, say, or is red, is in a position to make a judgement to that effect when an object

---

[6] J. Campbell, *Reference and Consciousness* (Oxford 2002) p. 6.

shows up in his awareness and he pays attention to it. What he predicates of the object is something he is at least capable of thinking of as true of other objects. Predicational capacity involves this kind of generality; the same concept can be applied to different objects, and different predicates can be applied to the same object. It is a general capacity in the sense that there is a gap or an open place within each of the potential thoughts or sentences the thinker remains poised to accept about something's being a chair or a red thing or whatever it might be, whenever an appropriate object shows up in his perception. He does not have to know or think anything about that object before it shows up in his awareness in order to come to have such a thought about it when he sees it. And when an object does show up, he does not always need to deliberate or weigh competing factors to determine whether a certain concept applies to it. 'Objectual' perception of an object by anyone who is already equipped in that way simply 'brings facts into plain view',[7] in John McDowell's phrase. A competent seer and judger can see and thereby know by perception alone that an object present to him has such-and-such a property.

It is tempting to think that there must be *some* concepts that we can *sometimes* see and thereby know by perception alone to be instantiated. If we could never know by perception alone that a certain concept applies to something we are aware of, it looks as if we could know such a thing only if we know that a certain other concept applies to the thing. And if that is true of every concept and every thing, it would go on forever; we could know nothing by perception alone about any object. Even those traditional theories that insist on a much more restrictive conception of the range of perceptual knowledge did not accept that consequence. They agreed that we can get knowledge of certain things by perception alone, but they denied that it is knowledge of anything that is so and would be so whether it is perceived to be so or not.

Those theories say the most you can know by perception alone is that an object *looks as if* it is red, say, or that *it seems* to be red, or that it *looks* or *seems as if* there is a red object there, or that your perception is *as of* a red object, or some such less committal thing. Even those particular ways of hedging might still be thought to be sticking one's epistemic neck out too far, but on views of this kind it is accepted that there is at least *something* we are directly aware of and know by perception alone.[8] What is in dispute is only the legitimate range of purely perceptual knowledge, not whether there is any such knowledge at all. But to know anything beyond that restricted range, those traditional theories say, we would need reason to believe that what we directly perceive is a reliable guide to the way things are. And given the restriction on purely perceptual knowledge, that is not something we could ever know by perception alone.

---

[7] J. McDowell, 'Conceptual Capacities in Perception', in his *Having the World in View* (Cambridge, Mass. 2009) p. 139.

[8] If what we are directly aware of in perception were only objects, and never *that* such-and-such is so, we would so far have no explanation of perceptual *knowledge* of anything, since 'objectual' seeing is consistent with knowing nothing about the object seen.

This is the two-step conception of perceptual knowledge of the world that I think we must overcome if we are to understand how we know anything at all about the world by perception.

We could begin to work towards overcoming that restriction by asking whether someone could recognize directly and without guidance or mediation that an object he sees *looks* or *seems* to be red if he did not at least understand what it is for an object to *be* red. And could someone understand that, and so be capable of having the thought that a present object is red, if he lacked the capacity ever to recognize, under any circumstances, that a present object *is* red? This is not a line of argument I will pursue further here. But I think it is the kind of (dare I say 'transcendental'?) investigation that could take us to the bottom of, and so put behind us once and for all, the appeal of the traditional restriction of perceptual knowledge to something always less than the world around us. This is where real work is needed: on the conditions of possessing and understanding the concepts needed even to be presented with the traditional episte-mological problem.

Suppose we found after extended reflection that it is not possible in general for someone to recognize that an object actually present to him in perception *looks* red without his also having at least a capacity to recognize, and thereby to know, that an object present to him *is* red. That would mean that anyone who becomes convinced that he can know by perception alone only how things *look* or *seem* to be, and not how things *are*, would in fact be capable of knowing things about the world by perception alone. He would be wrong to think he was faced by a general threat to his perceptual knowledge of the world. Even if he is somehow philosophically convinced to the contrary, he could in fact come to know that an object in the world is a chair, or is red, simply by seeing that it is.

I think that is the position we are actually in, and it can have a liberating effect to realize it. But even if that is true, I do not think that pointing out that we can and do know things in that way amounts to a straightforward answer to the traditional epistemological question. That question appears to require that knowledge of the world be satisfactorily explained only by identifying a reason or ground or justification for the knowledge-claim in question. It demands that there be something *on the basis of which* the believer justifiably accepts or believes what he does. And simply seeing and thereby knowing that a present object is red seems too close to the fact in question to satisfy that demand for justification; what is seen is the very thing the knowing of which is meant to be explained.

When I see and in seeing know that an object present to me is red, what I see to be so is not my 'basis' or 'reason' or 'justification' for believing that the object is red. What I see to be so is that the object is red. That is all it takes to know it. There can be no better or stronger position for believing or knowing something than seeing that it is so, right before your eyes.

But I think that does not mean that *what* I see to be so is *my* reason or justification or warrant. I think there is no such thing in this case. What I see and thereby believe and know is that the object is red. I come to know that that is so by seeing that it is so. It is *because* I see what I see that I know what I know. My seeing what I see explains *why* I believe or *how* I know what I do. It is in that sense the reason *why* I believe and know what I do. But my *seeing* that the object is red is not my reason or justification or warrant for believing that it is red. It is because I see what I do that I know and in that sense am justified or warranted in believing that the object is red. But there is nothing independent that serves as my 'basis' or 'warrant' or 'reason' for believing that.

When I say that I see and thereby know that there is a chair in this room, or that a certain object is red, and I do so not *on the basis of* anything I know or believe about the object, I do not mean that I could know what I know about the object even if I knew nothing else at all. I could not see and know that the object is red without having the concept 'red', and so without knowing what I am saying when I say that something is red. I need a rich conceptual repertoire to be able to see and thereby know that *p*, whatever the 'p' in question might be. And I think that in having the kind of conceptual repertoire we all have we thereby know, or are capable of knowing, a great many things about the world around us. Learning to understand and think certain thoughts and learning things about the world those thoughts are about go hand in hand. So I think anyone must know or at least believe many things about the world even to be capable of seeing and thereby knowing that a certain object is red, or that there is a chair in this room. One has to know what chairs are, for instance, and how they behave, and that involves a lot of other knowledge.

This is another reason why pointing out that we can sometimes see and thereby know that an object is a chair, or is red, would not be a satisfactory reply to someone facing the traditional problem of the external world. That problem is understood as completely general, concerned with any knowledge of the world around us at all. So if I am in a position to see and know, of an object I see, that it is red only if I already know many things about the external world, that would not be a satisfactory answer to that completely general question. It would not fulfil the demands built into the very form of that question.

It is remarkable that even many of those who claim to have no interest in that general epistemological question nonetheless seem to assume that someone's knowing something about the world can be satisfactorily explained only by finding something else, some separate basis or ground, on which the knowledge in question can be seen to rest. Some such assumption seems to be required by the possibility of error. It has to be admitted that we are not infallible in coming to see and know such things as that there is a chair in this room. It is perfectly possible to think and say that I see and thereby know that there is a chair in this room and be wrong. When I am wrong I of course do not know. And if I do not know, I do not *see* that there is a chair in this room either. This leads easily to the thought that I never *know* that there is a chair in this room *simply* by seeing that there is a chair. That is because, as the argument goes, I could have a perceptual experience of the very same kind when there only *looks* to me to be a chair in this room. And I can have that kind of perceptual experience even when there *is* no chair here.

I think it cannot be denied that the perceptual experience I have when I see and thereby know that there is a chair here is an experience of the same kind as I can have when I do not in fact see or know that there is a chair here. But every two things are of the same kind in some respects or other. So the similarity does not mean that there is not also a great difference between the two kinds of perceptual experience. There is a great difference, after all, between seeing and thereby knowing that there is a chair here and seeing and knowing only that there *looks* to be a chair here when there is not. It might be said that, at least as far as getting knowledge of the world is concerned, the two experiences are of the same kind. But that also seems wrong to me. The perceptual experiences are very different in that respect; in the one case you know and in the other case you do not.

But I think there remains the feeling that the two experiences are of the same kind, considered, so to speak, only as 'purely perceptual experiences'. There is a very strong tendency to think that *what* I see when I am wrong and do not know must be the same as *what* I see when I do know by seeing that there is a chair in this room. Otherwise, how could my error be explained? So it seems that what I *see* even in the case in which I do know cannot be that there is a chair in this room. This leads quickly down a very slippery slope, at the end of which we are thought to be able to know by perception alone only the very least committal thing we can be said to see and thereby know to be so without possibility of error. But there is no such thing we can see to be so, if the mere possibility of error is enough to disqualify something as not being *seen* to be so. This leads in turn to the thought that we make errors only in *judging* something to be so, not in perceiving itself, or in seeing what we see. Judgement, or propositional or predicational thinking, is then thought to be no part of 'the perceptual experience itself'.

This line of thought leaves us with a conception of 'the perceptual experience itself' as something from which all propositional thinking and the exercise of conceptual capacities have been removed. But then what is left? What is this thing called 'the perceptual experience itself', so understood? This is the idea of *a* perceptual experience, or even *an* experience, that has played such an important part in philosophy for a long time. But what is that idea?

I think my seeing and thereby knowing that there is a chair in this room is a perceptual experience. And *that* experience would not be what it is if I were not capable of propositional thought and the exercise of conceptual capacities in that very perception. Even when I see only that there *looks to be* a chair in this room, the perceptual experience I have also involves propositional thought and the exercise of conceptual capacities on my part. Are there perceptual experiences that do not involve any such capacities at all and yet can give us knowledge of something?

'A perceptual experience itself', thought of as something with no conceptual ingredients, would perhaps be a matter of being conscious and having your eyes open and seeing an object in the 'objectual' sense that does not imply that you know or believe anything about it. Objects seen in that way might include not only ordinary physical objects, but also colours, shapes, movement, and so on. Such things can be seen in the 'objectual' sense; it can be revealed in a creature's responses to the world that a colour is what its visual attention is drawn to, for instance, or that it is a certain shape that it discriminates from its surroundings, and so on. Things a creature is aware of in that way stand to the creature in the relation of being seen, but the creature does not need to know or think anything about those things for them to stand in that relation. The objects you see in that way might well be part of the world around you, but in that 'perceptual experience itself', understood in this austere way, you know nothing about the world by perception. So whatever you eventually come to know about the world could not be understood as something you know *on the basis of* what you know in perceptual experience alone, so understood. On this austere conception, there is nothing you know in having only 'the perceptual experience itself'. To have perceptual knowledge of anything at all, the perceptual experience in which you have it must involve some exercise of conceptual capacities involving propositional or predicational thought.

This requirement of the exercise of conceptual capacities seems unavoidable if we are ever to get any knowledge by perception. But that very requirement can seem to put perceptual knowledge of an independent world under threat from a completely different direction. John McDowell is one who thinks 'conceptual capacities are operative in our perceptual experience',[9] and he thinks, as he characteristically puts it, that 'there is justice in the thought that [that] idea can seem to work only in the context of an idealism'.[10] I think it would be disappointing to learn that the kind of perceptual knowledge I think we must have if we are to avoid the scepticism inherent in the traditional problem of the external world is available only at the price of idealism. But maybe all is well. McDowell says that 'any idealism with a chance of being credible...if thought through,...stands revealed as fully cohering with the realism of common sense'.[11] So in McDowell's own thinking he says he works to 'dislodge' from his idealism 'the appearance that it does not genuinely acknowledge how reality is independent of our thinking'.[12] Nonetheless, even when that independence is granted, he thinks his view is idealism 'in an obvious sense', 'the label is a good fit'.[13]

One thing McDowell is impressed by is the special role or position we 'rational animals' occupy in the world. We have a 'potential for self-determination', for doing and thinking what we in our rational capacity can ourselves determine to do or to think. This is something not just any creature 'whose senses inform it of things' can do.[14] So our 'rationality', our capacity for assessing the reasons for and against

[9] McDowell, 'Conceptual Capacities in Perception', p. 141.   [10] Ibid.
[11] Ibid.   [12] McDowell, 'Conceptual Capacities in Perception', p. 142.
[13] McDowell, 'Conceptual Capacities in Perception', p. 143.
[14] McDowell, 'Conceptual Capacities in Perception', p. 144.

something 'enters into the possibility of describing ourselves as accepting what our senses give us', as McDowell puts it.[15]

I agree that our having rational capacities enters into explaining how perception can provide us with something to accept. We have much richer and more varied conceptual capacities than other creatures. We can think, and think things to be true. And we can take one thing we think to be reason to believe something else we can think, and we believe it for that reason. That is how we, and not other creatures, can come to believe the sorts of things we do. But in appealing to our distinctive capacities to explain our achievements I do not see any need, or role, for idealism.

In the world we live in, perceivers with a capacity to think and reason and accept certain things as true can find that one thing they have come to think about the world is reason to believe another. That one thing is reason to believe another is something we find to be so in the world; it is part of what we take the world we believe in to be like. And in a world like that we can find by perception reasons to believe things about what that world is like. Other creatures cannot do that; they can perceive objects and respond appropriately, but do not have our kinds of capacities for thought and the recognition of reasons to believe things. We are naturally equipped to find out things about the world in ways that are impossible for other creatures.

Perhaps this is just the 'realism of common sense' that McDowell says his idealism 'fully coheres' with. But if that is so, I do not see what is left of idealism. McDowell sums up his view in the slogan 'The world is everything that is the case'. He says this expresses, truistically, what he calls an 'unimpeachable way to use the notion of the world'.[16] It is simply the idea of everything that is so—everything that can be truly thought or said. But he thinks this is idealism because 'on this conception', as he puts it, 'the world itself is indeed structured by the form of judgment'.[17] This is the point I do not get.

McDowell thinks his form of idealism fully acknowledges the independence of reality from our thought about it. That independence is preserved, he thinks, if we see and fully acknowledge that thought and the world are to be understood together, with neither thought of as prior to the other in the order of understanding. That seems right to me. I understand human beings as thinking and perceiving the kinds of things they think and perceive only because I have the conceptual and perceptual resources I have in the world in which we human beings find ourselves. But if what I and the rest of us can thereby think and perceive to be so is so, or not, independently of my, or anyone's, having or exercising those capacities, I do not see what is left of idealism.

But I strongly agree with McDowell in his stress on the importance of the idea that the world is everything that is the case. And I think he is right that it is a 'truistic' thought; there is no good reason to oppose it. I think the implications of that truistic thought have not really been seriously explored or faced. There has been an apparently

---

[15] Ibid.   [16] Ibid.

[17] McDowell, 'Conceptual Capacities in Perception', p. 143.

undying predilection in philosophy to look for, and to try to understand the world in terms of, *objects*—as if what objects there are is all we need to tell us what the world is like. But I take the slogan that the world is everything that is the case to be a way of saying that if there is a world at all, it is only because something or other is so—that the world is the totality of facts, not of things. Even if objects are essential to any world, that the objects have certain properties, that they stand in certain relations to one another, that they behave in certain ways, and so on, are all things that must be so if there is to be a world like that. And that world—understood as all those things' being so—cannot be simply a further object. So I think we need the idea that the world is everything that is the case in order to think of a world at all. But even when that idea is put together with a commitment to conceptual capacities as essential to perception of and thought about the world, I do not see how it amounts to any form of, or any encouragement to, idealism.

To say that the world is everything that is the case is not to deny that there are a great many things that are so that we cannot even think, let alone have reason to believe, right now. By enriching our resources for thinking and recognizing reasons we could perhaps discover what some of those things are, and so come to think and know much more about the world than we do now. But what we came to think and find out in those new ways would still be something we could think, then. Our being able to think it, and our having found things we recognize to be reasons to believe it, would explain our then believing what we do. None of that could be explained without appeal to our conceptual capacities. But just as the things that are so right now but that we cannot think right now do not depend on our having the conceptual capacities we do, so the things human beings come to think then, with expanded capacities, would not depend on people having the conceptual capacities they then have either.

I think not only the range of human propositional thought, but even the scope of propositional *perception* could be expected to expand in that way, and for the same reason. What you can see depends on what you can think and what you know about the world. We adults can see many things to be so that small children cannot see to be so. If you see my neighbour's car and thereby see that there is a car parked in my street, the chances are that you do not thereby see that my neighbour is at home, as I do. I am in a better position for seeing that than you are, even if we are standing next to each other. And a physicist who sees a marker moving on a computer screen can see much more to be so than I can see. Given his knowledge and his capacities, his seeing the marker is enough for him simply to see all those things to be so.

If the range of perceptual knowledge can be understood to expand in this way to include anything that an adequately equipped perceiver can come to recognize to be true of objects he perceives, there seems no hope of specifying in advance some determinate general limits to what can be seen and known about the world by perception. But the fact that a rich body of conceptual capacities is needed to make any such perceptual knowledge possible does not seem to me to support any form of idealism.

8

Causation in Commonsense Realism

Johannes Roessler

We think of perceptual experience as a source of propositional knowledge of the world around us. So we think of perceptual experience as a reliable source of true beliefs. Therefore, we must be thinking of perceptual experience as causally dependent on perceived objects. This is a rough sketch of a line of reasoning that plays a significant role in P. F. Strawson's defence of the causal theory of perception. In Strawson's words, it provides the 'rationale' for the causal theory of perception. The 'rationale' has been criticized by Paul Snowdon in a series of papers pioneering a 'disjunctivist' account of perceptual experience. Snowdon's central complaint is that the causal requirement has not been shown to be necessary, given that the causal theory is not without alternatives. For example, one might account for the reliability of perception by invoking a relational view of perceptual experience, on which mind-independent objects are constituents of the experience we enjoy in perceiving them.

Some philosophers have argued that the causal theory of perception and the relational view of experience are not in fact in conflict.[1] I think they may well be right, but the point does not resolve the dispute between Strawson and Snowdon. Even if we can consistently hold both views, we still face the question whether Strawson is right that a causal requirement on perception is somehow implicit in everyday explanations of what someone knows in terms of what they perceive. If he is, this would help to motivate, or even lend support to, the idea that such conditions are in some sense part and parcel of our very concepts of perception, or, as Strawson sometimes puts it, that they are a 'pre-theoretical commitment of commonsense realism'. It would present a challenge to sceptics, such as Snowdon, who think that an interest in the causal requirements on perception is, as it were, an acquired taste, not

* I am grateful to an anonymous reader for OUP for valuable comments on a previous version of this chapter. I would also like to thank Bill Brewer, Steven Butterfill, Naomi Eilan, Christoph Hoerl, Hemdat Lerman, Guy Longworth, and Matthew Soteriou for helpful comments and suggestions.

[1] For one version of this move, see Child (1994) and Child (this volume). For another, see Steward (this volume). For discussion of some of the differences between them, see my Introduction (this volume).

something that is integral to our very grasp of concepts of perception.[2] Now it seems to me that while Snowdon has certainly identified a gap in Strawson's argument, it may well be possible to amend the argument. On the other hand, I think Snowdon's response—at least the part of his response that turns on the availability of alternative ways of finding the epistemic role of perception intelligible—may be too concessive. An unargued assumption of Strawson's 'rationale' is that insofar as we, even 'pre-theoretically', think of perception as a source of knowledge, we are committed to conceiving of it as a source of *beliefs*, indeed as a source whose nature makes it *intelligible* that beliefs deriving from it constitute knowledge. My aim in this chapter is to question this assumption. Everyday explanations of perceptual knowledge, I will argue, may be more simple-minded than Strawson allows. My alternative suggestion will be this: we think of seeing an object as an immediate causal enabling condition of *seeing that* the object has certain features and falls under certain types. Such explanations invoke a primitive causal link between experience and knowledge, which should not be assumed to be intelligible in terms of causal relations between experience and beliefs. In section 2, I clarify Strawson's questionable assumption and set out my alternative analysis. In section 3, I argue that under this analysis, reflection on everyday explanations of perceptual knowledge provides a 'rationale' for the *relational view* of perceptual experience (rather than for the causal theory of perception). In section 4, I consider the broader issue of whether the simple-minded scheme can be defended against philosophical criticism. I begin by reviewing the dispute between Strawson and Snowdon.

1 Strawson's rationale for the causal theory of perception

Strawson's line of reasoning (to repeat) may be summarized as follows:

(1) We think of perceptual experience as a source of knowledge of the world around us.

So

(2) We think of perceptual experience as a generally reliable source of true beliefs.

Therefore,

(3) We must be thinking of our perceptual experiences as causally dependent on perceived objects.

I begin by examining Strawson's view of the relation between (2) and (3), and Snowdon's objection. In the next section, I will look at the credentials of (2).

Consider the following parenthetical remark, addressed to someone who accepts (2) but is doubtful about (3): 'Otherwise [if it were not part of "our ordinary scheme of thought" that perceptual awareness in general causally depends on the way perceived things objectively are] the normal truth or correctness of perceptual judgments would seem to be something inexplicable, an extraordinary coincidence' (Strawson 1992: 60). The idea here is that if the causal condition were not integral to our naïve concepts of perception, we would be committed to thinking of perceptual experience as generally reliable, yet lack the resources to make sense of its reliability. For example, we would be thinking of someone's experience of the shape of physical objects around her as a reliable source of true beliefs about the shape of physical objects. We would assume that if someone's perceptual belief that a certain object is square is caused by her experience as of a square object, then (supposing the experience to be a perception) the belief will very likely be correct. But the fact that this is so would be bound to look mysterious. It is not clear that this would amount to any formal inconsistency in the commonsense scheme.[3] But certainly our confidence in the reliability of perception would not look like reasonable confidence. It would resemble something like blind faith. The causal theory of perception enables us to give a more charitable interpretation of commonsense realism. Suppose we wonder how it is that visual experience is a reliable source of true beliefs about the shapes of objects in our visual field. The matter has a ready explanation if it is a conceptual truth that the experience involved in a visual perception of a physical object causally originates with the object, and that its phenomenal character causally depends on certain features of the object. For presumably beliefs generated by visual experiences of objects reflect the character of the experience. Given the causal condition, the character of the experience in turn can be seen to reflect the way the object is—for example, its shape. So there is nothing (in principle) mysterious about the normal truth of visually based beliefs about the shape of things.

One problem with this argument, as Snowdon points out, is that the correctness of the causal analysis is not the only way to make the reliability of perception intelligible (Snowdon 1998), Occasionalism (with its appeal to a common cause) would be one alternative. A relational view of perception would be another. According to the latter, a perceived mind-independent object is a constituent of the experience one enjoys in perceiving it. Accordingly, certain features of the object make an immediate difference

---

[3] Some of Strawson's formulations do encourage this stronger reading. In 'Causation in Perception' (1974) he writes that 'dependability in this sense *entails* dependence, causal or non-logical dependence on appropriate M-facts'(p. 79, my emphasis). Now perhaps it would indeed be incoherent simultaneously to think of perception as a reliable source of true beliefs and to regard the normal truth of perceptual beliefs as an 'extraordinary coincidence'. But the fact that in a certain situation we would have to regard the reliability of perception as *mysterious* does not license the conclusion that we would be committed to regarding it as a mere *coincidence* that perceptual beliefs tend to be true. For we might assume that there is in fact some kind of explanation of the reliability of perception, though not one (currently) within our ken.

One might wonder whether the weaker reading of the argument is not too weak for Strawson's purposes; in particular, too weak to warrant the conclusion that it is a *conceptual* truth that perception causally depends on perceived objects and their features. But notice that Strawson's 'rationale' is not intended to work in isolation. Its purpose might be characterized as that of linking the causal theory, originally supported by the traditional methods of conceptual analysis, to commonsense explanatory practice. It aims to show that the causal condition plays an important *role* in the commonsense psychology and epistemology of perception. (See Snowdon (1998) for illuminating critical discussion of the point of the rationale.) Relative to that aim, it is not essential that a denial of the causal condition can be shown to be incoherent.

to the phenomenal character of one's experience, not in virtue of being causally responsible for the occurrence of an experience with that character but in virtue of being (partly) constitutive of its character. Snowdon's point is that the relational conception of perceptual experience would enable us to make the reliability of perception intelligible without invoking a causal requirement on perception.[4] For example, the normal truth of perceptual beliefs about the shape of physical objects would be unsurprising if such beliefs were caused by experiences whose character is partly constituted by the actual shape of the perceived objects. Such beliefs would reflect the character of the experiences: *i.e.* the shape of perceived mind-independent objects.

In his response to Snowdon, Strawson expresses incredulity at the idea that mind-independent objects figure as constituents of perceptual experience. As Strawson understands it, this would amount to envisaging *logical* relations between 'natural items' (rather than between their descriptions); a claim he proceeds to dismiss as a 'category howler' (1998, p. 314). I take it this response is inadequate. Certainly the notion of constitution in general, and the idea of objects being constituents of experience in particular, stand in need of clarification, but they are not obviously nonsensical. One immediate clarification is provided by highlighting the modal implications of the relational view: if the character of one's visual experience of a square object is partly constituted by the shape of the object, the subject could not have enjoyed a qualitatively identical experience in the absence of the object or in a situation in which the object was differently shaped (even if, for some reason, it would still have looked square in that situation).

A better response, on behalf of Strawson's rationale, it seems to me, is the following. The response consists of two observations and one suggestion. The first observation is that Snowdon offers no reason to think that the relational view correctly articulates the way commonsense epistemology *in fact* understands the reliability of perception. The second observation is that there does not appear to be any such reason: either of the two explanatory schemes would enable us to demystify the normal truth of perceptual beliefs. The suggestion is that bearing in mind the principle of charity, the causal interpretation of commonsense epistemology may be defended on the grounds of greater parsimony. Seeing a square object in front of one is not the only kind of visual experience that, other things being equal, tends to give rise to the belief that there is a square object in front of one; optical illusions, or visual hallucinations, as of square objects have that same tendency. The causal theory would seem to offer a parsimonious conception of the causal-explanatory link between these sorts of experience and beliefs: experiences falling under one common kind are causally responsible for beliefs concerning the presence of square objects. The relational view, in contrast, is committed to positing at least two different kinds of explanatory

---

[4] My formulations here draw on Campbell (2002) and Martin (2006). Snowdon speaks of 'visible facts' being 'constituents of the experience'.

relations, corresponding to two different kinds of experience: in the genuine case, the belief is caused by one kind of experience (partly constituted by the perceived environment); in the other cases, by an experience of a different kind. The multiplication of kinds seems inelegant and unwarranted. (The point is familiar from the literature on disjunctivism: see e.g. Sturgeon 1998.)

I conclude, tentatively, that although Snowdon identifies an important lacuna in Strawson's rationale, a causal theorist remains on strong ground so long as our concern is merely with demystifying the reliability of perception. Even if this is disputed, it is clear that Snowdon's response does not (and is not intended to) amount to a positive case for the relational view. But perhaps Snowdon's response concedes too much. I want to argue that there are grounds for scepticism concerning (2); and that these grounds help to make a case for thinking that it is the relational view to which commonsense explanatory practice is committed.

2 A simple view of perceptual knowledge

We can distinguish two readings of (2). I will call these the analytic and the explanatory reading. Let it be agreed, at least for the sake of the argument, that the following are necessary conditions for A's knowing that p: A believes that p; it is true that p; and A is not merely 'flukishly right' in believing that p (Strawson 1974: 79). Suppose we also agree that it follows from this last condition that if perception is a source of knowledge, it has to produce a high ratio of true beliefs. (This is not to say that propositional knowledge can be reductively analysed as reliably true belief.) Then it may be argued that anyone who thinks of perception as the source of a given piece of knowledge is committed to thinking of that knowledge as involving a belief whose truth is unsurprising, given its derivation from perception. Let us call this the analytic reading of (2), and let us suppose that there is much to be said for (2), thus read. (2) might also be associated with a stronger claim. The idea here would be that there is a certain structure in the way we explain knowledge in terms of perception. If we find someone's knowing that p intelligible in the light of their current perceptual experience, this is because we understand two things: that her experience is causally responsible for her believing that p, and that the explanatory relation between the experience and the belief meets a certain general condition required for propositional knowledge (e.g. the condition that the belief not be 'flukishly' correct). On this view, our conception of the role of experience in explaining what someone believes is more basic than our conception of its role in explaining what someone knows: we find the latter *intelligible* in terms of the former. Call this the explanatory reading of (2).

To see why the distinction matters, consider an imaginary commonsense realist who rejects the causal requirement on perception. Strawson reasons that this person would have to regard the normal truth of perceptual beliefs about mind-independent objects as a coincidence, or at least as something inexplicable. He seems to suppose that if we confronted the anti-causalist with the question 'but *how is it* that perception is a dependable source of true beliefs about the mind-independent world?' she could only shrug her shoulders. Even setting aside the concerns raised by Snowdon, though, this is implausible. Here is something she could say: 'Of course perception is a source of reliably true beliefs—that is entirely unsurprising. After all, perception is a source of *knowledge* (and knowledge entails something like the absence of flukishness).' Note that this simple-minded response respects, indeed appeals to, the conceptual entailment affirmed by the analytic reading of (2). If the response strikes us as inadequate or question-begging this is because we assume the correctness of the explanatory reading of (2). We assume that understanding the epistemic role of perception must be underpinned by an *independent* explanation of the normal truth of perceptual beliefs, an explanation that does not simply help itself to the idea that perception is a source of knowledge.

The simple-minded response points to a further gap in Strawson's rationale for the causal theory. The analytic reading of (2) is plausible but too weak. If there is to be any prospect of reaching (3) it is the explanatory reading of (2) that is needed. The problem is that Strawson offers no support for (2) under that reading. Nor, I want to suggest, does the explanatory reading follow trivially or obviously from the analytic reading. It might be said that if we think of the acquisition of perceptual knowledge as a matter of acquiring reliably true beliefs, it can hardly fail to occur to us to ask what *explains* the normal truth of such beliefs, and once we ask *that* question, simply falling back on the knowledge-yielding role of perception would be an expression of blind dogmatism, hardly more rational than regarding the reliability of perception as 'inexplicable'. But I now want to argue that this line of reasoning begs the central question, of how we do find knowledge intelligible in terms of the subject's perceptual experience.

Consider Strawson's example of a 'non-philosophical observer gazing idly through a window' (1988). Suppose we ask him, not, this time, for a description of the character of his visual experience, but for an explanation of the source of his knowledge of certain facts. Suppose we ask him 'How do you know that the deer are grazing?' One thing he might say in reply is: 'I see that they are grazing.' This reply has its virtues. As Snowdon puts it, we treat it 'as totally unproblematic that someone's knowledge that p can be explained by saying they saw that p' (Snowdon 1998: 301). Part of what makes such explanations reassuring may be that they are, in Quassim Cassam's terms, 'knowledge-entailing'. (See Cassam 2008.) On the other hand, it has to be said that the reply is not particularly informative. The notion of epistemic seeing (or seeing-that) is used in many ways. Even discounting clearly metaphorical uses, appeal to epistemic seeing by itself has relatively little explanatory value. True, when you see that p, the source of your knowledge that p has something to do with vision. But it can draw on much else besides. One way of seeing that your neighbour is at home is to infer her presence from the observed presence of her bicycle. One way of seeing that the piano will not fit through that door is by engaging in a certain kind of imaginative exercise. Appeal to someone's seeing that p naturally prompts the question of how the subject is in a position to see that p—what *enables* her to see that p. Suppose we put this latter question to our non-philosophical observer. The natural reply is the same reply he gave to Strawson's request for a description of his experience: 'I see the deer.' Or: 'I see the deer grazing.' This provides a more illuminating explanation of the source of his knowledge. The reply leaves some important details implicit, though. Someone may see the deer grazing without being able to recognize the deer or their activity. They may be too far away or lighting conditions may be poor or he may lack the relevant visual recognitional capacities. Making the non-philosophical observer's point slightly more explicit, we might say this: he is able to see that the deer are grazing because (a) he sees the deer, and the event of the deer grazing, (b) he sees certain features of the deer, as well as relations to other objects, and (c) he has the visual recognitional capacities required for recognizing grazing deer and, in virtue of the truth of (a) and (b), is able on this occasion to exercise those capacities in the normal way.

We can summarize this sketch of the commonsense epistemology of perceptual knowledge by saying that we think of object perception as an enabling condition of epistemic perception. (Perhaps the *basic* enabling condition of epistemic perception, in the sense that the condition is indispensable to *any* explanation of how someone is in a position to perceive that p.) Now on the face of it, what is conspicuous by its absence in this picture is the notion of perceptual belief. If the sketch is at all on the right lines, we explain someone's non-inferential perceptual knowledge that p without even touching on the question 'why does he believe that p?'. We exploit explanatory relations between object perception and epistemic perception, and in that way explain the source of his knowledge. The attitude we aim to explain is conceived as someone's possession of a piece of knowledge or, more specifically, as a case of epistemic perception. The explanatory project does not require or involve thinking of the attitude as a case of believing that p. Of course, we can be induced to acknowledge certain entailments, such as that if the observer possesses perceptual knowledge that the deer are grazing he believes that they are grazing, and he must be non-flukishly right in believing this. But it does not follow that we account for his perceptual knowledge *by* explaining how he came by his belief. It is not clear that the structure revealed by conceptual analysis corresponds to any structure in our explanatory practice. If it does not, there will be no reason to suppose that a charitable interpretation of commonsense realism has to equip it with the resources to make sense of the reliability of perception. The question of what explains the normal truth of perceptual beliefs does not normally arise. If it is raised, commonsense realists may answer it by appeal to the fact that perceptual experience yields epistemic perception.

But how does perceptual experience explain knowledge, on the present analysis of commonsense realism? The natural answer is that reference to object perception provides a causal explanation of epistemic seeing and propositional knowledge. At least, this would be the most straightforward reading of the word 'because' in explanations such as 'He knows the deer are grazing because he sees them'. Note that we can manipulate his capacity to acquire knowledge by intervening on his visual experience of the deer. For example, we might intervene on his experience by improving lighting conditions, which in turn would enable the observer to acquire more detailed knowledge of the deer's activities. The obvious explanation of how this sort of manipulation is possible is that the experience is a causal enabling condition of the observer's coming to know various things. This gloss on the commonsense scheme would suggest that Strawson was right about the crucial importance of causal understanding to the commonsense realist conception of perception as an immediate awareness of mind-independent objects. Where the present analysis—call it the simple view of perceptual knowledge—differs from Strawson's is in envisaging just *one* sort of causal relation, between perceptual experience and knowledge, in place of the two causal relations featuring in Strawson's account, with perceptual beliefs produced by experience and the latter conceived as causally dependent on objects and their features.

Does the simple view of perceptual knowledge correctly articulate ordinary explanatory practice? It is of course not easy to settle this issue decisively. Here I can only sketch what seems to me a promising way to address it. I think an illuminating perspective on the issue is provided by Austin's well-known remarks about the difference between perception and evidence. Austin contrasted two cases: believing that there is a pig in the vicinity on the basis of clues, such as buckets of pig-food or the characteristic noises and smell of pigs, vs being confronted by the pig itself, standing there 'plainly in view'. In the latter case, Austin contended, our belief that the animal is a pig is not based on evidence. Rather, we 'just *see* that it is [a pig], the question is settled' (1962: 115). I think it is plausible that Austin has identified a salient feature of the 'manifest image' of perceptual knowledge. The question is, how should the putative contrast be articulated? According to one suggestive proposal, we credit perceptual experience with a distinctive causal power: we take it to cause perceptual beliefs in such a way as simultaneously to 'silence' any competing considerations. (See Campbell forthcoming.) It is not just that perceptual experience presents peculiarly powerful evidence of the pig's presence, outweighing other bits of evidence. Rather, other considerations cease to be even relevant once you see the pig. This analysis, though, raises the following question: how is it that perception has the power to 'silence' the rest of one's evidence? What is the ground of this remarkable disposition? It is natural to think that the answer has to do with the distinctive credentials of claims to direct perceptual knowledge. Thus it might be said that experience provides a special kind of justifying reason. As Martin puts it, 'for him [Austin], one might suggest, the reason for thinking that there is a pig there is simply the pig itself' (2002: 390). The idea that the source of perceptual knowledge can lie in the perceived object itself is one that seems to play an important role in Austin's discussion. But putting the point in terms of objects providing *reasons for* believing something has two unattractive consequences. One is that we would face the awkward task of explaining the sense in which mere *objects* can be thought of as justifying reasons for belief. The other is that we would have to make sense of the distinctive significance commonsense attaches to what would then appear to be merely a distinction between two kinds of justifying reasons (those provided by objects and those provided by what Austin describes as evidence). The simple view of perceptual knowledge offers a more straightforward gloss on Austin's contrast. The difference between the two cases turns on our conception of what is *explained* by appeal to evidence or experience, respectively. Possession of evidence concerning the presence of a pig most immediately explains your *belief* that there is a pig nearby (by providing a justifying reason for which the belief may be held). If the evidence is good enough, it may also, in turn, help to explain why your belief qualifies as knowledge. In contrast, your encounter with the pig itself, standing before you in full view, explains your *seeing that* this is a pig. Appeal to the experience yields an immediate answer to the question of how you *know that* the animal is a pig. It is in this way that it 'settles the question'.

3 A rationale for the relational view

Is the simple view of perceptual knowledge committed to a relational conception of the character of perceptual experience? The case for an affirmative answer may be set out as follows.

Suppose the correct account of what constitutes the character of your visual experience of a deer is neutral with respect to whether your experience is a veridical perception or an illusion or a hallucination. Given this account, the fact that your experience has the character it does will not, on its own, provide much of an explanation of how the experience puts you in a position to see that a certain animal in your environment is a deer. It can yield such an explanation, if at all, only in combination with what would be a further fact, that the experience in question is a veridical perception. Call this a composite account of the explanans. There is, of course, some explanatory work that the character of your experience, thus conceived, can do on its own. Even illusory or hallucinatory experiences have the power to generate *beliefs*. Moreover, the fact that your experience is a veridical perception does not cancel this explanatory potential of its character. So a defender of the composite account now faces a question. On her view, the character of your experience figures in two kinds of explanations: in the explanation of your *belief* that there is a deer in front of you and in the explanation of your *seeing* that there is a deer in front of you. How are these explanations related to one another? The natural analysis is that even in the second case, what's causally explained by the character of your experience is your belief. The explanation of your belief forms a proper part of the explanation of your seeing-that. The latter adds to this an account of what makes your belief knowledge. This suggests that a defender of a composite account of the explanans will find it difficult to resist a composite account of the explanandum. The latter, though, is inconsistent with the idea of a primitive explanatory link between experience of objects and epistemic perception, as posited by the simple view.

On the other hand, suppose we reject the 'highest common factor' conception of the character of perceptual experience and adopt a relational conception. Then the idea of a primitive explanatory link becomes intelligible; or at least, reflection on the explanatory potential of illusions and hallucinations no longer poses a threat to its intelligibility. If the character of your experience is determined or constituted by the real visible features of the deer, it provides for an immediate explanation of how you are in position to see that the deer has certain features. That your experience is veridical will not be a further fact, to be invoked alongside the character of your experience. So there will be no room for a composite account of the explanans, hence no pressure towards a composite account of the explanandum. Of course we still face a question over the relation between explanations of perceptual knowledge and belief. An illusory or hallucinatory experience that is subjectively indistinguishable from your visual experience of the deer can explain the subject's believing that there is a deer in front of her. Indeed one might insist that even in the veridical case, your belief can be made intelligible in the same way as in these other cases. But these points do not show that explanations of perceptual belief are *more basic* than explanations of perceptual knowledge. On the contrary, our understanding of the explanatory link between experience and *belief* may be said to be parasitic on our more basic grasp of the link between (veridical) experience and knowledge. In the case of illusion or hallucination, you have an experience that is subjectively indiscriminable from one in which you see a deer and which would put you in a position to see that there is a deer in front of you. No wonder, we might say, that you end up *believing* there is a deer in front of you—for you intelligibly *take yourself* to be able to *see* that this is so. The explanatory link between the illusory experience and your first-order belief turns on the fact that there is an intelligible link between enjoying an experience that is subjectively indiscriminable from a perceptual experience of a deer and believing that one is able to *see certain facts*, which in turn commits one to certain first-order beliefs, such as that there is a deer in front of one.

How successful is this argument? The argument is reminiscent of claims that have been made in other areas, to the effect that the explanatory role of some relational explanans is not to be understood in terms of a conjunction of facts. For example, it has been argued that the distinctive explanatory role of propositional knowledge cannot be matched by the role of belief conjoined with certain other conditions. (Williamson 1994) This latter argument, though, has no disjunctivist implications. The distinctive explanatory role of knowledge is consistent with the idea that knowledge and 'mere opinion' share a common element. Nor does it require that our understanding of the explanatory role of belief is parasitic on that of knowledge. That argument may block a composite account of the role of knowledge but it does not lead to a disjunctivist picture of belief. One might wonder, therefore, whether reflection on the explanatory role of experience (as conceived by the simple view) can yield a convincing rationale for the relational view of experience—a view notorious for its commitment to a disjunctivist conception of experience. The natural response is that there is a major disanalogy between the two cases. Propositional knowledge is not a type of experience. Questions about the nature of the subjective character of the explanans simply do not arise in the context of reflection on the explanatory role of knowledge. This response leads to a more serious concern, though. It highlights the importance of an assumption underpinning the whole argument, that everyday explanatory practice assigns a causal role to the character of experience. This assumption certainly requires clarification and defence.

One might suspect that the assumption reads into commonsense explanatory practice a distinctively philosophical doctrine, deriving from the foundationalist tradition in epistemology. Robert Brandom, for example, voices just this suspicion when he characterizes the idea as a 'residually Cartesian intuition'. (Brandom 2002: 98) One might elaborate the suspicion by noting that the range of properties and types whose instantiation we take to be manifest to us in perception far outstrips the sorts of features that can plausibly be held to constitute the character of perceptual experience. It cannot be right that when you gain direct perceptual knowledge that b is F, b's being F must be part of what constitutes the sensory character of your experience. As John Campbell puts it, 'there are plenty of cases in which we have perceptual knowledge of properties that are not making a difference to the nature of our experience' (in press). Recognizing a deer would seem to be a case in point.

To understand the disagreement here it is important to consider what might be the rationale for insisting that we ordinarily regard the character of experience as a relevant factor. I suggest the rationale is this: we take the explanatory link between your visual experience of b and your ability to see that certain things are true of b to be one that is intelligible not just to philosophers or cognitive scientists but, for example, to you. In recognizing a deer it is evident to you not only that the animal is a deer but also that you can see that it is a deer because you see the animal (in good lighting conditions, not too far away etc.). And it is not as if you merely think of your experience as something that, in virtue of some unknown underlying mechanism, has the disposition to facilitate epistemic perception of certain truths. The grounds of that disposition are manifest to you: as you might put it, you can see that it is a deer because it *looks like one*. This does not mean that the character of your experience has to be constituted partly by the species to which the object belongs. Your recognitional capacity can be intelligible to you through its dependence on certain lower-level features of the object that do make a direct difference to your experience—the characteristic shape of the animal, say, its colour pattern, its languid movements etc. One might say that this makes your knowledge depend on inference. I think that is the opposite of the truth. As I will argue in a moment, it is precisely because your recognitional capacity is intelligible to you in terms of the character of your experience that you are able to see without inference that the object is a deer.

The obvious test case for the proposed rationale is the familiar legend of the chicken-sexers, expert perceivers who have been trained to discriminate male from female hatched chicks. As Brandom tells the story, the chicken sexers 'have no idea what features of the chicks they are presented with they are responding differentially to' (2002: 97). They find themselves thinking 'this is female' or 'this is male' but their judgements are not intelligibly related to any features that make a difference to the character of their experience.[5] Of course they know that they have a reliable recognitional capacity. Otherwise they would attach no authority to their judgements (and would see no point in making them). I think the issue raised by this case is not whether the chicken sexers can have knowledge. Surely they can. The question is whether their knowledge has the same kind of source as ordinary perceptual knowledge. It might be said that it does: the difference is merely that in the ordinary case the source is evident to us insofar as we experience the features enabling us to perceive certain facts whereas the chicken sexers have no such immediate understanding of the source of their knowledge. I think resistance to this picture need not be underpinned by a dogmatic insistence that as a completely general matter, sources of knowledge have to be intelligible 'from within'. Suppose we allow that there might be wholly unreflective chicken sexers (for example, specially trained *chickens*). There is no reason to deny that their recognitional capacity might yield knowledge, despite their utter ignorance of its source. But the fact is that a rational chicken sexer is not like that. Mindful of his special skill, he will use his own spontaneous judgements as *evidence* concerning the sex of a chicken. As we have seen, without this background he could hardly be expected to make such guesses in the first place. Importantly, his grasp of this evidence, i.e. his ability to *infer* the chicken's sex from his spontaneous judgements, has to be a key factor when it comes to explaining the source of his knowledge. It would be quite irrational for him to reach beliefs in this area by relying on guesswork when he is actually in possession of compelling evidence. Such irrational beliefs would not amount to knowledge. Thus a reflective chicken sexer's knowledge will inevitably depend on inference. In this respect it differs from ordinary recognition-based knowledge that a certain animal is a deer. In the latter case, there is no need to rely on evidence. For in attending to the experienced object and its experienced features, you are aware of how you are in a position to acquire knowledge of it: you are aware that you see the object, that it looks like a deer, and that in this way you are able to see that it is a deer. There is no need to rely on evidence precisely because your capacity for epistemic perception is intelligible to you in this way. And of course there is no irrationality in your acquiring the non-inferential belief that it is a deer when it is evident to you how you can *see* it is a deer. That your recognition relies on certain experienced lower-level features does not necessarily make the resulting knowledge inferential. For it is not as if you first judged the animal to have a certain definite shape and colour and then concluded that therefore it is probably a deer. Your best effort at articulating the set of experienced features to which you are responding may well be in terms such as 'the characteristic shape and colour of a deer'. Your identification of the set of features may well draw on the very non-inferential recognitional capacity they help to make intelligible.

---

[5] Contrary to the philosophical legend, real chicken sexers do find their judgements intelligible in terms of their experience—specifically, in terms of the visible shape of the chicks' genital eminences. (Males tend to be described as 'round', females as 'pointy'.) See Biederman and Shiffrar (1987).

4 Knowledge and explanation

There are several reasons why it can seem hard to take seriously the idea of a direct causal-explanatory connection between perceptual experience and knowledge. I want to conclude by looking at two sources of resistance to the idea. We may call them the charge of psychological and epistemological irrelevance, respectively.

The first source of resistance stems from a particular conception of psychological explanation, encapsulated in Stephen Stich's remark that 'what knowledge adds to belief is psychologically irrelevant' (Stich 1978: 574). Discussion of this claim tends to focus on the role, real or apparent, of knowledge as an explanans in causal explanation; its role, for example, in explaining intentional actions. But Stich's slogan also bears on the role of knowledge as an explanandum of causal explanations. If the ideas behind the slogan are correct, apparently direct causal explanations of knowledge had better be something else, for example causal explanations of *belief*, in terms that simultaneously illuminate the epistemic status of the belief. I will not enter this debate here but it seems to me that the 'internalist' conception of psychological explanation has no more plausibility in the case of action explanation than in the case of explanations of perceptual knowledge. One way to challenge it, in the action case, is to advert to the distinctive sets of counterfactuals sustained by explanations in terms of knowledge, bringing out their distinctive explanatory value (Williamson 1994). A more radical move is to insist on the indispensable role of knowledge in reason-giving explanation: only explanations in terms of factual states, such as knowledge, accord an explanatory role to the facts that constitute justifying reasons for action (Hornsby 2008). It is not implausible to think that if we have learned to live with the psychological relevance of knowledge in the action case, we should not be too flustered by the idea of causal explanations *of* knowledge in terms of perceptual experience.

I think it is the charge of epistemological irrelevance that poses the deeper and more serious challenge to the simple view. In a discussion of the aspirations of a philosophical explanation of perceptual knowledge, Barry Stroud makes the following unflattering remarks about the explanatory scheme of what I have called the simple view:

> To say simply that we see, hear, and touch the things around us and in that way know what they are like, would leave nothing even initially problematic about that knowledge. Rather than explaining how, it would simply state that we know. There is nothing wrong with that; it is true, but it does not explain how we know even in those cases in which (as we would say) we are in fact seeing or hearing or touching the object. (Stroud 2000: 145)

It might be said that Stroud overstates the point. If you want to know how I know the deer are grazing, there *is* something that is initially problematic about my knowledge, viz. how I got it. If I say 'simply that I see the deer', or perhaps that I see (the event of) the deer grazing, this should put your mind to rest. Without some such account of the source of my knowledge, you cannot be sure that I was not merely guessing. My simple answer should do something to convince you that I am not; it can help to establish the credentials of my claim to knowledge. Of course, you may still be dissatisfied. My answer falls short of a full account of the enabling condition of my seeing that the deer are grazing, nor does it address potential worries about the satisfaction of relevant *disabling* conditions. What these points illustrate is that the explanatory role of object perception depends on various sorts of background conditions. But they provide no support for the prima facie surprising conclusion that appeal to object perception has no explanatory value whatsoever—that it fails to 'explain how we know even in those cases in which (as we would say) we are in fact seeing or hearing or touching the object'.

As Stroud himself emphasizes, it is relative to a certain *philosophical* conception of what counts as a good explanation of perceptual knowledge that the stronger conclusion appears plausible and perhaps inescapable. There are a number of philosophical reasons for thinking that the simple view is completely unsatisfactory, and that any genuine explanation of perceptual knowledge has to consist of an account of the explanatory relation between perception and *belief*, along with an account of how beliefs that are thus related to perception earn the 'status of knowledge'. These considerations support the following conditional: *if* object perception does indeed play some role in giving us knowledge of mind-independent objects it has to be possible to make that role philosophically intelligible by tracing it to the way object perception helps to satisfy certain general conditions on propositional knowledge. Now this demand is not trivial. For reasons discussed earlier, it cannot be motivated simply by reference to the entailment between knowing that p and believing that p. The question is why an *explanation* of someone's knowing that p should be expected to proceed via an explanation of her believing that p. One suggestion at this point might be that the answer lies in the 'slightest philosophy' Hume declared to be sufficient to expose the vulgar error that we are directly aware of mind-independent objects. What the arguments from illusion or hallucination show, it might be said, is that perceptual experience, subsuming as it does both veridical and illusory cases, can be *directly* explanatory only of belief, not knowledge. Arguably, though, the philosophical demand has sources that are deeper and perhaps less easy to resist. A central theme of Stroud's work is the connection between the traditional epistemological project and what is sometimes taken to be an implication or requirement of philosophical realism, the possibility of a *completely general* account of the credentials of claims to knowledge of the mind-independent world.[6]

But I think we can see the force of the philosophical demand even without a full understanding of its philosophical sources. The simple view appears to be committed to a position Quassim Cassam calls minimalism. According to minimalism, 'the connection between knowledge and perception is primitive and cannot be explained any further.' Cassam argues that minimalism is implausible, given that 'surely we want to

---

[6] See Stroud (1984: esp. ch. 2) and Stroud (2000: esp. chs. 8 and 10). Martin (2006: part 3) offers an illuminating discussion of Hume's 'slightest philosophy' and its relation to Cartesian scepticism.

say that perceiving is a way of knowing because, and only because, there are more general conditions on knowing that p that one satisfies in virtue of perceiving that p' (2008: 20). Why do we want to say this? One good reason is dialectical. It is not just that minimalism would deprive us of the intellectual satisfaction of understanding what it is in virtue of which the connection between perception and knowledge holds. We should like to think of our confidence in the epistemic role of perception as reasonable confidence, different in kind, say, from the confidence some people place in clairvoyance. The obvious way to debunk some putative source of knowledge is to show that beliefs flowing from that source violate certain completely general necessary (and jointly sufficient) conditions on knowledge. Correlatively, the obvious way to establish the epistemic credentials of perceptual experience is to satisfy ourselves that it does provide for the satisfaction of the conditions in question.

Cassam argues for what he calls a middle way between minimalism and the idea that 'a prior reductive analysis of the concept of knowledge is needed to make it intelligible that perceiving is a way of knowing' (2008: 21). The middle way proposes a limited elucidation of the epistemic role of perceptual experience, by reference to (merely) necessary conditions for knowledge. This is certainly plausible in as much as a good account of the necessary conditions for knowledge (e.g. reliability) would suffice to debunk certain putative sources (e.g. clairvoyance). Nevertheless, the middle way would fail to make the epistemic role of perception fully transparent to us.[7] One way in which this lack of transparency manifests itself is this. As far as the middle way is concerned, there could, on the face of it, be two sources of knowledge that are indistinguishable as regards the way they provide for the satisfaction of the necessary conditions for knowledge, yet intuitively count as importantly different sources. Consider the intuitive difference between knowing that a certain object is a pig by visually experiencing the object and knowing this on the basis of something like blindsight. On the face of it, the difference between explanations of knowledge in terms of the two sources could hardly be more profound. In one case, you know because the pig is there right in front of you, 'plainly in view'. The explanatory link between your visual experience and knowledge is peculiarly direct and intelligible. It is part of the 'pre-theoretical scheme of commonsense realism'. In the other case, you know because your guesswork is unwittingly controlled by your visual system. The explanatory link between blindsight and knowledge, such as it is, is part of a theory that is fully intelligible only to professional cognitive scientists. What is not clear, though, is that the difference between the two sources can be explained in terms of how they provide for the satisfaction of general necessary conditions for knowledge. Suppose it cannot be so explained.[8] The middle way, being concerned only with necessary conditions for knowledge, would have to acknowledge that the two sources are

---

[7] Cassam acknowledges that the middle way is 'very close to minimalism', insofar as it 'helps itself to the intuitive distinction between good and bad answers to the question "How does S know?"' (2007: 22).

[8] See Roessler 2009 for more detailed discussion of these issues.

distinct, but would provide no help in elucidating their difference. We would be reduced once more to the minimalist mantra that 'the connection between knowledge and perception (specifically, perceptual *experience*) is primitive and cannot be explained any further'.

There is no time for a detailed discussion of the numerous issues raised by minimalism. But I want to end by sketching a suggestion. It may be possible to go beyond minimalism, not by meeting the philosophical demand (even halfway), but rather by presenting grounds for resisting it. A basic assumption informing the demand may be put by saying that the concept of belief enjoys a certain explanatory independence, in the following sense. Understanding how someone knows what they know about a certain matter requires understanding the epistemic status of their beliefs in this area; specifically, understanding what confers the status of knowledge on their beliefs. An essential first step, then, is to identify the beliefs whose epistemic status is to be examined. Importantly, this is only a first step. As far as an explanation of the source of the knowledge in question is concerned, nothing has been settled by identifying the relevant beliefs. We can think about these beliefs in purely 'doxastic' or 'psychological' terms. Whether and how they have secured the status of knowledge will be a substantive further question, to be addressed by investigating whether they satisfy the general conditions for knowledge. Now in any particular case this seems a very sensible assumption to make. The question that I think is worth pressing is whether the assumption is still plausible when we reach the dizzyingly high level of generality at which the philosophical demand operates. Here is one reason to think the matter may not be straightforward. Consider what is involved in attributing to oneself and others beliefs involving perceptual demonstratives, such as 'this lemon is yellow'. To think of you as holding such a belief it is not enough to say that you believe of a certain object that it is yellow. We need to acknowledge that you think of the thing in a distinctive way, made available to you by your perceptual experience of it. Thus in the case of beliefs involving perceptual demonstratives, the idea of an explanatory link between your experience and your belief is integral even to the preliminary project of identifying the beliefs to be examined. (See Campbell 2002.) Suppose this is right. Then two questions arise. Can we coherently think of experience as a source of understanding perceptual demonstratives without simultaneously thinking of it as providing a good explanation of propositional knowledge? And if we cannot, what would be the implications for the philosophical demand?

Evidently grasping a perceptual demonstrative is consistent with having a lot of false beliefs about the object in question. It may even be consistent with having no propositional knowledge whatsoever of the object. Nevertheless, grasp of a perceptual demonstrative may essentially involve being in a position to gain some propositional knowledge of the object through one's experience of it. One way to support this claim would be to argue that perceptual demonstrative identification requires not just experience but selective attention, putting one in a position (at least under favourable conditions) to keep track of the object, and hence to gain propositional knowledge of its boundaries and identity over time. The upshot of such an argument would be that recognizing the explanatory link between experience and perceptual demonstratives commits one to acknowledging an explanatory link between experience and propositional knowledge. Then the second question is whether this result would be consistent with accepting the conditional demand, that if there is a genuine explanatory link between perceptual experience and knowledge, it has to be possible to make it intelligible in the light of the way experience provides for the satisfaction of the general conditions for knowledge. On the face of it, the result would call into question what I suggested is a basic assumption behind this demand, that identifying perceptual beliefs is merely a first step towards explaining how we know what we know. It would be mere pretence to proceed as if the idea that perceptual experience is a source of knowledge is to be justified (or debunked) by an investigation of whether and how experience helps to satisfy general conditions on knowledge. If we get as far as identifying the beliefs whose epistemic status is to be scrutinized we would already be committed to recognizing the explanatory link between perceptual experience and propositional knowledge. We would be so committed in virtue of the role experience plays in presenting us with the world around us and enabling us to have perceptual demonstrative thoughts about objects, independently of any underlying conception of how experience is linked to the general conditions for knowledge.[9] This would not prove minimalism correct. But it would disarm one kind of resistance to minimalism, and hence to the simple view of perceptual knowledge and the relational conception of experience.

References

Austin, J. L. 1962: *Sense and Sensibilia*. Oxford: Oxford University Press.

Biederman, Irving and Shiffrar, Margaret 1987: 'Sexing Day-Old Chicks: A Case Study and Expert Systems Analysis of a Difficult Perceptual-Learning Task', *Journal of Experimental Psychology: Learning, Memory and Cognition* 13, pp. 640–645.

Brandom, Robert 2002: 'Non-inferential Knowledge, Perceptual Experience, and Secondary Qualities: Placing McDowell's Empiricism', in N. Smith (ed.), *Reading McDowell*. London and New York: Routledge.

Campbell, John 2002: *Reference and Consciousness*. Oxford: Oxford University Press.

——in press: 'Visual Attention and the Epistemic Role of Consciousness', in C. Mole, D. Smithies, Wayne Wu (eds.), *Attention: Philosophical and Psychological Essays*. Oxford: OUP.

——forthcoming: 'Does Perception Do Any Work in an Understanding of the First Person?', in Annalisa Coliva (ed.), *The Self and Self-Knowledge*. Oxford: Oxford University Press.

---

[9] This account of the source of our commitment would not imply that the philosophical demand could not be met. (One elegant, if implausible, way to meet it would be to argue that something like acquaintance or intuition is a general condition for propositional knowledge.) But it would undermine an outlook that takes the rationality of the commitment to be dependent on the possible satisfaction of the demand. See Roessler 2009 for further discussion of this line of argument.

Cassam, Quassim 2007: 'Ways of Knowing', *Proceedings of the Aristotelian Society* 107, 339–358.

—— 2008: 'Knowledge, Perception and Analysis', *South African Journal of Philosophy* 27.

Child, William 1994: *Causality, Interpretation, and the Mind*. Oxford: Clarendon Press.

Hornsby, Jennifer 2008: 'A Disjunctive Conception of Acting for Reasons', in A. Haddock and F. Macpherson (eds.), *Disjunctivism*. Oxford: OUP.

Martin, Michael 2002: 'The Transparency of Experience', *Mind and Language* 17, 376–425.

—— 2006: 'On Being Alienated', in T. Szabó Gendler and J. Hawthorne (eds.), *Perceptual Experience*, pp. 354–410.

—— 2009: 'The Limits of Self-Awareness', in A. Byrne and H. Logue (eds.), *Disjunctivism*. Cambridge, Mass.: MIT Press.

Roessler, Johannes 2009: 'Perceptual Experience and Perceptual Knowledge', *Mind* 118, pp. 1013–1041.

Snowdon, Paul 1998: 'Strawson on the Concept of Perception', in L. E. Hahn (ed.), *The Philosophy of P. F. Strawson*. Chicago and Lasalle, Illinois: Open Court.

Stich, Stephen 1978: 'Autonomous Psychology and the Belief-Desire Thesis', *The Monist* 61, 573–591.

Strawson, Peter F. 1974: 'Causation in Perception', in *Freedom and Resentment*. London: Methuen.

—— 1988: 'Perception and its Objects', in G. McDonald (ed.), *Perception and Identity: Essays presented to A. J. Ayer*. London: Macmillan, pp. 41–60 (1979). Reprinted in J. Dancy (ed.), *Perceptual Knowledge*. Oxford: OUP.

—— 1992: *Analysis and Metaphysics*. Oxford: OUP.

—— 1998: 'Reply to Paul Snowdon', in L. E. Hahn (ed.), *The Philosophy of P. F. Strawson*. Chicago and Lasalle, Illinois: Open Court.

Stroud, Barry 1984: *The Philosophical Significance of Scepticism*.

—— 2000: *Understanding Human Knowledge*. Oxford: Oxford University Press.

Sturgeon, Scott 1998: 'Visual Experience', *Proceedings of the Aristotelian Society* 80, 185–216.

Williamson, Timothy 1994: 'Is Knowing a State of Mind?', *Mind* 104, 533–565.

9

Perceptual Concepts as Non-causal Concepts

*Paul Snowdon**

Although philosophers traditionally attempt to construct theories about the nature of causation by asking and attempting to answer questions about claims containing the *general* notion of causation—say, such a question as: what entailments does a singular causal judgement of the form 'x caused y' have?—it has also, ever since Anscombe's famous paper 'Causality and Determination', seemed good sense to scrutinise and analyse what are sometimes called specific causal concepts, concepts such as those of killing, cutting, knocking over, breaking, drying, bending, and so on.[1] Doing so, there is some reason to say, has had one major *epistemological* consequence. Anscombe made it very clear that the tendency to agree with Hume that we, mature and normal human adults, do not observe that causal facts or processes obtain may seem justified when we consider general causal facts, but it is highly implausible when we consider singular and specific types of causation. Thus, you need to have the capacity to deny the obvious if you wish to say that we cannot observe that someone broke a window, or scratched a car, or amused someone else.[2]

To be somewhat more precise, it is not that what I have called specific causal concepts always pick out causal links that are always observable, or even that they all pick out causal links of a type which are at least sometimes observable, but that it is obvious that

* I am very grateful to have been asked to contribute to this volume. A version of this paper was originally presented at Warwick and I would like to thank David Smith, Bill Brewer, Naomi Eilan, Johannes Roessler, and Hemdat Lerman, and others there, for very helpful comments. I also presented it at UCL and would like to thank Mike Martin, Mark Kalderon, and Rory Madden (and others) for comments that I feel I have not been able to properly respond to.

[1] See Anscombe (1971; 1975 reprint).

[2] Sadly, the capacity to deny the obvious is, perhaps, one of the leading characteristics of philosophers. It is true to say of some causal links that we cannot observe them to hold. Thus, we do not observe smoking causing cancer, nor do we observe low interest rates causing inflation, nor do we observe consumption of alcohol to cause liver damage. Causal information of this character has to be based on inferences, themselves resting on data. In contrast, causal processes that are faster and which involve observable aspects of things, are ones that we can tell to obtain by observation.

some of them sometimes do. Anscombe herself cites the example of infecting as a specific causal link which does not normally represent something that can be observed to obtain. What is surely clear, though, is that many such specific causal concepts do sometimes apply to causal links or processes that are observable by us. It might in fact be even more accurate and precise to suggest that strictly it is not the existence of the specific causal vocabulary that makes it clear that Hume's view on the non-observability of causation is wrong but rather the failure to notice that certain causal facts can be observed to hold, and this could have been noticed even if we, as English speakers, had chosen to report them *using the general notion of causation*. We could have said 'S caused the scratch on the car' rather than 'S scratched the car'.[3] Anscombe herself makes the following claim which if true would run counter to the last proposal:

[T]he word "cause" can be *added* to a language in which are already represented many causal concepts. A small selection: *scrape, push, wet, carry, eat, burn, knock over, keep off, squash, make* (e.g. noises, paper, boats), *hurt*. But if we care to imagine languages in which no special causal concepts are represented, then no description of the use of a word in such a language will be able to present it as meaning *cause*.[4]

Anscombe, however, gives no reason for believing what she claims, and it is not obviously true, nor does she properly explain quite what her thinking is. Presumably, her idea is that unless the language contains a variety of specific causal terms, which are recognised as entailing the application of a general causal relation, then there could not accrue to any general term in the language enough to identify it as the general notion of causation. One has to respond by asking why not? Why could not speakers of this imagined restricted language link their use of the term 'cause' to enough multiple facts of causation, and acknowledge enough of the logic as applying to their term that the corresponding general term for causation has in our language, so as to fix its interpretation as being the same as our term 'cause'?

About what might be thought of as the Anscombean advice to concentrate on such specific causal concepts I want to make three remarks. (1) Despite its attraction and value as a strategy we should not think that general talk of causation is uncommon and not standard. We are completely happy to ask whether smoking is a cause of cancer, or low interest rates a cause of inflation, and whether bankers' bonuses were a cause of the current economic crash, and so on. We tend to employ that way of speaking when we have in mind one *general* process and another *general* process or condition and are interested in their relation. Is one a cause of the other? The general notions of a cause and of causing are therefore ones we often employ in normal talk. Such a general notion should not, therefore, be thought of as akin to highly general categories that philosophers have introduced and use, categories such as material continuant, or

---

[3] Hume's claims about observation had in fact already been effectively challenged by Ducasse in his (1975) article, which in fact appeared in 1926, without the emphasis on specific causal concepts.

[4] Anscombe (1971; repr. 1975) pp. 68–69.

abstract entity, which themselves do not figure in ordinary thought. (2) What, indeed, is a specific causal notion? A first step at answering this question would be to say that it is a notion the correct application of which entails or requires the presence of a causal connexion. This explanation itself employs the very *general* notion of causation. So the category towards which we are advised to attend as opposed to the general one, is itself a category that we can only specify by ourselves *employing* the general one. (3) If the strategy is to be carried out insightfully and correctly it is, of course, vital that the chosen examples are indeed properly speaking causal concepts. That is the issue that I shall focus on here. My question is: is it right to say that the concepts of perception *are* causal concepts? So I am not accepting the invitation to carry out the Anscombean programme, fruitful though I believe it undoubtedly is. I want, rather, to clarify and illuminate the nature of our perceptual concepts and, equally, to shed some light on the notion of a causal concept, by asking whether perceptual concepts would be suitable ones to attend to if one was minded to carry out the Anscombean programme. To that question the title of my paper gives away my preferred answer.

My preferred answer is, of course, that perceptual concepts are not causal concepts, and I hope in this paper to provide *some* justification for that preference, along with some clarification of what the issue is. I do not think, though, that I have my hands on a proof that the answer I prefer is correct. My strategy is, rather, to clarify the issue, and to cast some aspersions against some arguments for the causal view, and to sketch a non-causal conception that seems to me not obviously incorrect. The project might, therefore, be described as one of assumption loosening. I aim primarily to weaken the tendency simply to *assume* that a causal analysis is correct. It is worthwhile posing the following question at this stage. I shall assume for purposes of posing this question that the idea of *analysing concepts* relates to what necessities about the concept's application conditions can be established a priori. Suppose that there is a general agreement that it is a conceptual truth that the truth of sentence S requires the truth of sentence S★, but that you are inclined to doubt that that is so. How can you support your doubt? You might be able to locate a possible case which people can agree on where S is true but S★ is not. But that need not be possible. Maybe there are no such *possible* cases. It would remain an open question whether the relation was a priori determinable. There is, though, no obvious way to settle that issue. One has to look at the arguments offered, and query them, and make alternative suggestions, and so on. The point is that there will be no demonstration of the falsity of the normal view, even if it is false. So, I am suggesting, there is bound to be something inconclusive about presenting a case of the sort I incline to. That the case is not decisive is, then, no defect, but rather, an inevitable aspect of presenting such a case.[5]

---

[5] There is another reason why the present discussion will be inconclusive, and that is that I cannot engage with all the arguments that are relevant, including some central and highly influential ones. In effect, this paper should be read as continuing the developments of themes earlier contributions to which are Snowdon (1981), (1990), and (1998). In particular I am not dealing with the main argument for the causal analysis as

In focussing on this question about our perceptual concepts, I do not mean to imply that I think that either the sole business, or even the most important business, of what we might call the philosophy of perception is conceptual analysis. We can distinguish between the task of constructing a theory of *perception* (in its many aspects) and the task of giving an account of our *perceptual concepts*. And so we can distinguish between the task of determining what role causation should have in the correct account of perception from the task of determining the involvement of the notion of causation in our perceptual concepts. I am merely assuming that we have an understanding of what talk of specific causal concepts amounts to, in which case there is the question whether our perceptual concepts are such concepts (whatever the importance of this question in the overall scheme of things).

1 Some clarifications

We might be prepared to say, as I have done, that we have an understanding of talk of *causal concepts*, but the ground needs to be prepared a little before we venture onto it.

First, I am going to assume that we understand each other well enough when we talk of *causal* conditions or facts. I shall not try to define or analyse what being a causal condition or fact is. It is a notion to be taken as understood here.[6]

Second, what is meant by 'perceptual concepts'? In this paper I am restricting that to such notions as seeing, hearing, smelling, touching etc., plus that of perceiving itself, where the notion relates a subject to an object (of some kind or other). The kind of claim then that I am scrutinising would include: S saw O, S heard O, or S heard sound O*, etc. Clearly, under the general category—perceptual concepts—many other notions can quite legitimately fall, but they are not my present concern. In particular I am not including under 'perceptual concepts' what might be called *action concepts* related to perception—concepts such as 'looking at' or 'listening to' and so on. I am interested only in concepts which record basic perceptual relations.[7] This should become clearer as we proceed.

Third, what more precisely is meant by a causal concept? This is a tricky question because it is hard not to think that there are variations in the way it is understood. Indeed, there seem to be variations along a number of dimensions. Let me start with one dimension. I want to propose that there are three dominant ways to take talk of the causal character of a concept, or at least three discernible directions of interpretation.

developed by Grice (and endorsed by many others) since I have already spilt much ink on that, in the cited articles. And, second, I do not want to repeat my main reasons for not accepting Strawson's type of argument, which are contained in Snowdon (1998).

[6] We are therefore to be in the position of causal theorists prior to them developing a theory; we understand causal talk, but do not have an elucidation of it.

[7] Some conversations with Craig French have convinced me that it is hard to say anything too definite about the meaning of these expressions which I am calling action concepts. It may be that they do not always signify actions. I leave that issue open.

The first is this: C counts as a causal concept just in case it is an a priori truth that a (positive) judgement containing the notion C necessarily requires for its truth, that is to say entails, that a (certain sort of) causal condition obtains. This places talk of causal concepts in a context of a priori determinable entailments. I shall label this way of taking the notion 'causal concept$_1$'. It seems to me that it corresponds to the central understanding of 'causal concept' amongst people who describe themselves as analysing such concepts as those of perception, or action, or memory etc.

The second notion of causal concept is that of a concept such that it is a necessary condition for a subject to count as having that concept that she or he holds that the concept applies only if a causal link of some kind obtains. Let us call this a 'causal concept$_2$'.

How do the first and second notions of causal concepts relate? It seems clear that if a concept is causal$_1$ it need not be causal$_2$. It may be a priori determinable that a concept can apply only if a causal link obtains without it being necessary that anyone who has the concept must have recognised that requirement. It seems clear, in fact, that the highly complex causal entailments that analyses were supposed to unearth (in the golden age of conceptual analysis) were not supposed to be already recognised or accepted by everyone with the concept. That is why arguments were offered to persuade readers of the entailments. Further, strictly speaking there is no entailment for being a causal concept$_2$ to being a causal concept$_1$. It might be for some reason that people who have the concept must believe that it applies only if a causal link obtains, even though there is no entailment from the application of the concept to the presence of a causal link. In some contexts this might be an important contrast but with our debate people tend to accept that perceptual concepts are causal$_2$ only if they accept that they are causal$_1$.

I want to mark out a third notion labelled causal concept$_3$; this is vague but I have in mind the idea that by and large any relatively mature person with the concept takes it that it applies only if a (sort of) causal link obtains. This is a weaker notion than the second one, but I include it on the list because it seems to me to correspond to a use that is encountered in discussion of these matters. In particular it corresponds to the idea which seems present in the writings of developmental psychologists that with certain mental concepts children characteristically acquire a causal understanding of the phenomenon in question, an understanding which underpins their ability to think straight about the phenomenon in question. It would be quite natural to describe such approaches as holding that the concept in question is a causal one, even though in so doing they are not committed to the entailment thesis nor to counting someone who does not think this way as not having the concept in question.

I have drawn these distinctions because they seem to me to correspond to lines of thinking about our perceptual concepts. I shall though be mainly concerned with the notion of a causal concept$_1$. I had hoped to say more about the third notion, but have not managed to consider enough evidence yet.

There is a final and important clarification I wish to make. The bulk of the clarification so far concerns the status of the causal requirement. But one might ask: what *sort of causal relation* are we concerned with? It would be agreed by most of us that the concept of hearing a physical object, say a particular piano, involves the notion of the piano giving off a sound, and the notion of giving off seems to be a causal concept. So in one sense the concept of hearing a physical object incorporates a causal condition. But my focus is on the idea that such a concept as that of seeing involves a causal relation going from the object seen to the subject who is seeing. In this general sense of a causal relation the relation of hearing is not established as such by its involving a causal relation between object and sound. So the issue is whether the concept of seeing involves (in one of the ways distinguished above) a causal relation *of that sort*. This also means that it would not make the concept of seeing a causal notion in the relevant sense should it turn out that seeing an object requires standing to it in a certain relation which itself causally issues in or generates a subjective state (perhaps a belief). That again would not mean that there has to be a causal relation going from the seen object to the subject. There are then plenty of senses in which, say, seeing might be a *causal notion* with which I am not concerned here.

2 Causal concepts

There is no doubt, I think, that many philosophers think that our perceptual concepts are causal concepts$_1$, and plenty who think they are causal concepts$_2$. In the face of this opinion we can begin by asking whether there is any obvious general reason to treat that as the view we should somehow expect to be true, so that opposing it is both surprising and requires one to undertake some substantial intellectual obligations? We can note that people who are suspicious of the idea of conceptual analysis should be suspicious of the idea that perceptual concepts are causal ones. For them, such a view has no claim to be the default approach. Second, once the contrast between conceptual analysis and genuine scientific theorising is to hand, there is no obvious reason to suppose that because the phenomenon that a concept picks out is best theorised about as a causal process that the concept picking it out should rank as a causal concept in the relevant sense. Third, suppose we grant that what is sometimes called objective thinking requires causal thinking, and credit that idea with the status of being a major insight, it does not follow from it that all concepts that figure in our objective thinking are causal concepts, since it is obvious that they are not. For example such an important concept as 'being longer than' represents an objective feature, but does not amount to a causal concept. It captures a feature of spatial comparison, not of causal linkage. So from that supposed insight about objective thinking nothing follows about such central concepts as our perceptual ones. I do not think, though, that we should regard it as obvious that what might totally reasonably be called objective thinking (or speech) has to involve causal thinking. It would seem reasonable to say that someone whom we regard as thinking about some of the objects in space and recognising objective properties that they have should be credited with objective thinking. But it would seem possible for creatures to have attained that status without attending to causal features or causal questions. Thus if a child plainly entertained thoughts expressible in such words as 'Mummy is here' or 'Daddy is laughing' or 'That is black' then the child is entertaining objective thoughts, thoughts about external objects, attributing objective features to them, whether or not they have raised causal questions or noticed causal facts. These remarks are too sketchy to settle anything but we should not rush to endorse the view that objective thinking requires causal thinking, and certainly not assume that if objective thinking does require causal thinking then that would mean that our perceptual concepts themselves have to represent causal features.

I have not here, perhaps, illuminated all the factors that might be inclining people to hold the causal analysis as more or less the default view, but to the extent to which I have I cannot see that they provide any real justification for according it that status.

Now, it is obvious that perceptual concepts pick out a relation that the subject stands in to the relevant object. The fundamental question is what restrictions or limitations on that relation are imposed by the concept, or in some sense, built into it. It can also be pointed out that a remark to the effect that someone has perceived (in some way) a certain object does not convey much information about the details of the occurrence. It conveys nothing as to how much of the object was perceived nor how it appeared to the subject. But is it an a priori truth that the relation has to be a causal one?

I want to start considering the question whether perceptual concepts are causal in any of these senses by looking at cases of concepts which more or less everyone would agree are causal in something like senses 1 and 2. The most obvious examples are the notion expressed by certain verbs. Consider the verb 'kill'. Everyone would agree that for it to be true that S kills O then O must die but also S must be the cause of the death. Consider also the case of 'dries' in its use as a transitive verb. If S dries O then O must get drier, but, further, S must be bringing that change about. Finally, consider the claim that S opened the door O. For this to be true O must have opened and S caused that to happen. It seems clear that with such verbs there is an identified result (namely, with these examples, dying, drying, opening) and the idea of an agent bringing it about. Now, I am not claiming that we can say that the elements so far identified exhaust the content of what these verbs express. Further, although I have talked here of agents, this should not be taken to pick out agents in any heavy philosophical sense. We allow that a boulder can kill someone, the sun dry something, and the wind open a door. There are also lots of verbs with a similar structure where no one would be tempted to think of them as applying only to agents in the strong sense, such verbs as scratching, crushing, and nourishing. We can, though, quite naturally describe the subjects in such sentences as the agents. Note that characteristically verbs like this do not convey anything precise about the way the agent produced the result. We fill in such details by appending 'by' descriptions. For example, we can say S opened the door by pushing it. Or we might have a verb which conveys the method. For example, we can say that O blow-dried the table.

We can agree that with such sentences if they are to be true it is required that some causal link obtains, and, moreover, it would not be unreasonable to claim that unless this requirement was appreciated by someone using the word they did not properly understand it.

The question I want to ask is whether we can fit our perceptual verbs into the model applicable to such verbs? Now, there is, of course, an immediate disanalogy between our perceptual verbs and the verbs just described. In these sentences the subject is the agent, but in perceptual ascriptions the normal thought is that the object of perception corresponds to the agent, and the result is something about or in the subject. However, I want to ignore that difference. The question is whether we can discern a requirement for the truth of perceptual sentences which has a similar structure to that discernible with the previous verbs even if the direction of causation is differently related to grammar.

At this point, though, I want to highlight one feature of such notions, at least something that is characteristic of them. Their application requires the presence of an effect or result, plus the bringing about of that result. The result itself is a discrete element in the required situation, which can be focussed on and considered independently of the agent producing it. So what I am currently considering is whether we can understand our perceptual concepts in line with that model.

The chief problem that I want to suggest is that with perceptual verbs there is no obvious discrete result involved in their applying to a situation.

What are the *candidates* for being the result in a causal analysis? One candidate is that if S sees O then the result is that O is seen by S. It is clear though that O's being seen by S is not a result involved in S's seeing O in the way that O's dying is a result involved in S's killing O. Basically, there is an equivalence between S's seeing O and O's being seen by S, which does not hold between S's killing O and O's dying. With result cases the truth of the claim requires the result plus that the agent is responsible for the result; whereas nothing more is needed for S to see O than for O to be seen by S.

The second candidate for result would be—that S is having a visual experience. Now, we can allow that if S sees O then it is true that S has a visual experience; that is therefore like the requirement that if S kills O then O dies. The question that remains though is what kind of entailment we have in the perceptual case. There is a conception of this entailment in the perceptual case which treats it as similar to the following entailment: if there is a cat in my garden then it follows that there is an animal in my garden. The presence of the animal is not a result of the (presence of the) cat doing something or producing something; rather it is true that the presence of the cat involves the presence of an animal because the cat just is an animal. So we might think that S's seeing O requires that S have a visual experience because to see is to have a (visual) experience. On this conception—no seeing without an experience—is like— no cat without an animal—and not at all like—no killing without a death.

So the agreement that for there to be a sighting by S of O S must have an experience allows of two understandings. It is required because a sighting is an experience or it is required because for there to be a sighting there must be an experience for S as a separable result of the object O. There are two things to say. First, to adopt the causal understanding of the role of experience in the requirements imposed by the concept of seeing needs the provision of an argument ruling out the other option, and that remains to be given. Second, it seems to me alien to the phenomenology of perception to suppose that in situations thought of as sightings (or perceptions in general) the ordinary person is so thinking of it as to be committed to there being an experiential effect generated by the sighted object in the situation. Rather, given that one's eyes are open and an object O sighted the only discrete element available to the subject is the object O. It seems quite unnatural to think of the situation as involving O plus a discrete effect of an experience sort generated by it.

I think in the light of these points that we should conclude at this stage that it is simply not obvious that our perceptual concepts are parallel to such concepts as killing by way of being linked to the achievement of an effect.

There is an important question to which I want to link these remarks. It is worth asking why is the causal nature of such verbs as 'kill' and 'dry' so obvious to us. This is not an easy question. However, I want to propose an answer. My answer is that it is obvious to us as people who understand such verbs that their correct application requires the presence of what I might call an outcome. Thus if S kills O then it must be that O dies, and if S dries O then O must become drier. Now, I am not saying how that is obvious to us, but rather relying on the fact that it is. Once one has noticed that requirement another question occurs: what must that outcome have to do with the subject S for the verb to relate S to O? The proposal is that there is no other candidate for that link that suggests itself other than a causal link. If I am right about this explanation and also right that our perceptual verbs are not obviously linked to any outcome (of the right kind) then it will not be obvious for them that they are causal, or at least, it will not be obvious in the way it normally is.

Another clear category of causal notions are those like sun-burn, footprint and, perhaps, signature of S. These notions are characteristically linked to nouns that apply to something, say, a certain indentation in the ground, in virtue of its causal origins. Thinking of our causal concepts as similar to these involves thinking of them as applying to something in virtue of that thing's causal origins. Now, the chief problem in such a suggestion is, I suggest, the same as, or very close to, that raised in relation to the first model. I do not think that there is any obvious thing, in the broadest sense of 'thing', the causal origins of which are in question when we are deciding whether we are seeing something or not. Thus, I might say: when I open my eyes something happens. Something happens, but maybe I am seeing some external object, or maybe I am hallucinating. Now, in thinking about that choice is there some given thing that is undoubtedly there, manifesting its presence to me, and on the causal origins of which the issue depends (in the way that, say, a mark is undoubtedly there whether or not it is S's signature)? I want to say that I myself cannot work out what that might be. The line of thought that I want to propose to generate some sympathy for my attitude is this. We are agreed that something is happening, but let us suppose that what is happening is that I am seeing O, and not hallucinating. Now, on that assumption I can do what I would describe as fixing my attention on a certain thing, namely, what is granted to be O. But I cannot draw my attention back into myself (or closer into myself, on a supposed line of causation running from O to me) and locate something distinct from the object O such that I have now determined its status as an effect of O. I may be suffering from a certain sort of blindness here, but nothing in my experience of the situation seems to have that status.

The point of these remarks is not to demonstrate that the causal view is mistaken. It may well be that the issue whether an occurrence satisfies the conditions imposed by our concept of seeing amounts to whether a causal link is present where, however, the putative effect is not itself one which the subject can locate or attend to, in the way that the mark on a piece of paper is detectable or something that can be attended to in considering whether it is S's signature. The point is rather to show that the situation of the subject when engaging with issues to do with the application of the concept of vision is unlike the situation we are in when dealing with the application of what are standard causal concepts. Why then should we suppose the fundamental condition for correct application is a causal one?[8]

I have argued that there is nothing about the idea of objective thinking that creates a presumption that our perceptual concepts are causal, and that they do not seem to be embedded in a conceptual structure that makes them appropriately similar to standard examples of causal concepts.

There is, finally in this section, another argument I wish briefly to comment on.[9] It is claimed that we count a subject watching a television on which an object O is being depicted as seeing O, whereas we do not count a subject who sees a picture depicting O as seeing O. If so this contrast needs an explanation. The obvious explanation is that in tele-visual depiction there is what we might call an active causal link between the object O and the depiction, whereas there is no active causal link in the pictorial case. It is then suggested that this supports the causal theory of the concept seeing. The step I wish to query here is the last one. This phenomenon (assuming it is real) illustrates that we allow, for some reason yet to be articulated, that seeing an object suitably causally linked to another counts as seeing the second item. But from this it does not follow that the basic concept of seeing itself imposes a causal requirement.

---

[8]   A nice example to scrutinise here is that of 'a viral infection'. This surely expresses a causal notion (that of an infection caused by a virus), but infections are not themselves things we attend to in our naïve experiences. Rather the notion of an infection represents an explanatory postulate, linked to more observable features such as having a temperature, and lacking energy, and feeling unwell. But the notion of an infection introduces what we might call a discrete element causes of which can be sought. So we can have discrete elements which are not themselves attendable to. The question in the perceptual case is what the (perceived) object independent element is.

[9]   I am grateful to Mike Martin for bringing this line of thought to my attention.

3 Perceiving and causal factors

The argument that has been developed is intended to make it seem implausible to model our perceptual concepts on some obvious specific causal notions. It is clear, though, that even if these arguments have supported the existence of such a contrast it does not follow that perceptual verbs are not causal. One reason for saying this is that they are not the only causal concepts there are. One further example is such a judgement as 'O had an effect on S'. This is clearly a causal notion but its application does not entail the presence of a certain type of effect. Certainly, therefore, no general conclusion has been demonstrated. What I want to do briefly in this section is to consider how our perceptual thinking links to our causal thinking and see if a way of understanding that link can be proposed which is plausible without going the whole way to thinking of our perceptual concepts as causal concepts.

Our perceptual verbs stand for relations in which subjects can stand to objects. When they obtain these relations typically afford us the opportunity to gain information about our environment. We also grade our perceptions in ways that are relevant to this. We speak of being able to see O well, or clearly, and we talk of not getting a good view of O. Now, we are creatures that inevitably develop an awareness of the factors that affect both the quality and the occurrence of perception. We quickly learn that the quality of the light, and state of our eyes, the distance away of the object, etc., all affect both the possibility of (say) vision and its quality. It is, further, completely natural to envisage this growth of understanding about perception as itself the growth of a causal theory. We can think of these factors as ones that have an influence on our perceiving. We embed our conception of perception within a network of information about causal dependencies. It is low-grade and pre-scientific information. However, there is no pressure generated by these remarks to suppose that the relation that such factors impinge on must itself be conceptualised as a causal relation. What the nature of the concept capturing it is remains open even once we have acknowledged its embedding within causal information.

We not only develop a theory about factors affecting vision, we also develop notions about the effect of different sorts of vision. Thus we might say that O dazzled S (or that O deafened S). Now these seem to be causal notions, with a certain sort of interference to the perceptual system being the effect. But the obvious account of such a notion is that we think of a perceptual relation of a certain character as itself having an effect. We might say S was dazzled by his sighting of O. In this way we assign the sighting a causal role, but again we need not in consequence assign the notion of a sighting itself a causal structure.

It would also be important not to exaggerate the degree to which we all form the same embedding causal theory. A beautiful illustration of this is given in John Hull's account of his blindness in his book *Touching the Rock: An Experience of Blindness*. Hull recounts that he survived in his home environment by knowing where everything was. He knew the layout of the furniture etc. His children did not know that he was blind, but realised that he manoeuvred his way around successfully even when the light was not on. This created a problem for them, which they solved by developing the theory that their father could see in the dark, even though they could not. People, then, need not share the same embedding theory. What is developed is dependent on the evidence and experience available to the theoriser.

My aim in these remarks is to prevent a slide from the correct idea that we place perception within a causal body of information to the, in my view, questionable idea that the very concept of perception is itself a causal one.

What character then does the notion or concept at the centre of this evolving web have? The way I want to suggest that we fix on the concept of the relation in question, that is to say the relation of seeing, is best brought out by considering the role of our thought about perception in the first person situation. Suppose that you are having a visual experience which is as of a cat. As we say, it looks to you as if there is a cat. Now the question is: are you seeing a cat or not (in which case you may be hallucinating a cat).[10] The character of the concept picking out the perceptual case is surely illuminated by what is crucial to you settling the question you face. The concept may be regarded as the concept of the relation that is fixed as present by the type of questioning you there and then would engage in. The crucial question that you face, I want to suggest, is this: essaying a thought at the supposed object indicated as present before you, you ask: is that a cat? The fundamental task that you, the subject, face is deciding what the answer to that question is. Note that this is not a causal question; it is not deciding whether something has a certain causal position. It is an identificatory question. The crucial issue is: what is that? The subject decides that as best they can, by, as we might say, deciding whether the theory that it is a cat is better than the theory that it is not true that it is a cat.[11] In a broad sense it seems to me quite fair to think of this procedure as an inference to the best explanation; the explanation proceeds by identification. If this seems the basic issue raised then there are two things to stress. The fundamental question is not a causal question, but rather a question about identity. Second, it suggests that we capture the relevant relation under the notion of being the one in which we can stand to objects which enables such types of thought to have a true application. This proposal says nothing about what the notion of it as *visual* perception amounts to, but an account of that needs to be grafted on to the present proposal. Further, we can in effect entertain the idea of the same relation in third person thinking; in thinking of someone else as perceiving I am thinking of them as so

---

[10] The illustration of the fundamental choice faced by the theorising experiencer is somewhat streamlined. That that is not a cat would not mean that there was an hallucination. I am assuming that the reader will read it in the right spirit.

[11] I adopt this rather convoluted way of speaking because I do not wish to subscribe to the view that if there is no physical object identifiable in the situation then there is another type of object. The suggestion that the essayed demonstrative fails of reference is, I believe, plausible. So the conclusion when the outcome is negative is not so much—that is not a cat—as—it is not that that is a cat—a negation consistent with reference failure.

related to external objects that they can make such true identity claims. (I do not mean such that they will have the evidence or understanding to do that.)

I am here sketching in rather broad terms. But the idea is that we capture the notion of a perceptual relation in this quasi-functional manner. Having got the idea of this relation, we embed it within a structure of causal information, primarily causal information that might be of practical relevance. My suggestion, then, is that we have here a way of thinking how content is conferred upon our perceptual concepts which stops short of having to treat them as causal concepts, but which can make sense of how our thought embeds thought about perception within causal information.

4 Child's arguments

An important contribution to the debate about whether our perceptual concepts are causal is that by William Child.[12] Child's most important insight is the point that the disjunctive account of perceptual experience is not itself inconsistent with the idea that perceptual concepts are causal concepts. The reason for saying this rests on two steps. The first step is that it is consistent to suppose both that in a perceptual experience the perceived object is both a constituent within the experience itself (and hence the experience cannot be conceived of as separate from the object or its status as a perceptual experience), and that the object is the, or an element in the, cause of such a fact obtaining. The support for this claim lies in examples where it seems that there is a state of affairs in which a certain object is a constituent and which is brought about by that object. An example of this kind would be that the wind can be the cause of a wind-vane's pointing in the direction of the wind. Here the effect is a matter of the way the vane relates to the wind and the cause is the wind itself. Or again, a man can be the cause of his being heavier than another man, say by eating a large amount. In each case, the state of affairs which is the effect involves the object which is the cause. Second, if that is consistent then it is equally *consistent* to suppose that there is an a priori discernible requirement that if the case is one of perception then this causal dependence must obtain. It seems to me that both these two steps are correct, and so that Child's idea that a disjunctive conception of experience is compatible with the a priori status of the causal requirement is plausible.

However, although that seems *consistent*, it remains to decide whether that is the best account in the light of the evidence we can come up with about our perceptual concepts.

I wish, therefore, to consider whether the two main arguments that he advances in favour of saying that our perceptual concepts are causal are persuasive. I am unable to

---

[12] See Child (1994) ch. 5. It needs stressing that my discussion here focusses exclusively on William Child's earlier discussion of these issues, and does not relate to his paper in the present volume. The considerable interest of his earlier thoughts is not diminished by his having had more since.

consider every aspect of Child's interesting arguments, but I hope that my treatment covers the major points he makes.

Child describes the first argument as 'show(ing) that grasp of the idea that something which is seen is causally affecting the subject is an essential part of mastery of the concept'.[13] Child's claim is, then, that our perceptual concepts are causal concepts in sense 2 (and, of course, in sense 1). In outline Child's first argument is that if one denies that the concept of perception is causal that will mean that one must adopt a certain sort of analysis or account of the concept of perception, which is untenable. To avoid this untenable conception we must therefore adopt a causal theory of the concept. When characterising the account that someone who rejects the causal approach must adopt Child says that it is 'that we have a concept of vision which can be specified in mental terms, without making any particular assumptions about causation in general, or physical causal processes in particular. Mastery of the concept of vision, therefore, gives us the resources to say what is involved in S's seeing O without assuming anything about causation or the physical'.[14] Now, as far as I can see, it is quite difficult to specify limits on what analyses someone who does not wish to include the standard causal condition can propose. In the first place it is not obvious that someone denying the causal analysis needs to provide an analysis at all. Maybe the concept is a primitive one. But if they are offering an analysis why should it be supposed that it cannot include physical conditions? Further why should it be assumed that their analysis cannot include causal conditions or notions at some point? There is, I suggest, no obvious answers to these questions and the difficulty of answering them makes Child's argumentative strategy questionable. Indeed, the only available way, it seems to me, to support a causal analysis is to argue directly that a causal condition is correct, rather than to argue indirectly that all non-causal analyses share some general defect or defects.

However, let us allow that Child is right and that these two features must be part of any non-causal analysis. Why does that show that a non-causal analysis is *wrong*? What exactly is wrong with an analysis that does not require that seeing has a physical nature? Child remarks that there is 'no prospect for an account of what it is to be a perceiver which does not include the fact that perception has a physical nature.'[15] As a remark about the only available direction for a full and informative theory about perception, the complex phenomenon, Child's remark is totally reasonable. However, it seems no more cogent a reason to include this requirement of a physical nature into the analysis of the concept than it would be to include in the analysis of the concept of pain the requirement that it is a physical state on the grounds that any informative theory of pain must treat it as physical. Normally, that is taken as a reason to be a physicalist rather than a reason to analyse the concept of pain as itself requiring that pain has a physical nature. A further problem with Child's line of thought is that it seems to require more than

---

[13] Child (1994) p. 164.   [14] Ibid.   [15] Child (1994) p. 165.

ordinary causal analyses deliver. They normally leave open what the *nature* of the causal process is.

Further, what exactly is wrong with failing to require the causal condition in one's analysis? Child says this:

[I]f one has the concept of vision, one must know that S will stop seeing something if she shuts her eyes, or if we interpose something opaque between her and the object, or if the object is moved away; and to know that is to know that something cannot be seen if it is prevented from, or cannot be, causally affecting S.[16]

Now, there are two doubts that need voicing at this point. In effect, Child is simply claiming that there are certain relatively specific conditions for seeing or truths about seeing that must be acknowledged by anyone with the concept of vision, and he is further claiming that if one acknowledges those things then one must also acknowledge that O cannot be seen (by S) if it 'cannot be ... causally affecting S'.[17] The first doubt is whether Child is right to claim that anyone with the concept of vision must acknowledge those relatively specific things. The second query is what follows if they must acknowledge those things.

I am, I confess, quite unconvinced by Child's suggestions as to what anyone with the concept of vision must believe. For example, it would hardly discredit someone as a possessor of the concept if he should think that some people can see through their eyelids. Maybe some animals can see through their eyelids. Maybe we can see through our eyelids in certain lighting conditions. And if someone held some such view it would hardly discredit them from knowing what seeing is. Again, someone can have a theory of vision and seeing that holds that ordinary objects can bend light and enable us to see objects behind intervening objects. Although these are not the only kinds of case to keep in mind we should remember members of the conceptual community who are at an early stage; they can surely be credited with knowing what vision is and so understanding of 'vision' talk, but be relatively uninformed about factors affecting visibility, and we should also remember more advanced members who might have developed non-standard theories of vision which deny some of these commonsensical platitudes. There is a further worry that the conditions for vision are specified in a trivial manner. Thus the idea of an intervening object might be characterised as the presence of an object through which one cannot see and round which one cannot see. So characterised anyone with a modicum of logical acumen can work out that the occluded object cannot be seen, but that does not represent any significant condition for vision.[18]

---

[16] Ibid.   [17] Ibid.

[18] It may also be the case that someone without a modicum of inferential ability could not work this out even though they possessed the concept of vision. But my objection to Child's claim does not rest on that possibility.

Finally, it seems to me that a far more plausible picture of the status of such information, such as the fact that we cannot see through our eyelids, is that it is empirically grounded. We note that closing our eyes means that we cannot see external objects. We note too that as objects move further and further away we cease to be able to see them. Such principles represent very low-level empirical truths.

There are two more things to add. It might be felt that the introduction of possibility into the expression of these truths about seeing (which I am suggesting are low-grade empirical generalisations) implies that the relation of seeing is a causal relation. That, I believe, is a mistaken response. Consider this parallel case. I am trying to get within 10 metres of someone. The density of the surrounding crowd might make it impossible for me to be within 10 metres of the person. It hardly follows that the relation—being within ten metres of—is a causal relation.

The second extra point is that Child's own position faces a problem. He argues that the notion of seeing is causal because this is implied by certain other truths that anyone with the concept must accept. But the question that this approach faces is, supposing that the concept of seeing is a causal concept, how does the concept possessor learn the other more specific truths about the causal process. Simply having mastered a causal concept in itself does not acquaint them with the specific causal factors bearing on the possibility of the causal relation in question. Thus, it is one thing to know that seeing involves a causal relation and another to know that the causal relation in question is blocked in certain specific circumstances. Child does not explain how this specific information is derived. Of course, this question is not faced because Child argues from the supposedly agreed necessary specific conditions to the general conclusion. However, once the general conclusion is agreed it becomes hard to know how and why the specific conditions must be known to the concept possessor.

I have tried to counter the main elements in Child's first argument and to raise some difficulties for his approach, I need finally to say two things about the way he continues his argument. First, Child in effect is claiming that anyone with the concept must accept the notion of causation as entering into some agreed necessary condition on perceiving or seeing. One respect in which it enters in, according to Child, is that one cannot see an object if *it is such that it could not have been the cause of the experience*. I, however, find it hard to see how this principle yields his conclusion about the causal status of the concept of seeing. The reason it does not imply the conclusion is that it may be that the fact that O could not have been the cause of P's visual experience itself implies certain things about the relation of O and P's experience, such as that the experience could have happened without O, since something else was causing it, which implied consequence means that O could not be seen. It need not be that the reason O is not seen in such circumstances is that it is not the cause. Second, Child seems to assume that the non-causalist must agree that the specific causal dependencies relating to, say, vision are a priori, and so must suppose, rather implausibly, that the concept is simply one into which it is a priori built that certain causal factors defeat it. But this reductio overlooks that the non-causalist need not view the status of such defeating conditions in that way, as I hope to have already made clear. It is also not explained how Child's own view avoids a similar problem.

My general conclusion is that Child does not in this argument present convincing evidence for his conclusion, and, moreover, that his own conception faces certain problems.

Child's second argument is one he calls the Kantian Argument. He defends an argument devised by P. F. Strawson, which starts from the idea, roughly, that perception is a basic way of gaining knowledge about the world and concludes that the concept of perception is a causal concept. I shall respond to this in a rather brief way, since I have discussed different aspects of it elsewhere, and want here merely to add two more thoughts.[19] This means that I shall not give the argument the attention that I agree it deserves. The argument starts from the claim, in Strawson's words, that 'we think of perception as a way, . . . , of informing ourselves about the world of independently existing things'.[20] However, we need to be careful about where exactly the argument starts. As Strawson expresses it the fundamental conviction about perception is simply that it is a way of informing ourselves about the external world. But such a conviction cannot tell us anything about the *concept of perception*, since it is simply a conviction about perception. In order to relate to the concept the conviction must be something like: it is an a priori truth that perception is a way of informing ourselves about the external world. The problem that arises is that no evidence is presented to suppose this is an a priori truth, nor that we generally think that this is an a priori truth. So there is a serious deficiency relating to the status of the first premise. Second, there is something doubtful about the link between perception and knowledge. The problem is that we can, say, see an item in circumstances and in a way that does not obviously enable us to gain information about it. We might have very bad eyesight, the object might be in mist, and all sorts of distorting factors be at work. In these circumstances the object is, ex hypothesi, seen, but information is in very short supply, and maybe there is no supply. If then the argument works by extracting conditions for information being available, there is no obvious reason to suppose those conditions are conditions for *perceiving*. Third, suppose we set those two caveats aside, and we allow that simply perceiving must a priori deliver conditions for knowing, it still remains for a proponent of the argument to identify what those conditions are. This presumably is extracted by working out what it is about perception which explains the availability of knowledge. I remain unsure how to do that. Suppose, for example, that someone proposed the explanation that perception yields knowledge because in perception an object and some of its properties are presented to the subject. By being presented they are available to be known. The explanation is in terms of presentation, and not causation. Why is this not a potential account of what perception is which yields an explanation of its informativeness? Of course this is not a mode of explanation that would appeal to a

---

[19] See Snowdon (1981) section II, and Snowdon (1998) passim.
[20] Quoted in Child (1994) p. 167.

current psychologist, and that may be because it is not scientifically adequate, but it is not clear why we need to read in to our *concepts* conditions that mirror those that the scientist would appeal to. It remains hard to see what the final step is here.

We can, I want to suggest, relate this issue to a more general aspect of how to think about psychological notions and explanations. When we reflect about ourselves in the way non-scientific and normally curious people do, we explain many of our achievements in psychological terms. How did P know that S was the answer to that question? We reply that he remembered that it was. How did P know that the ball was there? We reply that he saw that it was. Now, it need not strike us at all that this psychological explanation is not the absolute terminus of explanation. Of course, we can ask how the psychological achievements themselves occurred, but not everyone realises that can be asked. There is what we might call 'problem blindness'. However, once we have seen the problem we cannot simply explain these processes in psychological terms. We need to go to a new explanatory level with a new vocabulary, and to postulate new causal processes. But we as theorists of our shared psychological concepts should refrain from treating them as if they contain conditions which more or less demand that we move to the exploration of underpinning causal processes. We should treat that as a response to a problem that dawns on us, rather than as where simple possession of the concept should take us.

5 Conclusion

I am conscious that there is a certain looseness and speculativeness about some of these reflections, but I hope that at least some food for thought has been presented to make the conviction that our perceptual concepts are causal$_1$ or causal$_2$ seem less compelling than it often is taken to be.

References

Anscombe, G. (1971) 'Causality and Determination', reprinted in Sosa (ed.) (1975) pp. 63–81.

Child, W. (1994) *Causality Interpretation and the Mind* (Oxford, Clarendon Press).

Ducasse, C. J. (1975) 'On the Nature and the Observability of the Causal Relation' in Sosa (ed.) (1975) pp. 114–125.

Sosa, E. (ed.) (1975) *Causation and Conditionals* (Oxford, Oxford University Press).

Snowdon P. F. (1981) 'Perception, Vision and Causation' in *Proceedings of the Aristotelian Society* 81, pp. 175–192.

Snowdon, P. F. (1990) 'The Objects of Perceptual Experience' in *Proceedings of the Aristotelian Society Supp. Vol. 64*, pp. 121–150.

—— (1998) 'Strawson on the Concept of Perception' in L. E. Hahn (ed.) *The Philosophy of P. F. Strawson* (Chicago and Lasalle, Illinois, Open Court).

10

Perception and the Ontology of Causation

Helen Steward

From time to time in the literature on the Causal Theory of Perception,[1] something called 'the Humean Principle' is invoked. Mostly, it is offered in an attempt to place conditions on the 'effect' end of the causal chain which, it is presumed, the causal theorist will want to argue that any true instance of visual perception must, as a matter of conceptual necessity, involve.[2] An effect, it is said, and its cause, must be 'distinct existences'—or, more fully 'if X is the cause of Y, then it is logically possible for Y to exist without X and vice versa'.[3] But then, so a plausible line of thinking goes, the causal theorist is bound to end up committed to an understanding of the nature of perceptual experiences according to which those very experiences might have occurred even in the absence of the objects of which they *are* perceptual experiences. The object perceived will have to be one 'distinct existent' and the experience of it another, logically capable of existing in the complete absence of the perceived object itself. And therefore, those who have been inclined towards the view known as disjunctivism in the philosophy of perception have sometimes thought that the Causal Theory of Perception is a view which cannot coherently be held in conjunction with their own. For it is crucial to disjunctivism that real perceptions are characterised as instances of relations borne to worldly objects, instances of relations which could not exist if their relata did not.

Some have suggested that this reasoning is mistaken and that there is, after all, no conflict between disjunctivism and the causal theory.[4] I think that conclusion is correct. But those who have made this suggestion have tended, I think, to make too

---

[1] I really mean by this (as do most of those who use the phrase) the Causal Theory of *Vision*. I think it remains an open question how plausible it might be to extend some version of the Causal Theory to the other sensory modalities.

[2] The point about conceptual necessity is important. No one denies that as a matter of empirical fact, perception is underpinned by causal relations. The question is whether there is something in the very idea of perception, in the very concept, which connects it to causation.

[3] See e.g. Hyman (1992), p. 283.

[4] See e.g. Child (1992); Baldwin (1997).

many concessions to Humean ways of thinking about causation along the way, and as a result, the reconciliations they have provided have not been altogether convincing. In this paper, I shall try to offer—and defend the importance of offering—a less concessive reconciliation. I shall not be arguing that the Humean Principle is straightforwardly *false*—for the Principle itself is, I think, too vague for us to be able to know what exactly would constitute its refutation. But I shall try to suggest that it can only really be worked up into something that looks as though it might conceivably be defensible if one supposes that the ontology of causation must be, always and everywhere, an ontology of particulars—a supposition I shall call *causal particularism*. And it will be the contention of the large, central part of the paper that causal particularism is not true. Causation, properly understood, I shall argue, has *no* distinctive ontology—it is a *category* which subsumes a large number of ontologically various relations and relation-*ships*, including, of course, certain relations between particulars, but by no means confined to such. And it is this recognition, I want to suggest, that may eventually provide the key to seeing how causalist and disjunctivist are to be reconciled.

I The Humean Principle

Some considerable work has already been done in the literature on perception to elaborate on, and clarify, the Humean Principle, and what it does, and does not, imply. Strawson considers it briefly, but suggests that it presents no 'serious difficulty' for the philosopher who wishes to combine causalism with recognition of the fact that 'the correctness of the description of a perceptual experience as the perception of a certain physical thing *logically* requires the existence of that thing'—since, as he notes '(t)he situation has many parallels':

Gibbon would not be the historian of the decline and fall of the Roman Empire unless there had occurred some actual sequence of events more or less corresponding to his narrative. But it is not enough, for him to merit that description, that such a sequence of events should have occurred and he should have written the sentences he did write. For him to qualify as the *historian* of these events, there must be a causal chain connecting them with the writing of the sentences. Similarly, the memory of an event's occurrence does not count as such unless it has its causal origin in that event. And the recently much canvassed 'causal theory of reference' merely calls attention to another instance of the causal link which obtains between thought and independently (and anteriorly) existing thing when the former is rightly said to have the latter as its object.[5]

Strawson's point here seems to be the correct one that it may often be logically required, in order that something (Gibbon's writing of certain sentences, my memory of a party I once attended, my utterance of the word 'Aristotle' on a given occasion) qualify for a *description* of a certain sort, that the thing in question be causally related in a certain way to something else (a series of historical events, the party itself, the

---

[5] Strawson (1988), p. 52.

'baptismal' event at which Aristotle originally received his name). But of course, Gibbon's writing of his sentences is a distinct event from those he is writing about; and the occurrence of a memory of the party is a distinct event from the party itself; and my referring to Aristotle is a distinct event from the 'baptismal' event at which Aristotle received his name. The Humean Principle, correctly understood, is therefore preserved in all these cases—and, Strawson implies, can be preserved also in the perceptual case, despite the fact that nothing can count as a seeing of something unless there is something there to be seen. As Strawson puts it, 'Only someone temporarily blinded by philosophy could dream of denying that when a subject S sees an external object O, the visual experience enjoyed by the subject S is one thing or occurrence in nature and the object seen is another and distinct thing in nature'.[6]

But this simple point has not been enough to silence the worries of disjunctivists. Why not? One important strand of disjunctivist thinking that has impeded the Strawsonian reconciliation, I think, is the desire of at least some disjunctivists to maintain the view that seeing might be an *essentially* relational affair—that no descriptions of seeings as merely qualitative states, states of the sort which might equally have been produced by such things as direct cortical stimulation, hallucinatory drugs, whatever brain mechanisms give rise to dream imagery—are available. As Hyman puts it, the question is whether one may '"conceptually skim off" a purely psychic event from the exercise of a perceptual power, an event which can also occur when a person perceives nothing whatsoever'.[7] And at least some disjunctivists will tend to think that the answer to this question is 'no'. *Seeing* is the basic state, she will say, and seeing is irreducibly relational. Not only is there nothing that can be correctly *described* as a seeing that is not the seeing of some thing or other (however murky, vague, and indistinct it may be), but seeings simply do not *have* descriptions which do not involve essential reference to the thing perceived (any more than, say, carryings have descriptions which do not involve essential reference to the thing carried, or lookings after have descriptions which do not involve essential reference to the thing(s) looked after).[8] Our talk of having a 'visual experience', in the opinion of the disjunctivist, is a sophisticated philosophical construct, designed specifically to allow us to talk of something which might indifferently have been produced by any one of a number of radically different sorts of cause. And her view is likely to be that to introduce this construct is to forsake the natural ontology of mind for a philosophers' highly misleading term of art, with its roots in a bad and perhaps ultimately self-destructing epistemology. We ought, in the disjunctivist's opinion, to get away from having visual experiences and back to plain old seeing.

---

[6] Strawson (1979), p. 314.

[7] Hyman (1992), p. 283.

[8] If carryings and lookings after are actions, and actions are bodily movements, one might doubt that what I have said of carryings and lookings after here is true. On the other hand, one might be encouraged by the plausibility of the idea that carryings and lookings after are essentially relational entities to wonder whether it is true that all actions really *are* bodily movements.

It is a mistake, though, I believe, for the disjunctivist to think that the proper appreciation of this point cannot be made to cohere with causalism. Others have made the same claim of course[9]—but none of the defences of which I am aware explicitly makes the move which in my estimation is central to an adequate solution, and are therefore subject to certain forms of unclarity and implausibility. Child's preferred reconciliation, for example, involves the suggestion that an essentially relational state of affairs, such as o's looking F to S (or presumably S's seeing o), might nevertheless be caused by o.[10] I do not want to insist that the suggestion itself must be a bad one—indeed, the view I shall defend entails that there is nothing in the least problematic about such claims as these—but the analogy Child offers to help us understand how a causal relation *could* hold here is unhelpful, because it retains a conception of causation which is basically particularist. Child notes, as though it might serve as a helpful parallel, that the bombing of Pearl Harbor might be said to be the cause of the Pacific War of which it is also a part. But even if we accept that a part of an event may cause the whole of which it is a part, the analogy with the perceptual case is surely problematic; both the bombing of Pearl Harbor and the Pacific War are *events*, while in the perceptual case, the relation we are asked to regard as causal holds between a persisting *object*, on the one hand, and a relational *state of affairs*, on the other. Child speaks as if we could think about the relational state of affairs which is constituted by someone's seeing something as though it were 'a (larger-sized) event. . .which itself consists in the whole chain of physical events (not merely events *within* S) by which o causally affects S'[11]—as though it were a mereologically complex, but nevertheless still *particular* entity. But (a) this is not obvious, states of affairs arguably bearing much closer relations (perhaps the identity relation) to *facts* than they do to particular events;[12] (b) even if it were so, Child's response invites the retort from event theorists of causation that it is not strictly o which is causing the relational state of affairs to obtain, but rather some ostensibly more event-like entity, such as o's *reflecting light in the direction of S*, say; and (c) once we say this, it looks as though the causal relations which really obtain in the case are just those which are revealed by the *empirical* investigation of vision, not causal relations of a kind it might be plausible to think are part of the very concept of perceiving.[13] And it is usually thought to be essential to the Causal Theory of Perception that the causal connection between o and S's seeing o is supposed to be a part of the very concept of seeing—not merely something we can infer only from what we know empirically about how seeing in fact works. It is arguable, then, that Child's

---

[9] In particular, Child (1992) and Baldwin (2007).

[10] Child (1992).

[11] (1992), p. 309.

[12] For arguments to this effect, see my (1997), ch. 5.

[13] Child appears to concede this, noting in a footnote that 'the possibility of a compatibilism of this sort is not something which Snowdon would contest' (p. 310), Snowdon being an adherent of the view that though it may be a matter of empirical necessity that we cannot see anything that does not affect us causally, it does not seem to be a conceptual truth.

attempt at reconciliation cannot really be judged a success, because it seems ultimately to forsake the idea at the heart of the causal theory that causality is something conceptually (and not merely empirically) central to seeing.

Thomas Baldwin is another philosopher who has sought to reconcile causalism with disjunctivism. Baldwin accepts the Humean principle that cause and effect must be separately describable in terms of 'causally relevant natural properties' but thinks it may be possible to defuse the disjunctivist's worry about whether perception can be described in such a way as to accord with the principle by insisting that there is no reason to find the relational description to be 'second-rate' or 'non-fundamental'.[14] But this will not meet the disjunctivist's concern if that concern is that there may simply be *no* description of S's seeing O as 'a sensory state of S induced by O'[15]—that no non-relational description whatever may be available. The disjunctivist may well think not merely that the relational description of perceiving is fundamental; she may think, more radically, that seeings are simply not the sorts of things that *have* non-relational descriptions at all.

It may be that this point has been insufficiently appreciated because it has been thought simply absurd to suggest that there are no descriptions of seeings in terms of 'causally relevant natural properties', and so that no one could really wish to maintain such a view.[16] But we must be careful here. It would certainly be absurd to suggest that there is no *explanation* of the phenomenon of seeing which does not invoke the causally relevant natural properties of a large number of natural objects (cells, photons, retinas, etc.). What is not obligatory, though, is the more properly *ontological* decision to regard seeings as particular *events*, or such event-like things as 'token states' are generally supposed to be, which can be picked out by means of 'natural' descriptions, just as well as they can be picked out by the ordinary vocabulary of seeing. It may help to see just how heavy are the commitments incurred by this sort of particularist naturalism to think about how hard it would be, not just in practice, but also in principle, actually to *supply* such descriptions:[17] which bits of the underlying physiology of my seeing a tree, say, are parts of that (token) seeing itself? How about events involved in blood supply to the visual cortex? Or is that just a service industry, not part of the real business of seeing? What about events in the retina and optic nerve? Are they just causes of the seeing event itself, rather than its parts? More importantly, perhaps: why on earth should we think we have any obligation to answer such questions as these? But we *do* have such an obligation if we commit to the view that each seeing is identical with, or constituted by, some mereological sum of underlying processes. For the problem is not

[14]   Baldwin (2007), pp. 24–5.

[15]   p. 25.

[16]   Cf. Strawson's remark quoted above that one would have to have been 'temporarily blinded by philosophy' not to accept that a visual experience was a 'thing in nature' distinct from the thing it is an experience of.

[17]   See Hornsby (1980–1) for a parallel argument against a parallel sort of identity theory in the case of actions.

just vagueness at the edges (such as might exist if one were asked to identify the set of particles making up a table at some particular time)—it is massive, radical under-determination of the answer, by the sum total of further facts of kinds we might think pertinent to it. And in the face of such radical underdetermination, we surely have the right to ask whether it makes sense to assert the identity of seeings with particular events specifiable in non-relational ways, nonetheless.

There is no absurdity, then, in the disjunctivist's refusal to specify descriptions of seeings in terms of 'causally relevant natural properties', if what that means is descrip-tions couched in the vocabulary of the physiological sciences. But nor does this refusal necessarily bring with it a rejection of the causal theory of perception, or so I would like to maintain. If causation has to fit the particularist conception, then true enough, the disjunctivist may be correct if she thinks that she cannot at the same time be a causal theorist. For a particularist causalist will want to know what the particular event, or event-like thing may be that is to be the effect of the causation presumed to be operating in the perceptual case—and if we say that it is a seeing event or a token state of seeing, or some such (rather than a 'visual experience'), in an attempt to respect the disjunctivist's preference for our natural ontology, we face a dilemma. Either such seeing events are essentially relational and so not capable of existing in the absence of their relata (in which case we will have violated the Humean Principle)—or we will have to revert to a non-relational conception of seeing after all, according to which a seeing is an event of a sort which might go on in the absence of anything seen. The kind of disjunctivist I am currently considering will certainly not want to do the latter. But then the only alternative is violation of the Humean Principle. And it has to be confessed that when thought of as a principle concerning events, the Humean Princi-ple is quite an attractive one. Can there really be *causal* relations between particulars which do not *have* descriptions under which they are revealed to be separate, natural entities, capable of existing in independence from one another?

Perhaps the rejection of the Humean Principle for particular causes is not unthink-able. But a much better solution, in my view, lies in the recognition that not all causal relationships *are* relations between particulars—and that the Humean Principle is simply not applicable to those that are not. In the next section of the paper, I shall set out some arguments for the view that there is really no such thing as 'the' ontology of causation—that things of a very wide variety of kinds may be causes—and in particular, that *facts* are amongst them. The idea that facts can stand only in the different relation of *causal explanation* and that causation itself is a relation which holds only between particulars will be argued to be a serious error; moreover, I shall show that there is no hope of finding each instance of 'p because q', in which the 'because' is adjudged causal, to be founded on the relation Strawson calls the 'natural' relation of causation.[18] The fact is that causation is not a relation in the strict sense at all. And once

---

[18] Strawson (1985), p. 115.

this is seen, the way will be open, I think, to reconcile disjunctivist and causalist, in the way they ought to be reconciled—that is, without insisting that the disjunctivist surrender the essential relationality of seeing.

II   Is there an ontology of causation?

Is there an ontology of causation? There are plenty of people who think there is. Well-known arguments exist in the literature, for example, for all of the following views: that the ontology of causation is an ontology of events; that it is an ontology of facts; that it is an ontology of processes; that it is an ontology of things and their powers; that it is an ontology of tropes; that it is an ontology of properties; that it is an ontology of 'facta'. And a conscientious trawl through the literature would doubtless yield up yet other suggestions. But before embarking on a choice amongst these alternatives, we need to ask why it is obligatory to suppose that causation *has* an ontology in the first place. After all, (as is frequently observed), items in almost all the ontological categories it is possible to think of are *spoken* of as causes—objects, persons, events, facts, states, properties, and so on. Why think that any of these ways of speaking can be sensibly thought of as revelatory of *the* ontology of causation? Might not the simple truth be that we need a plurality of irreducibly distinct ontological categories to do justice to the totality of causal phenomena?

In insisting that this is indeed, the simple truth, I do not mean to offer merely a counsel of despair with respect to the question whether we can, as philosophers, bring any order to the chaos of causal discourse. On the contrary, there *is* plenty of order to be discerned—I only wish to claim that it is not order of the sort that can be dealt with by means of the invocation of entities of an entirely homogeneous sort. What I shall suggest instead is that we need to recognise at least a three-fold ontological categorisation to capture and account for the different types of thing we call 'causes' (and, relatedly, the different sorts of relationship we recognise as causal).[19] I call these three types of cause *movers*, *matterers*, and *makers-happen*. None of the types, I maintain, can be dispensed with in favour of the others—though there are important relations between the types which can, to a certain extent, be mapped. But the really important thing, in my view, is that we must not get the categories *mixed up*, and assimilate them wrongly to one another, in the service of a chimerical uniformity.[20] My overall aim is to suggest that an honest recognition of the multiplicity of ontological categories we need to catalogue all the sorts of causal relationship there are, is preferable to an attempt to iron

---

[19] I focus here on causes. Effects can, I think, be readily accommodated within the ontological categories I shall argue are needed to deal with causes—indeed, they can be more simply dealt with, for in their case, I do not really think there is anything which corresponds properly to the category I call 'mover'.

[20] In my view, it is our having got them mixed up that is largely responsible for the existence of a number of artificial ontological categories for which I have yet to be persuaded that there is any genuine need—token states, tropes and facta, to name but three.

out the differences in favour of an entirely spurious standardisation—and in particular, that this can help us in the perceptual case.

It would take too long and anyhow would be too tedious to examine the individual claims of all the various pretenders to the throne of unique causal relatum. I shall content myself with a look at two of the most popular—events and facts— and explain why I think it is obvious that in the end, neither can perform all the duties required of a universally adequate causal ontology. Then, at the end, I shall move on to outline my positive view which recognises at least a three-fold distinction in the ontological types of cause, and explain how it can help us reconcile causal theorist and disjunctivist.

(i) Why events will not suffice

One has to be very careful when speaking of events. The term has been used by philosophers to refer to entities of very different sorts indeed—so let me be clear that I am using the term 'event' here in what might be thought of as a Davidsonian way to refer to a range of genuinely particular, multi-propertied (though not necessarily easily localisable) *happenings*, of which some examples might be: the moving of some pebble in response to the impact of a wave, the birth of an eland, a landslide, the explosion of a star.[21] Davidson's view, as is well known, is that it is entities of these sorts which are the only causes and effects.[22] He accepts, of course, that we do sometimes speak in ways which might make it *appear* as though we recognise causal relationships which require an alternative ontology. There is, for example, the fact that we express many—indeed, most—of our causal claims by way of the sentential connective 'because'. One might say, for instance, that the match lit because it was struck. And this appears to be a causal claim, a claim which might perhaps be recast in the following way: 'The fact that the match was struck caused it to be the case that the match lit'. And so here we might seem on the face of it to have a way of speaking about causation which makes it seem as though it is such things as facts, rather than such things as events, which stand in causal relationship to one another. But it was not really *the fact that the match was struck* which was the cause of the match's lighting, according to Davidson. The true cause in this case was a particular event—the particular striking of a particular match.

What, then, is the connection between the fact-citing claim:

(F1)   The fact that the match was struck caused the match to light;

—and the event-citing claim:

(E1)   The striking of the match caused the lighting of the match?

which, according to Davidson, is the linguistic form which reveals the true relata of the causal relation in this particular case? The natural thing for a Davidsonian to think[23] is

---

[21] Taken from Davidson (1970).

[22] He is not easy to pin down on the question whether there are also stative causes (and effects). In some places, he appears to prefer the idea that it is always a change in a state (hence an event) which is the real cause; in other places he appears more relaxed about the idea that token states might in effect be a species of event.

[23] Given the views expressed in Davidson (1967).

that the fact-citing explanation is, in effect, an existential generalisation over the sorts of singular causes and effects which are mentioned by (E1)—and so that its logical form should be represented in something like the following way:

$$\exists x \; \exists e' \; \exists e'' \; [[Struck \; (x, \; the \; match, \; e') \; \& \; Lit \; (the \; match, \; e'')] \; \& \; Caused \; (\; e', \; e'')]$$

What (F1) says, one might think, is effectively that there was a striking of the match and there was a lighting of the match and the one caused the other. If this were correct, it would be plausible to suppose that metaphysically speaking, claims like (F1) are at bottom dependent in general for their ontological grounding and causal character on singular causal claims like (E1)—and so that there is no need to treat fact-citing claims like (F1) as revelatory of a real ontological relationship of a causal kind amongst facts, or fact-like entities. Rather, on this view, fact-citing claims are simply existential general-isations over the only true sorts of causal relation we need to recognise—the tidy two-place relation represented by the predicate 'caused' as it occurs in sentences like (E1).

It would be nice if this Davidsonian story were true. But unfortunately, it cannot be the right way to think about the relation between fact-citing and event-citing causal explanations. Next, I shall offer three arguments for this conclusion. I offer here only brief summaries of lines of reasoning that I—and others—have developed with more care and more detail else-where[24]—but I hope I shall say enough, at any rate, to make persuasive the idea that we cannot manage with a causal ontology which contains only Davidsonian events.

(a) Negative explanantes
Consider the following explanation:

(F2) The match did *not* light because it was *not* struck.

My inclination is to say that this is a causal explanation; it is just as causal, indeed, as 'the match lit because it was struck'. But what are the events which are the causes and effects in virtue of which it is true? Surely it is obvious that there are none—indeed, that there was *no* striking and *no* lighting is part of what the sentence tells us. So how can its status as a causal explanation be dependent on the existence of a relation of causation existing between particular events?

One reaction to this want of particular causes (and effects) might be to introduce negative events—events of not-striking and not-lighting to stand in the wanted causal relations. But this is, to my mind, grotesque. It would be like representing the claim that no one came to my lecture by means of the following notation:

$$\exists x \; (x \; came \; to \; my \; lecture \; \& \; x = no \; one)$$

And negative events are in no better standing than negative persons. Absences, lacks, failures to happen, and the like are simply not events at all—and we need to face up

---

[24] See my (1997), ch. 5.

properly to the fact that the only sensible way we have of speaking of the causal relevance of such things is by means of connectives which are basically *sentential*. We simply cannot do the same job with a couple of singular terms and a two-place predicate; we need whole propositions and sentential connectives to do justice to what we wish to say when we attribute an effect to something's *not* being the case.

Another reaction might be to deny that the fact-citing explanation in question—that the match did not light because it was not struck—is causal in the first place—precisely *because* there are no particular causes here. But would it not be curious if the 'because' which figures in the sentence 'the match lit because it was struck' was a causal usage of 'because', while that which figures in the sentence 'the match did not light because it was not struck' was not? Surely these two sentences must be doing much the same kind of job—if one is a causal explanation, it seems bizarre to deny that the other must be a causal explanation too. But then their status as causal explanations cannot be dependent upon their relation to a singular causal relation of the sort described by (E1). And as will be seen shortly, it is not only negative explanantes which cause problems here—if we insist that singular causes and effects have to be found to underwrite every case of causation, we are going to find ourselves denying that all kinds of relationships are causal that we might have thought, initially, should count.

(b) Stative explanantes

For instance, a similar though more complex argument can be generated from the consideration of fact-citing explanations where the *explanans* is a stative predication, rather than an event predication like 'it (the match) was struck'. Take, for example, an explanation like

(F3)   The match lit because it was dry.

Again, it seems to me that this is a perfectly good causal explanation (albeit one that might require a certain context in order to become a very natural offering—one, for example, where most of the matches in the vicinity are damp). But if one were to attempt to convert it into the fact-citing form, one would arrive at:

(F4)   The fact that the match was dry caused it to be the case that the match lit.

And what is the event that is available to serve as underlying singular cause in this case? There is the match's dryness, perhaps—or its being dry. But the match's dryness is not an event at all in the original Davidsonian sense—dryness is not a happening but a property or state.

Now, it might be tempting to think that this little problem ought not to be allowed to get in the way of the overarching metaphysical strategy here—which is to attempt to replace all appearances suggestive of causal relationships between facts with *bona fide* relations between particulars, which we might think we should really prefer. What we need to recognise, it might be said, is that the range of particulars we need is wider than we thought at first—that Davidsonian events alone will not do the job. We need events, it might be thought, that are perhaps more like Kim's exemplifications of properties at times,[25] in order to enable us to include stative features as well as true events in the category of particular causes. But this move, which is extremely common in the literature, is much more significant, it seems to me, than it is sometimes represented as being, mainly because Kim's events are much more different from Davidson's than they are sometimes represented as being. On Davidson's view, an event is a properly *particular* entity, capable of being singled out by a genuine singular term and susceptible of informative re-description. But 'the match's dryness at *t*' is not a genuine singular term. For a start, 'dryness' is not a count noun, as 'striking' is. Moreover, strikings, on the original Davidsonian conception of events, and the event individuation criteria that went with it, could potentially be identical with such things as movements of arms and alertings of prowlers. Depending on the contingencies of the situation, re-description by means of semantically utterly unrelated predicates is possible for a Davidsonian particular event. But what sorts of re-description are possible for exemplifications of properties at times? Only, it would seem, re-descriptions which exploit identity relations which are at the level of the properties by means of which they have to be referred to in the first place—for example, an instantiation of dryness could also be an instantiation of aridity or dessication or H_2O-lessness. But instantiations of dryness do not seem to be individual enough to sustain informative identities in virtue simply of their own particularity. They are property-dependent entities, which cannot be singled out at all except by reference to a specific property. They are, as it is often put, 'fine-grained'—they are not the multiply re-describable entities in whose relations with one another Davidson hoped to ground causality in the world. The move to exemplifications of properties at times represents, then, I think, not so much a generalisation of the Davidsonian strategy, as an abandonment of it.

So what, it might be asked? Surely what reflection on the above example shows is simply that Davidson got the nature of the wanted particulars wrong—that we *need* to move towards a more fine-grained conception of events if we are going to do justice to the variety of things that can be causes. Since exemplifications or instances of states or properties like dryness can cause things, it will be said, we have simply discovered that it was something like the category of property exemplification or property instance or trope that was really needed here all along. A strict conformity to a conception of events which insists that they are things which *happen* must simply be forsaken for the sake of the generality we require in an ontology that will subserve the causal relation in all of its forms. But this move, which, again, is extremely common in the literature on causation, is one of the places where it seems to me we are in danger of getting distinct types of causal relationship mixed up; specifically, that we are in danger of mixing up truly singular causal claims, in which a genuinely particular event is said to make another happen, with an utterly different sort of claim, in which a feature or aspect or

---

[25] See e.g. Kim (1969, 1973, 1976).

property of some thing or situation is said to matter causally, to be causally relevant, to the fact that some outcome occurred. Recall that the claim for which we are trying to provide an ontological grounding is that the match lit because it was *dry*. The present proposal is that we are to understand the causality which is presupposed by this claim as rooted in a causal relation between a match's exemplification of dryness at a time and its exemplification of lighting at a slightly later time. But what is an exemplification of dryness at a time, exactly? Is it—like a Davidsonian event—a multi-propertied entity, capable of significant re-description which does not simply exploit a property-level identity? I have argued already that it is not, but even if someone thought that that was a mistake, a dilemma now threatens. Suppose the instantiation of dryness is an individual that *can* thus be informatively re-described in some way. If it is, how can we guarantee that its machinations will secure what we need to secure in this case— viz., the fact that it was that state's being, specifically, a token state of *dryness* that mattered causally for the match's lighting, as the original explanation—that it lit because it was dry—seemed to tell us? How can the fact that a multi-propertied entity stands in an extensional relation to another guarantee what we really seem to need to have guaranteed here—the causal relevance of the fact that the match was, specifically, *dry*? If token states or property instances of dryness are themselves the sorts of things that have many properties, then their being token states or property instances, specifically of *dryness* will presumably, be merely one amongst many possible descriptions by means of which we might single them out—and then there seems to be no way that the mere truth of the purportedly extensional causal claim we are to envisage as underwriting the original fact-citing one can guarantee the preservation of the causal relevance of the property of dryness. But if instead we capitulate here and confess that the token state is *not*, after all, a multi-propertied entity, capable of significant re-description, in order to permit ourselves to be secure about the causal relevance, specifically, of the fact that the match was *dry* to the event of its lighting, we have effectively abandoned the Davidsonian strategy of attempting to root all causal truths in ontologically unproblematic relations between true particulars. The fine-grainedness of the entities we seem in the end to need here should alert us, I think, to the fact that we have not properly moved any true distance away from what we appeared to have started with—a causal relationship holding between things which either are, or are extremely close relations of, the *facts* with which we began.

(c) Event predications

Indeed, the final nail in the coffin of what I have called the Davidsonian strategy comes with the recognition that it does not work even in the case for which it seems most alluring—cases of the type with which we began our discussion, where the *explanans* is a well-behaved event predication like 'The match was struck'. The trouble is that on the Davidsonian view, the singular causal claim (E1) ought to imply the sentential claim (F1)—if the form of (F1) really is the existential generalisation I suggested earlier. But it seems not to do so. For we can imagine a case in which we wanted to say that the striking of the match, conceived of as a particular event, caused the lighting of the match all right and yet not in virtue of the fact that it was a *striking*, so that it is not correct to say that the match lit because it was struck. Here is a somewhat far-fetched example[26] which, I think, proves the point. Suppose someone is attempting to invent, for some reason, a procedure for igniting matches by remote control, and tests of the mechanism are under way. One experimenter is holding one of the specially designed matches in his hand. At a signal from this first experimenter a second experimenter, who is sitting beside a button which triggers the remote control ignition mechanism is supposed to press the button. The signal arranged is an up and down motion of the hand. The first experimenter gives the signal a number of times, but the attention of the second experimenter has temporarily wandered, and he does not immediately notice that the signal has been given. The first experimenter, who is holding the box from which the match came in his other hand, while attempting to signal more vigorously, strikes the match he is holding accidentally against the box, though too lightly to cause it to ignite. It just so happens that the up and down motion of his arm is noticed this time by the second experimenter, who presses the button and the match lights as a result. In such a situation, it seems true that the striking of the match—which happened also in this instance to be a signal to the first experimenter—caused the lighting of the match. But it is not true that the match lit because it was struck. It is irrelevant that it was struck—any one of the other up and down motions of the experimenter's arm might have caused the lighting. The singular causal claim is true, but the sentential one, which was supposed to be a mere existential generalisation of it, is not.

What these various arguments show, it seems to me, is that it is always futile to attempt to root the claims we make about the causal relevance of facts (or equivalently, properties) to the occurrence of effects, in the causal machinations of particulars. For if the particulars really are particulars, the question will always remain open: in virtue of which of *their* properties did the particulars produce the effects they did?—there is simply no way of securing, if we stick to the machinations of mere particulars, precisely what we need secured if the fact-citing claim is to be true—namely the *relevance,* the *mattering* of the property or fact with which we started and from which we conjured a referring expression for a supposed particular in the first place. The basic problem is a straightforward failure to understand that particular causes and causes which are facts are irreducibly distinct and different from one another. The effectiveness of a causal 'token', if it really is a token, can never guarantee to carry with it the relevance of the property by which that token happens to be singled out. True tokens, true particulars can, of course, make things happen—indeed, particular events, are, I should say, the paradigmatic makers-happen of causal reality, the triggers which serve to bring further happenings about. But the import of a fact-citing causal claim can never be represented properly solely by a proposition about which particular events made which other

---

[26] Taken from Steward (1997), p. 155.

particular events occur. If fact-citing causal claims really do represent real causal relationships, then it is causal relationships of another sort entirely that they must represent.

(ii) Why facts will not suffice

At this point, one might reasonably think that the error of the Davidsonian was to have backed the wrong horse in a two-horse race. Events will not do all the work required of a uniform causal ontology. But perhaps facts could do so? D. H. Mellor[27] is perhaps the best-known champion of the view that if we are to represent causation adequately we need to recognise that relations between facts—facts representable by means of propositions of the form 'E because C'—are the primary causal relations. But even he cannot quite bear just to say so and leave it at that. For there is an obvious problem about facts. Facts do not seem—at least on very many conceptions of what they are— to be the sorts of thing that could actually *do* anything. Facts exist (on many concep- tions, Mellor's and my own included) merely in virtue of the truth of propositions— they are not properly conceived of as things in the world at all. And this gives even Mellor, perhaps their most determined champion, pause for thought—and indeed ultimately causes him to back down from his original claim that the ontology of causation is an ontology of facts, and to introduce the curious ontology of 'facta' with which he is preoccupied during the final four chapters of his book.

I will not go into much detail about what facta are supposed to be—for the details are not very important for my purposes. Roughly speaking, facta are particulars having properties—though Mellor distinguishes them from tropes because he insists that they are essentially structured entities containing universals, whereas he regards tropes as essentially unstructured—but that, for present purposes, is a debate we need not enter into. I will also not say a great deal about Mellor's official motivation for introducing them, which is the worry that otherwise, there would be no truthmakers for claims of the form 'C because E', since whether or not one is likely to be sympathetic to *that* reasoning is going to depend a great deal on how sympathetic one is in general to the idea that truths require truthmakers and that is too big a debate in its own right to enter into here. I merely want to point out that there is something about the idea that facts might be the only ultimate relata of the causal relation which is unsatisfying, even for those (like me) who remain to be convinced that there is any entirely *general* need for such things as truthmakers are normally supposed to be. The pressing difficulty is that an important aspect of our conception of causation seems to involve the idea that causes *do* things—that they make things happen in particular times and places. And facts seem royally unsuited to playing any such role as this, at any rate on many common sorts of understanding of what they are. Facts are about the world, they are not in it. They do not have causal powers, they do not literally have interactions with anything, they are

---

[27] See, in particular, Mellor (1995).

not causal agents. They simply cannot fulfil our requirement that at least some causes get involved in pushing and pulling and bumping and grinding—for if it is right to think of them as entities at all, it would seem that they simply do not have the requisite concreteness to enter the fray.

Mellor's solution to the problem of the unworldliness of facts is to invent a sort of hybrid category—the category of facta—things which are supposed to be worldly in a way that facts themselves are not, but which are nevertheless somewhat fact-like, fact-like enough, at any rate, to stand in some sort of correspondence relation to the facts in terms of which he thinks we must ultimately express the causal claims of the form 'E because C' which he believes, quite correctly in my view, to be an uneliminable and irreducible part of our causal talk. But I think this is the wrong solution. Ontologically speaking, it is to diversity rather than to hybridity that we should look, in order properly to understand how to fit together the different aspects of our concept of causation. The answer is not to invent strange new categories of entity in which we attempt confusedly to combine all the properties we might think we want a cause to have, but rather to see that there is more than one kind of cause.

Why don't I like the hybridity strategy? I should own at this point that I suspect myself of *some* motivations here which are perhaps not strictly kosher, being more aesthetic and ideological than they are philosophical. Facta seem to me to be ugly and unintuitive entities whose nature I find it difficult properly to understand; moreover, I have a general distaste for the introduction of too many new types of metaphysical entity—if we can get by with a few old favourites like substances and properties, then I should prefer to do so, particularly since it would seem to me to be surprising if it were to turn out that philosophical reflection on an everyday notion like causation turned out to require for its metaphysical underpinnings entities that have never, so far as anyone knows, been mentioned or referred to by any non-metaphysician. But I think it is also possible to provide a justification for thinking that hybrid entities like facta are not the answer, which is less encumbered by such general metaphysical prejudices. The main problem, I think, is that Mellor's hybridity strategy ends up misunderstanding the import and significance, the *meaning* of the types of causal claim he quite rightly insists must be central to any acceptable account of causation—causal explanations of the sentential form 'E because C'. It misunderstands what is required to be the case in order for a claim such as this to be true.

Let us return to the claim that the match lit because it was dry. What is it telling us? I am quite happy to accept for present purposes a great deal of what Mellor says it is telling us—let us agree with him for argument's sake that one thing that it is telling us that the fact that the match was dry raised the chances of its lighting. If we need to, indeed, we can say more about this—we can say more about what made it the case that the fact that the match was dry raised the chances of its lighting—for example, we can say that water absorbs the heat produced by the friction of the strike; that this is in turn because water has a very high heat capacity; that moreover, water makes the match-head weak so that rubbing just turns it into wet powder instead of producing the friction required for a successful strike, etc. These are some of the reasons why the fact that the match was dry is causally relevant in a positive way to the fact that the match lit, why it *mattered* causally. But what it is important to realise, I think, is that the relationship which our claim seeks to record—that the match lit *because* it was dry— is not itself a transactional one, and does not need to be in order for the claim to count as causal. It *relates* to a transaction, of course, but the transaction to which it relates is a transaction between a matchhead and some sandpaper, neither of which are entities about whose concrete particularity we need be in any doubt. The relationship our claim seeks to record, I repeat, is not itself transactional but is rather true in virtue of a relationship which is ultimately *functional*—a relationship between variables. The relationship in question is this: the damper a match head, the more of the energy generated by striking it will be siphoned off to evaporate the water, and the less will be available to set that match head alight. But this functional relationship is a *general* one. It only obtains in general, naturally, because it obtains in particular instances—this much explanatory priority we must allow to the individual cases in which the functional relationship can be discerned. But we do not need in addition to insist that this general functional relationship be grounded in individual *transactional* relationships relating to one another entities of the sort required to be arguments of the function—degree of dryness, and amount of energy required for lighting, for instance. That a match is dry matters to the fact that it lights, but not because little entities, little instantiations of dryness or 'facta' are hard at work in all the individual cases, pushing and shoving, doing what is so often and so misleadingly called 'causal work'. To think that it must be so is to mistake a cause that is what I call a *matterer* for a cause of another sort entirely. The crucial point is that not everything that matters causally, matters because it *does* something, because it *acts*.

One can see this particularly clearly when one reflects on the fact that absences, lacks, and omissions can matter causally—but they are obviously not the right sorts of thing to do any causal pushing and shoving, not being around to do any in the first place. But if matterers need not also be doers, need not also be agents, there is also no need for them to be ontologically particular or concrete or local. And if there is no need for matterers to be ontologically particular or concrete or local, there seems no need to replace facts with facta when we try to say what sorts of ontological relationship underlie claims of the form 'C because E'. Indeed, the paradigm matterers, in my view, are precisely things which are *not* ontologically particular or local—the paradigm matterers are facts. But this need not disturb us unduly. Non-particularity, non-concreteness might get in the way of something's being what I call a *mover* and might also prevent it from being what I call a *maker-happen*. But the fact that the match was dry is neither of these things—it is a *matterer*. I propose now briefly to explain this three-fold distinction between movers, makers-happen and matterers, and then to return, finally, to the case of perception, to show how the reconciliation between causalism and disjunctivism can be effected by a proper understanding of these distinctions.

III Movers, matterers, and makers-happen

I have not said anything yet about the category of mover, and for reasons of space, will not say much about it. But roughly speaking, movers are *things*. They are such entities as stones and masses of air and water, and animals and persons, as well as some of the smaller entities that go to make them up—like molecules and ions. It might be objected that fundamental physics may ultimately recognise no entities of the sort we generally suppose enduring things like this to be—I reply that fundamental physics, as is often observed, has no use for the concept of causation either. I claim only that at the levels at which we *do* find it useful and important to speak of causation, we also find it useful and important to single out powerful particulars which *do* things, which act and are acted upon.

Makers-happen, roughly speaking, are proper Davidsonian events. They are triggers, and therefore must be happenings. Strikings of matches are makers-happen—though the fact that a match was struck is not. A caution is perhaps necessary that of course my terminology is technical—not everything of which we might say in everyday life that it made something happen counts as a maker-happen, in my sense. We might, for instance, say that a stone (which, in my terminology, is a mover) made the breaking of the window happen; or that the fact that the match was dry (which in my terminology is a matterer) made it light. But these things are not makers-happen in my technical sense; a maker-happen, in my technical sense, can only be an event.

The same caution applies also in the case of matterers. We use the verb 'matter' of course in connection also with movers and makers-happen—the stone (a mover) matters, in a sense, to the breaking of the window (if it breaks it) and so does my throwing of it (a maker-happen). But one can perhaps get a sense of my motivation for employing the word 'matterer' specifically to pick out causes which are facts, or equivalently, causes which are aspects, or features of things situations, by reflecting on the point that actually, it was really the fact that a projectile of a certain mass was thrown at a certain speed at the window that mattered to the fact that it broke—the particularities of individual stone and individual throwing are neither here nor there. Another projectile and another throwing meeting given criteria would have done as well. It is the meeting those criteria that matters for the production of the effect.

Of course, it is incumbent upon a proponent of a pluralistic view like this one to say something about what unites these various kinds of cause. It must be explained what makes them all *causes*; what makes the relationships between a mover and what it moves, and a maker-happen and what it makes happen, and a matterer and what it matters to, all *causal* relationships. And I have not provided any such account; nor, I confess, am I in a position to provide anything of a well-worked-out kind which would meet this explanatory need. But in my defence, let me say first that it is important to see that the arguments I have provided in section II against causal particularism are quite independent of the production of a positive alternative view of what unifies these ontologically multifarious sorts of causation. I think it is possible to see (by way of those arguments) that relations between events, or event-like entities, are not capable of grounding the totality of relationships we regard as causal, even without having decided what might be the best alternative account of causation. And second, though the task of providing a general account of causation is a large one which I cannot hope to take on here, I do not in the least despair of being able to provide something plausible to plug the gap left by the manifest inadequacies of the so-called 'natural' relation. One promising possibility, for instance, is the manipulability conception of causation, recently developed in great detail by James Woodward.[28] The crucial thing, I think, is to get away from the picture of causation as a monolithic natural force, like electromagnetism or gravity, with its own essence and physical character—for it is this picture which I think brings with it the idea that it must possess a uniform ontology of its own. The thing to recognise is that causation is not a force, but a *category* in terms of which we think. As such, it can encompass a wide range of ontologically different sorts of relationship. This does not make causal claims any less true, and it does not imply that causation is a creature only of the mind, or anything similar. It only means that the correct account of what makes all causal claims *causal* (not, note, what makes them *true*) may be something which has more to do with us than it has to do with mind-independent reality.

IV The case of perception

What, then, is the relevance of all this for the prospects of a reconciliation between causalism and disjunctivism in the theory of perception? The crucial benefit, I think, is that we are freed from the particularistic conception of causation which insists that 'because' is merely the indicator (at best)[29] of causal *explanation*, and that we must look elsewhere than to the propositional elements that it relates for the true causal relata in any given case. I have argued that it cannot be true in general that what makes a given 'because' sentence causal is that it is underwritten somehow by the obtaining of a particularistic causal relation between events. And so we do not need any longer to agonise about what particular event exactly is to serve as the effect end of the causal chain allegedly involved in vision. There need be no such event—indeed, there need not be anything describable as a causal 'chain' at all, so far as what is given to us by an understanding of perception uninformed by the results of scientific investigation is concerned. For the metaphor of a 'chain' is really a metaphor suited to the understanding of causal relations amongst event-particulars. And not all causation need involve chain-like phenomena—think, for example, of what is involved, for example, in the claim that the earth goes around the sun because of gravity, or that the oil floated on the water because it was less dense. These are causal claims, but they do not fit neatly

---

[28] Woodward (2003).
[29] 'At best', because of course there are many sorts of explanation which are not causal at all.

into the picture whereby causation always has to involve the occurrence of one 'distinct existent' followed by another. Rather, they are claims about general relationships of dependency between different kinds of *facts*, relationships whose causal status does not need to depend on any transactional relationships between particulars.

So too in the perceptual case, I suggest, instead of causal relata which are particulars, we have causes and effects which are best regarded as facts. We may say that in the case of perceiving an object o, the relevant effect is simply 'that I see o', an unashamedly propositional entity, a fact, which bears its relational character on its face, and which there is no temptation to suppose must have a 're-description' in terms of 'causally relevant natural properties' (though no doubt it has an *explanation* in such terms). And the causal platitudes which it is plausible to think of as coming along with the very concept of perception can then simply be such things as these: 'I see o (on this occasion) because it is there to be seen right in front of me'; 'o looks F to me (on this occasion) because it *is* F'; and so on.[30] No complicated empirical investigation is needed to establish that claims such as these are true. They are the sorts of claims that go hand-in-hand with the idea that Strawson has stressed that we think of perception as a way of informing ourselves about a publicly available, mind-independent world—that 'the presence of the thing as accounting for, or being responsible for, our perceptual awareness of it is implicit in the pre-theoretical scheme from the very start'.[31] The causal relationship is precisely that between 'the presence of the thing' (= the fact that it is present) and 'our (my) perceptual awareness of it' (= the fact that I can see it). We do not need to convert this relationship of dependency into a transactional relation between particulars, even if, as a matter of empirical fact, there could be no perceiving unless certain events brought others about. The relation between the facts themselves is *itself* a causal one.

It might be objected at this point that more must be said about the nature of causal mattering or relevance, the causal relationship I have suggested can hold between facts, before we can judge whether it is a relationship that holds between such things as the fact that an object is present before me and the fact that I can see it. It may be obvious that the fact that an object is there in front of me helps *explain* why I can see it—but what is it, exactly, that makes this explanation count as *causal* if it is not some 'natural' relation obtaining in the case? I have already confessed to not having a well-worked-out answer to this question. Counterfactuals are doubtless *part* of the story—but it seems most unlikely that they can do all the work that needs doing alone, since 'q would not have been the case if p hadn't been the case' can be true in all kinds of cases

---

[30] Of course, I can sometimes see things even though they are not right in front of me and things can look F to me even though they are not F. But this does not in the least undermine the idea that when I *do* see things that are right in front of me, I see them (in the normal case) because they are there; or that when F things look F to me and they *are* F, that (very likely) they look F because they are F.

[31] Strawson (1979), p. 51.

in which the relation between p and q is not intuitively causal. But I have already suggested that perhaps we might look to a manipulability account of causation to help us answer the question what unites the various sorts of causal relation and relationship—perhaps what is crucial to the concept of causation is the idea of altering or changing one thing by manipulating another. Thus, for instance, we might say that the reason the presence of the object before me *causally* explains why I am able to see it is because moving it away from that prime position makes it progressively more difficult for me to see it, and will eventually prevent me from doing so. Some work would have to be done, no doubt, to ensure that all the many cases of causation in which actual, practical manipulation is unfeasible and perhaps even inconceivable could be brought under the umbrella of the account. But it may not be implausible that there are analogues and extensions of the idea of manipulation that could be used in such cases. But in any case, I would want to resist the suggestion that we cannot accede to the account I have offered of the perceptual case until we have the wanted full account of the category of causation in the palm of our hand. For even if we cannot be sure precisely *why* it seems right to say that an object's being present before me is part of what causally explains why I can see it, I think we can be sure that it *is* part of what causally explains this (albeit platitudinously). The only reason we had for doubting the platitude in the first place, I think, was the worry that we might involve ourselves, by agreeing to it, in a bad metaphysics and epistemology of perception, which requires states of seeing to be describable in other terms. But it has been the aim of this paper to suggest that this worry is unfounded, and in its absence we should be free to embrace the powerful pull of the causalist's view.

We have, then, I think, respected the main points dear to the causalist's heart. But equally, we have properly allowed for the disjunctivist's claim that seeing is *essentially* relational. The fact that I see o is essentially a relational fact—one which could not obtain unless o existed. We have not attempted to 'skim off' any purely psychic events, because we have rejected the need to deal in events at all. The effect of the causation in the case is a fully relational fact—that I see the chair—which cannot obtain in the absence of the relevant relata—and that the chair is right there in front of me *matters* causally—is *relevant* to—the fact that I see it; as well as being logically necessary in order that I should count as seeing it. And to those who are inclined to wheel out their Humean Principle at this point, we should just reply that the Principle is not applicable where the causal relationships involved hold between facts rather than events—that we cannot even make proper sense, in this case, of the relevant notion of 'distinct existences'. And we might point out, in addition, that the situation 'has many parallels'[32] It may be causally necessary, in order that I should score a goal in a game of football, for me to touch the ball; it is also logically necessary for me to do so, for

---

[32] To quote Strawson's earlier comment.

nothing could *count* as my scoring a goal which did not involve my touching the ball; it is causally necessary for me to grieve that I should believe that something tragic has happened, but it is also logically necessary, for nothing can count as grieving which is not a response to something believed to be a tragedy. A causal relationship between *facts* can perfectly well coexist with a logical relation between them. If the Humean Principle has any value, it is tenable only in relation to true 'distinct existences' such as events are generally supposed to be. But the ontology of causation is not, or is not only, an ontology of events, as I have tried to show.

In conclusion, then, I should like to suggest that the best way forward for the disjunctivist who also wishes to be a causal theorist lies with the denial of causal particularism. Powerful arguments of an entirely general kind suggest that it cannot be true. That its rejection might provide us with the means of reconciling two theories of perception which have much, independently, to recommend them, is yet a further argument for attempting to loosen ourselves from its powerful grip.

References

Baldwin, T. (2007), 'Perception, Reference and Causation', *Proceedings of the Aristotelian Society* 107: 1–26.

Child, W. (1992), 'Vision and Experience: the Causal Theory and the Disjunctive Conception', *Philosophical Quarterly* 42: 297–316.

Davidson, D. (1967), 'The Logical Form of Action Sentences', in N. Rescher (ed.) *The Logic of Decision and Action* (Pittsburgh: University of Pittsburgh Press), reprinted in Davidson (1980).

Davidson, D. (1970), 'Events as Particulars', *Nous* 4, reprinted in Davidson (1980).

Davidson, D. (1980), *Essays on Actions and Events* (Oxford: Oxford University Press).

Hornsby, J. (1980–1), 'Which Physical Events are Mental Events?', *Proceedings of the Aristotelian Society* 81: 73–92.

Hyman, J. (1992), 'The Causal Theory of Perception', *Philosophical Quarterly* 42: 277–296.

Humphreys, P (1989), *The Chances of Explanation* (Princeton, NJ: Princeton University Press).

Kim, J (1969), 'Events and their Descriptions: Some Considerations', in N. Rescher (ed.) *Essays in Honor of Carl G Hempel* (Dordrecht: Reidel) 198–215.

Kim, J (1973), 'Causation, Nomic Subsumption and the Concept of Event', *Journal of Philosophy* 70: 217–236. Repr. in Kim, *Supervenience and Mind* (Cambridge: Cambridge University Press, 1993) 3–21.

Kim, J. (1976), 'Events as Property Exemplifications', in M. Brand and D. Walton (eds.) *Action Theory* (Dordrecht: Reidel). Repr. in Kim, *Supervenience and Mind* (Cambridge: Cambridge University Press, 1993) 33–53.

Mellor, D. H. (1995), *The Facts of Causation* (London: Routledge).

Steward, H. (1997), *The Ontology of Mind: Events, Processes and States* (Oxford: Oxford University Press).

Strawson, P. F. (1979), 'Perception and its Objects', in G. McDonald (ed.) *Perception and Identity: Essays Presented to A.J. Ayer with his Replies* (London: Macmillan) 41–60.

Strawson, P. F. (1985), 'Causation and Explanation', in B.Vermazen and Merrill B. Hintikka (eds.) *Essays on Davidson: Actions and Events* (Oxford: Oxford University Press)115–135.

Strawson, P. F. (1988), 'Reply to Paul Snowdon', in L. E. Hahn (ed.) *The Philosophy of P. F. Strawson*. Chicago and Lasalle, Illinois: Open Court.

Woodward, J. (2003), *Making Things Happen* (Oxford: Oxford University Press).

11

Vision and Causal Understanding

William Child★

When we see an object, it causally affects us. It reflects light towards us; the light strikes our retinas; that causes impulses to be sent down our optic nerves; and so on. Without those causal processes, we could not see. But that is a scientific thesis: something we learn *a posteriori*, long after we have the concept of vision. There is nothing distinctively philosophical about this scientific thesis. And it seems clear that, when philosophers argue for or against a causal theory of vision, they are not arguing about the truth or falsity of the scientific thesis. What, then, are they arguing about? The causal theory of vision has been formulated in various ways. But there is a common basic intuition: according to the causal theory, the idea that our perceptual experiences are causally explained by the things we see is part of our ordinary thought about vision; it is an element of our naïve, pre-theoretical view of the world, rather than a feature only of a more sophisticated, scientific view.

That basic intuition has been expressed in various ways. H. P. Grice sees the causal theory as part of an attempt 'to elucidate or characterize the ordinary notion of perceiving a material object' (Grice 1961, 121–2). He concludes that the theory must not contain 'material of which someone who is perfectly capable of using the ordinary notion might be ignorant' (Grice 1961, 143). In defending a version of the causal theory, P. F. Strawson says that 'the general idea [of] causal dependence' is 'implicit' in 'the naïve or unsophisticated concept of perception' (Strawson 1974, 83, 82); and, again, that 'the idea of the presence of the thing as accounting for, or being responsible for, our perceptual awareness of it is implicit in the pre-theoretical scheme from the very start' (Strawson 1979, 51). Paul Snowdon says that, for the causal theorist, it is a conceptual truth that seeing is a causal process. That implies, he says, that the causal claim can be supported by appeal to data 'that are relatively immediately acknowledgeable by any person, whatever their education, who can count as having

★ Earlier versions of this paper were presented at the Warwick Workshop on Understanding Perception and Causation in April 2007, and at the Catz Work in Progress Group. I am extremely grateful to the participants in those discussions, and to an anonymous referee, for very helpful comments.

the concept in question' (Snowdon 1981, 176). Or again: the causal theory is concerned with the 'analysis of the *concepts* of perceiving and seeing'; so a defence of the theory cannot rest only on 'arguments relying on what are, broadly, empirical considerations' (Snowdon 1990, 121–2). And Helen Steward, in her contribution to the present volume, writes that 'it is usually thought to be essential to the Causal Theory of Perception that the causal connection between *o* and *S's seeing o* is supposed to be a part of the very concept of seeing—not merely something we can infer only from what we know empirically about how seeing in fact works' (Steward 2011, 142).

The point of these characterizations of the status of the causal theory is broadly similar: they aim to distinguish the philosophical claim that seeing is a causal process from a scientific claim. But the ways in which that distinction is drawn in the passages just quoted are not equivalent. The implication of Grice's comments is that the truth of the causal thesis is known by everyone who is capable of using the ordinary notion of vision. (An elucidation of the ordinary notion, he says, must not contain material that someone who grasps that notion might be ignorant of. So if the causal thesis figures in a correct elucidation of the ordinary notion, users of that notion must know that the causal thesis is true.) Snowdon's requirement that a defence of the causal thesis must not rely on 'empirical considerations' is less demanding: for even if the truth of the causal thesis could be established without relying on empirical evidence, it would not follow that the thesis must be known to be true by everyone who grasps the ordinary concept of vision. Strawson's idea that the causal thesis is 'implicit in' the ordinary concept of perception is weaker still. It is weaker than Grice's condition: for something might be implicit in the ordinary concept without being known by everyone who possesses that concept. And, on the face of it, the idea that the causal thesis is 'implicit in the pre-theoretical scheme' is also weaker than Snowdon's requirement. After all, much of our pre-theoretical scheme—our naïve way of thinking of the world—seems to involve knowledge that is, in some sense, empirical; it is acquired on the basis of our experience of the behaviour of things in the world around us. (Think, for example, of the principles that govern the mechanical interactions of physical bodies.)

So the characterizations offered by Grice, Strawson, and Snowdon are not equivalent. Furthermore, there is room for debate about what it takes for those characterizations to be satisfied. What makes it correct or incorrect to include the causal thesis in an elucidation of the ordinary notion of vision? What does it take for the causal thesis to be 'implicit in the pre-theoretical scheme', or to be 'a part of the very concept of seeing'? Without an answer to those questions, we do not know exactly what the causal theory of vision is claiming. There remains a strong intuition that there is room for a distinctively philosophical debate about the role of causation in our thought about perception: a debate that is not settled by the universal acceptance of the scientific thesis with which we started. But resolving that debate requires greater clarity about the intended content of the philosophical theory.

Philosophers recently have been increasingly interested in questions about the character of philosophy. What is the nature of philosophical reasoning and of philosophical theories? What distinguishes them from scientific reasoning and scientific theories? In what sense, if any, is philosophy concerned with the analysis of concepts? Is philosophy a distinctively *a priori* discipline? The questions we have just been raising about the status and nature of the causal theory of vision are instances of such questions about the status and nature of philosophical theories in general. Many of the classic writings on the causal theory of vision date from a period when it was taken for granted that the business of philosophy was conceptual analysis, and that philosophical theories are to be assessed by purely *a priori* reasoning. Philosophers nowadays tend to reject that conception of philosophy. How (if at all) and in what form does the causal theory of vision survive that change?

I want to approach those questions from three related directions. In part 1 of this paper, I respond to an objection raised by Helen Steward against some earlier work of mine; she suggests that my account of the causal theory of vision 'forsake[s] the idea at the heart of the causal theory that causality is something conceptually (and not merely empirically) central to seeing' (Steward 2011, 143). In part 2, I consider the objection that the causal thesis cannot be part of the ordinary concept of vision, since it is perfectly possible for someone to grasp the ordinary concept without accepting that seeing something involves being causally affected by it. In part 3, I reflect on the causal theory of vision in the light of psychological work on causal understanding. What light does experimental work on the origin and nature of causal thinking cast on the question, whether our ordinary thought about vision is a form of causal thinking?

1 Mentalism, physicalism, and the causal theory

In an influential paper published in 1981, Paul Snowdon argued that the causal theory of vision is undermined by the possibility of taking a disjunctive view of visual experience.[1] His argument was this: The causal theory of vision treats the experience S has when she sees an object as an effect; the effect-end of a causal chain initiated by the seen object. But if a disjunctive, or relational, view of experience is correct, then it is wrong to treat experience in that way. For the disjunctivist, the experience S has when she sees an object is not an inner effect that is produced in S by the object. It is, instead, a relational state of affairs: the state of affairs of o's looking some way to S (or equivalently: the state of affairs of S's seeing o as being that way). Now the object, o, is a component of this state of affairs. And an object cannot be the cause of a state of affairs of which it is a component. So, if the disjunctive view of experience is correct, it is wrong to treat the experience S has when she sees o as something that is causally produced by o; and in that case, the causal theory must be rejected. Snowdon does not argue that the disjunctive view of experience *is* correct. His argument is less ambitious: the disjunctive view, he says, is not ruled out by the concept of vision; it cannot,

---

[1] See Snowdon 1981. The argument is further explored in Snowdon 1990.

therefore, be a conceptual truth that our visual experiences causally depend on the objects we see; but the causal theory holds that that is a conceptual truth; hence, Snowdon concludes, the causal theory is false.

In a response to Snowdon, I argued for the *compatibilist* view that there is no conflict between the causal theory of vision and a disjunctive or relational view of experience.[2] The disjunctivist conceives the experience *S* has in seeing *o* as a relational state of affairs: the state of affairs of *S*'s seeing *o*. That view of experience, I argued, is quite compatible with the causal theory. For there is no difficulty in holding that an object, *o*, causally explains, or is causally responsible for, the state of affairs of *S*'s seeing *o*.

Someone might object to this compatibilist view on the ground that it violates a Humean requirement that causes and effects must be distinct existences. A relation between *a* and *b* can only be a causal relation, Hume thought, if *a* and *b* are 'distinct existences': if it is possible for each to exist without the other. If the existence of *a* entailed the existence of *b*, he thought, the relation between them would be a logical relation (or, in his terms, a relation of ideas) not a causal relation. (The event of my sister's giving birth and the event of my becoming an uncle, for example, are not distinct existences; that shows that the first is not the *cause* of the second.) But the object, *o*, and the state of affairs, *S*'s seeing *o*, are not distinct existences; the existence of the state of affairs entails the existence of the object. So if we accept the Humean constraint, the objection goes, we cannot regard the relation between *o* and *S*'s seeing *o* as a causal relation.

How should the compatibilist respond? I explored two ways of developing a compatibilist position: a *mentalist* view and a *physicalist* view. On the mentalist view: 'The entire causal story implicit in saying that something is a case of vision can be told in mental language; in showing how vision is causal, we do not need to rely on any non-mental characterizations'; in particular, 'we do not have to appeal to a description of *S*'s experience as a physical state or event' (Child 1994, 156). On the physicalist view, by contrast, 'the causal element in vision can be made intelligible only if we draw on physical facts about the subject' (Child 1994, 156).

Suppose we take the mentalist view. One way of responding to the Humean argument is simply to deny that the Humean constraint applies to causal relations involving mental phenomena. The Humean constraint, we might argue, derives from reflection on causal relations between physical entities. And a crucial feature of the physical is that it is 'a realm of autonomous entities, things whose intrinsic natures are independent of any other things' (Child 1994, 159). But the mental is not a realm of autonomous billiard-ball-like entities; that is part of the point of the disjunctive view of experience. So in the case of mental causation we should reject the Humean constraint altogether. The fact that the existence of the experience, *S*'s seeing *o*, constitutively depends on the existence of the object, *o*, is then no barrier to the presence of a causal relation between them.

---

[2] See Child 1992. A revised version appears as chapter 5 of Child 1994.

This mentalist view has much in common with Steward's position. Steward, too, thinks that the Humean constraint does not apply in this case. And she, too, holds that there is no need for the causalist to appeal to a physical characterization of the effect in order to make sense of the causal element in vision. On Steward's view, the causal relation holds between two *facts*: the fact that o is located where it is, and the fact that S sees o. And the effect—the fact that S sees o—is essentially relational; it 'could not obtain unless o existed' (Steward 2011, 158). But, she insists, it is a mistake to think that, in order for this to qualify as a genuinely causal relation, there must be some non-relational, presumably physical, characterization of the effect. For, she argues, 'the [Humean] Principle is not applicable where the causal relationships involved hold between facts rather than events' (Steward 2011, 158). Steward's reason for holding that the Humean constraint does not apply to the causal relation in vision is different from the reason given by the mentalist I have described. But the two positions are pushing in the same general direction. Had I endorsed the mentalist view, the distance between Steward and me would have been relatively small.

But I favoured the physicalist view. Exploring the reasons for that preference sheds light both on Steward's critique of my position and on the questions about the status of the causal theory with which we began.

On the physicalist view, I said, 'a full understanding of causal relations involving mental phenomena . . . must relate them to physical phenomena and to physical causality' (Child 1994, 110). In particular, 'the causal element in vision can be made intelligible only if we draw on [such] physical facts about the subject' (Child 1994, 156). Why should we accept that claim? It is sometimes suggested that we need to appeal to a physical characterization of the effect in vision in order to show how the causal relation in vision satisfies the Humean constraint—to show that an object and the experience it causally explains are suitably distinct existences. I made some comments that were sympathetic to that suggestion (see Child 1994, 117, 160). But that was not my main argument. And I would not now put any weight on it.[3] My main reason for preferring a physicalist view stemmed from the thought that the mental supervenes on, or is determined by, the physical. Causality is involved in many mental phenomena: action, perception, memory, and so on. But these phenomena do not involve a *sui generis* sort of causation: something whose operation is a basic, autonomous feature of the world, independent of the production of physical effects by physical causes. On the contrary, it is over-whelmingly plausible that mental causation is realized by, or constituted by, more basic

---

[3] In the first place, the fact that an object can exist without being seen is already sufficient to satisfy any legitimate requirement that causes and effects must be distinct existences (a point that I noted, but did not sufficiently stress). In the second place, the version of physicalism we get from this suggestion construes a visual experience as an event or state of affairs *in S*; on this view, the phrase 'S's seeing o' picks out an inner event in terms of its cause. But, on a wholeheartedly disjunctive view, the experience S has when she sees o is not an inner event; it is a relational state of affairs of which o is a component. And a relational state of affairs cannot be shown to be independent of its cause by being redescribed in physical terms; however we describe that state of affairs, its existence requires the existence of the object.

processes of physical causation. And if that is right, I argued, it is not intellectually satisfactory to say simply that *o* causes *S*'s seeing *o* and to leave it at that. A full understanding of the causal element in vision must say something about how the causal relation between an object and a person's seeing that object relates to the underlying physical causal processes; it must say something about how the effect in vision is brought about by the cause. Unless we do that, we do not fully understand the idea that seeing is a causal process. That, I argued, is why we should prefer the physicalist version of compatibilism.[4]

Against this position, Steward objects that the truth of physicalism is not built into the concept of vision. The physicalist, I said, holds that the mental state of affairs, *S*'s seeing *o*, 'consists in the whole chain of physical events . . . by which *o* causally affects *S*' (Child 1994, 161). But, Steward observes, the events mentioned in that causal story are events such as *o*'s reflecting light in the direction of *S*. And 'once we say this, it looks as though the causal relations which really obtain in the case are just those which are revealed by the *empirical* investigation of vision, not causal relations of a kind it might be plausible to think are part of the very concept of perceiving' (Steward 2011, 142). So, she argues, the physicalist view 'forsake[s] the idea at the heart of the causal theory that causality is something conceptually (and not merely empirically) central to seeing' (Steward 2011, 143).

I shall make three points in response to that objection. First, my reasons for favouring the physicalist over the mentalist view were not supposed to be *a priori* or non-empirical. An essential premise in the argument was that the mental supervenes on the physical. And, as I said, that is plainly not something that we know *a priori*.[5]

Second, and relatedly, the case for a physicalist version of the causal theory should be seen as having two parts. The first part is an argument for the claim that our ordinary thought about vision is a form of causal thinking. (I shall explore that part of the argument in section 2, below.) That is a point about our ordinary thinking. There is, as we saw at the beginning of the paper, a question about how exactly to understand that claim. On one view, the key idea is that the causal claim is, as Steward puts it, 'conceptually central to seeing'; on a different view, the idea is that the causal claim can be known to be true without empirical evidence; on a third view, it is that the causal claim is implicit in the pre-theoretical scheme; and so on. But whichever formulation we prefer, and however we understand it, it seems clear that we can endorse this first point without yet taking a position on the issue of physicalism. The second part of the case for physicalism is an argument that, since vision is a causal process, and since there are good reasons for thinking that all causation is realized by underlying physical causal processes, there is good reason for accepting a physicalist version of the causal theory. At no stage of the argument is it claimed that it is built into the ordinary concept of

---

[4] See Child 1994, 115–16, 159.   [5] See Child 1994, 116, 75.

vision that seeing involves the specific kinds of physical events it actually does involve: events involving light waves, optic nerves, and so on.

So the argument for a physicalist version of the causal theory, taken as a whole, does not forsake the idea that causality is central to our ordinary way of thinking of vision. On the contrary, the first stage of the argument explicitly endorses that idea. What the argument does repudiate is an assumption fundamental to much writing on the causal theory of vision: that the causal theory is or should be concerned only with conceptual analysis. Suppose, for the sake of argument, that we have a clear grasp of what is and is not part of the ordinary concept of vision. And suppose that it is not part of the ordinary concept of vision that seeing involves the kinds of physical events it actually involves; or even that it involves any physical events at all. It does not follow that there is no properly philosophical argument for a physicalist version of the causal theory. For the proper business of philosophy is not confined to the analysis of our ordinary concepts. As I said:

Philosophy has a legitimate interest not just in understanding the concept of [vision] but also in understanding the relations between different sorts of concepts which apply to subjects, and between different levels of description; and in that way it has an interest in understanding the phenomenon of [vision] itself.[6] (1994, 115)

In particular, philosophy has a legitimate interest in the relation between the causal story we can tell about vision in mental terms and the underlying physical causal processes. It is that concern, I claim, that makes the physicalist version of the causal theory preferable to the purely mentalist version.

Third, I said that, on the physicalist view, the causal element in vision cannot be 'made intelligible' without drawing on physical facts about the subject (1994, 156). In saying this, I did not mean that it would be literally *meaningless* to hold that there are no physical causal processes involved when someone sees an object, or to remain agnostic on the matter. (Cartesian dualists deny the physicalist view. But even if dualism can be shown by purely *a priori* reasoning to be incoherent, statements of dualism are not meaningless. So dualism is, in that sense, intelligible.) The point is, rather, that given the general reasons for accepting physicalism, it is not intellectually satisfactory simply to say that the objects we see are causally responsible for our visual experiences and to leave it at that. We need also to say something about how these causal processes relate to physical causal processes.

To take stock: (1) I agree with Steward that the kinds of physical event or process that will be mentioned in the physicalist's account of what is involved in S's seeing o are not plausibly 'part of the very concept of perceiving'. But, for the reasons given, I do not see that as an objection to the physicalist view; the causal theory of vision need not confine itself to elements that are parts of the concept of vision. (2) As we have seen,

---

[6] The quoted passage focused on the causal theory of memory rather than the causal theory of vision. But the same considerations apply in each case.

the central claim of the causal theory has been variously formulated. Some say that the causal element in vision is part of the ordinary concept of vision; others say that it is implicit in the pre-theoretical scheme; others say that our ordinary thinking about vision is a form of causal thinking; and so on. Two questions have emerged very clearly in the discussion so far. First, which of these formulations should the causal theorist be aiming to defend? Second, why should we believe that the causal theorist's central claim, thus formulated, is true?

2 Conceptual truth and our ordinary thought about vision

On one way of formulating the causal theory, the central claim of the theory is that it is a conceptual truth that seeing an object is, or involves, being causally affected by it. And on one reading of that central claim, it follows directly that one cannot grasp the ordinary concept of vision without accepting the causal thesis. We saw above that Grice seems to endorse that view. But, understood in that way, the causal theory faces an obvious objection: that it seems perfectly possible for someone to grasp the concept of vision without accepting the causal thesis.

Timothy Williamson has recently argued that there are no conceptual truths. There is, he thinks, no truth that one has to accept in order to count as grasping the concepts it contains.[7] So (applying that view to our case) there is no truth about vision that one is required to accept in order to grasp the concept of vision. Williamson's argument focuses in the first instance on grasping the meanings of words. Understanding the English word 'see', on his view, requires being a sufficiently fluent member of the practice of using that word. But someone can be sufficiently fluent in using the word 'see' to count as understanding it, even if she holds bizarre views about vision and, as a result, denies what the rest of us take to be very basic and simple truths about vision; extreme eccentricity in some elements of her use of the word can be compensated for by her normality in other parts of its use.[8] And, on Williamson's view, what goes for understanding the word 'see' goes equally for grasping the concept *see*. If someone understands the word 'see', she understands the concept it expresses: the concept *see*. So, just as she can understand the word 'see' without accepting that seeing is a causal process, so she can grasp the concept *see* without accepting that seeing is a causal process. Of course we could decide to individuate concepts in some other way; and some ways of individuating concepts would indeed make acceptance of the causal thesis a necessary condition for grasp of the concept *see*. But, Williamson argues, we would need an intellectually respectable rationale for individuating concepts that way, and it is hard to see what that rationale would be.[9]

---

[7] See Williamson 2007, ch. 4.   [8] Williamson 2007, 90.
[9] For more detail, see Williamson 2007, ch. 4, section 5.

Williamson's argument is extremely plausible. It is easy to produce actual or imaginary examples of people who plainly possess the concept of vision, but who hold views about vision on which there is no causal relation running from an object to the subject who sees it. For example, we can imagine someone accepting a 'searchlight theory' of vision. She thinks that the eye sends out visual 'rays' that range over the objects in one's environment. When an object lies in the path of these visual rays, the person's mind encompasses the object and she sees it. On this view, vision is a causal process; but the causality runs from the perceiver to the object, rather than the other way round. Or again, philosophical occasionalists hold that the objects we see do not themselves cause the experiences we have when we see things: they are only the occasions for God to produce those experiences in us. It is overwhelmingly plausible to say that the searchlight theorist and the occasionalist have the concept of vision. After all, they know what vision is; they can identify cases of seeing as well as any one else, and distinguish seeing from not seeing. They understand the causal claim about vision—which, of course, they reject. Their own false theories are clearly false theories *about vision*. Given all that, it would be implausible to say that the searchlight theorist and the occasionalist do not grasp the concept of vision. But they reject the causal theorist's claim that seeing something involves being causally affected by it. So, it seems, grasping the concept of vision does not require accepting the causal claim.

How should the causal theorist respond? The right response, I think, is to give up the idea that one cannot grasp the concept of vision without accepting that vision is a causal process. What the causal theorist should be defending is a more modest claim: that our ordinary thought about vision is a form of causal thinking. A successful defence of that claim must do three things. It must say what it takes for someone to think of vision in causal terms, or to think of vision as a causal process. It must defend the claim that we do ordinarily think of vision as a causal process. And it must show that that way of thinking of vision is part of our naïve, intuitive view of the world, rather than being a feature only of a more sophisticated, scientific view of the world.

The causal theory, on this conception, is distinct from any scientific thesis about vision. No doubt there is no sharp distinction between our naïve, intuitive view of the world and a more sophisticated, scientific view of the world. But there is a distinction. And the causal theory is concerned with our naïve thinking about vision: the thinking involved when, for example, we consider what we and other people can or cannot see ('Which of those two people is she seeing?', 'Can he see this thing from where he is standing?'), when we explain why we cannot see something ('It's too dark', 'It's too far away', 'There's something in the way'), when we explain why it looks as if things are thus-and-so, and so on. We can engage in that thinking without having any scientific knowledge about the causal processes involved in seeing—about light waves, optic nerves, the visual cortex, and so forth. The point of the causal theory, on the current conception, is that this ordinary thinking is a form of causal thinking. That is analogous to the claim that our naïve thought about the behaviour of physical objects is a form of causal thinking; or to the claim that our naïve thought about the growth of plants is a form of causal thinking. In both of those cases, too, we can distinguish our naïve thinking from more sophisticated, scientifically-informed thought. In both cases, we can engage in the naïve thinking without having any relevant scientific knowledge. And in both cases, it is a non-trivial claim that the naïve thinking is a form of causal thinking.

I have allowed that someone may have the concept of vision without accepting that seeing something involves being causally affected by it. The searchlight theorist and the occasionalist are cases in point: they grasp the concept of vision; but they explicitly deny that we are causally affected by the objects we see. If we hold, with the causal theorist, that our ordinary thinking about vision is a form of causal thinking—that our ordinary thought represents objects as causally responsible for our perception of them—what are we to say about the searchlight theorist and the occasionalist? There seem to me to be two possibilities. (i) We might say that, though our ordinary, naïve way of thinking about vision is a form of causal thinking, it is possible for someone to think about vision in a different way, which does not represent our visual experiences as causally dependent on the things we see. So, in particular, the searchlight theorist and the occasionalist have ways of thinking of vision that do not so represent it. An analogous position concerning our thought about physical objects would be this: 'Our naïve thought about the behaviour of physical objects is a form of causal thinking: when one object collides with another and sets it in motion, we think of the first object as causing the movement of the second; when a ball hits a window and the window breaks, we think of the ball as causing the window to break; and so on. But there could in principle be ways of thinking about these kinds of relations that did not represent them in causal terms; for example, a way of thinking that represented events of the relevant kinds as constantly conjoined without representing them as causally related.' (ii) We might, instead, take a more ambitious view. In thinking of something as a case of vision, we might say, one is thereby thinking of it in causal terms. The searchlight theorist and the occasionalist have theories of vision that explicitly deny that seeing something involves being causally affected by it. Nonetheless, their basic, ground-level thought about vision still represents it in causal terms. So there is a tension in these theorist's thought: their explicit theories of vision deny that it has a feature that their ordinary thought about vision represents it as having. An analogous proposal in a different area would be this: 'When one thinks of x as breaking y, one thereby thinks of x as causing y to break. Nonetheless, someone may have a bizarre theory that denies that x's breaking y involves x's causally affecting y. Perhaps she is an occasionalist: x does not causally affect y; it is simply the occasion for God to produce a change in y. Or maybe she thinks that what happens when x breaks y is this: y spontaneously disintegrates and draws x into contact with it. Such a person has the concept of breaking: she can pick out cases of breaking, and her use of the word "break" passes muster in the community. But there is an internal tension in her thought: in thinking that x breaks y, she represents x as causally affecting y; but her explicit theory of breaking denies that x's breaking y involves x's causally affecting y.'

This second, more ambitious, view seems right for the case of breaking; in representing something as a case of x's breaking y one really is thereby representing it as a case of x's causally affecting y. But I am inclined to think that the first, less ambitious, view is more plausible for the case of seeing. That is to say, it is possible to represent S as seeing o without representing S as being causally affected by o. My reason for distinguishing the two cases in that way is the following. Suppose the bizarre theory about breaking turned out to be true: suppose that, in cases that we ordinarily call 'instances of x breaking y', what happens is not that x causes y to break; instead, y spontaneously disintegrates and draws x into contact with it. What we would have discovered would not be that the process of one thing's breaking another was very different from what we had thought: that it did not, after all, involve x causally affecting y. Rather, we would have discovered that the cases we ordinarily regard as ones in which x breaks y are not cases of x's breaking y at all. But things seem different for the case of vision. Suppose the searchlight theory or the occasionalist theory of vision turned out to be true: it turns out that, in cases that we ordinarily regard as instances of a person's seeing an object, there is no causal relation running from object to perceiver. Should we conclude that these cases that we ordinarily regard as instances of seeing have turned out not to be instances of seeing at all? Or should we rather conclude that, contrary to what we ordinarily thought, seeing something turns out not to involve being causally affected by it? My own sense is that this latter view is more plausible. But if that is right, then it is not true that, in representing something as a case of someone's seeing an object, one cannot fail to be representing it as a case of the object's causally affecting the person.

Some philosophers would object that, if we concede this much, then we are no longer defending a philosophical causal theory of vision. Once we allow that someone may have the concept of vision without accepting that seeing something involves being causally affected by it, the objector will say, and once we allow that someone may represent something as a case of vision without thereby representing it as involving causation, all we are left with is the claim that our ordinary, pre-theoretical way of thinking about vision does as a matter of fact represent vision as involving the causal dependence of our experiences on the things we see. And, it may be said, there is nothing philosophical about that: it is just an empirical claim about the way we think. I do not agree that the concessions I have made leave us defending a claim with no philosophical content. For one thing, the question, what it takes for a given way of thinking to be a form of causal thinking, is not an empirical question; it is a distinctively philosophical question. And in considering whether our ordinary thought about vision is a form of causal thinking, part of what we are considering is precisely that question. For another thing, the project of charting the most general features of our conceptual scheme—the project of descriptive metaphysics—has a distinguished history as part of philosophy. It is no shame for the causal theory of vision to be part of such a project.

The causal theorist claims that our ordinary, pre-theoretical thought about vision is a form of causal thinking. What can be said in favour of that claim? Consider, for example, how we tell which of two similar objects someone is seeing. We move them about, one at a time, and see which movement makes a difference to the person's experience. That procedure, the causalist says, is exactly the same as the procedure we adopt in any other case where we are testing which of two things produces a given effect. Suppose we want to know which of two switches controls the light. We press each in turn, and see which of them makes a difference to the state of the light. In that case, we are testing for the presence of a causal relation. And the same is true in the case of vision; testing which thing S is seeing is testing which thing is causally affecting S: which thing is causally responsible for S's experience. Similarly, the causalist says, thinking about vision involves thinking about the enabling and defeating conditions of vision. When we think about vision, we do not just have thoughts of the form 'I am seeing x', or 'She is seeing y'. We also think about what we and others can and cannot see: 'She can't have seen the object, because it wasn't there, or it was too far away, or there was something in the way, or the room was too dark'; 'This must be the object she was seeing because this is the one that was in her line of sight'; and so on. And these enabling and defeating conditions are causal conditions: they are conditions on an object's causally affecting a person. Reasoning of this sort about vision is ubiquitous in our ordinary thought. And, the causalist says, in reasoning in these ways, we are engaged in causal reasoning—just as we are engaged in causal reasoning when we think that it cannot have been the ball that broke the window because the ball is too light, or because it did not hit the window sufficiently hard, or because something stopped it hitting the window at all.

The non-causalist rejects this argument. She agrees that vision is a causal process; that, she thinks, is an undeniable empirical truth. But she denies that our ordinary, pre-theoretical thought about vision represents it as a causal process. Similarly, she agrees that, in reasoning about the enabling and defeating conditions of vision, we are reasoning about what are in fact causal conditions. But she denies that we ordinarily represent those conditions as causal conditions. All that is built into our ordinary thought, she suggests, is a set of simple principles about the conditions under which one can see things: one cannot see something if it is not there, or if it is too far away, or if it is blocked from view, or if there is insufficient light, and so on. We accept those principles about vision and we reason in accordance with them. But it is no part of the pre-theoretical scheme that these principles have anything to do with causation. Similarly, when we test which of two objects someone is seeing, we are in fact testing for the presence of a causal relation. But we do not ordinarily think of what we are doing in those terms.

What should the causal theorist say in response? An ambitious causalist might respond that it is just not possible to think about the enabling and defeating conditions of vision in non-causal terms; in representing them as enabling and defeating conditions of vision, one is perforce representing them as causal conditions for someone's seeing something. But I shall not defend that view. My causal theorist thinks that, though our ordinary pre-theoretical thought about vision is a form of causal thinking, it is possible for someone to represent something as a case of S's seeing o without thereby representing it as a case of o's causally affecting S. And likewise for the enabling and defeating conditions of vision. For her part, the non-causalist insists that our ordinary, naïve thought about vision does not represent it in causal terms. But she will of course agree that it is possible to think of vision in causal terms, and to do so without adopting a distinctively scientific viewpoint. For we can know that objects are *causally* involved in our seeing them simply on the basis of our naïve experience of the world, without engaging in science—just as we may know on the basis of ordinary experience that moisture, light, and soil are causally involved in the growth of plants.

At this stage, the debate between the causalist and the non-causalist may seem to degenerate into an uninteresting verbal dispute about what to count as our ordinary pre-theoretical thinking about vision. The causalist agrees that vision *can* be thought of in non-causal terms; the non-causalist agrees that it *can* be thought of in causal terms; they simply disagree about which way of thinking is the ordinary, naïve, pre-theoretical way of thinking about vision. I think that view of the debate is too pessimistic. There is, as I have already said, a substantive philosophical issue about what it takes for a kind of thinking to count as causal thinking. The lower we set the threshold for something to count as genuinely causal thinking, the easier it will be to show that our ordinary thought about vision is a form of causal thinking, and the more plausible the causalist's position will be. The higher we set the threshold, the harder it will be to show that our ordinary thinking is a form of causal thinking, and the stronger will be the non-causalist's position. But we do not have a free hand to set the threshold wherever we want: there are plausible and less plausible views about what it takes for something to be a form of causal thinking. We should look for the best view of what causal thinking involves. Having done that, we may find that it is quite clear that our ordinary thought about vision qualifies as causal thinking, or that it does not. My own view is that our ordinary thinking about vision plainly is a form of causal thinking.

What, then, does it take for a kind of thinking to qualify as causal thinking—for it not merely to represent phenomena that are causal, but to represent them as causal? I have only a preliminary and sketchy answer to offer to that question. But I offer the following suggestion.

In the first place, it is overwhelmingly plausible that the concept of cause is basic and unanalysable. That means that we cannot give a completely non-question-begging explanation of what it takes for our thinking about some domain to be a kind of causal thinking. We might say, for example, that in order for someone to represent the relation between x and y as a causal relation, she needs to represent x as bringing y about, or as influencing or affecting y. But, while those formulations may be true, and while they may be helpful in reminding us what causal thinking involves, they do not give us an *analysis* of what it takes to be thinking in causal terms: for the notions of 'bringing about', 'influencing', and 'affecting' are themselves causal notions.

Second, a concept may be a causal concept—it may represent the relations it picks out as causal relations—even if those who possess the concept do not possess any general concept *cause* that they are prepared to apply in every case in which they apply one or another more specific causal concept. In practice, it seems clear that children do grasp all-purpose, domain-general causal and causal-explanatory concepts like 'make' and 'because' at an early stage. But there seems no reason in principle why it should not be possible for a child to grasp a range of specific causal concepts—such concepts as *crush, break, spill, sting, wash, switch on*, and so forth—and to use those concepts in thinking about phenomena in genuinely causal terms, without having any more general causal concept that she can use to classify these specific kinds of causal action or causal process as instances of the same general kind—i.e. as instances of causation.

What, then, makes these concepts causal concepts? What makes the thinking that employs them causal thinking? Strawson writes:

'[C]ause' is the name of a general categorial notion which we invoke in connection with the explanation of particular circumstances and the discovery of general mechanisms of production of general types of effect. (Strawson 1985, 135)

On this view, what makes a concept a causal concept is just that it has to do with explaining why something happened; why an event or state of affairs occurred, or came about, or persisted; what produced some event or state of affairs; why a particular thing behaved as it did, or why that kind of thing generally behaves as it does; and so on. That is a very plausible view. And by that standard, what makes our ordinary thinking about vision a form of causal thinking is that the 'because' in our reasoning about seeing ('She couldn't see it because it was too far away', and so on), has to do with the explanation of why something happened (or did not happen). In our ordinary thought about vision, we are concerned with the occurrence or non-occurrence of natural phenomena: someone's seeing this, or failing to see that. In the same way, when we reason about the enabling and defeating conditions of vision, we are reasoning about why something happened or persisted, or why something of a certain sort failed to happen. That is enough for this reasoning to be a form of causal reasoning.

3 Psychologists' understanding of causal understanding

We have been considering whether our naïve, pre-theoretical thought about vision is a kind of causal thinking. In this connection, I want to consider work from developmental psychology on questions of exactly that form, about the nature and acquisition of causal understanding. I can only scratch the surface of that work here. But even a brief and incomplete comment on some psychological literature will be helpful from a philosophical point of view—as well as raising questions about some claims that have been made in the developmental literature.

In the psychological literature, the phrase 'causal understanding' is used with at least two different senses. In some cases, psychologists who consider the question, whether S has a causal understanding of x, are considering whether S represents or thinks of x in causal terms. In those debates, the question 'Does our thought about x involve a causal understanding of *x*?' is equivalent to my question, 'Is our thought about *x* a form of causal thinking?' In other cases, psychologists who ask whether *S* has a causal understanding of *x* are asking whether *S* knows, or understands, the kinds of causal processes involved in *x*. To have a causal understanding of something in this second sense one must have a causal understanding in the first sense too: one cannot have knowledge of the causal processes that produce something without thinking of that thing in causal terms. But the opposite is not true: one could on the face of it think of the relation between *x* and *y* as a causal relation without knowing anything at all about how *x* produces *y*.

Susan Carey's work on naïve biology provides an example of this second use of the phrase 'causal understanding'.[10] Her aim is to show that naïve biology is a much later-developing element in our thinking than either folk psychology or naïve mechanics. These latter, she argues, unlike naïve biology, are 'core cognitive modules'. Part of Carey's argument is that someone only qualifies as having a naïve *biology* if she has a causal understanding of biological processes. And, she maintains, a causal understanding of biological processes is lacking even in children as old as 6 or 7 years old. She writes:

Until the child has constructed an intuitive theory of how bodily processes mediate between eating and growth, or eating and becoming fat, knowledge of mere 'input-output' relations does not constitute causal understanding ... It is unlikely that the pre-school child knows of any biology-specific causal mechanisms relevant to bodily phenomena; these may just be facts that the child has observed about his and others' bodies. Animals and people grow, the heart beats, we become sleepy even if we want very much to stay awake, etc. (Carey 1995, 284–5)

The child who does not know of any biological causal mechanisms, then, does not have 'causal understanding' of the relation between eating and growth.

But Carey does not think that one needs a theory of the causal mechanisms relevant to bodily growth in order to think of the relation between eating and growth as a causal relation at all. She is happy to allow that someone can think of a relation as a causal relation even if she has no idea at all of any mediating causal mechanisms. She writes, for example:

[K]nowledge about the relation between eating and growth ....may be mere knowledge of an input-output relation, such as knowledge that turning on a light switch *causes* a light to go on. Such knowledge is probably acquired through being told about input-output relations explicitly ('If you don't eat your vegetables, you won't grow into a big strong girl ...) ... The pre-school child has no clue as to any bodily mechanism which mediates between eating and growing. (Carey 1995, 286–7, my emphasis)

Or again:

[P]re-school children's understanding of disease, like their understanding of ... growth and bodily processes, is limited to knowledge of input–output relations—dirt, poisons, going outside with no coat on, and germs *cause* disease. (Carey 1995, 292, my emphasis)

---

[10] See Carey 1995.

In these examples, Carey treats knowledge of 'input–output' relations as causal knowledge. So when she says that the pre-school child lacks 'causal understanding' of the relation between eating and growth, she does not mean that the child does not think of the relation between eating and growing as a causal relation at all. She is talking about causal understanding in the second of the two senses distinguished above: knowledge of causal mechanisms.

But what about the other sense of causal understanding? Carey allows that knowledge of an input–output relation may be causal knowledge. But what makes it causal knowledge rather than mere knowledge of an association? Could there be a stage in a child's development at which she grasps that eating is associated with growth, and extrapolates that association to new cases (if A eats, he will grow; if B does not eat, he will not grow); but at which she does not think of the association in causal terms at all? If not, why not? But if there could be such a stage, what makes it the case that a child at a later stage of development is engaging in causal thinking rather than merely thinking about regularities?

These questions receive some treatment in an interesting literature about infants' perception of causation, which explores the extent to which very young infants perceive interactions of various kinds as causal interactions.[11] The primary focus of this work is the *perception* of causality, rather than the more general issue of what it is to *represent* a relation as a causal relation. But work on the perception of causation must take a position on the more general question. For in order to explore the extent to which infants perceive certain relations as causal relations, we must know what it takes for a perception to have causal content; and answering that question requires some answer to the question, what it takes for representations in general to have causal content.

I want briefly to explore some issues about the bearing of this work on our earlier discussion of the causal theory of vision. I focus on the overview offered in Saxe and Carey's paper, 'The perception of causality in infancy' (Saxe and Carey 2006).

Saxe and Carey accept, for the sake of argument, the view taken by Michotte (whose work they are discussing): that we have an innate representation of cause.[12] Their own view is that it is an empirical question whether or not the representation of cause is innate. But, they think, it is a live possibility, compatible with current evidence, that 'representations with the content *cause* [are] innate' and are 'part of a central conceptual system that integrates information' provided by different sources of information about causality (Saxe and Carey 2006, 163). Even if our concept of cause is innate, we can still ask what makes that concept a concept *of causality*. Possible answers to that question would include that the innate representation is a representation *of causality* in virtue of being reliably triggered by exposure to causal relations; or in virtue

---

[11] For two early contributions to that literature, see Leslie 1982, and Leslie and Keeble 1987. For a comprehensive recent survey, see Saxe and Carey 2006.

[12] Saxe and Carey 2006, 148. For Michotte's work, see Michotte 1963.

of its biological function; and so on. But Saxe and Carey do not address that question. So as far as their 2006 paper goes, all we are told about what it takes for someone to represent a relation as a causal relation is this: to represent a relation as a causal relation is to represent it in a way that employs one's innate *cause* representation. The main focus of their discussion is the question, what reason we have for thinking that infants do represent events of various kinds in causal terms: Do the experimental data support the claim that infants represent the world in causal terms? Or are the data consistent with the hypothesis that infants represent the world only in some more basic, non-causal way?

The psychological literature that Saxe and Carey bring together does not, then, directly address the question, what it takes for our thinking about some domain to be a form of causal thinking. But it may still deliver insights that are relevant to our question. For one thing, we can infer something about what psychologists take causal representation to involve from what they regard as strong evidence for the presence of such representation. For another thing, if we are convinced by psychologists' case for saying that infants as young as 6 or 7 months old do represent their environment in causal terms, that will imply that the threshold for a representation's counting as a causal representation is relatively low. That in turn will make it easier to show that the causal theorist is right to say that our ordinary, pre-theoretical thought about vision represents seeing in causal terms.

Saxe and Carey argue that the studies they review do indeed 'suggest that young infants (by 6–7 months of age) perceive and interpret' events of various kinds causally (Saxe and Carey 2006, 162). What evidence do those studies provide?

There are simple situations that adults reliably perceive in causal terms: e.g. when adults are shown a scene in which an object, A, approaches and makes contact with another object, B, and then B immediately moves off, they reliably perceive this as A's causing B to move—as A's 'launching' B. Other similar situations are not perceived by adults as involving causality: e.g. if A approaches B but stops before it makes contact, whereupon B starts moving, we do not see A as launching B; and similarly in cases where A does come into contact with B but there is a short delay before B starts moving. Taking sets of cases like these, experimentalists then ask whether infants reliably distinguish between the kinds of events that adults perceive as launching events and the kinds of events that adults do not perceive as launching events. If infants do make such a distinction, that is taken as evidence that, like adults, they perceive the relation as causal in the first kind of case but not the second.

However, as Saxe and Carey observe, the fact that infants make such a distinction is not by itself conclusive evidence. For infants might perceive the two kinds of case differently without the difference in the contents of their perceptions being a *causal* difference. 'The challenge for researchers remains to show that infants perceive these events in terms of *caused* motion (rather than merely predicted motion)' (Saxe and Carey 2006, 151). They argue, however, that the hypothesis that infants do indeed perceive such events in causal terms is strongly supported when we take account of further evidence. I shall mention two of the kinds of evidence Saxe and Carey cite.

First, 'infants categorize different spatiotemporal patterns together on the basis of whether they specify a causal interaction or not' (Saxe and Carey 2006, 151). That is to say, infants distinguish events that adults perceive as launching events from events that adults perceive non-causally; but they do not distinguish amongst the different kinds of events that adults perceive non-causally (those where A stops before it hits B; and those where A hits B but there is a delay before B starts moving).[13] That, it is said, shows that the difference between causal and non-causal cases is in itself a salient difference for infants. And that in turn, say Saxe and Carey, is evidence that they are representing the causal cases in terms of causality.

Second, a range of experiments show that infants have a 'systematic and pervasive sensitivity to the dispositional causal status of the entities involved in the interactions' they observe (Saxe and Carey 2006, 162). That is to say, their expectations about the behaviour of objects involved in events of various kinds—including the kinds of launching events described above—are sensitive not just to the objects' spatiotemporal properties, and not just to physical properties such as size and weight, but also to the kinds of objects they are. For instance, if A and B are inanimate objects, infants are surprised by scenes in which A moves towards B, stops without hitting B, and B then starts moving. But if B is a person, infants are unsurprised by that sequence of events. The obvious explanation is that infants are sensitive to the fact that people but not inanimate objects have the capacity to move themselves.[14] The fact that infants' expectations are sensitive in quite subtle ways to the effects of combining a range of causally relevant properties, argue Saxe and Carey, provides further evidence that infants have representations with causal content. This sensitivity, they write:

bolsters our interpretation that infants are reasoning causally—they are reasoning about the causes of motion of entities, and consider that the motion of dispositionally inert objects must be caused by contact with a moving entity, and that dispositional agents are better candidate causes of motion than are dispositionally inert objects. (Saxe and Carey 2006, 162)

The studies that Saxe and Carey describe are certainly suggestive. But I want to register a note of caution; do the data Saxe and Carey cite really demonstrate that young infants represent the world in causal terms?

The studies Saxe and Carey discuss do show that infants are sensitive to more than just constant conjunction: for infants distinguish constant conjunctions that adults represent in causal terms from non-causal conjunctions. And they show that the expectations infants form are sensitive to the interactions of a range of causal factors, in a fairly complex and subtle way. But does that give us compelling reason to think that infants represent those factors as causal factors? Could not an infant form all the

---

[13] Saxe and Carey cite Oakes and Cohen 1990.
[14] See Spelke, Phillips, and Woodward 1995.

expectations that Saxe and Carey describe, and be sensitive to all the features they mention, without yet representing these interactions as causal interactions? Carey warns elsewhere against what she calls the 'fallacy of theory-laden attribution'.[15] She says, for example, that it is a fallacy to infer from the fact that pre-school children distinguish animals from other things that they have the concept *animal*. But is it not equally fallacious to infer, from the fact that infants distinguish causal relations from non-causal ones, that they have the concept *cause*? I raise this point not as a serious argument against Saxe and Carey's view but as a challenge to be answered—and as a request for more discussion and more justification. Without a fuller account of what it takes for a representation to be a causal representation, my suspicion is that they set the standards for causal representation too low.

Suppose, however, that we accept Saxe and Carey's argument for the conclusion that infants as young as 6 or 7 months old represent the behaviour of animate and inanimate objects in causal terms. What if anything would that suggest about the issue we have been discussing: whether our ordinary thought about vision is a form of causal thinking? Saxe and Carey do not address that issue. But their position, applied to the case of vision, would undercut the non-causal view. The non-causalist holds that our ordinary thought about vision involves the mastery of enabling and defeating conditions. She accepts that these conditions are in fact causal conditions; conditions for the causal production or prevention of an effect. But, she says, one can grasp and manipulate those conditions without thinking of them as causal conditions. So our ordinary thought about vision is not essentially causal. If we adopt Saxe and Carey's approach, however, that position seems untenable. The non-causalist agrees that we reliably classify instances as cases of seeing or not seeing; and she agrees that, in doing so, we are sensitive to the interactions of a varied and complex range of causal factors. On Saxe and Carey's approach, however, that in itself is compelling evidence that our ordinary thought involves representations with causal content—that it is a form of causal reasoning. To defend her position, therefore, the non-causalist needs to set out and justify a different and more demanding standard of what it takes for a representation to be a causal representation.

My own view, as I have said, is that Saxe and Carey do set the standard for causal representation too low. But, as I argued in section 2, even when we adopt a higher standard of what is involved in causal thinking, it remains the case that our ordinary thinking about vision is a form of causal thinking.

References

Carey, Susan (1995) 'On the Origin of Causal Understanding', in Sperber, Premack, and Premack 1995.

---

[15] Carey 1995, 279–80.

Child, William (1992) 'Vision and Experience: The Causal Theory and the Disjunctive Conception', *Philosophical Quarterly*, 42, 297–316.

Child, William (1994) *Causality, Interpretation, and the Mind*, Oxford: Oxford University Press.

Grice, H. P. (1961) 'The Causal Theory of Perception', *Proceedings of the Aristotelian Society, Supplementary Volume*, 35, 121–68.

Leslie, A. (1982) 'The Perception of Causality in Infants', *Perception*, 11, 173–86.

Leslie, A. and Keeble, S. (1987) 'Do six-month-old infants perceive causality?', *Cognition*, 25, 265-88.

Michotte, A. E. (1963) *The Perception of Causality*, transl. T. R. Miles & E. Miles, London: Methuen.

Oakes, L. and Cohen, L. (1990) 'Infant Perception of a Causal Event', *Cognitive Development*, 5, 193–207.

Saxe, R. and Carey, S. (2006) 'The Perception of Causality in Infancy', *Acta Psychologica*, 123, 144–65.

Snowdon, Paul (1981) 'Perception, Vision and Causation', *Proceedings of the Aristotelian Society*, 81, 175–92.

Snowdon, Paul (1990) 'The Objects of Perceptual Experience', *Proceedings of the Aristotelian Society, Supplementary Volume*, 64, 121–50.

Spelke, E., Phillips, A., and Woodward, A. (1995), 'Infants' Knowledge of Object Motion and Human Action', in Sperber, Premack, and Premack 1995.

Sperber, D., Premack, D., and Premack, A. (1995) *Causal Cognition: A Multidisciplinary Debate*, Oxford: Oxford University Press.

Steward, Helen (2011) 'Perception and the Ontology of Causation', in J. Roessler, H. Lerman and N. Eilan (eds) *Perception, Causation, and Objectivity*, Oxford: Oxford University Press.

Strawson, P. F. (1974) 'Causation in Perception', in his *Freedom and Resentment*, London: Methuen.

Strawson, P. F. (1979) 'Perception and its Objects', in G. F. Macdonald (ed.) *Perception and Identity*, London: Macmillan.

Strawson, P. F. (1985) 'Causation and Explanation', in B. Vermazen and M. Hintikka (eds) *Essays on Davidson: Actions and Events*, Oxford: Oxford University Press.

Williamson, Timothy (2007) *The Philosophy of Philosophy*, Oxford: Blackwell.

12

The Perception of Absence, Space, and Time

Matthew Soteriou★

As Ryle (1949) noted, certain of our verbs of perception, such as 'see', 'hear', 'detect', 'discriminate', and others, are generally used to record perceptual success. Not all perceptual experiences are to be counted as cases of perceptual success. In discussion of what is distinctive of those that are, it is often suggested that there is a causal requirement on perceptual success: the subject's perceptual experience must causally depend, in some appropriate way, on what is perceived. Discussion of this idea usually focuses on our perception of objects and their features. Here I want to consider what we should make of the idea when applied to the claim that there are respects in which we can perceive absence, space, and time.

In the first section of this chapter I compare the suggestion that there is a causal requirement on perceptual success with the suggestion that there is also a causal requirement on episodic recollection. The aim is to bring out a distinctive way in which the causal requirement might be thought to apply in the case of perception, as opposed to episodic recollection, by highlighting a distinctive respect in which successful perception is passive to its objects. I then consider how these causal considerations might be thought to apply in certain putative cases of the perception of absence—in particular, in putative cases of hearing silence and seeing darkness. In sections 2 to 4 I argue that the key to providing the right account of the respect in which we can perceive silence and darkness lies in providing the right account of the respect in which we can have conscious perceptual contact with intervals of time and regions of space within which objects can potentially be perceived. In the account I propose, a significant explanatory role is assigned to comparatively invariant structural features of our conscious perceptual experience of regions of space and intervals of time. In section 5, I consider how the explanatory role assigned to these structural features

★ For very helpful discussion of these issues I am grateful to Bill Brewer, Steve Butterfill, Tom Crowther, Naomi Eilan, Christoph Hoerl, Hemdat Lerman, Guy Longworth, Ian Phillips, and Johannes Roessler. I should also like to thank an anonymous referee for helpful comments on an earlier draft of this paper.

might affect our view of the causal requirements on perceptual success. Finally, in section 6, I consider some of the differences between the ways in which our conscious perceptual awareness of space and time are structured, and I suggest ways in which these differences may be relevant to some of our different intuitions about space and time themselves.

1

A common assumption in philosophical discussions of perception is that our perceptual experiences are part of the natural causal order, and thereby subject to broadly physical and psychological causes. Following M. G. F. Martin I shall call this view 'experiential naturalism'.[1] A further assumption that is often made is that whether a perceptual experience counts as successful perception crucially depends on its causal pedigree. In particular, the suggestion is that in order to successfully perceive the world the subject's experience must causally depend, in some appropriate way, on what is perceived.[2] There are various considerations one might appeal to in support of the claim that there is a causal requirement on perceptual success. For example, one might think it part and parcel of the idea that perception is a receptive faculty that provides us with a source of knowledge of contingent truths about the mind-independent world. The thought here being that our perceptual sensitivity to contingently existing, and placed, items and features in our environment provides us with a central source of knowledge about them, and the aspects of our environment we are perceptually sensitive to can only be those that our perceptual systems are causally sensitive to. One might also think that the appropriate causal dependence of perceptual experience on what is perceived plays a crucial role in fixing for us which particular individuals are perceived on any given occasion. The idea here is that when we perceive our environment we stand in a distinctive epistemic relation to particular individuals in our environment, one which allows us to think about those individuals demonstratively, and the fact that we stand in this perceptual relation to those particular individuals, rather than any others, is determined, at least in part, by the fact that the perceptual experience we undergo causally depends on those particular individuals, rather than any others.

Similar considerations are sometimes invoked in discussions of episodic recollection—i.e. the perceptual recollection of particular past events we have witnessed or

---

[1] As M. G. F. Martin expresses the view, 'Our sense experiences, like other events or states within the natural world, are subject to the causal order, and in this case are thereby subject just to broadly physical causes (i.e. including neuro-physiological causes and conditions) and psychological causes (if these are disjoint from physical causes)' (2004, p. 39).

[2] For agenda-setting arguments for the view, see Grice 1961, Pears 1976, and Strawson 1974. One issue I will not be engaging with here is the question of how we ought to understand the status of the claim that there is this causal requirement for perceptual success—in particular, whether or not it is right to claim that it is part of our ordinary, common sense concept of perception. For criticism of standard arguments for the claim that it is, see Snowdon 1980–81, 1990, and 1998. For a response to Snowdon, see Child 1992 and 1994.

performed.[3] A common background assumption is that an analogue of experiential naturalism applies: episodes of recollecting past events are, like other occurrences, part of the natural causal order, and subject to broadly physical and psychological causes. Our talk of a subject 'recollecting' or 'remembering' some past event records success, as does our talk of a subject seeing or hearing something. And, as in the case of perception, it is often assumed that a requirement on such success centres on the causal pedigree of the episode of recollection—the episode of recollection must causally depend, in some appropriate way, on the event recollected, otherwise the episode will be a merely apparent, but not genuine, case of recollection. Again, a consideration one might appeal to in support of the assumption is the idea that when we episodically recollect a particular past event, we stand in a distinctive epistemic relation to the items recollected—one that enables a distinctive form of demonstrative thought about those items. And the fact that we stand in this distinctive epistemic relation to those particular items, rather than any others, when we recollect them is determined, in part, by the fact that the episode of recollection causally depends on those particular items, rather than any others.

However, even if one is sympathetic to the general line of thought just sketched there is reason to think that despite the similarities between perception and episodic recollection, there are significant differences between the cases that need to be reflected in the way these causal considerations apply. It is these differences that I want to focus on now. I shall be suggesting that what lies behind these differences is a respect in which episodic recollection does not share the passivity and receptivity of perception.

A familiar strategy of arguing for the causal requirement for successful perception is to exploit the background assumption of experiential naturalism and consider the circumstances under which it might be possible, in principle, to induce in a subject a hallucinatory experience. A suggestion that is sometimes made is that it may be possible in principle for a neuroscientist to induce in a subject a hallucination, through suitable stimulation of the subject's sensory cortices, and possible manipulation of the subject's psychological condition, despite the fact that the experience induced matches the scene before the subject—i.e. despite the fact that the scene before the subject really does contain the sorts of objects and features his perceptual experience suggests.[4] What we are invited to speculate here is that the neuroscientist's direct causal intervention on the subject's perceptual system prevents the sort of causal dependence of the subject's perceptual experience on the scene before him that is required for perceptual success. This thought experiment is supposed to support the idea that the occurrence of a perceptual experience that matches the subject's environment is not in itself sufficient for perception of the environment, and that the appropriate causal dependence of the subject's perceptual experience on the items perceived is the further necessary condition required.

---

[3] See C. B. Martin and Deutscher 1966.   [4] See Grice 1966.

Let us now compare our intuitions about the sorts of circumstances under which it might be possible for a neuroscientist to induce in a subject a merely apparent, but not genuine, episode of recollection of a past event. Here, I suggest, it is far from clear what would be required in order to induce in the subject a merely apparent, but not genuine, episode of recollecting a past event, if the sort of event in question is one that the subject has in the past perceived. The problem here is that in such circumstances it is not clear that the neuroscientist's causal intervention on the subject would not have the effect of inducing in the subject a genuine recollection of some previously witnessed event. Of course it may be possible, in principle, to induce in a subject a merely apparent, but not genuine, recollection of a past event that the subject has never perceived, but once a subject has perceived an event of a given kind, what kind of manipulation of the subject's brain might induce a merely apparent, but not genuine, recollection of that event? This, I suggest, is something our intuitions do not speak to directly.

In the case of the thought experiment concerned with perception, our intuition is supposed to be that the neuroscientist's causal intervention on the subject will be sufficient to sever the sort of causal connection between the environment and the subject's perceptual experience that is required for the subject to perceive it. However, in the case of episodic recollection, it is not clear that the neuroscientist's causal intervention on the subject will be sufficient to sever the kind of causal connection between the episode of apparent recollection and the past perceived event that may be required for the subject to recollect it. Why is this?

One thing to say here is that some of the temporal considerations that distinguish perception and episodic recollection are relevant to differences in the ways these causal considerations apply. In the case of episodic recollection the putative causal connection between the past event and the later episode of recollecting it is not generally thought to be of special significance when it comes to accounting for the temporal location of the episode of recollection (except in the general sense that the episode of apparent recollection can only be a genuine case of recollection if it occurs some time after the event recollected). While it may be tempting to think that some kind of causal connection between a past event and the episode of recollecting it must play some role in determining that it is that particular past event that is recollected, rather than any other, we do not tend to think that this putative causal connection between the episode of recollecting and the past event recollected need play a significant role when it comes to explaining why the episode of recollecting occurs *when* it occurs. That is to say, there is no reason to think that an explanation of the particular temporal location of an episode of recollection should appeal to the temporal location of the event recollected. There might be any number of different explanations that could be offered as to why a particular episode of apparent recollection occurred when it occurred that are consistent with that episode being a genuine case of recollection— including an explanation that appeals to the fact that the subject was caused to recollect the event on that particular occasion as a result of a neuroscientist's intervention. In this respect the case of perception is somewhat different. In the case of perception, the causal connection between the object perceived and the perception of it *is* usually thought to be of special significance when it comes to accounting for the temporal location of the perception.

What lies behind this difference between perception and episodic recollection is a respect in which episodic recollection does not share the passivity of perception. There can of course be an active element to perceptual success. For example, one can choose what to look at and when to look at it, and one can choose to continue to actively scrutinise some object. But still, the success of such agential perceptual activity depends upon the occurrence of passive perceptual events whose inception and duration depend upon the object perceived. The same is not true of episodic recollection. When one tries to recollect some past event, and one mentally reaches for some patch of the past, that past episode cannot initiate and causally sustain some current episode of recollecting what was there. In the case of perception, in contrast to episodic recollection, there is a sense in which the temporal location of the mental episode involved is passive with respect to the temporal location of its object.

This is connected with a respect in which the phenomenology of episode recollection and perception are different. Discussions of the conscious character of perceptual experience often appeal to its 'transparency'. The idea is sometimes expressed in terms of the claim that introspection of one's perceptual experience reveals *only* the objects, qualities, and relations one is apparently perceptually aware of in having that experience. Perceptual experience is 'transparent' or 'diaphanous' to the objects of perception. A weaker version of the claim is that when one attempts to attend introspectively to what it is like for one to be having a perceptual experience it seems to one as though one can only do so through attending to the sorts of objects, qualities, and relations one is apparently perceptually aware of in having the experience. It does not seem as though one can focus solely on the conscious character of one's experience without attending to the nature of the objects of apparent perceptual awareness—the objects that one's experience is an experience of.

A further claim we might add here is that the temporal location of one's perceptual experience seems to one to be transparent to the temporal location of whatever it is that one is aware of in having that experience. Introspectively, it does not seem to one as though one can mark out the temporal location of one's perceptual experience as distinct from the temporal location of whatever it is that one is perceptually aware of. Moreover, it seems to one as though the temporal location of one's perceptual experience depends on, and is determined by, the temporal location of whatever it is that one's experience is an experience of, so there's a respect in which the temporal location of one's perception seems to one to be passive with respect to the temporal location of its object.

In this, perception is quite unlike episodic recollection. Introspectively, it does not seem to one as though the temporal location of one's act of recollection is, in the same way, transparent to the temporal location of the event is one is recollecting, for one can mark out the temporal location of one's act of recollecting as distinct from the temporal location of whatever it is one is recollecting. Introspectively, an episode of apparent episodic recollection does not strike one as being the kind of event that depends on the current presence of its object.

When one perceives an unfolding occurrence (e.g. the movement of an object across space), it seems to one as though one's perceptual experience has the temporal location and duration of its object, and it seems to one as though the temporal location and duration of each temporal part of one's experience is transparent to the temporal location and duration of each temporal part of the unfolding occurrence one seems to perceive. In this respect perception is also quite unlike a present-tensed conscious act of judging—e.g. an act of judging that 'The hurricane is now passing over Haiti'. In the case of the judgement, it does not seem to one as though the duration of one's act of judging depends on, and is determined by, the duration of whatever it is that one's judgement represents.

There is a special significance to the way in which the temporal location of a perception is determined by the temporal location of its object, and this is not true of episodic recollection. This is connected with a distinctive respect in which perception is passive and not subject to the will. Even when successful perception involves agential perceptual activity, such as looking, watching, etc., one's successful perception depends upon the occurrence of perceptual experiences whose inception and course are determined by the temporal location of the object perceived. One might think, then, that there is a distinctive sense in which such perceptual occurrences are to be thought of as the passive effects on us of the objects we perceive. This in turn might invite the following causal proposal: Any successful perception of the world depends upon the occurrence of perceptual experiences whose inception and duration are causally determined by the temporal locations of events involving the items perceived.

However, what should we say about the applicability of such causal considerations in the following kind of case? You wake up in a dark, silent room. There is nothing wrong with your senses of sight and hearing, and you notice that the room is dark and silent. Is this something you discover by perceptual means? Do we have here a case of perceptual success? In particular, when you wake up, do you hear the silence and see the darkness that surrounds you? If so, how does this affect the applicability of the idea that any successful perception of the world depends upon the occurrence of perceptual experiences whose inception and duration are causally determined by the temporal locations of events involving the items perceived?

In the next section I shall primarily be focusing on the question of what should be said about putative cases of hearing silence. Before doing so I make some brief general remarks on the perception of absence.

2

Roy Sorensen (2008) has recently defended the claim that we perceive absences and that the fact that we perceive absences is perfectly compatible with a causal requirement on perceptual success. Sorensen considers the proposal that some of the things we ordinarily take ourselves to perceive do not seem to cause our perceptual experiences of them. For example, the black letters on this page are seen in virtue of the light they absorb, and not the light they reflect. So one might be tempted to say that you see the black letters on this page in virtue of the *absence* of a causal connection between the letters and your experience of them. The shadows that objects cast are also among the things we ordinarily take ourselves to perceive. Shadows are absences of light, and since absences do not transmit energy, they cannot owe their visibility to any positive occurrence on their part. So again, one might be tempted to claim that the successful perception of a shadow cannot be caused by the perceived shadow.

In response, Sorensen claims that some absences can cause, and that this is supported by our ordinary talk of prevention and omission.

Many commentators on causation reluctantly concede that submarine crews die from lack of oxygen and that astronauts can be killed by empty space. Physicists have long marveled at the power of vacuums to explain how thermos bottles insulate...Road engineers explain traffic accidents by appealing to shadows. For instance, the Blue Ridge Mountains shade patches of nearby roads thereby allowing the formation of 'black ice'. Since this thin layer of refrozen snow looks like damp blacktop, motorists continue at a high speed and lose control. The shadows of the Blue Ridge Mountain are deadly. (2007, p. 28)

Sorensen (2008) notes that as there are many more ways for something not to happen than to happen, it is often simpler to focus on the positive, and he remarks that as we are "metaphysically uncomfortable" with absences, positive substitutes are usually offered (p. 217). However, he defends a line on absences taken by C. B. Martin (1996) and Kukso (2006), who hold that absences are objective, causally relevant and perceptible, and have locations in space and time. According to C. B. Martin, absences are non-abstract, localized spatio-temporal states of the world, which are causally relevant.

In discussions of whether absences can cause, a distinction is sometimes drawn between the 'causally relevant' and the 'causally operative'. According to Molnar (2000), operative causality is a natural, mind-independent relation that relates naturally occurring entities. He claims that absences are not causally operative. It is causally operative entities that add 'biff' to the world, and absences do not. Kukso (2006) concedes that Molnar is correct to say that absences are not causally operative, but he holds that they are, nonetheless, 'causally relevant'. According to Kukso, if we consider causal relevance in terms of making a difference to the causal order of the universe, an entity's absence has as much causal relevance as the entity's presence, for it is both the existence *and absence* of entities that makes a difference to the causal order of the universe. He argues as follows. The way we determine whether the presence of something is causally relevant is by comparing two situations: one in which the thing is present and the other in which it is not. The difference in the causal order of the universe is a difference *between* the thing's presence and its absence. Since both the presence and the absence are required for there to be a difference, both presence *and* absence are causally relevant.

In defending Martin and Kukso's line on absences and their causal powers, Sorensen (2008) argues that the claim that there is a causal requirement on perceptual success makes 'bold and correct predictions' about what we perceive 'when unencumbered by a metaphysical outlook skewed in favour of positive things' (p. 6). The most profound instance of the perception of absence, he suggests, is hearing silence.

Sorensen argues that one can non-epistemically hear silence. According to Sorensen, hearing silence is not a matter of inferring an absence of sound from one's failure to hear a sound, for one can hear silence while being neutral about whether one is hearing silence—e.g. when wondering whether or not one has gone deaf. He suggests that there can be creatures that hear silence despite their inability to introspect. Just as animals stop and orient to an unexpected sound, they often stop and orient to an unexpected silence. He also suggests that different people's experience of silence can be caused differently—for example, by different local conditions when different people hear silence in different places.

Are we to understand this suggestion in terms of the idea that when one hears silence an auditory perceptual experience occurs whose inception and duration are causally determined by the absence of sound in one's local environment? If so, how is this to be reconciled with the intuitive thought that in such a case there are no causally operative events involving an object of experience, which could have the effect of producing and sustaining one's auditory experience of it?

Here it might be thought that a defender of the claim that we can hear silence should resist the initial assumption that an auditory perceptual experience actually occurs when one hears silence. It is not tempting to say that no visual experience occurs when one sees shadows, or the black letters on a page, or holes. For example, when we see shadows it is clear that a positive visual occurrence is involved, for when we see shadows we also see positivities—objects in our environment and their features. Furthermore, we can cite causally operative events involving these positivities—events that causally affect us—when explaining why a particular perception of a shadow occurs when it occurs, and when explaining what causally sustains our perception of it, for such things are seen in virtue of the contrasts they make with their illuminated environment. However, in the case of hearing silence, it is more open to question whether there really does occur a positive, auditory, experiential event, for it is not clear that one hears *any* positivities when one hears silence.

Sorensen claims that hearing silence is the most negative of perceptions, for when one hears silence 'there is nothing positive being sensed, and no positive sensation representing absence' (2008, p. 272). According to Sorensen, there is no sensation of silence to introspect. You instead introspect the absence of auditory sensation. This observation might lead one to reason as follows: If hearing silence does not involve the auditory perception of any positivities, then we cannot cite any causally operative events involving what is heard when it comes to explaining why an auditory experience of silence occurs when it occurs, and when explaining what causally sustains that auditory experience. So the appropriate response should be to deny that a positive auditory experiential event occurs when a subject perceives silence. We should rather say that a subject can be said to hear silence when the subject does not have any auditory experiences despite the fact that he is perceptually sensitive to sounds. When it comes to explaining why a subject perceives silence when he does, we should be seeking to explain why the subject does not have any auditory experiences at that time despite the fact that he is perceptually sensitive to sounds at that time, and here we can cite the absence of audible events in the subject's surroundings at that time.

However, I think that as it stands, this proposal does not yet provide us with an adequate account of hearing silence, for the following reason. We are reluctant to say that a subject hears the silence that surrounds him when he is asleep, even if it is true that were sounds to occur during that time he would wake up and have auditory experiences of them. Is it possible to refine this proposal about hearing silence in a suitable way by simply adding to it? O'Shaughnessy's account of what is involved in hearing silence might be regarded as just such a modified proposal.

O'Shaughnessy (2000) thinks that no auditory experience occurs when one hears silence. He accepts that there is a distinction to be drawn between hearing silence and simply not hearing anything. However, O'Shaughnessy's account of what is involved in hearing silence is rather different from Sorensen's. O'Shaughnessy thinks that a *cognitive* attitude, with silence figuring in its content, is a necessary condition for hearing silence. On his view hearing silence is logically equivalent to, and identical with, a variety of hearing *that* it is silent. It is a special case of coming to know that it is silent which arises out of an absence of auditory experience: 'Whereas there is both a hearing-of a whistle and a hearing that the whistle sounds, there is only hearing that it is silent. There is no such thing as the hearing-of silence. There is merely the absence of hearing-of anything, occurring in a self-conscious setting which is such that a cognitive experience occurs which refers to the prevailing silence' (2000, p. 333).

Should we accept O'Shaughnessy's proposal and hold, against Sorensen, that a cognitive attitude with silence featuring in its content is a necessary condition for hearing silence? O'Shaughnessy's discussion of hearing silence arises in the context of a discussion of whether negation features in the content of experience. Once one thinks of the issue in such terms, one might think that one can strengthen the case for thinking that (a) no auditory experience actually occurs when one hears silence, and (b) a cognitive attitude with silence featuring in its content is necessary for hearing silence. One might reason as follows. Either we accept that when a subject hears silence, a positive auditory experience occurs with negation featuring in its content (e.g. 'it is not the case that there are sounds'), or we accept that no such event occurs, and hold instead that negation features in the content of a cognitive attitude. Silence is the absence of sound. Our perceptual system is incapable of speaking to the question of whether there is an absence of sound everywhere. It can only speak to the question of whether there is an absence of sound within a certain region. But within which region?

Is this something that our auditory system really specifies? Should we not rather say that one's auditory system simply speaks to the question of whether there are sounds near enough and loud enough for one to hear? And does not this simply amount to the idea that one's auditory system simply speaks to the question of whether one is currently hearing anything? So if a positive auditory experience occurs when one hears silence, with negation featuring in its content, 'hearing' will also need to feature in its content—e.g. 'it is not the case that a sound is heard'. But it is more plausible to hold that no such positive perceptual event occurs, and instead hold that negation and hearing feature in the content of a cognitive attitude. When one hears silence one becomes cognitively aware that one is not hearing anything, and one assumes that this is because there are no sounds near enough and loud enough for one to hear.

I want to suggest that there is reason to be dissatisfied with the conclusion of this line of reasoning, and that this should lead us to question certain assumptions on which the line of reasoning depends.

Although Sorensen claims that there is an absence of auditory *sensation* when one hears silence, he does appear to be committed to the claim that a positive auditory experience occurs when one hears silence. For he suggests that it is possible for one to hallucinate silence. It is difficult for one to make sense of this suggestion without assuming that there is such a thing as a positive auditory occurrence as of silence. Here is Sorensen's example of the veridical hallucination of silence.

Consider a man who experiences auditory hallucinations as he drifts off to sleep. He 'hears' his mother call out his name, then wait for a response, and then call again. The cycle of calls and silence repeats itself eerily. As it turns out, his mother has unexpectedly paid a late-night visit and is indeed calling out in a manner that coincidentally matches the spooky hallucination. The hallucinator is not hearing the calls and silence of his mother. (2008, p. 269)

A significant feature of the example is the fact that the silences are gaps between *positivities*—sounds—that the subject hallucinates. Let us assume that when a subject hears a sequence of sounds with silent gaps between them, the subject has a positive auditory experience of the positivities sensed—i.e. the sounds he hears. Should we also assume that the subject has a positive auditory experience of the silences between the sounds?

If the subject does not have an auditory experience of the silences between the sounds, then arguably the subject does not hear the temporal boundaries of the sounds—i.e. the starting and stopping of the sounds. For the subject will need to experience the silence before a sound starts and after the sound stops in order to hear its stopping and starting. Compare here Smith's discussion of the experience of hearing the tone of a melody begin sounding:

Starting to experience in a certain way does not obviously entail experiencing something of a certain sort starting. I need to have now, as the first note begins to sound, an awareness that just before now I was aware of silence. (2003, p. 88)

On the auditory experience of a series of discrete pips, he writes:

[S]uch pips are presented to us as discrete only in virtue of each one being preceded and followed by a relevant silence. We have to be aware of this silence, this non-sounding, as such if we are to be aware of the discrete sounding pips. And the pips will be perceived as further apart or closer together in time depending on how long these silences are. Perceiving silence is not the absence of any awareness, but is itself an intentional achievement. (2003, p. 88)

O'Shaughnessy claims that 'Real perceiving is invariably of the concrete...It is of phenomenal realities. And thus invariably of what one might call "positivities"' (2000, p. 333). What Smith's remarks highlight is that our perception of the boundaries of such positivities may in certain circumstances require the perception of absence as well—the perception of when and where things are not.

C. B. Martin claims that absences are needed as much as entities for the edges, limits or bounds of entities. For example, he writes:

The concept of an edge is the concept of a limit of where something is and where something isn't...The reference of the referring term 'world' is divided into presences whose limits are drawn by absences. (1996, p. 60)

This suggests that the experience of absence is not of marginal significance. If the perceptual experience of the boundaries of some positivity is itself a positivity, then that positive perceptual occurrence may necessarily involve the experience of absence as well.

However, this still leaves us with the following question. Should we accept the claim that negation features in the content of such positive perceptual occurrences? In particular, should we accept something like the following picture of the successful perception of silence: due to the absence of causally operative events involving objects of audition, an auditory perceptual experience occurs which has a negative representational content?

In what follows I will be defending the claim that we can accommodate the idea that when we perceive the boundaries of positivities there is a sense in which we perceive absence as well, without having to commit to the claim that such experience has a negative representational content. The key to avoiding the commitment, I shall be suggesting, lies in considering the respect in which we can have conscious perceptual contact with regions of space and intervals of time within which the boundaries of such positivities can be perceived.

In the next section, I shall be discussing what we should say about our visual experience of the regions of space within which we seem to see bounded objects. This will then lead to a discussion of our experience of the intervals of time within which we seem to hear sounds, which in turn will lead to an account of hearing silence. Only then will we be in a position to re-consider the question of how the claim that there is causal requirement on perceptual success might apply in the case of the perception of absence. For intimately bound up with this issue, I shall be suggesting, is the position we take on the causal requirements for our perceptual awareness of the regions of space and intervals of time within which we seem to perceive objects, events, and their features.

3

In work comparing sight and touch, M. G. F. Martin invokes a notion of the 'visual field' that he takes to be a phenomenological feature of visual experience. In articulating the notion he has in mind, Martin writes:

> We can think of normal visual experience as experience not only of objects which are located in some space, but as of a space within which they are located. The space is part of the experience in as much as one is aware of the region as a potential location for objects of vision. (1992, p. 189)
>
> One is aware of the location of visual objects not only relative to other visually experienced objects, but also to other regions of the spatial array—regions where nothing is experienced, but where something potentially could be. (*ibid*. p. 188)

To help clarify the suggestion being made here, consider first the Kantian thought that when looking straight ahead, any region of space in front of you that you are thereby aware of is presented as a sub-region of a region of space that has that sub-region as part. As the relevant spatial region is presented as a *sub*-region of space, it might be said that when you are visually aware of a region of space in front of you there is a sense in which it thereby seems to you as though there are *other* regions of space that are potential locations for objects of vision—'regions where nothing is experienced but where something potentially could be'. Yet these other regions of space—e.g. regions of space behind your head—are not regions of space that you are visually aware of, in the relevant sense. So what more can be said about the way in which you are aware of the region of space in front of you, which is not a way in which you are aware of these other regions of space—e.g. a region of space behind you?

When Martin says that in normal visual perception one is aware of 'regions where nothing is experienced, but where something potentially could be', we should understand this not in terms of the idea of there being an absence of the experience of things, but rather in terms of there being the experience of the absence of things.[5] When looking straight ahead you may be aware of regions of *empty* space—i.e. regions of space that are empty of visible objects. When looking straight ahead you are not aware of a region of space behind your head in that way—i.e. as empty of visible objects.

One might then think that a crucial component of the right characterisation of the way in which we are visually aware of regions of space, when we are aware through vision of the spatial locations of objects, should accommodate the idea that this can involve the visual registration of an absence—one's perception of regions of space as

---

[5] See especially Martin 1999 and Richardson 2009.

empty of visible objects. And it is this that allows us to visually perceive the boundaries of objects, by allowing us to perceive where things are not, as well as where they are. However, I want to suggest that it would be a mistake to think that in order to accommodate this idea we need to assume that visual experience has a negative representational content. The key to avoiding the mistake is to note that the conscious character of a normal visual experience is not *solely* determined by the sorts of objects and events one is apparently aware of in having that experience. For it is also determined, in part, by the way in which one's visual awareness of those objects and events seems to be structured, and we should appeal to these structural features of visual awareness when accounting for the sense in which it seems to one as though one is visually aware of regions of space that are empty of visible objects.

Consider again the idea that when looking straight ahead, any region of space in front of you that you are thereby aware of is presented as a sub-region of a region of space that has that sub-region as part. The region of space in front of you that you are aware of does not strike you as being some object or thing that has boundaries you are visually aware of. There may be a sense in which there are boundaries to be identified in your visual awareness of the region of space in front of you, for it may be said that you are visually aware of something like a cone of physical space in front of you, and we might think of the boundaries of this cone as the boundaries of your visual field. But the boundaries of your visual field do not seem to you to be the boundaries of some thing you are visually aware of that happens to move around with you; and changes in the boundaries of your visual field (e.g. when you half close your eyes, or close one eye) do not seem to you to amount to changes in the boundaries of some thing that you are visually aware of—some thing that you are aware of as changing size and shape.

Rather than thinking of the boundaries of the visual field as boundaries of some thing one is sensing, we should think of the boundaries of the visual field in terms of one's sensory limitations. That there are limits to what can now be sensed that are due to one's sensory limitations, rather than due to the limits of whatever it is that one is now sensing, brings with it the idea that there is more to be sensed beyond those sensory limits, hence the idea that your visual awareness of the region of space in front of you is in some sense an awareness of the region *as* a sub-region of a region of space that has that sub-region as part. That you visually experience a region of space in front of you in this way is an important part of the conscious character of visual experience. The existence of some kind of sensory limitation features as an aspect of the conscious character of the visual experience.

Earlier I distinguished a stronger and weaker version of the claim that the conscious character of perceptual experience is transparent to its objects. According to the stronger version, introspection of one's perceptual experience reveals *only* the objects, qualities, and relations one is apparently perceptually aware of in having the experience. According to the weaker version, when one introspectively attends to what it is like for one to be having a perceptual experience, it seems to one as though one can only do so by attending to the sorts of objects, qualities, and relations one is apparently perceptually aware of in having that experience. The fact that the visual field is a phenomenological feature of visual experience gives us reason to reject the stronger version of the claim. The boundaries of one's visual field are not features of some object one is visually aware of in having a visual experience. One cannot directly attend to them in the way in which one can directly attend to the objects and features that fall within them. But they do nonetheless feature in the conscious character of one's visual experience, and one can become aware of them when attending to the objects that fall within them. For in attending directly to objects of visual awareness, one can reflect on the way in which one's visual awareness of those objects seems to one to be structured.

In saying that an aspect of the conscious character of normal visual experience is to be accounted for by appeal to some structural feature of the experience, I am suggesting that there is an aspect of the conscious character of the experience that can be common to various visual experiences but which is not to be accounted for by appeal to the fact that these experiences are as of the same kinds of objects and features. As these aspects of the conscious character of experience are relatively invariant, and as one cannot directly attend to them in the way in which one can directly attend to the objects one is apparently aware of in having that experience, they go largely unnoticed. However, we can, nonetheless, introspectively reflect on these relatively invariant aspects of the conscious character of visual experience, common to one's conscious visual experience of all sorts of different objects, which are determined by the ways in which one's conscious visual awareness of those objects seems to be structured. The relatively invariant structural feature of the conscious character of visual experience that is of relevance here is that when one has a visual experience of the spatial locations of objects, it seems to one as though one is visually aware of a region of space within which those objects are located, where the boundaries of the relevant region of space are determined by one's sensory limitations, rather than the limits of some thing one is sensing.

Not all modes of conscious awareness have the same structure. For example, the structural feature of normal visual experience that accounts for the existence of its spatial visual field is lacking in the form of bodily awareness involved when one feels a located bodily sensation—e.g. a painful sensation in one's knee. When you have a visual experience, you seem to be aware of objects that fall within a region of space that you are aware of in having that experience, where the bounds of that region of space seem to you to be determined by your sensory limitations, rather than by the limits of some thing you are sensing. In contrast, in the case of the experience of located bodily sensation the boundaries of any spatial region you are aware of, within which things are experienced to be, *do* seem to you to be set by the limits of some *thing* you are sensing that moves around with you (i.e. your body), rather than by your sensory limitations. The fact that the experience of located bodily sensation lacks the structural feature of visual experience that provides visual experience with its spatial sensory field, is connected with the fact that when bodily sensations are felt to be located, it seems to one that one is aware of a region of space within which they are located only in so far as one is aware of some *thing* occupying that region of space. Hence the fact that one does not feel these sensations to be in space but not in a body.[6]

Some of the differences between the conscious character of visual awareness and bodily awareness are to be explained in terms of the different ways in which one's conscious awareness is structured in these different modalities. One such difference is the fact that in the case of normal vision, when one experiences the spatial locations of objects, it seems to one as though one is aware of a region of space within which those objects are located, where the boundaries of the spatial region one is aware of seem to one to be determined by one's sensory limitations, rather than the limits of some thing one is sensing. As the relevant spatial region is experienced as a region whose bounds are determined by one's sensory limitations, there is a sense in which one visually experiences a spatial region, delimited by one's sensory limitations, as a region within which objects must fall if they are to be seen. In consequence there is a sense in which one experiences a spatial region as a region within which objects *can* be seen. This is what accounts for the sense in which, in vision, one can be consciously aware of a region of space as a region within which there are no objects to be seen, but within which objects potentially can be seen.

So the correct explanation of the respect in which we can be consciously aware, in vision, of absence—e.g. of regions of space as empty of visible objects—will sometimes need to appeal to relatively invariant structural features of such conscious awareness. I now want to suggest that a similar story can be told concerning the perception of silence. I shall be suggesting that auditory experience has a temporal sensory field, analogous to the spatial sensory field in vision. When we hear sounds we are consciously aware of intervals of time within which these sounds fall. And the correct explanation of the respect in which we can hear silence—intervals of time as empty of audible sounds—will need to appeal to relatively invariant structural features of such conscious awareness—the way in which such conscious awareness is structured.

4

There are reasons to think that the things we perceive are perceived as filling, occupying, or having some location within, an interval of time, just as the objects we see are generally seen as filling, occupying, or having a location within a region of space. Consider, for example, our experience of events. In certain cases one's introspection of the conscious character of one's experience seems to one to require attending to the occurrence of events that are distinct from the experience itself, and furthermore, in such cases, the occurrences one thereby seems to be attending to seem to one to have temporal extension. In a given case, it may be that it does not seem to one as though one is thereby attending to all of the temporal parts of that occurrence,

---

[6] This discussion follows Martin 1995.

however, it seems to one as though one cannot attend to the occurrence without attending to *some* temporal part of it and, moreover, some temporal part of the occurrence that has temporal extension. If one tries just to attend to an instantaneous temporal part of the occurrence, without attending to a temporal part of the occurrence that has temporal extension, then one will fail. By analogy, in the case of one's experience of the spatial objects one seems to be attending to in introspecting the conscious character of one's experience, it may be that it does not seem to one as though one is attending to all of the spatial parts of the object, however, it seems to one as though one cannot attend to the object without attending to *some* spatial part of the object, and, moreover, some spatial part of the object that has spatial extension.

Instantaneous events may also feature in the conscious character of experience, for example the event of an object starting to move, but when they do, it seems to one as though one cannot attend to them without thereby attending to something that has temporal extension, for example the object moving. By analogy, it seems to one as though one cannot attend to the spatial boundary of an object of experience without thereby attending to some spatial part of the object that has spatial extension.

We can add that your experience of the event of an object starting to move appears to entail both your experience of the object moving and your experience of the object at rest. If you do not experience the object at rest, then you cannot experience it start to move, and if you do not experience the object moving you will not yet have experienced it starting to move. If you experience the instantaneous event of an object starting to move, then your experience of that event must also have been an experience of the object at rest *and* in motion, and so your experience of the instantaneous event requires the experience of something that is not instantaneous—it requires the experience of something occupying an *interval* of time, an interval of time that spans both a time at which the object is at rest and a time at which the object is moving.

We can think of this sort of instantaneous event as marking a temporal boundary of a time-occupying entity—i.e. a temporal boundary of the time-occupying occurrence that is the movement of the object. Similar remarks apply to the instantaneous event that marks the point at which the object comes to rest. We can regard instantaneous events of starting and stopping as marking the temporal boundaries of time-occupying entities. In vision we seem to be aware of such instantaneous events, and hence aware of temporal boundaries of time-occupying entities, through being aware of intervals of time that span these relevant temporal boundaries. We seem to be aware in vision of a temporal interval within which such instantaneous events can occur—an interval of time within which the temporal boundaries of time-occupying entities can be experienced.

There is also reason to think that the temporal interval that we can perceive something as filling, or occupying, is of limited extent—even when we continue to perceive that thing for an indefinite period of time. Sometimes, no matter how carefully we attend to a continuously moving object we fail to perceive the event of it moving, even if we continue to scrutinise it for hours (e.g. the movement of the hour hand of a clock). We may be able to see that it has moved, but we never see it moving. Our finite capacity to perceive the spatial location of an object is insensitive to very slight variations in the object's location, so the movement of an object across a very short distance may be imperceptible to us. A continual series of such imperceptible movements may constitute the movement of the object across a much greater distance, and yet still we may be unable to perceive the object moving across that greater distance, no matter how carefully we continue to scrutinise it, and no matter for how long. This suggests that in certain cases the continual movement of an object may be imperceptible to us because it is too slow. And this in turn can be explained by the idea that the temporal interval that we can perceive something as filling, or occupying, is of limited extent. For over that limited temporal interval the movement of the object may be too slight to be perceived. In which case, we will be unable to perceive any of the temporal parts of the event of the object moving. And if we cannot perceive any of the temporal parts of the event of an object moving, then the motion of the object will be imperceptible to us, no matter how long we continue to observe the object.

So to summarise, we have reason to think that (a) the things we perceive are perceived as filling, occupying, or having some location within, an interval of time, and (b) the temporal interval that we can perceive something as filling, or occupying, is of limited extent.

With this in mind, let us now reconsider what to say about the perception of silence—starting with what we should say about our perception of the silences between sounds that we hear. Earlier I suggested that if a subject does not have an auditory experience of the silences between such sounds, then the subject does not hear the temporal boundaries of the sounds—i.e. the starting and stopping of the sounds. For the subject will need to experience the silence before a sound starts and after the sound stops in order to hear its stopping and starting.[7] Applying the idea that the things we perceive are perceived as filling, occupying, or having a location within, an interval of time, we might say that our auditory experience is not only of sounds that are located in time, but also of a temporal interval within which they are located. The claim that in auditory perception we hear a sound as having a temporal location within an interval of time that we are consciously aware of can accommodate the fact that we can hear the temporal boundaries of a sound—the stopping and starting of the sound. For it can accommodate the idea that one can be consciously aware, in having auditory experience, of the temporal locations of sounds relative to other experienced sounds, and also to other regions of time where no sounds are experienced, but where other sounds potentially could be experienced.

That we are consciously aware, in auditory experience, of intervals of time, of limited extent, within which sounds can be heard, is an invariant feature of the way in which such conscious awareness is structured. In this respect we might say that

---

[7] Consider Sorensen's remark that animals can stop and orient themselves to an unexpected silence. Presumably here they hear the sudden stopping of sounds.

auditory awareness has a temporal sensory field analogous to the spatial sensory field in vision. In accounting for the sense in which we can be consciously aware of silence, we should appeal to this invariant, structural feature of auditory awareness. In the case of auditory perception one can be consciously aware of an interval of time as an interval within which sounds can potentially be heard, even if no sounds can actually be heard to fill that temporal interval, just as in vision one can be consciously aware of a region of space as a region within which objects can potentially be seen, even if no objects can actually be seen to occupy that region. When we hear silence we hear an interval of time as empty of audible sounds, just as in vision we can see regions of space as empty of visible objects.

To summarise, according to the proposal I am recommending, the successful perception of silence does involve a positive perceptual occurrence, and it does not require the acquisition of a cognitive attitude with silence featuring in its content. Furthermore, when one hears silence something positive is experienced—namely an interval of time, of limited extent, within which no sounds are heard. We do not need to commit to the idea that the positive perceptual experience involved has a negative representational content, explicitly representing the fact that there are no sounds to be heard during that interval of time. In explaining the sense in which one can have conscious auditory contact with an interval of time during which no sounds are heard, we should, rather, appeal to relatively invariant structural features of conscious auditory awareness—its possession of a temporal sensory field. In the case of auditory perception, in virtue of its possession of a temporal sensory field, we can have conscious contact with intervals of time, of limited extent, within which sounds can be heard *or potentially heard*. Just as in the case of visual perception, in virtue of its possession of a spatial sensory field, we can have conscious contact with a region of space, of limited extent, within which objects can be seen, *or potentially seen*.

This account accommodates the respect in which hearing silence is not simply a matter of absence by omission—i.e. the fact that hearing silence is not simply a matter of a case in which an absence of auditory experience is to be explained by an absence of sound. It accommodates the fact that one cannot hear silence when asleep, despite the fact that there may be a sense in which one's auditory system is sensitive to sounds in one's environment when one is asleep. In order to hear silence one must have conscious perceptual contact with an interval of time, of limited extent, within which sounds potentially can be heard. One only has this form of conscious perceptual contact with time when awake.[8]

---

[8] When you are awake and you have conscious perceptual contact with a silent interval of time, what makes it appropriate to regard your perceptual experience of that interval of time as an auditory one? There may be reason to think that it is only appropriate to regard the perceptual experience involved as an auditory one if the following counterfactual is true: if sounds were to have occurred during that interval one would have heard them. For instance, I suspect that there are no distinctively auditory phenomenal properties that the experience has that would allow one to differentiate a case in which one is temporarily deaf from a putative case of the occurrence of a hallucinatory experience of silence. This is not to deny that it is possible to

5

In the first section of the paper I tried to identify a distinctive sense in which successful perception is receptive, and passive to its objects. In the case of perception, in contrast to episodic recollection, there is a sense in which the temporal location of the mental episode involved is passive with respect to the temporal location of its object. Some find it intuitive to think that successful perception depends upon the occurrence of perceptual events whose inception and duration depend upon the object perceived. I suggested that one might think, then, that there is a distinctive sense in which such perceptual occurrences are to be thought of as the passive effects on us of the objects we perceive. And that this in turn might invite the following proposal: any successful perception of the world depends upon the occurrence of perceptual experiences whose inception and duration are causally determined by the temporal locations of events involving the items perceived. We are now in a position to consider what to say about the applicability of such causal considerations in a putative case of the perception of absence—when one wakes up in a dark, silent room and perceives the darkness and silence that surrounds one.

I have said that in virtue of its possession of a temporal sensory field, in auditory perception we are aware of intervals of time, of limited extent, within which sounds can be heard, *or potentially heard*—and this is an invariant structural feature of such conscious awareness. Our conscious auditory contact with an interval of time, of limited extent, within which sounds can potentially be heard, does not depend on our actually hearing some sound filling that temporal interval. And so it does not depend on our being causally affected by some sound that falls within that temporal interval. If no sounds are heard to fall within such a temporal interval, then we can hear the silence that fills that limited interval of time.

Analogous remarks apply in the case of vision. In virtue of its possession of a spatial sensory field, in vision our conscious visual contact with a region of space, of limited extent, within which objects can potentially be seen, does not depend on our actually seeing some object occupy that spatial region. And arguably, it does not depend on our seeing light fall within that spatial region either. And so it does not depend on our being causally affected by objects, or light, that fall within that spatial region. If no objects and no light are seen to fall within such a spatial region, we see the darkness that fills that limited region of space.[9]

When one hears silence and sees darkness one has a positive perceptual experience of some positivity.[10] When one hears silence one perceives some positivity—namely an

---

hallucinate silence—e.g. when one hallucinates successive sounds with silent gaps between them. And note that nothing that I have said rules out the possibility of hallucinating darkness. For further discussion of the hallucination of silence see Phillips forthcoming.

[9] For defence of this claim see Sorensen 2008.

[10] I have argued that hearing silence is not simply a matter of absence by omission, and there are similar reasons for thinking that seeing darkness is not simply a matter of absence by omission either. That is, seeing

interval of time, of limited extent, which one hears to be silent. And likewise when one sees darkness one also perceives some positivity—namely a region of space, of limited extent, which one sees to be dark.[11] There remains a sense in which one can only successfully perceive a region of space, or interval of time, if one's perceptual system is causally sensitive to what does and does not fall within it. So when one perceives such absences, the absence perceived is causally relevant to one's experience.[12] However, when one sees darkness, the inception and duration of the experience involved is not determined by the temporal location of causally operative events involving the positivity one perceives, namely the relevant region of space. There is a sense, then, in which the occurrence of the perceptual experience involved is not a matter of one's perceptual system being causally responsive to whether or not there is such a region of space to be aware of.

Similar remarks apply in the case of hearing silence. Suppose that you woke up and heard silence. When you woke up, you had conscious auditory contact with an interval of time, of limited extent, within which sounds potentially could be heard. You had such conscious contact with that interval of time because you woke up when you did. But there would be something odd in the suggestion that that interval of time caused you to wake up and have conscious auditory contact with it. There are of course causal explanations to be offered as to why a subject might be roused into the state of wakeful consciousness when he is, as there are causal explanations to be offered as to what might sustain the 'ticking over' of such a state of wakeful consciousness. And such causal explanations will appeal to the occurrence of events that fall within the intervals of time we are consciously aware of when awake. But when one wakes up, and one's state of wakeful consciousness is sustained by the occurrence of such events, it does not seem

---

darkness is not simply a matter of a case in which an absence of visual experience is to be explained by the fact that there is an absence of suitably placed illuminated items in the environment of the perceiver. Consider a subject who can only sleep with his eyes open in a dark room. If there were illuminated items suitably placed in the environment of the perceiver, then he would wake up and perceive them. In this case we would not say that the subject could see the darkness surrounding him when he was asleep.

[11] Sorensen (2008) writes, 'There is a reliable connection between each portion of one's visual field being black and there being an absence of light in the corresponding region of the environment' (pp. 257–8). 'If the universe goes dark the observer sees the darkness of the universe. He does not see all of the darkness because his range of vision is limited. The limit is not imposed by an obstruction. The observer has limited acuity, like a man amid the vast expanse of the ocean' (p. 263).

[12] An anonymous referee suggested that it might be possible for there to be a subject who is able to hear silence despite the fact that that subject cannot hear sounds because of the enormous fragility of his auditory system. My intuition is that if the subject does not have an auditory system that enables him to hear sounds— and so if he does not have an auditory system that can register any difference between sounds and silence— then the subject is deaf and incapable of hearing silence. Another suggestion made by the same referee is that a subject might hear silence in a vacuum in which no sounds can be heard. I agree that a subject might hear silence in a vacuum. I also think it is true that if the subject were to hear sounds during that interval of time he would not be in a vacuum. But this I take to be consistent with the claim that when hearing the silence in a vacuum the subject has conscious auditory contact with an interval of time within which sounds could potentially be heard.

right to think of this as a matter of one's perceptual system being causally responsive to whether or not a temporal interval is present.

There is a sense, then, in which one's perceptual system is not causally sensitive to certain ubiquitous, invariant aspects of our environments—the presence of intervals of time and regions of space. But, it nonetheless represents them, in so far as it makes presuppositions about them in representing the contingent aspects of the environment to which it is causally sensitive. For our conscious awareness of these invariant, ubiquitous aspects of our environment is due to the invariant structural features that condition our conscious awareness of the contingencies to which our perceptual systems are causally sensitive.

Much of what is being proposed here echoes some remarks that Kant (1998) makes in the metaphysical expositions of space and time in the Transcendental Aesthetic, where Kant marks a distinction between the 'matter' and 'form' of appearances, and argues that space and time are 'pure forms of sensible intuition'. I do not propose to enter into any detailed comparison with Kant's views here, nor will I be discussing the question of the legitimacy of the conclusions that Kant draws about the status of space and time. However, I do want to close by briefly touching upon one aspect of Kant's account—that aspect of the Kantian account that I alluded to in the discussion of the spatial sensory field in vision. There I suggested that in vision, any region of space we perceive is perceived as a sub-region of a region of space that has that sub-region as part. I suggested that in explaining this aspect of the phenomenology of visual experience we should appeal to certain structural features of conscious visual experience. Kant assigns a similar explanatory role to the forms of intuition in his suggestion that space and time are given to us in experience as unitary and unbounded. In the final section of the paper I shall be suggesting that there are some significant differences between the way in which we experience space as unitary and unbounded and the way in which we experience time as unitary and unbounded. There are some significant phenomenological differences between the cases that are reflected in differences in the ways our conscious spatial awareness and our conscious temporal awareness seem to us to be structured. These differences, I shall be suggesting, are relevant to differences in some of our intuitions concerning space and time themselves.

6

Let us return to the suggestion that there is a respect in which in vision, any region of space you are aware of is presented as a sub-region of a region of space that has that sub-region as part. I suggested that when you are visually aware of a region of space in front of you, that region of space does not strike you as being some object or thing that has boundaries that you are aware of. I suggested that there is, nonetheless, a sense in which there are boundaries to be identified in your visual awareness of that region of space. It seems to you as though you are aware of something like a cone of space. We can think of the boundaries of this cone as the boundaries of the spatial sensory field of vision.

I suggested that as the boundaries of this spatial sensory field do not seem to you to be the boundaries of some thing that you are visually aware of, we should think of these boundaries in terms of your sensory limitations. In vision, the region of space in front of you is experienced as a region whose bounds are determined, or delimited, by your sensory limitations. That there are limits to what can be sensed that are due to one's sensory limitations, rather than due to the limits of whatever it is that one is sensing, brings with it the idea that there is more to be sensed beyond those sensory limitations (i.e. other regions of space, even if there are no objects to be perceived as falling within those other regions of space). Hence the idea that there is a sense in which your visual awareness of the region of space in front of you is an awareness of the region as a sub-region of space.

The boundaries of one's visual field do not seem to one to be features of some object that one is visually aware of, but they do nonetheless feature in the conscious character of one's visual experience. I suggested that although one cannot directly attend to them in the way in which one can directly attend to the objects and features that fall within them, one can become aware of them when attending to the objects that fall within them, through reflecting on the way on which one's conscious awareness of those objects seems to one to be structured. Because one's conscious visual experience has such invariant structural features, implicit in the phenomenology of visual experience is the idea that whatever region of space you visually experience will be experienced as a sub-region of a region of space that has that sub-region as part. Arguably, as this region of space is experienced as the sub-region of a region of space that you are not visually aware of, also implicit in the phenomenology of visual experience is the notion that the relevant sub-region of space is independent of your awareness of it. (Of course, even if such notions are implicit in the phenomenology of experience, what it may take to grasp them in thought may be a further matter.)

Earlier I offered reasons for thinking that conscious perceptual awareness has a temporal sensory field analogous to the spatial sensory field in vision. There are reasons to think that the things we perceive are perceived as filling, occupying, or having some location within, an interval of time, and there are reasons to think that the temporal interval that we can perceive something as filling, or occupying, is of limited extent. I suggested that we understand this aspect of the conscious character of conscious perceptual experience in terms of an invariant structural feature of conscious perceptual awareness. Up until now I have been treating the spatial and temporal cases as analogous. However, there are some significant disanalogies between the cases that are worth noting.

In characterising Kant's view of the way in which we experience space as unbounded, Melnick (1973) writes: 'We do not perceive spatial regions…that are limitless or without bounds. Rather, we perceive space under the pre-conception (or better, under the "pre-intuition") that the bounded spatial extents we do perceive are parts of a limitless or unbounded space' (p. 11). According to Kant we arrive at the notion of such bounded sub-regions of space through the 'introduction of limitations' to the all-embracing space. I have argued that in the case of visual awareness these limitations are manifest in the conscious character of experience, and, moreover, that they are presented to one as one's own sensory limitations. However, it is not clear that analogous remarks apply when it comes to our conscious awareness of the intervals of time, of limited extent, within which we seem to perceive objects and events.

In the case of spatial visual awareness one can say something, at least very roughly, about the extent and shape of the region of space (delimited by one's sensory limitations) that one is visually aware of. One has the impression that it remains relatively fixed over time, and so one has the impression that one can take one's time in attending to it. One can also notice that it seems to shrink when one closes an eye. Our conscious perceptual awareness of time is somewhat different.

Firstly, there does not appear to be any temporal equivalent of the act of closing of one eye that one can perform which makes a discernable difference to the extent of the temporal interval one is consciously aware of. Secondly, and more importantly, when we are consciously aware of an interval of time, of limited extent, within which we seem to perceive objects and events, it does not seem to us as though we are aware of that interval of time from a point in time that is distinct from it—e.g. from a point in time that falls within that interval of time. This is something I remarked upon when I suggested that the temporal location and duration of one's perceptual experience seems to one to be transparent to the temporal location and duration of the objects of perception.

Introspectively, it does not seem to one as though one can mark out one's own temporal location as distinct from the temporal location of whatever it is that one is perceptually aware of. It does not seem to one as though one is perceptually aware of an entity occupying some temporal location that is distinct from the temporal location *from* which one is perceptually aware of it. Since the temporal location and duration of perceptual awareness seems to one to be transparent to the temporal location and duration of what one perceives, the temporal phenomenology is that of being aware of an interval of time over that interval of time. In consequence, there is a sense in which one's perceptual access to an interval of time does not seem to one to be perspectival— for it does not seem to one as though one has perceptual point of view on an interval of time from a temporal location that is distinct from it. As the phenomenology of conscious temporal awareness lacks this perspectival aspect, it does not seem to one as though one can identify, in conscious experience, a perceptual point of view on an interval of time—a perceptual point of view with manifest boundaries that one can discern, and which seem to be delimited by one's sensory limitations.

It remains true that there are reasons to think that we are perceptually aware of intervals of time, of limited extent, within which objects and events are perceived. But the extent of the temporal interval one is aware of does not seem to one to be determined by one's sensory limitations. In this respect, one's conscious perceptual experience of limited temporal intervals is quite unlike one's visual experience of bounded regions of space.[13] This difference in the phenomenology of temporal and spatial perceptual awareness might have some role to play in explaining some of the ways in which our intuitions about time can differ from our intuitions about space. For example, while it is intuitive to think that the fact that one cannot see a larger region of space from one's spatial location is something that is to be explained by one's sensory limitations, it is less intuitive to think that the fact that one cannot hear the whole one hour symphony from one's temporal location is something that is to be explained by one's sensory limitations.

There are further consequences to note. The phenomenological fact that it does not seem to one as though the extent of the temporal interval that one can have perceptual access to is something that is determined by one's sensory limitations might make intuitive the thought that the extent of the temporal interval that one can have perceptual access to is something that is determined by facts about that temporal interval that are independent of one's sensory limitations. Whether entities are perceptually accessible to one depends in part on whether those entities fall within an interval of time that one is perceptually aware of. The phenomenological fact that it does not seem to one as though one's sensory limitations determine whether entities fall within an interval of time that one is perceptually aware of might make intuitive the thought that whether entities are perceptually accessible to one depends in part on temporal facts about those entities that are independent of one's sensory limitations. This in turn might make intuitive the thought that whether entities are perceptually accessible to one depends in part on whether they fall within an interval of time that is *temporally present*, where this is thought to be a non-perspectival temporal fact about those entities that is independent of one's sensory limitations.

The entities one is perceptually aware of are experienced as occupying an interval of time. Everything one is perceptually aware of seems to one to be concurrent with one's awareness of it. It does not seem to one as though one has a perceptual point of view on an interval of time that is distinct from that interval of time. So in that sense, everything that one is perceptually aware of is experienced as occupying an interval of time that is temporally 'present'. Each sub-interval of that interval of time seems to one to be concurrent with one's awareness of it, and so in that sense, each sub-interval of time seems to one to be temporally 'present'. Those sub-intervals of time seem to one to be successive, in so far as it seems to *take* time to be perceptually aware of their sum—i.e. the interval of time that is determined by the extent of one's temporal

[13] One could add that it is also quite unlike one's experience of the spatial region within which one experiences one's bodily sensations to be located. I said that in the case of one's experience of located bodily sensations the region of space within which one experiences such sensations to be located seems to one to be determined not by one's sensory limitations but rather by the spatial limits of some thing one is sensing—i.e. one's body. So the region of space within which one can experience sensations to be located seems to one to be determined by the contingencies of the size of one's body. In contrast, the extent of the temporal interval one can be perceptually aware of does not seem to one to be determined by the contingencies of the temporal extent of some entity one is perceptually aware of.

sensory field, and which those sub-intervals of time together constitute. So there is a sense in which the interval of time that falls within one's temporal sensory field seems to one to be made up of *successively* present times. As a result, the phenomenology is something like the continual and successive unfolding of present times.[14] And it is this that accounts for the respect in which we might be said to experience time as unbounded.

So there is, I think, quite a significant difference between the way in which we might be said to experience space as unbounded and the way in which we might be said to experience time as unbounded. These phenomenological differences, which can lead to quite different intuitions about space and time themselves, are due to significant differences in the ways our conscious awareness of space and time are structured. To accept this much, however, still leaves open the further question of the extent to which these relatively invariant structural features of conscious perceptual awareness reflect the real objective nature of space and time themselves.

References

Fine, K. (2005). 'Tense and Reality', in *Modality and Tense: Philosophical Papers*. Oxford University Press.

Grice, H.P. (1961). 'The Causal Theory of Perception', *Proceedings of the Aristotelian Society Supplementary Volume* 35: 121–52.

Kant. I. (1998). *Critique of Pure Reason*. Ed. and trans. Paul Guyer and Allen W. Wood. Cambridge: Cambridge University Press.

Kukso, Boris (2006). 'The Reality of Absences', *Australasian Journal of Philosophy* 84/1: 21–37.

Martin, C. B. (1996). 'How It Is: Entities, Absences and Voids', *Australasian Journal of Philosophy* 74/1: 57–65.

Martin, M. G. F. (1992). 'Sight and Touch', in T. Crane ed. *The Contents of Experience*. Cambridge: Cambridge University Press.

Martin, M. G. F. (1995). 'Bodily Awareness: A Sense of Ownership', in J. Bermudez, A. Marcel, and N. Eilan eds. *The Body and the Self*. MIT Press.

Martin, M. G. F. (1999). 'Sense Modalities and Spatial Properties', in N. Eilan, R. McCarthy, B. Brewer eds. *Spatial Representation: Problems in Philosophy and Psychology*. Clarendon Press.

Martin, M. G. F. (2004). 'The Limits of Self-Awareness', *Philosophical Studies* 103: 37–89.

Martin, C. B. and Deutscher, Max (1966). 'Remembering', *Philosophical Review* 75: 161–196.

Melnick, A. (1973). *Kant's Analogies of Experience*. Chicago: University of Chicago Press.

Molnar, G. (2000). 'Truthmakers for Negative Truths', *Australasion Journal of Philosophy*, 78/1 (March): 72–86.

---

[14] As Fine (2005) remarks,

The passage of time requires that the moments of time be *successively* present and this appears to require more than the presentness of a single moment of time...Even if presentness is allowed to shed its light upon the world, there is nothing in this metaphysics to prevent that light from being 'frozen' on a particular moment of time...So clearly something more than an equitable distribution of presentness is required to account for the passage of time. (p. 287)

O'Shaughnessy, B. (2000). *Consciousness and the World*. Oxford: Oxford University Press.

Pears, David F., (1976). 'The Causal Conditions of Perception', *Synthese* 33 (June): 25–40.

Richardson, L. (2009). 'Seeing Empty Space', *European Journal of Philosophy*.

Ryle, G. (1949). *The Concept of Mind*. University of Chicago Press.

Sorensen, R. (2007). 'The Vanishing Point: The Self as Absence', *Monist* 90/3.

Sorensen, R. (2008). *Seeing Dark Things*. Oxford: Oxford University Press.

Smith, A. D. (2003). *Husserl and the Cartesian Meditations*. Routledge.

Snowdon, P. (1980–81). 'Perception, Vision and Causation', *Proceedings of the Aristotelian Society*. 81: 175–92.

Snowdon, P. (1990). 'The Objects of Perceptual Experience', *Proceedings of the Aristotelian Society Supplementary Volume* 64: 121–50.

Snowdon, P. (1998). 'Strawson on the Concept of Perception', in L. Hahn (ed.) *The Philosophy of P. F. Strawson* (Chicago and Lasalle: Open Court): 293–310.

Strawson, P. F. (1974). 'Causation in Perception', in P. F. Strawson, *Freedom and Resentment*. Methuen.

13

Perception, Causal Understanding, and Locality

*Christoph Hoerl**

1 Introduction

Locality, as I will understand the term in this paper, is the view that causal relations are always subject to spatial constraints in the following sense: For any case in which there is a causal relation between two spatiotemporal particulars,[1] that causal relation would not have obtained if certain spatial parameters of the situation had been different (e.g. had one of the two particulars been located elsewhere).

The issue as to whether locality is true is arguably central to recent philosophical debates about causation. Theories that seek to analyse causal relationships in terms of the notion of a mechanism, or so-called process theories of causation appear committed to locality. Put briefly, such theories maintain that causation involves the presence of a spatiotemporally continuous empirical feature connecting cause and effect, i.e. a feature which is also present at points intermediate between cause and effect—be this a concrete object travelling between cause and effect, or radiation, or the existence of a magnetic or gravitational field (Salmon, 1984, pp. 208ff.).[2] This rules out what is typically referred to as action-at-a-distance, that is, alleged cases of causation that violate locality. Thus, such theories rule out, for instance, the idea that a 'powder of

* An early version of this paper was presented at Sydney University, a later one to the Wednesday philosophy group at Warwick University. By and large, the comments I received on each of the two occasions came from two very different sides, but I found them equally helpful. I am also grateful to the AHRC for its support—both for the AHRC Project on Causal Understanding, in the context of which I was prompted to write this paper, and for a term's research leave, during which much of the writing took place.

[1] I am using the phrase 'a causal relation' in a loose sense here, which is not meant to imply a commitment to a specific philosophical view of the ontology of causation. The kinds of cases I have in mind might, for instance, be described by saying that x's ϕ-ing caused y's ψ-ing, or by saying that the fact that x ϕ-ed caused the fact that y ψ-ed, where x and y are the relevant spatiotemporal particulars. Thus, localism, as I understand it, is a thesis about token or singular causation, but it is otherwise neutral as to what entities such causation ultimately relates (e.g. events vs facts).

[2] This characterisation will do for the moment. In section 3, I will suggest that the key intuitions behind causal process views of causation can also be accommodated by a slightly more liberal formulation.

sympathy', applied to a weapon that had caused a wound, could heal the wound purely in virtue of the past contact between the knife and the wound, and irrespective of where the wounded person was located now.[3]

By contrast, if regularity theories or counterfactual theories of causation are correct, the truth of locality, and the non-existence of cases of action-at-a-distance, seem at best interesting empirical facts about our world. The truth of locality has nothing to do with what, according to these theories, causation is. Indeed, the alleged conceivability of action-at-a-distance, as illustrated by the example above, has sometimes been claimed to provide an argument in favour of adopting one of these latter types of theory.

In this paper, I want to suggest that we can extract from the existing philosophical literature on perception, and perceptual judgement, materials for an argument to the effect that a commitment to locality *is* part of our common-sense concept of causation. I will also suggest that this literature can help to bring out a specific kind of role this commitment plays in our reasoning about causal relationships. However, in order to make the connection between the two different areas of philosophy—the philosophy of perception and the philosophy of causation—we also need to have in place a particular way of thinking of what is at stake, in general, in philosophical debates on causation. Thus, a second aim of the paper is metaphilosophical: to articulate and defend a specific philosophical approach to causation.

Along with other philosophers working on causation, I will take my task to be that of providing (part of) an account of the meaning of 'our' concept of causation. In the existing literature, authors often explicitly state their aim in those terms.[4] However, it also seems implicit in the predominance of a particular type of methodological tool: this is an area of philosophy where the use of examples and thought-experiments proliferates, i.e. where many of the arguments proceed by trying to show that the theory put forward is one that best accords with our intuitive causal judgements about a range of actual or imagined scenarios.[5] Use of this method would seem to be to the

---

[3] Another example would be the idea that a person could be brought to harm by damaging an object representing them, purely in virtue of the representational relationship between the object and the person. It is important to note, though, that not all historical accounts of such 'sympathetic' action do in fact conceive of it as involving action-at-a-distance in the sense at issue here. (Thanks to John Sutton for pointing this out to me.) For instance, Kenelm Digby's (1658) account of the effectiveness of the 'powder of sympathy' is cast entirely in terms of corpuscular-mechanical principles. According to him, as the powder mixes with the blood on the weapon, particles of medicine mixed with blood are released in the air, which then find their way to the wound (see Mercer, 1998). For more discussion of the notion of action-at-a-distance, in the philosophically relevant sense, see Hall (2002) and Frisch (2010).

[4] One exception here is Dowe (2000), who describes himself as offering an 'empirical analysis of causation' (ibid., p. 2), aimed to uncover 'what causation is in the objective world' (ibid., p. 1). He specifically contrasts this with the task of 'elucidat[ing] our normal concept of causation' (ibid., p. 1). The latter, he claims, is exemplified by Strawson's (1959) project of 'descriptive metaphysics'. Some of what follows is inspired by Strawson's project, and I will make use of Dowe's theory in a way that is against his own stated metaphilosophical intentions. However, I think this would be objectionable only if I ended up criticising Dowe's theory for failing to do a job that it is not intended for, which I will not.

[5] Collins, Hall, and Paul (2004) include a separate index for the examples used in that volume, which runs to several pages.

point only if the target of the theory is the concept of causation mobilised in such intuitive judgements.

Yet, whilst the widespread use of examples and thought-experiments in the philo-sophical literature on causation may indicate that the target explanandum is indeed our common-sense concept of causation, we can still ask how good they ultimately are as a tool for probing that concept. When the question as to what it is to have a certain concept is raised in philosophy, it is usually assumed that a subject can possess a concept and yet misapply it on occasion. If this is true, perhaps some of the scenarios appealed to in the existing literature mislead us about the nature of our concept of causation, if there are features of such scenarios that make us more prone to misapplying that concept. Suppose, on the other hand, we take the particular causal judgements people do in fact make as the ultimate arbiter in determining the nature of their concept of causation. In that case, it is unclear whether we can still be said to be carrying out a distinctively philosophical project of conceptual analysis. Instead, we seem to have strayed into the territory of anthropology.

Put very broadly, what we need, it seems, is some principled way of singling out specific types of reasoning about causation as central to our possessing a concept of causation, or at least a way of distinguishing between more or less central types of such reasoning. This, I believe, is where some thoughts familiar from the literature on perception might be brought to bear on the debate, in the philosophy of causation, about the status of locality.

Beyond these programmatic remarks, to see how exactly the connection might be made, some stage setting is required. In the next section, I present one way of looking at a key debate in contemporary work about causation. In section 3, I argue that the (or, at any rate, a) central issue on which that debate turns is best described in terms of the question as to what place (if any) locality has in our ordinary thinking about causation. In section 4, I discuss a suggestion recently made by James Woodward as to how questions such as this are best approached, and offer an alternative. It is not until section 5 that I get to the link with the philosophy of perception. In that section, I draw on an influential type of argument to the effect that perceptual judgement recruits a certain basic form of causal understanding. In the context of the present paper, the aspect of the argument that will be of particular interest is that the causal understanding that, according to the argument, is recruited in perceptual judgement does seem to involve a commitment to locality. In the final two sections, I show how analogous arguments in other areas might be used to draw a more general conclusion.

2 The debate between difference-making and causal process theories of causation

Contemporary philosophical debates on causation are dominated by the two broad types of theoretical approach to causation that I mentioned at the beginning of this paper, which are sometimes called difference-making and causal process approaches, respectively. Both types of approach have been developed to a considerable level of sophistication, but the basic idea behind each is relatively simple to explain. What is proving to be a rather recalcitrant problem, by contrast, is how exactly the dialectic between the two types of approach is to be understood. There is an obvious sense in which difference-making and process theories make quite different claims about causation. What exactly the difference between them comes to, however, depends on what we take to be their respective explanatory aims. Indeed, it has been suggested that there may be no conflict between them, because they are trying to account for two different types of thing (see the opening methodological remarks in Dowe, 2000, and Woodward, 2003, for discussion).

In what follows, I will suggest that perhaps a more fruitful way of construing the dialectical situation between difference-making and causal process theories of causation is by seeing them as articulating two conflicting sets of ideas about the meaning of ordinary causal thought and talk.

According to one prominent way of thinking, a key part of the task of a philosophical theory of causation is to provide an account of what distinguishes causation from mere correlation. Typically, when the need to distinguish causation from correlation is raised in the context of scientific investigation, the thought is as follows. A statistical correlation between A and B implies only that there is *some* sort of causal connection between the two; but it is compatible with a number of quite different causal scenarios—e.g. A causing B, B causing A, or both A and B being effects of a common cause.[6] This is the key problem that has led, for instance, to the development of the Bradford Hill criteria in epidemiology (Hill, 1965). These are concerned with the evidence on which we ought to decide which particular causal scenario is present in a given case. However, we can also ask what the difference between these different causal scenarios consists in in the first place.

As I will interpret them, process theories of causation start off from a line of thought that runs roughly as follows (though see the next section for an important qualification). If the choice is, e.g. between a situation in which A causes B and a situation in which A and B are effects of a common cause, A causes B only if there is a process, a spatiotemporally continuous empirical feature, that directly links A with B. In the relevant sense of 'directly', there is no such process linking A directly with B if A and B are effects of a common cause; instead there are separate processes linking the common cause with A and with B. Further details will need to be added, e.g. to distinguish between a situation in which A and B are effects of a common cause, and a situation in which A causes an event which, in turn, causes B. But the basic thought is that spelling out these details is just a matter of characterising in more detail the process in operation (e.g. introducing the idea of a direction intrinsic to a process). It is thus that a person's

[6] I leave to one side here the possibility of statistical correlations in the absence of any sort of causal connection.

grasp of the notion of a process is implicated in their ability to distinguish mere correlation from causation; or so the thought goes.

As soon as the basic thought behind process theories of causation is spelled out in these terms, however, it may look as though the proponent of such a theory starts off on the back foot. For one thing, it may seem that the general notion of a process, as used in the preceding paragraph, is little more than a placeholder. For another, there are in fact a variety of philosophical accounts that seem to be able to distinguish, say, between a cause–effect relation and a common cause relation, without making any appeal to the notion of a process, thus understood.[7] Instead, the distinction is couched in terms of the idea that a particular kind of counterfactual relationship holds between A and B only if A causes B, and is absent if A and B are effects of a common cause. The most developed account of this kind is typically referred to as interventionism or manipulationism. The basic intuition behind interventionism is that for A to cause B is for there to be an association between A and B that remains invariant under (a range of) interventions on A—where this is to be contrasted specifically with three other cases in which any association between A and B will be broken by interventions on A: (a) there is no causal connection; (b) B actually causes A, rather than vice versa; (c) A and B are joint effects of a common cause. Of course, a lot more has to be said about the key notion of an intervention here, but I will assume that we can find the necessary refinements in the work of theorists such as Pearl (2000) and Woodward (2003), who have offered detailed accounts of that notion. In other words, I will assume that interventionism does indeed provide a way of distinguishing, say, between the case in which A causes B and the case in which they are both effects of a common cause, without using the notion of a causal process.

Where does this leave the dialectic between difference-making and causal process accounts of causation? According to the process theorist, our common-sense view of causation involves a metaphysical commitment to a particular kind of empirical feature the presence of which makes causal statements true, viz. a causal process. This, by itself, does not force the process theorist to deny that interventionism can provide a way of distinguishing a case in which A causes B from a case in which both are the effects of a common cause without making reference to that empirical feature. What the process-theorist will maintain, though, is that interventionism should be seen as giving an account of certain (idealised) ways of deciding whether certain causal statements are true, rather than of what makes those statements true. In other words, the process theorist can invoke a distinction between an epistemic account of the methods by which to arrive at certain causal judgements, on the one hand, and our grasp of what it

---

[7] At least that is what I will assume for the sake of the argument. One stubborn problem for counterfactual accounts such as Woodward's is how to account for certain cases of preemption. Woodward's own analysis of such cases involves the idea of an intervening variable in between the cause and effect. The idea that there *must* be such intervening variables, however, seems to involve theoretical commitments that go beyond the basic idea of analysing causation in terms of certain counterfactuals and is in tension with the view that, e.g. action-at-a-distance is possible.

is for those judgements to be true, on the other. In this respect, from the causal process theorist's point of view, the debate between causal process theories and difference-making theories of causation resembles the debate between, say, a realist concerning statements about the past (of the type represented by, e.g. Peacocke, 2005), and a justificationist approach to such statements (of the type represented by Dummett, 2005).

From the point of view of an interventionist, by contrast, the existence of relationships that are invariant under interventions is not just evidence for the existence of causal relationships, but is the very feature of reality that causal talk aims to get at. The interventionist's diagnosis of where the process theorist goes wrong runs roughly as follows. There are, the interventionist can admit, legitimate ways of spelling out the notion of causal process, such that many instances of causation will in fact involve the operation of such processes. In the interventionist literature, instances of causation that do involve causal processes in the relevant sense are often also referred to as ones where there is a *mechanism* present. The interventionist can also admit that there are various reasons why identifying such mechanisms can be of scientific interest. Yet, he will insist that the existence of a mechanism mediating the causal connection between A and B is simply a matter of there being separate parts of the relationship between A and B which can themselves be described in terms of interventionist counterfactuals (cf. Woodward, 2007). The mistake made by the process theorist, thus, is to confuse our legitimate interest in mechanisms with an insight into what makes the relevant relationship causal. If A causes B, the existence of a mechanism between A and B is simply a (contingent) further fact about the causal relation between them. Indeed, on this way of construing the notion of a mechanism, it is actually ruled out that causal relationships are always mediated by mechanisms. As Campbell (2007, p. 65) puts the view, '[e]xplanation by means of mechanisms must bottom out somewhere, and then we are left with the bare facts about what would happen under interventions'.

3 Locality and negative causation

I have sketched one way of understanding of what is at stake in the debate between difference-making and causal process approaches to causation. Put schematically, according to the first type of approach, our common-sense concept of what it is for A to cause B involves a commitment only to the holding of certain counterfactual relationships involving A and B. According to the second, the relevant counterfactuals point to some of the reasons why we might endorse the claim that A causes B; to capture what it is for A to cause B, though, we have to appeal to the idea of a causal process.

In the previous section, I spelled out the latter thought in a way that implies a commitment, on the part of the causal process theorist, to the idea that causes are physically connected to their effects, as it is sometimes put. In other words, as I have characterised the causal process theorist so far, she holds that appealing to the idea of a causal process mediating between cause and effect must take the form of claiming that there is an actual spatiotemporally continuous empirical feature connecting cause and effect. In fact, however, I believe that the substance of the dialectic between difference-making and causal process approaches that I have sketched is not well described by saying that it turns on the question as to whether causes are physically connected to their effects in this sense. The dialectic still arises for a weaker form of causal process theory that is not committed to this claim, which I will outline below. Correspondingly, I will suggest that rather than concentrating on the question as to whether causes are physically connected to their effects, a better question to focus on in evaluating the two sides of the dialectic is that of locality.

Against specific theories fleshing out a causal process approach, such as the conserved quantity theory (Salmon, 1984; Dowe, 2000), it is sometimes held that there is a class of cases which common-sense seems happy to classify as cases of causation, but which do not involve any physical connection along which a physical quantity such as energy or momentum could be transmitted between cause and effect. The cases at issue here are ones that exemplify what is sometimes called 'negative causation', that is, causation in which absences act as causes or effects. A paradigmatic example are cases of double prevention, such as the following. I remove from the side of a road a traffic sign that warns of a narrow bend further down the road; minutes later a car takes the bend too fast and crashes, because the driver was unaware that there was a bend coming up. There is an intuition here that I caused the accident, or was at least in some sense causally involved—an intuition that might manifest itself in the feeling that I should be punished for what I did.[8] Yet, were we to ask how I caused the accident, we could point to nothing concrete in the space between where the traffic sign used to be and where the car is travelling that could provide the answer; there is no physical connection between my actions and what happened to the car.[9]

One option for a defender of a causal process theory, in response to examples of this kind, is to deny that they are *bona fide* examples of causation. Dowe (2000), for instance, takes this line, arguing that intuitions in fact vary across different cases of alleged causation involving absences. However, if our main interest is in the dialectic between difference-making and causal process approaches as described in the previous section, it is not obvious that siding with a causal process approach requires taking this (somewhat heroic) line.

As Dowe himself notes, in as far as there is indeed an intuition, in response to examples of double prevention like that given above, that we are dealing with a case of causation, it is because the initial action disrupts a physical connection that would otherwise have been in place. To make intelligible the sense in which I am causally

---

[8] Examples of structurally identical cases that invite even stronger intuitions (if they are not strong enough in this case) can be found in Woodward (2003) and Schaffer (2004).

[9] Or so I will assume. Frisch (2010) explores one interpretation of the notion of a field that might allow us to speak of the obtaining of a physical connection even in cases such as this.

involved in the occurrence of the car crash, it seems we have to bring in the idea that, had I left the traffic sign alone, there *would have been* a physical connection between the sign and the subsequent behaviour of the driver (involving, e.g. the physical processes that make it possible for the driver to *see* the sign), such that the car would have made it safely around the bend.

What this observation suggests, in my view, is that a simple-minded version of a causal process approach, which demands that cases in which A causes B must involve an actual physical connection between A and B, is untenable, but that we can nevertheless hold on to the spirit of a causal process approach if we formulate the relationship between the idea of a causal process and that of a physical connection in slightly more complex terms.

Part of what causal process accounts of causation are trying to get at, on the view I have in mind, is the idea that, with respect to any case in which A causes B, we assume that it makes sense to raise the question as to *how* A causes B. On this view, causal process accounts can accommodate cases of negative causation, provided that we allow that the answer to the how-question sometimes needs to be framed in counterfactual terms. Note that the relevant counterfactuals here are still quite different from the counterfactuals appealed to by proponents of difference-making approaches such as interventionism. The counterfactuals needed to explain our causal intuitions regarding cases of negative causation seem to be able to do so only because they mention physical connections that would have obtained if a certain event had not taken place. In other words, we can hold on to the view that causal relations always involve causal processes, and also that detailing a causal process by which A causes B is always a matter of appealing to some sort of physical connection, as long as we allow that the latter can sometimes take the form of appealing to a physical connection that would have obtained had a certain event not happened. Thus, even though the resulting theory has to introduce a counterfactual element into the analysis of negative causation, it is still a theory that takes the notion of a physical connection as primitive to our understanding of causation.

On this way of dealing with cases of negative causation, one particular issue emerges as central to the debate between causal process approaches and difference-making approaches to causation, viz. the issue of locality. Note that there is one crucial feature that cases of negative causation have in common with cases of positive causation, in which there is an actual physical connection between cause and effect: due to the role that actual or counterfactual physical connections play in each case, it will be true for both of them that A would not have caused B, had certain spatial parameters of the situation been different. As I will also express it, on the kind of view I have sketched above, both positive and negative causation are subject to spatial constraints. By contrast, at least on the face of it, there is no room for mentioning spatial constraints in counterfactual theories such as Woodward's interventionism. In its most simple form, interventionism simply says that what there is to causation is the holding of certain interventionist counterfactuals. It seems to be a consequence of such a view that it should be possible for there to be causal relationships that are not subject to any spatial constraints—the theory itself makes no mention of space at all.[10]

Thus, one way to pursue the basic dialectic between difference-making and causal process approaches to causation, understood along the lines sketched in the previous section, is by asking whether we need to see it as an integral part of our concept of causation that causation is always subject to spatial constraints, or whether we should treat this feature, which is present in the cases of both positive and negative causation that we are familiar with, as a dispensable feature. Specifically, my interest in the following will be in the question as to the grounds on which one might adopt one rather than another answer to this question.

4 'Practical' and 'impractical' accounts of causation: A misleading dichotomy

I have suggested that we should think of one, if not *the*, key issue at stake in the debate between causal process accounts and difference-making accounts of causation in terms of the question as to whether a commitment to locality is part of our common-sense concept of causation, i.e. whether that concept implies that causal relations are always subject to spatial constraints. It might of course be agreed upon on all sides that, as a matter of fact, the only kinds of causal relations we are familiar with are ones that involve such spatial constraints, and that action-at-a-distance, violating locality, does not in fact exist. The issue, though, is whether this is merely a contingent, empirical matter regarding the world we live in, or whether action-at-a-distance is somehow ruled out by our very concept of causation.

In outlining a possible defence of the claim that locality is indeed an ingredient in our common-sense concept of causation, I want to make use of a type of methodological consideration used by Woodward, even though it will lead me to a position that disagrees with his. Woodward, perhaps slightly tongue-in-cheek, writes the following:

> Broadly speaking, philosophical theories of causation fall into two main camps [...]. Some theories, call them 'impractical,' provide accounts that fail to make it understandable how knowledge of causal relationships has any practical utility at all. Other theories, call them 'practical,' do provide (or are naturally interpretable as providing) accounts that connect causal knowledge with some goal that has practical utility [...]. My suggestion is that [...] we have strong prima-facie reasons to prefer practical to impractical theories. (Woodward, 2003, p. 30)

He then goes on to argue that causal process theories should be counted as impractical theories. The example he uses in this context is the conserved quantity theory of Salmon (1984) and Dowe (2000). He writes:

---

[10] Indeed, Woodward explicitly takes it to be a virtue of his theory that it can allow for 'action-at-a-distance'. See, for instance, Woodward, 2003, p. 148 and p. 353.

[T]he conserved quantity theory, as it stands, fails to explain the practical point of (the benefit that would follow from) the ability to distinguish between interactions that involve the exchange of energy and momentum and those that do not. Needless to say, animals, small children, and many adults do not possess the concepts of energy, momentum, and conservation laws and are not motivated by a disinterested intellectual concern to classify interactions into those that do and those that do not involve the transfer of energy and momentum. (Woodward, 2003, p. 30)

I take it that Woodward's remarks here are meant to extend also to other theories that imply locality, as opposed to theories such as his own version of interventionism, which he thinks provides a straightforward and plausible answer to the question as to what the point of our having the notion of causation is. Put crudely, the thought is that the distinction between causal and noncausal relationships matters to us because it is only causal relationships that we can exploit practically, in the sense of, say, bringing about the effect by bringing about the cause.

I want to take from Woodward the idea that an account of the concept of causation has to earn its keep, at least in part, by making plausible why we have that concept in the first place. I want to argue, though, that there is something potentially quite misleading about the way Woodward sets up the alternatives here, in particular if the passages above are read as a general critique of causal process accounts of causation.

First of all, it is not obvious that a defender of the type of causal process view I have outlined in the previous section cannot tell a story as to how distinguishing between causal and noncausal relationships might be of practical relevance for us. For instance, if causal relationships are subject to spatial enabling conditions, grasp of such enabling conditions might, on occasion, allow us to prevent A from causing B, or to enable it to do so, by changing some spatial parameters of the situation. This is an issue I will return to.

However, I think there is also a deeper methodological problem with the way in which Woodward appeals to a dichotomy between disinterested intellectual concern and practical interests. Woodward describes himself as being motivated by questions such as the following: 'What is the point of our having a notion of causation (as opposed to, say, a notion of correlation) at all? What role or function does this concept play in our lives?' (Woodward, 2003, p. 28). I want to suggest that these questions in fact call for an answer that comes in two parts, only one of which Woodward seems to focus on, to the exclusion of the other. The point that Woodward makes, which I am happy to agree on, is that any plausible account of the concept of causation needs to show what sort of practical payoff there might be for us in carving up the world into causal vs noncausal relations. Yet, an issue Woodward seems to ignore is that being able to carve up the world into causal vs noncausal relations may not always require the use of a *concept* of causation. Thus, when we ask about the role or function that concept has in our lives, part of what needs to be explained is also what benefit there is for us in drawing the contrast between causal and noncausal relations in conceptual terms. In other words, what I am urging is that we need to draw a further distinction between what might be called a '*purely* practical' and a 'theoretical' grasp of causal relationships, where this distinction turns not on the idea that the latter is impractical, but on the idea that, in contrast to the former, it involves an exercise of the *concept* of causation.[11]

If what I have just said is along the right lines, it suggests a certain strategy in tackling the question as to whether locality is indeed part of our common-sense concept of causation. In deciding this question, we need to look at contexts in which it is plausible to think that the subject does not just have to be sensitive to certain *de facto* causal relations, but in which the subject's employing a *concept* of causation seems to play a crucial cognitive role. The question we should then examine is whether, in these contexts, the role that the concept of causation plays is tied to a commitment to the idea that the causal relations at issue are subject to spatial constraints.

5 Causal understanding and perceptual judgement

I think it is at least arguable that one context in which it is crucial for us not just to be sensitive to certain causal relations, but also to be able to think of them in causal terms is that of perceptual judgement. I should make clear that what I will say on this issue does not aspire to any originality, and is heavily based on the work of others.[12] My aim is not to provide an argument of my own for the claim that perceptual judgement recruits causal reasoning abilities, but to find out what the motivation might be for making such a claim, and then see whether this motivation might give us a lead on the question as to what role causal concepts, more generally, play in our cognitive lives.

The precise way in which one might think of perception itself as involving a causal relation is of course the subject of considerable debate in philosophy, as some of the other chapters in this volume attest. But not all aspects of this debate are relevant for our present concerns. I will focus primarily on two types of considerations, both of which can be extracted from the following quotation from Peter Strawson:

[W]e think of perception as a way, indeed the basic way, of informing ourselves about the world of independently existing things: we assume, that is to say, the general reliability of our perceptual experiences; and that assumption is the same as the assumption of a general causal dependence of our perceptual experiences on the independently existing things we take them to be of.... It really should be obvious that with the distinction between independently existing objects and perceptual awareness of objects we already have the general notion of causal dependence of the latter on the former, even if this is not a matter to which we give much reflective attention. (Strawson, 1979, p. 54)

One question that Strawson is concerned with here is the question as to what it is for perception to *be* a reliable way of informing ourselves about the world around us, and there is clearly a suggestion in play that, in order to answer that question, we need to

---

[11] On related issues, see Hoerl (2011) and Peacocke (forthcoming).

[12] Some key influences here are: Campbell, 1995; Eilan, 1998; Roessler, 1999. See also Johannes Roessler's Introduction to this volume, and the chapters by Naomi Eilan and William Child.

appeal to something like the idea that perceptual experience causally tracks the state of the world. The first thing to note about this suggestion is that it ties in quite naturally with an interventionist account of causation such as the one offered by Woodward. Arguably, what matters for reliability is the obtaining of what Woodward calls invariant relationships, i.e. a relationship between experience and the world such that differences in the way the world is make a systematic difference to what we experience. However, the question that concerns us at the moment is not just whether a certain *de facto* feature of perceptual experience, such as its reliability, calls for an explanation in causal terms (perhaps along interventionist lines), but whether there are any reasons for thinking that the subject herself must be able to think of certain relations in causal terms in order to, say, arrive at perceptual judgements. And here it does not look likely that considerations about the reliability of perception can supply us with such a reason. Specifically, it cannot be that the subject must first establish, say, the obtaining of certain invariant relationships between her experiences and the world before she can rely on her perceptual experiences in informing herself about the world around her. Otherwise, it could not be true that perception is the most basic way we have of informing ourselves of the world, and on this Strawson is surely right.

I think a more promising context in which to look for a reason for thinking that the ability to make perceptual judgements involves a grasp of causal concepts is provided by Strawson's remark that 'with the distinction between independently existing objects and perceptual awareness of objects we already have the general notion of causal dependence'. In other words, one key motivation behind the idea that perceptual judgement involves a grasp of causal concepts is that we need to use such concepts to make intelligible to ourselves, in making perceptual judgements, how perception can present us with objects whose existence is independent of being perceived. An idea along those lines stands behind Gareth Evans' claim that perceptual judgement recruits a *simple theory of perception*. Evans puts the claim as follows:

Any thinker who has an idea [. . .] of a world of objects and phenomena which can be perceived but which are not dependent on being perceived for their existence [. . .] must be able to think of his perception of the world as being simultaneously due to his position in the world, and to the condition of the world at that position. The very idea of a perceivable, objective, spatial world brings with it the idea of the subject as being in the world, with the course of his perceptions due to his changing position in the world and the more or less stable way the world is. (Evans, 1982, p. 222)

There is considerable scope for debate as to what exactly we should take to be the upshot of the line of thought Evans is describing here. What seems clear is that the kind of reasoning described by Evans, in terms of which the subject makes intelligible to himself how it can be that an object he currently perceives does not depend for its existence on being perceived, employs some basic causal concepts and involves a capacity to give causal explanations of a certain kind. Amongst philosophers who invoke the notion of a simple theory of perception, however, we can find a range of different answers as to the exact role that such causal reasoning abilities are meant to play in the context of perception. At one end of the spectrum is the idea that there is a sense in which the very ability to perceive mind-independent objects as such requires possession of (at least a rudimentary) simple theory of perception. Or the thought is that making perceptual judgements in which concepts of particular mind-independent objects figure requires a grasp of such a theory. In its weakest form, at the other end of the spectrum, the claim is that possession of the general concept of an objective reality, at any rate, requires a simple theory of perception.

My own interest, for present purposes, is not in where along that continuum the right answer lies (assuming it does lie on that continuum).[13] That question is one about the particular role that accounts invoking the idea of a simple theory of perception assign to the capacity to engage in causal reasoning in the context of perceptual judgement. My point is rather that, irrespective of what the answer to that question is, these accounts can also be seen to provide us with a model of what the capacity to engage in such causal reasoning consists in. That is to say, they give us one way of spelling out what is involved in going beyond merely relying on the *de facto* obtaining of certain causal relations, and instead engaging in reasoning about such relations.

What kind of theory is the simple theory of perception? Note that, as described by Evans, the theory is not so much concerned with the fact that, generally, our perceptual experiences causally track the way the world is, and are, in this sense, reliable. In a way, that sort of causal dependence is already taken for granted. Instead, what the simple theory of perception is concerned with is why some particular instances of that general causal dependence obtain and others not, i.e. why I can perceive certain items but not others.[14] And here it seems that the idea that causation, at least in the case of perception, is subject to spatial enabling conditions plays a crucial role: On each given occasion, what I can perceive is determined, in part, by my own position in space, my orientation, and such things as the absence of barriers between me and the thing perceived. In other words, the way we give substance to the general idea that there are further enabling conditions to be fulfilled, apart from the actual existence of an object, before we can perceive that object, is in spatial terms.

We can perhaps clarify further the nature of the reasoning capacity at issue here, and the role that a grasp of spatial enabling conditions plays in it, by considering a passage from William Child's contribution to this volume. In the context of defending the view that our ordinary thinking about seeing is a form of causal thinking, Child discusses the idea that

what makes a concept a causal concept is just that it has to do with explaining why something happened; why an event or state of affairs occurred, or came about, or persisted; what produced some event or state of affairs; why a particular thing behaved as it did, or why that kind of thing

---

[13] See Naomi Eilan's contribution to this volume for a discussion of these issues.

[14] Compare Campbell, 1995, p. 208: 'The actual explanations [provided by the simple theory of perception] are all at the level of the concrete particular.'

generally behaves as it does; and so on. [...] And by that standard, what makes our ordinary thinking about vision a form of causal thinking is that the 'because' in our reasoning about seeing ('She couldn't see it because it was too far away', and so on), has to do with the explanation of why something happened (or did not happen). In our ordinary thought about vision, we are concerned with the occurrence or non-occurrence of natural phenomena: someone's seeing this, or failing to see that. In the same way, when we reason about the enabling and defeating conditions of vision, we are reasoning about why something happened or persisted, or why something of a certain sort failed to happen. That is enough for this reasoning to be a form of causal reasoning. (Child, this volume, p. 174)

The issue Child is concerned with in this passage is somewhat different from the one at issue in the present section. However, I believe the connection he draws between causal reasoning and the explanation of particular occurrences is also relevant to our current concerns. Indeed, the difference might be put as a mere difference in emphasis. What Child, in effect, is suggesting is that a subject is engaged in *causal* reasoning to the extent that she is concerned with the explanation of *particular occurrences*. An idea that is implicit in the line of thought that I have sketched above might similarly be put by saying that a subject is engaged in causal *reasoning* to the extent that she is concerned with the *explanation* of particular occurrences. Thus, the strength of the thought that perceptual judgement, for instance, involves causal reasoning abilities turns on the idea that it requires that the subject be able to grasp why the same object can sometimes be seen and sometimes not.

The idea behind the claim that perceptual judgement recruits a simple theory of perception, then, is that a simple theory of perception can furnish the subject with the required kind of explanation. However, it seems to be able to do so only because within the simple theory of perception, perception is conceived of as involving causal relations that are subject to spatial constraints. What does explain why I can sometimes see an object and sometimes not, according to the simple theory of perception, is that, apart from the object being present, I must also stand in the right sort of spatial relation to it. Thus, in as far as accounts of perceptual judgement that invoke the notion of a simple theory of perception make a plausible case for the idea that (an element of) perceptual judgement recruits causal reasoning abilities, rather than just a sensitivity to the *de facto* obtaining of causal relations, those reasoning abilities turn on a commitment to a version of locality, at least in connection with the causal relations involved in perception.

6 Causal understanding and agency

It is easy to imagine someone agreeing, at least in broad outline, with the line of thought just sketched, but arguing that it tells us more about the concept of perception than about that of causation. In other words, it may well be that, in the context of talking of the way in which we think of perception as a causal phenomenon, we also need to bring in the idea that it is subject to spatial enabling conditions. However, it clearly does not follow from this that this idea always has to be brought in when we think of a phenomenon in causal terms.

Furthermore, it might be held that a more natural (or at least equally natural) starting point in considering questions about subjects' grasp of causal concepts is by looking at their ability to recognise their own actions as being effective. For instance, Menzies and Price (1993, p. 187) claim that 'the ordinary notions of cause and effect have a direct and essential connection with our ability to intervene in the world as agents'. More specifically, on their view, we can explain how subjects come to have causal concepts by pointing to features of their own experiences as agents. They explain:

[F]rom an early age, we all have direct experience of acting as agents. That is, [. . .] we all have direct personal experience of doing one thing and thence achieving another. We might say that the notion of causation thus arises not, as Hume has it, from our experience of mere *succession*; but rather from our experience of *success*: success in the ordinary business of achieving our ends by acting in one way rather than another. It is this common and commonplace experience that licenses what amounts to an ostensive definition of the notion of 'bringing about'. In other words, these cases provide direct non-linguistic acquaintance with the concept of bringing about an event. (ibid. p. 194f.)

At least part of the proposal Menzies and Price put forward here fits in quite well with an interventionist approach to causation. We can make sense of the idea of a distinctive experience of success, as they call it, if we think of that experience as reflecting the detection of patterns of invariant relationships of the type that interventionist accounts of causation focus on.[15] Arguably, some such ability to detect patterns of invariant relationships is key to the very possibility of agency. Using the technical notion of 'wiggling' (Lewis, 2004, p. 91), Price elsewhere explains that '[t]he task of an agent is to find out what else wiggles, in response to her possible present actions' (Price, 2007, p. 13). Without being able to register, at least on occasion, whether or not her actions make a systematic difference to aspects of her environment, a subject would not have any grip at all on how to bring about events.

In what follows, I thus want to grant the idea that agency involves something like direct acquaintance with the phenomenon of bringing something about, understood along interventionist lines. However, I want to argue that in the context of agency, too, grasp of causal *concepts* involves theoretical commitments that go beyond those recognised by interventionism. More specifically, my claim will be that an agent's ability to use causal concepts in thinking about her own actions turns on her possessing a simple theory of action akin to the simple theory of perception discussed in the previous section. Furthermore, as with the simple theory of perception, the specific role that the simple theory of action plays in an agent's reasoning seems tied to a commitment to a version of locality, i.e. the thought that the causal relations exploited in one's actions are subject to spatial constraints.

---

[15] See also Woodward, 2007, p. 29.

Perhaps the most vivid way of bringing out the key issue that is at stake here is by considering the possibility of what Woodward (2007) calls *purely egocentric* instrumental behaviour and learning. In such purely egocentric instrumental behaviour and learning

the agent grasps (or behaves as if it grasps) that there are regular, stable relationships between its manipulations and various downstream effects but stops at this point, not recognizing (or behaving as though it recognizes) that the same relationship can be present even when it does not act, but other agents act similarly or when a similar relationship occurs in nature without the involvement of any agents at all. (Woodward, 2007, p. 32)

As Woodward points out, it has been suggested that primates, for instance, do not go beyond this basic level of learning. Consider the following passage from Tomasello and Call (1997, p. 389):

[S]uppose that an individual ape, who has never before observed such an event, for the first time observes the wind blowing a tree such that the fruit falls to the ground. If it understands the causal relations involved, that the movement of the limb is what caused the fruit to fall, it should be able to devise other ways to make the limb move and so make the fruit fall. [...] We believe that most primatologists would be astounded to see the ape, *just on the basis of having observed the wind make fruit fall*, proceed to shake a limb, or pull an attached vine, to create the same movement of the limb.

The type of limitation Tomasello and Call talk about here is meant to stand in stark contrast with primates' other learning abilities, e.g. when it comes to trial and error learning. To use Price's phrase, primates are in fact very capable of finding out what else wiggles, in response to their own actions.

Woodward contrasts purely egocentric instrumental behaviour and learning with what he calls a fully causal viewpoint, which involves, for instance, the ability to move between classical conditioning and instrumental conditioning, or, in other words, 'the ability to use information learned about causal relationships through passive observation to guide interventions and vice versa' (Woodward, 2007, p. 35). This is one way of characterising what the limitation here comes to, which turns on the question as to which sources of information a subject can exploit. However, if Tomasello and Call's description is correct,[16] there is clearly also a sense in which we are dealing with a limitation on the conceptual level. That is to say, the ape described by Tomasello and Call lacks the conceptual resources to give substance to the sameness between the causal relations that are involved in its own interactions with the world and those involved in natural occurrences in which it is not itself the agent.

This poses a difficulty for the idea that the general concept of bringing about an event, or similar causal concepts, could simply be ostensively defined with reference to a characteristic experience of success in the way suggested by Menzies and Price. Arguably, a creature in possession of a such a concept should have some way of giving

---

[16] See Povinelli, 2000, p. 314, for some scepticism as to whether it is in fact empirically true.

substance to the idea that the same causal relationship that governs its own actions can also be present in events in which it is not itself involved. But this is precisely what the ape described by Tomasello and Call seems to lack. And the trouble is that it is hard to see how having a characteristic experience of success could play any role in overcoming that lack. If there is such a thing as an experience of success, as envisaged by Menzies and Price, there seems to be no reason to deny that the ape has such experiences, and that they play a key role in the learning abilities it does possess. Yet, they play a role only in enabling it to learn from its own actions.

I think it is worth noting, at this point, a structural similarity between the issue that has come to the fore in the preceding paragraphs, and the issue that prompted the idea, in the last section, that perceptual judgement recruits a simple theory of perception. There, the question was how a subject, in making perceptual judgements, can make sense of the idea that the very objects that she can perceive are not dependent for their existence on being perceived. The issue that has emerged from the above discussion of Menzies and Price's proposal, in effect, is what it takes for a subject to make sense of the idea that the very kinds of causal relations that she can exploit in acting on her environment can obtain without her acting.

To put the matter slightly differently: The point Evans and others have been making in the case of perceptual judgement is that we need a substantive account of what it is in virtue of which the subject can appreciate that the same object can exist perceived or unperceived. In a similar way, I am now arguing that, in the case of causal judgement, we need a substantive account of what it is in virtue of which the subject can appreciate that the very same causal relationships governing her own actions can also be present in natural occurrences that do not involve agents. Only then can we say that she is not merely sensitive, in some way, to the *de facto* obtaining of certain causal relations, but also that she is capable of thinking about them in terms of causal concepts.

If the line of thought discussed in the previous section is at least roughly along the right lines, a natural suggestion, at this point, is this: it is a grasp of a simple theory of action, akin to the type of simple theory of perception appealed to in the accounts of perceptual judgement I have discussed, that is required to give substance to the idea that the same kinds of casual relations that are exploited in one's own acting can also govern events in which no agent is involved. Again, the idea would be that such a simple theory of action furnishes the subject with an explanation of particular occurrences (and non-occurrences), reflecting the fact that, e.g. one's own actions have certain outcomes only under certain conditions. It is this idea that then also allows for the thought that the same type of outcome could depend in the same way on causes that are not actions, if its occurrence is subject to the same conditions. In other words, what makes available to the subject the thought that the same type of event can be brought about in the same way by her own actions as well as by naturally occurring events is the idea that the same explanation can be given for the occurrence or non-occurrence of this type of event in each case.

Just as in the case of the simple theory of perception, though, it seems that the idea that causal relations are subject to spatial enabling conditions has a crucial role to play in how a simple theory of action can provide for the type of explanation called for here. Consider again the example of Tomasello and Call's ape. What seems to be missing in this example is any kind of indication that the ape grasps *why* the wind, in the particular situation it witnesses, has the power to make the fruit fall. This is why it cannot connect the familiar fact of the wind blowing with the falling of the apple in a way that might also make it realise implications for its own actions. At its most basic, though, such a transfer between observation and action would seem to require a grasp of the fact that the wind can only make the fruit fall because it is acting on the limb. Thus, the reasoning required for the ape to give substance to the idea that the same causal relations at work in the events it witnesses could also be exploited in its own actions turns crucially on the idea that those causal relations are subject to certain spatial enabling conditions.

If this line of thought is along the right lines, it suggests that, just as in the case of perception, giving causal reasoning capacities and a grasp of causal concepts a role to play in agency is tied to the idea that the agents in question can engage in a form of reasoning that trades on an assumption of locality. My argument has been that we require a substantive account of how a subject with causal concepts makes intelligible to herself that the same such concepts can be applied to its own interactions with the world as well as to events in which it is not an agent. What I have suggested, in short, is that we can see how the subject can do so if we credit it with the idea that the same spatial constraints govern the occurrence of particular types of outcome, no matter whether they are being brought about by the subject herself or in some other way. Thus, in the context of agency too, it seems, making plausible the idea that a subject engages in genuine causal reasoning, rather than merely being sensitive in some more primitive way to the *de facto* obtaining of certain causal relations, seems to be bound up with the idea that the reasoning in question involves a commitment to locality.

7   Causation, space, and practical interests

In section 4, above, I outlined a strategy for resolving the question as to whether a commitment to locality should be seen as being part of our common-sense concept of causation. The strategy I recommended was to look at types of reasoning that are arguably central to having causal concepts in the first place, and to see to what extent, if any, these types of reasoning turn on an assumption of locality. I subsequently discussed two reasoning contexts that might, with some justification, be held to be fundamental to our grasp of causal concepts. I suggested that making perceptual judgements and insightful causal learning both mobilise a simple theory (of perception and action, respectively), in which the idea that the causal relations at issue are subject to spatial constraints plays a crucial role. Thus, I have argued that at least two types of causal understanding that have some claim of being central to our understanding of causation generally turn on the assumption of locality.

I do not mean to suggest that what I have said about the case of perception and the case of agency is already sufficient to establish that an assumption of locality is part of our common-sense concept of causation, quite generally. However, in this final section, I wish to draw out three key issues that emerge from what I have argued, which at least offer starting points for working towards a more general conclusion.

First, when discussing Woodward's distinction between what he calls 'practical' and 'impractical' theories of causation, I said that Woodward's way of setting up this distinction ignores a further distinction that we might want to draw between what I called a 'purely practical' and a 'theoretical' grasp of causal relations, where only the latter involves the use of causal concepts. I think that both the case of perception and that of action provide plausible examples of contexts in which we do indeed need to invoke a distinction of this kind.

I take it that there are creatures who do not possess what I have called a simple theory of perception, but who can nevertheless use their sense organs to find their way around the terrain, locate food, etc. Similarly, I take it that there are creatures who do not possess a simple theory of action, but can nevertheless engage in purposive behaviour (if Tomasello and Call, 1997, are right, apes are an actual example). Arguably, there is a sense in which these creatures exploit just the same causal connections in perception and action that we do in making perceptual judgements and engaging in insightful causal learning. But they do so in a way that does not need to involve the use of causal concepts at all. My argument has been that it is not perception or agency as such that demand the possession of causal concepts and the ability to engage in the kinds of causal reasoning that a simple theory of perception or action provides for, but more specific abilities, such as the ability to form judgements about a mind-independently existing world on the basis of perception, or the ability to think about one's own actions in the same terms as about happenings that do not involve agents.

Second, just how does grasp of a simple theory of perception and action go beyond a mere practical sensitivity to causal relations and instead involve the subject herself thinking of those relations in causal terms? To repeat, grasping a simple theory of perception is a matter of grasping that what we can perceive is the joint upshot of what there is in the world and our own position in the world, thus making intelligible how the very objects we can perceive are, at the same time, not dependent for their existence on being perceived. Similarly, grasp of a simple theory of action is, in part, a matter of grasping that what particular outcomes we can bring about is a matter of what kind of thing can cause what kind of other thing and where we are located, thus making possible the idea that the very same causal relationships we can exploit in our actions can obtain independently of us acting. I think one way of describing the general kind of causal reasoning at issue here is by saying that it is concerned with the relationship between general and singular causation in the case of perception and action. It involves, for instance, both the idea of a general causal dependence of perceptual experience on the world, and the idea of particular instances of a feature of the world causing a particular perceptual experience, and provides an explanation of what else it takes, apart from the former, for the latter to occur.

I think the general moral in the offing here is that causal concepts generally only come into play once a subject faces an explanatory task of this particular type. That is to say, there may be various ways in which a subject is able to exploit the fact that As cause Bs without the subject herself using causal concepts. But such concepts do seem to be required if the subject has to grasp what else has to be the case, given the fact that As generally cause Bs, for a particular A to cause a B. Yet, note that this explanatory task already presupposes that there must, in each case in which an A causes a B, be an answer to the question how it does so that also makes intelligible how, sometimes, an A can occur but without causing a B. Thus, the subject's use of causal concepts, in this context, is tied to the idea that the question of how A causes B always has an answer—and, as I have suggested in section 3, above, this is just one way of understanding the idea that causation involves causal process.

Finally, once we put the point of having a concept of causation in the way just sketched, we can perhaps also see how what I have called a theoretical grasp of causal relations need not just be a matter of mere disinterested intellectual concerns, as Woodward calls it, but can be of practical relevance. Understanding why, even though As generally cause Bs, they can only do so if certain conditions are met, also involves understanding what can prevent A causing B on a given occasion, or how a change in conditions might enable it to do so, and the notions of preventing and enabling, in this sense, are clearly of practical relevance.[17] Note also, though, that the notions of preventing and enabling, understood in this sense, do not seem to apply to putative cases of action at a distance, such as the workings of the 'powder of sympathy' described at the beginning of this paper. Or, at any rate, we have no idea as to how we could apply them. That is to say, there does not seem to be any intelligible account we could give of why such actions might work on a given occasion but not another. And this might indicate a sense in which we do not just think of the possibility of action-at-a-distance as far-fetched, but in which the idea of action-at-a-distance violates a basic feature of our common-sense concept of causation.

References

Anscombe, G. E. M. (1971). Causality and determination. Reprinted in: P. Van Inwagen and D. W. Zimmermann (eds.) *Metaphysics: The Big Questions* (pp. 244–258). Oxford: Blackwell 1998.

Campbell, J. (1995). *Past, Space and Self*. Cambridge, MA: MIT Press.

[17] I believe that, understood in the way indicated here, concepts such as 'prevent' and 'enable' form an important, and generally neglected, middle ground between what Anscombe (1971) calls special causal concepts, such as 'scrape, push, wet, carry, eat, burn, knock over', and the general concept 'cause'. This issue is discussed in further detail in Hoerl (2011).

—— (2007). An interventionist approach to causation in psychology. In: A. Gopnik and L. E. Schulz (eds.). *Causal Learning: Psychology, Philosophy, and Computation* (pp. 258–266). Oxford: Oxford University Press.

Collins, J., Hall, N., and Paul, L. A. (eds.) (2004). *Causation and Counterfactuals*. Cambridge, MA: MIT Press.

Digby, K. (1658). *A late discourse made in solemne assembly of nobles and learned men at Montpellier in France, touching the cure of wounds by the powder of sympathy*, 2nd edn, trans. R. White. London: R. Lowdes.

Dowe, P. (2000). *Physical Causation*. New York: Cambridge University Press.

Dummett, M. (2005). The justificationist's response to a realist. *Mind* 114, pp. 671–688.

Eilan, N. (1998). Perceptual intentionality, attention and consciousness. In: A. O'Hear (ed.) *Contemporary Issues in the Philosophy of Mind*. (pp. 181–202) Cambridge: Cambridge University Press.

Evans, G. (1982). *The Varieties of Reference*. Oxford: Clarendon Press.

Frisch, M. (2010). Causes, counterfactuals and non-locality. *Australasian Journal of Philosophy* 88, pp. 655–672.

Hall, N. (2002). Non-locality on the cheap? A new problem for counterfactual analyses of causation. *Nous* 36, pp. 276–294.

Hill, A. B. (1965). The environment and disease: association or causation? *Proceedings of the Royal Society of Medicine* 58, pp. 295–300.

Hoerl, C. (2011). Causal reasoning. *Philosophical Studies* 152, pp. 167–179.

Lewis, D. (2004). Causation as influence. In: J. Collins, N. Hall, and L. A. Paul (eds.) *Causation and Counterfactuals*. Cambridge, MA: MIT Press.

Menzies, P. and Price, H. (1993). Causation as a secondary quality. *British Journal for the Philosophy of Science* 44, pp. 187–203.

Mercer, C. (1998). Digby, Kenelm. In E. Craig (ed.), *Routledge Encyclopedia of Philosophy*. London: Routledge.

Peacocke, C. (2005). Justification, realism and the past. *Mind* 114, pp. 639–70.

—— (forthcoming). Representing causality. In: T. McCormack, C. Hoerl, and S. Butterfill (eds.). *Tool Use and Causal Cognition: Issues in Philosophy and Psychology*. Oxford: Oxford University Press.

Pearl, J. (2000). *Causation*. Cambridge: Cambridge University Press.

Povinelli, D. J. (2000). *Folk Physics for Apes: The Chimpanzee's Theory of How the World Works*. Oxford: Oxford University Press.

Price, H. (2007). The effective indexical [Draft at November 23, 2007]. Retrieved from http://philsci-archive.pitt.edu/archive/00004487/01/EffectiveIndexical.pdf

Roessler, J. (1999). Perception, introspection and attention. *European Journal of Philosophy* 7, pp. 47–64.

Salmon, W. (1984). *Scientific Explanation and the Causal Structure of the World*. Princeton: Princeton University Press.

Schaffer, J. (2004). Causes need not be physically connected to their effects. In: C. Hitchcock (ed.). *Contemporary Debates in Philosophy of Science* (pp. 197–216). Oxford: Blackwell.

Strawson, P. F. (1959). *Individuals: An Essay in Descriptive Metaphysics*. London: Routledge.

—— (1979). Perception and its objects. In: G. McDonald (ed.). *Perception and Identity: Essays presented to A. J. Ayer* (pp. 41–60). London: Macmillan & Co.

Tomasello, M. and Call, J. (1997). *Primate Cognition.* Oxford: Oxford University Press.

Woodward, J. (2003). *Making Things Happen: A Theory of Causal Explanation.* Oxford: Oxford University Press.

—— (2007). Interventionist theories of causation in psychological perspective. In: A. Gopnik and L. Schulz (eds.). *Causal Learning: Psychology, Philosophy and Computation* (pp. 19–36). New York: Oxford University Press.

14

Causal Perception and Causal Cognition

*James Woodward**

1 Introduction

What is the role of causal perception in learning about causal relationships and in achieving causal understanding of why things behave as they do? Of course, perception plays a role in the acquisition of much and perhaps all causal knowledge. (Think of using sight to read a text in which one is told about a causal relationship by a reliable authority or of using some statistical or causal modeling procedure to reach a causal conclusion on the basis of data produced by an "observational" study.) My interest in this essay, however, is in a much narrower class of cases which are often described as involving the "perception of causation." Very roughly, it is characteristic of these cases that it appears one can "read off" certain causal relationships from perceptual cues (often but not always visual cues involving spatio-temporal relationships).[1] Moreover, one does this in a way that, phenomenologically at least, seems to have the directness, immediacy, and non-inferential character of other cases in which one detects properties and relations through sensory experience. The perception of causation in a simple collision, in which one appears to see the impact of one billiard ball cause another to move, is a paradigmatic example, but there are many more—it appears one can see one object push or pull another along or see the impact of a moving object (a thrown stone)

* I have benefited greatly from comments and discussions from Jim Bogen, David Danks, Alison Gopnik, Chris Hitchcock, Dave Lagnado, Andrew N. Meltzoff, and Anne Schlotmann. Some of the ideas in this paper were presented at a workshop in honor of John Watson at the Center for Advanced Studies in the Behavioral Sciences at Stanford in March, 2008. I am grateful to the audience there for many helpful suggestions. I am also grateful to members of the Warwick philosophy department, including Stephen Butterfill, Naomi Eilan, Christoph Hoerl, Hemdat Lerman, and Johannes Roessler, for many helpful comments on a longer version of this ms.

[1] In part for reasons of space, I follow the common practice (within both the philosophical and psychological literature) of focusing almost entirely on the role of visual cues in causal perception. It is important to realize, however, that other sorts of sensory modalities—e.g., haptic and auditory—can also play an important role.

cause another (a bottle) to break (cf. Scholl and Tremoulet, 2000). Similarly one can apparently see that one object is supported by another, that a moving ball has been blocked by a solid barrier and will not pass through it, that a key will or will not fit into a lock of a certain shape, and so on.[2]

By no means all causal relationships seem to be detected in this way. Suppose that I am interested in whether a drug will cure a certain illness. I conduct a randomized controlled trial in which the drug is supplied to a treatment group with the illness and withheld from a control group also with the illness. If I observe a higher incidence of recovery in the treatment group, I may be entitled to infer that the drug does indeed cause recovery but in reaching this conclusion I do not seem to rely on causal perception in the sense illustrated above—whether the drug is efficacious is not something that I can read off from geometrical or spatio-temporal cues in the way in which I can apparently read off the role of the impact of the first billiard ball in causing the second to move.

My interest in this essay is in the relationship between the kinds of causal learning illustrated by these two examples—billiard balls and drug efficacy—and more generally in the way in which the experience of causal perception influences causal cognition and the way we conceptualize causation. I shall suggest that the differences between the abilities that, on the one hand, are exhibited in tasks involving causal perception, and, on the other hand, causal judgment tasks like the inference to drug efficacy closely tracks two very different ways of thinking about causation (and about causal learning and causal representation) that one finds in the philosophical and psychological literatures.

In speaking of these "two different ways of thinking" about causation, I emphasize that what I have in mind is, in the first instance, how various *researchers* (particularly in philosophy and psychology) *conceptualize* (or theorize about) causal relationships them-selves as they exist in the world or about the causal concepts/representations that people employ. At this stage, I want to leave it open, as a further, independent question, whether these conceptualizations are accurate or defensible. Whether plausible or not as general accounts of causation and causal representation, I believe it is nonetheless true that an important part of the *motivation* for each of these ways of thinking about causation can be found in the psychological phenomena and capacities for causal learning that I shall be describing.

The first approach, which I take to be grounded in part in experiences having to do with causal perception, involves what I shall call a *geometrical/mechanical conception* of causation.[3] This way of thinking about causation focuses on cases in which there is a physical process connecting cause and effect and, more broadly, on phenomena that are

---

[2] Although some are skeptical, I assume in what follows that it is legitimate to characterize such episodes as involving the perception of causation—for discussion, see Beebee (2003), Menzies (1998), Butterfill (forthcoming).

[3] I do not claim that causal perception is the only source of geometrical/mechanical ideas. In the philosophical literature, physical ideas grounded in special relativity have played an important role in motivating causal process theories (cf. Salmon, 1984)

mediated by contact-mechanical forces and in which spatio-temporal or geometrical relationships play an important role. Causal interactions themselves are conceptualized in terms of contact forces and energy/momentum exchange. This contrasts with a second way of thinking about causation involving a *difference-making conception*. This second conception focuses on causal judgments that are sensitive to *contingency* or difference-making information (roughly, information that compares what happens to the effect in the presence versus the absence of its putative cause). Such judgments may not be guided, at least in any direct way, by spatio-temporal or contact-mechanical information. The randomized trial involving the drug provides an illustration—the trial shows that the drug makes a difference to recovery but does not exhibit a connecting process or contact forces mediating the relationship between drug and recovery.

As we shall see, at least as presented in the philosophical literature, there are deep conceptual differences between geometrical/mechanical and difference-making approaches to causation and these lead, in certain cases, to strikingly different causal judgments. Notoriously, these conceptual differences have made it difficult for philosophers to combine the two approaches into a single, integrated account of causation.[4] Parallel to this, there is also empirical evidence for various sorts of dissociations between judgments guided by causal perception (and based on geometrical/mechanical cues) and judgments based on difference-making or contingency information: that is, the psychological structures that underlie causal perception seem to be at least in part distinct from those that underlie causal judgments based on difference-making considerations and these different structures can lead to judgments or outputs that conflict with each other. My conjecture is that this parallelism is not accidental—I think that various features of causal perception help to motivate or make plausible the intuitions that seem to support geometrical/mechanical accounts of causation, while the kinds of judgments that are based on information about difference-making play a similar role in motivating difference-making theories. The difficulty of putting these two philosophical approaches together into a single integrated account of causation is connected to (and is in part a reflection of) the fact that the psychological processes and judgments with which they are associated also differ in important ways. Nonetheless and despite these facts, adult human causal thinking is characterized by an ability to (often) move back and forth relatively smoothly between these two conceptions—they are relatively well-integrated in adult causal thinking. (There is nothing inevitable about this—as we shall see, in non-human primates and perhaps in human infants, these two conceptions may not be well integrated).

These considerations lead to a number of questions, of both philosophical and psychological interest, that will be explored in this essay. Is one of these two ways of thinking about causation more fundamental than or prior to the other, either

---

[4] For discussion, see, for example, Hall (2004).

developmentally or conceptually? For example, is it true, as some psychologists claim, that a broadly geometrical/mechanical way of thinking about causation, derived from experiences with causal perception, and leading us to conceptualize causation in terms of "forces," serves as a basis for all human causal cognition, including cognition based on difference-making considerations? Or is the difference-making conception and the kind of contingency-based learning associated with it instead more fundamental? Or, as a third alternative, is it more accurate to think of the two conceptions and the abilities associated with them, as instead developing in tandem, mutually influencing or boot-strapping one another? More generally, my hope is that a better understanding of the relationship, both conceptually and developmentally, between the way of thinking about causation naturally suggested by causal perception and the way suggested by difference-making causal judgments will help to clarify both approaches.

The remainder of this essay is organized as follows. Sections 2 to 5 set out some of the differences between difference-making and geometrical/mechanical accounts within philosophy, the (apparently) very different intuitions on which they draw, and the different core phenomena they attempt to describe. Parallels with theories within psychology that focus on causal perception (broadly understood) and theories that instead emphasize contingency based causal judgment are noted. Sections 6 to 8 then describe some relevant psychological results concerning dissociations between causal perception and contingency-based causal judgment and between causal percep-tion and action and attempts to connect these with the ideas introduced in Sections 2–5. Section 9 then takes up some more general issues about the significance of causal perception for our understanding of causation and our capacities for causal cognition.

2 Difference-making theories

As I shall understand *Difference-making* (DM) theories of causation, they rely on the guiding idea that, at least in many paradigmatic cases, and perhaps always, causes must make a difference to their effects.[5] Typically such theories conceive of causal claims as at least implicitly contrastive or comparative in the sense that they imply that there is some possible state which is an alternative to the presence of the cause (a state in which the cause is absent or "different") such that in that state the effect is or would be absent or different (or perhaps its probability would be different). In other words, the presence of the cause makes a difference to the effect in the sense that in a situation in which cause is appropriately different, the effect will or would be different. In philosophy, this difference-making relationship is explicated in variety of different ways—for example,

---

[5] Simple forms of difference-making theories face well-known difficulties in cases involving pre-emption and over-determination, among others. But more sophisticated versions of difference-making theories have been extended to cover such cases, by (roughly) taking the cause to be a difference maker for the effect, conditional on certain other assumptions which either characterize the actual situation or an allowable departure from it—for details see Hitchcock (2001), Woodward (2003).

in terms of relations of necessity, sufficiency, and non-redundancy among factors figuring in regularities, as in Mackie's *INUS* condition account (Mackie, 1974); in terms of a relationship between the probability of the effect conditional on the cause (and other factors) and the probability of the effect conditional on the absence of the cause (and other factors) (Eells, 1991; Eells and Sober, 1983); and in terms of counter-factuals concerning what would happen to the effect if the cause were to occur and how this compares to what would happen to the effect if the cause were not to occur (Lewis, 1973). These differences will largely not matter to what follows.

Some difference-making accounts are "Humean" in the sense that they take causal claims to be fully reducible to claims about regularities or patterns of covariation, but not all difference-making accounts have this feature. (For example, the Eells/Sober, 1983 account and the interventionist theory of Woodward (2003) described below are non-Humean difference-making theories) Moreover, since the difference-making theories described above are theories of what causation is, rather than theories about how one learns about causal relationships, they are also not committed to the claim that the only way that we can learn about causal relationships is through the observation of regularities or patterns of covariation. However, in what follows, I shall assume that difference-making accounts *are* committed to the claim that information about patterns of covariation (including covariation generated by interventions) is one important source of information about causal relationships; that is, I take such accounts to assume that causal judgments will at least be *sensitive* to covariational information, even if such information may not by itself be enough to fully fix which causal judgments are accepted or correct.

As an empirical matter, the claim that causal judgment is (at least sometimes) sensitive to covariational (or as it is sometimes called in the psychological literature "contingency") information does not seem controversial. As Schlottmann and Shanks (1992) remark, there is a huge body of experimental evidence supporting this claim. It is one of the virtues of difference-making accounts that they seem to provide a natural explanation of why covariational information is relevant to causal judgment. By contrast, as we shall see, accounts that instead focus on the role of connecting processes (and geometrical/mechanical information) have a more difficult time making sense of the role of covariational information.

As remarked above, I regard interventionist accounts of causation as one particular kind of difference-making theory. According to interventionist accounts, causes make a difference to their effects in the sense that if an intervention (roughly, an idealized experimental manipulation) were to occur which changes the value of a cause variable (e.g., by introducing the cause into an appropriate situation in which it was previously absent or removing it from a situation in which it was previously present) this would make a difference to the value of the effect variable. Interventionist theories do not claim that the only way to learn about causal relationships is to actually perform interventions—they agree that one can sometimes learn about causal relationships from passive observation (typically these will be observations that provide covariational information). However, they hold that the causal claim one learns in such a case has an *interventionist interpretation*—roughly, it is information about what would happen if one *were* to perform an intervention. Interventionist accounts thus make the potential role of causal claims in guiding action and manipulation central to understanding the content of those claims. As we shall see (Section 8), this feature of interventionism puts it in some tension with at least some accounts that take causal perception to be central to the acquisition of causal knowledge.

As remarked above, the philosophical treatments of causation just described are intended, in the first instance, as accounts of what causation is or of what causal claims correspond to "in the world." By contrast, psychologists interested in causation tend to focus, unsurprisingly, on causal *cognition*: on such issues as how causal relationships are represented, learned, reasoned about, and so on, both by humans and other animals. Nonetheless, many, perhaps most philosophers working on causation have also held views about human causal cognition and, depending on the details of their views, have often moved back and forth between worldly claims about what causation is and psychological claims about the nature of causal cognition. This is unsurprising: To the extent that one thinks that human causal thinking, at least sometimes, accurately tracks or reflects causal features of the world, as described by one's philosophical theory of causation, one also will likely think there is some relation between these worldly features and what goes on in people's heads when they engage in causal thinking and learning. For example, if one thinks that causal relationships are best represented in terms of relationships among conditional probabilities, then it is likely to seem plausible that successful causal cognition in some way involves the mental representation of facts about conditional probabilities.

Similarly, suppose as some theorists in the causal process tradition claim (Salmon, 1984), that whether c causes e has to do only with the presence or absence of a "causal process" connecting c to e and not with the truth or falsity of comparative claims concerning whether e would or does occur in situations in which c is absent. Then, prima facie at least, to the extent that human causal judgment is accurate or represents the causal facts as they actually are, one would not expect it to be sensitive to such comparative information. To the extent that causal judgment is sensitive to such information, it would seem natural to conclude that either (i) people are making a mistake of some kind (their causal judgments are influenced by information that is irrelevant to the truth of those judgments) or else (ii) the causal process account is not the whole story about causal relationships, as they are in the world.[6] For these reasons, although it is of course true that causation is one thing and our representations or judgments about it another, I believe it is illuminating to group together philosophical accounts of what causation is with psychological accounts of causal cognition and

---

[6] Of course there are other possibilities: perhaps the comparative information somehow conveys evidence about a causal process connecting c to e, but not by conveying information about what would happen if c were different etc. (since the latter information is supposed to be irrelevant to the truth of causal claims). Needless to say, the details of this would require some spelling out.

representation insofar as these focus on the same sorts of information about or features of causal relationships.

Proceeding in this way, one may identify a number of influential theories of causal learning and judgment within empirical psychology that also seem to embody a broadly difference-making conception of causation or of causal representation. These will include accounts that take causal learning and judgment to involve the representation of contingency information (understood as having to do with a comparison between the frequency of the effect in the presence of the cause with the frequency of the effect in the absence of the cause). Examples include accounts of judgments of causal strength according to which this depends on $\Delta p = P(O/A) - P(O/-A)$ (where A is some action the subject chooses and O an outcome) and Patricia Cheng's causal power theory. Accounts according to which causal representation has the structure of a Bayes net (and/or according to which causal learning involves learning the structure of a Bayes net) are also naturally understood as difference-making accounts, since they make predictions about claims about how values or expectation values of effect variables will change depending upon changes of various sorts in the value of cause variables.

3 Geometrical/mechanical theories

Standing in contrast to difference-making theories are geometrical/mechanical theories. These focus on the role of connecting processes or more broadly on the role of what Scholl and Leslie, 1999, call "contact mechanical" relationships between cause and effect.[7] "Mechanical" in this context is not easy to define, but, roughly, it at least includes, at the level of folk physics, those causal relationships which physical objects enter into in virtue of their possession of properties like solidity, rigidity, and impenetrability. Usually the idea is that the presence of such a contact mechanical relationship is signaled by the holding of a rather specific spatio-temporal relationship between cause and effect. On some versions of this idea, there is a single characteristic spatio-temporal signature (e.g spatio-temporal contiguity) that is common to all causal relationships; on other versions, it is held, more plausibly, that different causal relationships will have different spatio-temporal signatures—collisions will differ in this respect from, say, support.

In the philosophical literature, the most familiar recent examples of geometrical/mechanical theories are the *causal process* or *conserved quantity* theories of Salmon (e.g, 1984) and Dowe (2000). Here the guiding thought is that some particular event c

---

[7] Although the phrase "contact mechanical" captures many of the relationships that fall into the geometrical/mechanical category, it is overly narrow in the sense that there can be perception of causation even in the absence of overt evidence of spatial contact, as in the case of "pulling." Nonetheless, the label is a useful one since it correctly suggests that the interactions in this category are mediated (even if this is not apparent) by contact forces, such as those involved in collisions, pushing, support, and so on.

causes some other event *e* if and only if there is a connecting causal process from *c* to *e,* where this means roughly that there is a spatio-temporally continuous process linking cause and effect that transmits a conserved quantity such as energy and/or momentum. A paradigmatic example of such an interaction is one rigid object striking another and causing it to move, as when two billiard balls collide.

Within empirical psychology, there are a number of theories and research programs that draw on ideas that are broadly similar to those on which causal process theories focus. It thus seems natural to group these within the general category of geometrical/ mechanical accounts. These approaches downplay the significance of covariational or contingency information (including covariational information generated by interventions) in causal learning and judgment and instead focus on the role of spatio-temporal cues that are readily perceptually accessible and/or on "mechanical" information which seems to be associated with such cues.

One of the most straightforward examples of psychological research focusing on geometrical/mechanical causation is so-called "causal perception" in connection with collisions or "launching events"—phenomena which have been extensively studied by Michotte (1963), Leslie (e.g., 1995), and others. Here the details of the spatio-temporal relationship between colliding objects guide the perception (or not) of a causal interaction and, as we shall see, at least under some conditions, this perception apparently does *not* depend on contingency or difference-making information about how these or similar objects would have moved in the absence of spatio-temporal contact. But within the general category of the geometrical/mechanical, one might also include interactions having to do with solidity, occlusion, support, containment, entrainment, and impenetrability. Our understanding of such phenomena again seems to involve, at least in adults, causal knowledge of some form which is strongly guided by spatio-temporal or geometrical cues that are readily perceptually accessible.[8]

Consider support. Adult humans easily recognize (e.g., on the basis of visual inspection) that an apparently solid physical object at rest on a solid surface in such a way that the boundaries of the surface extend beyond the object (e.g., a plate on a table) is typically supported by that surface and will move with the surface if the latter is not moved too abruptly. This seems to involve recognition of a causal relationship between the surface and the object. Adults (but not sufficiently young children—see below) also recognize that not just any kind of spatial contact between surface and object is sufficient for support and can sometimes determine from visual inspection whether the contact is of such a character as to provide support. In all of these cases,

---

[8] For reasons that are unclear to me psychologists often restrict the notion of causal perception to phenomena like collisions and pushing and do not describe perceptual recognition of support, impenetrability of barriers, and so on as involving "causal perception." Perhaps in some cases this reflects an implicit theory that the perceptual mechanisms underlying the former are different from those underlying the latter, although a number of prominent psychologists (e.g. Leslie, Spelke) seem to suggest that the same mechanisms or implicit theory underlie both. In this paper, I shall group both sets of phenomena together, leaving open the extent to which underlying mechanisms may be the same or different.

causal relationships between the object and its support seem to be read off from their geometrical relationship (via visual perception) in a straightforward way.

Within psychology, subjects' understanding or representation of phenomena like those just described (collisions, support, etc.) is often taken to involve notions like "force transmission" (Leslie, 1995) or "force dynamics" (Wolff, 2007) or to involve the deployment of a "theory of body" (Leslie again) or various "core physical principles" (Spelke et al., 1995) which specify, for example, that moving solid objects follow spatio-temporally continuous paths and cannot pass through each other. Often this is accompanied by the claim that the concepts and principles deployed in the recognition/understanding of mechanical interactions like those described above serve as the basis for more general notions of causation and causal mechanism, which are then taken to be central to causal cognition in other circumstances as well—in other words, the experience of causal perception and the processes and representations associated with this somehow give us the concepts and capacities that underlie adult causal cognition. For example, Schlottmann and Shanks (1992), suggest that the "mechanism of causal perception . . . would provide a robust intuitive understanding of the concept of cause that is not fraught with the ambiguities encountered when trying to define cause" (p. 341). Similar suggestions can be found in Pinker (2007), Spelke et al. (1995), Wolff (2007).

Although this is not made explicit in the psychological literature, presumably part of the motivation for invoking notions like "force transmission" (rather than the narrower notion of "causal process" described by Salmon, and Dowe) is that many paradigmatically mechanical phenomena do not seem to be very adequately captured by accounts of the latter type. Seeing that a table supports a (stationary) plate does not (at least prima facie) involve tracing causal processes and their intersections since there is no energy or momentum exchange involved in the support. The table and apple do, however, exert forces on one another and it is presumably this that prompts psychologists like Leslie to attempt to subsume such phenomena under the broader category of "force transmission." Of course, according to current physical theory, forces are not literally "transmitted" but the basic idea that phenomena like support (and for that matter, collisions) are to be understood in terms of contact forces is certainly correct.[9]

I emphasized above that to the extent that causal perception involves vision, it seems to be based largely on spatio-temporal or geometrical cues. However, as already intimated, the way in which adult humans conceptualize or understand (at a common-sense or folk level) mechanical phenomena like collisions, support, and so on

[9] In both the philosophical and psychological literatures there are also discussions of a more general and diffuse notion of mechanism which is not limited to examples involving straightforward contact mechanics and which is intended to cover (among other things) talk of neural and biochemical mechanisms—see e.g., Machamer, Darden, and Craver (2000) and Bechtel (2006). The arguments of this paper are not intended to engage with issues about this broader notion of mechanism; I observe only that its connection with the narrower contact mechanical notions on which I focus is far from transparent. The broader notion does share with the narrower the idea that spatio-temporal relations and organization matter.

seems to involve ideas about the solidity, rigidity, and impenetrability of bodies, as well as an appreciation of facts about their spatio-temporal relationships and relative motions. Such facts about rigidity, solidity, and so on do not seem to be reducible to facts about spatio-temporal relationships. Conceptually, it seems to be one thing for an object to be at rest on a larger surface and another thing for the object to be *supported* by the surface—the latter requires not just that the object be in spatio-temporal contact with the surface but also that the surface be strong or rigid enough to support the object and that the object be maintained in that position by forces exerted by the surface, rather than by some other set of forces. (This is part of the folk or common-sense conception of support, but it is also true from the point of view of physics.) Parallel remarks apply to collisions, blocking of the path of one object by another, and so on.

This distinction between mechanical and spatio-temporal properties also has an empirical psychological component. It is widely thought to be possible for the visual system to process (see) phenomena that appear to violate naïve physics expectations involving mechanical properties—for example, one can see one solid object apparently pass through another, even while recognizing that this is "physically impossible" (Leslie, 1995). This has suggested to a number of writers that the neural systems that process information about trajectories and spatio-temporal relationships are in some respects distinct in their operation from the systems that process mechanical features like impenetrability. For example, Leslie suggests on this basis that we possess a "theory of body" that characterizes various simple mechanical features of objects that is distinct from our understanding of the purely spatio-temporal aspects of object behavior.[10]

How then are mechanical and spatio-temporal properties related in causal perception? Very roughly, what often seems to happen is this: we operate in an environment in which many of the objects we view have mechanical properties like rigidity etc. (This is not to say, of course, that we necessarily "assume" that this is the case, at least in any sense that implies conscious or explicit entertainment of this assumption. Adult humans may make such assumptions but perhaps infants do not.) Because objects have these features, it is possible to read off (or perceive) causal relationships from information about their spatio-temporal relationships in a fairly reliable fashion. If the objects with which we were dealing did not have features like rigidity and solidity, spatio-temporal information would often be a much less reliable source of causal information—thus spatio-temporal contact between two objects that are not solid may tell us little about whether the motion of one causally influences the motion of another, we cannot read off from the shape of a non-rigid key whether it will open a lock, and so on. Of course it is also true that sometimes the absence of rigidity will show up in spatio-temporal clues: the object will deform etc.

---

[10] It is also relevant in this connection that mechanical properties seem to be (or are naturally thought of as) cross-modal or amodal, or at least not tied to a single sensory modality like vision. For example, haptic experiences seem relevant to the assessment of objects as rigid.

Although writers like Leslie might claim otherwise, I think that one implication of the distinction between the spatio-temporal and the mechanical is that we should be wary of moving too readily from the observation that a subject is capable of causal perception in the sense of reliably discriminating between causal and non-causal relationships on the basis of spatio-temporal cues to the conclusion that the subject must be explicitly conceptualizing those causal relationships in terms of mechanical categories like rigidity and force. Reliable discrimination may require nothing more than that the objects with which we are dealing have certain mechanical properties and that certain spatio-temporal relationships are recognized, not that the subject possesses explicit concepts of such mechanical properties or their causal role.

4 The relationship between DM and GM theories

How are difference-making and geometrical/mechanical ways of thinking about causation related to each other? Let us begin by noticing some differences.

4.1 Type versus token

There are a number of difference-making (DM) accounts of so-called token (or singular) causation, both in the philosophical literature and elsewhere, with David Lewis' (1973) version of a counterfactual theory of event causation being perhaps the most prominent. Nonetheless, the most natural domain of such theories seems to be so-called type causal claims—claims that some type of factor C causes or is causally relevant to another factor E, where C and E are kinds that may be repeatedly realized. This in turn is presumably connected to the fact that contingency or difference-making information is most naturally described in terms of relationships among types of repeatable events.

By way of contrast, geometrical/mechanical (GM) theories seem to apply in the first instance to particular causal interactions involving individual events or occurrences—to token causation—although attempts have been made to extend them to contexts involving type causal claims. This is presumably because it is particular pairs of events that are connected by causal processes and particular objects which stand in geometrical/mechanical relationships involving contact forces. As a matter of phenomenology, it also appears that one first detects such particular causal interactions on the basis of perceptual cues (causal perception) and only later, if at all, generalizes to type relations involving other cases—any generalization follows the awareness of the particular case, rather than preceding it. (See below for experimental evidence supporting this picture.) It is thus not surprising to find such experiences are one of the primary sources of so-called "singularist" views about causation (cf. Armstrong, 2004).

4.2 Domain-general versus domain-specific

Difference-making theories are *domain-general* in the sense that virtually any kind of event, or factor which is capable of variation may (in principle) stand in a difference-making relationship to another such event or factor. (Of course, it is an empirical matter which such relationships in fact hold in any particular case.) This is a reflection of the fact that difference-making relationships (whether understood in terms of regularities, conditional probabilities, or counterfactuals) do not restrict the content of causal claims in the sense of excluding certain kinds of items as candidates for causal relata on *apriori* grounds. Thus difference-making causal relationships can hold between physical items like billiard balls, but also between mental items like beliefs, between mental and physical items (beliefs and behavior) between social and economic variables, and so on.

In contrast, geometrical/mechanical theories are *domain-specific*. The natural domain of application of such theories concerns the interactions of solid objects bearing specific spatio-temporal relations to one another, and which we are able to describe in terms of processes like energy/momentum transfer or physical forces involving contact between objects or surfaces. It is not obvious how to apply geometrical/mechanical theories to causal relationships between factors that lack these features such as relationships involving mental events or economic variables (e.g., increases in the money supply cause increases in inflation).

4.3 Comparative versus non-comparative

Conceptually one of the most obvious differences between difference-making ac-counts and causal process accounts is that the latter (at least in standard philosophical formulations, such as those due to Salmon and Dowe) do not conceive of causal claims as comparative in the way that the former do. According to causal process accounts, whether *c* causes *e* on some particular occasion depends just on whether the appropriate connecting process or contact relationship linking *c* to *e* is present on that occasion. In particular, whether *c* causes *e* on that occasion does *not* depend on what happens or would happen with respect to *e* or *e*-like events on other occasions—either on other occasions in which *c* or *c*-like events occur or in cases in which they are absent. Indeed, it is a common claim of causal process theorists (and many others who are sympathetic to geometrical/mechanical approaches to causation) that allowing such dependence would violate the (apparently natural) intuition that whether *c* causes *e* should depend just on the "local" or "intrinsic" character of the connecting relationship between *c* and *e*: facts about what would happen to *e* if *c* had not occurred or if *c*-like events had or had not occurred on other occasions seem "extrinsic" to whether or not there is a causal relationship between *c* and *e* on this particular occasion.

I believe that this feature of causal process theories is paralleled by our common-sense picture of what is involved in particular examples of causal perception. Suppose that we see a moving billiard ball strike a second stationary ball and then see the latter begin to move, the spatio-temporal parameters governing the collision being such that we perceive that the collision caused the second ball to move. Our common-sense picture is that all that we need for this perception (and the judgment that we base on it) is contained in "local," non-comparative information about the trajectories of the balls, their spatial contact, and the almost immediate subsequent motion of the second ball.[11] In particular, this perception does not seem to require that we compare the actual motion of the balls that we perceive with some alternative—e.g., that we consider what would happen to the trajectory of the second ball if there was no collision. Indeed, it appears that we can perceive/judge/know that the collision with the first ball caused the second to move, even if we do not know how or whether the second ball would have moved in the absence of the collision (for all we may know, collision with a third ball would have caused the second ball to move even in the absence of a collision with the first). In other words, the perceptual judgment that the collision caused the second ball to move does not seem to be based on considerations having to do with difference-making. Of course, in many ecologically natural circumstances (e.g., if no other cause of motion of the second ball is present and if it does not move spontaneously), adults will readily (and correctly) connect this perceptual causal judgment based on geometrical/mechanical cues to a difference-making judgment: they will judge that the second ball would not have moved if the collision with the first ball had not occurred and so on. So in such cases, at least, we are willing to move relatively seamlessly from perceptual causal judgments to judgments about difference-making. Nonetheless, the latter judgment seems (that is, from the point of view of our folk psychology of causal judgment which may of course mislead us) independent of the former; it seems like an *additional* thought that follows from the perception of causation, rather than serving as a basis for it.

4.4 Additional differences between the two accounts

A number of other observations from the philosophical literature seem to support this picture according to which ordinary causal judgment is guided by two (at least) partially distinct ways of thinking about causation.

First, as a conceptual matter, geometrical/mechanical causal connectedness (or the operation of contact forces) is apparently not necessary for difference-making. This is shown by the observation that it seems prima facie possible that one factor should act as a difference-maker for another even if there is no connecting process or spatio-temporal contact between the two. Theories that postulate action at a distance, such as Newtonian gravitational theory, provide an illustration of difference-making without contact action.

Second, geometrical/mechanical causal connectedness is also not sufficient for difference-making. Basically, this is because the presence or absence of such connectedness is too coarse-grained to capture the judgments of causal relevance that difference-making accounts embody. If I rub the tip of a cue stick in blue chalk, use the stick to strike the cue ball, which in turn strikes the eight ball, sending it into the corner pocket, the blue chalk may be transferred to the eight ball, via a spatio-temporally

---

[11] This intuition is apparently not correct for more complex causal perception cases involving several launching-like events—see Scholl and Nakayama (2001)

continuous process in which energy and momentum is conserved, but the presence of the blue chalk is not what made the difference for whether or not the eight ball drops and still less is it responsible for the detailed behavior of the eight ball—its velocity when it falls into the pocket and so on (Hitchcock, 1995). Similarly, when I bounce a tennis ball against a brick wall, there is a connecting causal process from the motion of my hand to the wall, but this motion and the impact of the ball do not make a difference for whether the wall stands up.

As these examples illustrate, the true claim that there is a causal process linking X and Y does not tell us which features of X make a causal difference for various features of Y. Indeed, the presence of the connecting process does not even ensure that there is some feature of the process that makes a difference to the particular feature of Y that is of interest. This seems connected to the point that even veridical causal perception often does not disclose fine-grained difference-making information. For example, the experience of seeing that a collision with one billiard ball has caused another to move does not disclose what properties of the first ball are causally relevant to the details of the subsequent motion of the second ball—it does not tell us that the energy and momentum of the first ball are the crucial difference-making variables. Similarly, seeing that one object supports another does not tell us in any detailed way which features of their relationship make a difference for successful support—for example, it does not tell us about the relevance of the position of the center of gravity of the supported object. One implication of this that is relevant to psychology is that the fact that a subject is sensitive to, e.g., the difference between collisions involving causal interactions and sequences that do not involve causation does not automatically ensure that the subject has a detailed understanding of the difference-making features of the collision.

Despite this, it is worth noting that when there is a causal process or a geometrical/mechanical connection between X and Y, it is often heuristically useful to examine X or this connecting process in order to locate difference-making features for Y (even if the mere existence of the connection does not tell us what those features are). In other words, when there is such a "physical" connection, some feature of X *may* be one locus of the difference-making; in the absence of such a connection it will often be plausible to conclude that the difference-making features for Y are not contained in X. Thus, if one perceives that a collision with X causes Y to move, it will be a good bet that there are properties of X that are difference-makers for Y's subsequent movement, even though this perception does not by itself tell us what these features are and they instead must be identified in some other way. For example, to understand the breaking of a bottle in detail, one should focus on features of the rock that hit it and the interaction of this rock with the bottle rather than on the rock that missed it. I shall suggest below that this has implications for one possible role of causal perception in development: causal perception can tell us where to look for more fine-grained difference-making features, without requiring that we have already identified those features.

In addition to the conceptual differences between GM and DM described above, they seem to lead to different causal judgments about particular cases, such as those involving causation by omission and double prevention. This is a familiar theme in the philosophical literature (cf. Hall, 2004), but I shall use results from a recent series of psychological experiments to illustrate the point. Walsh and Sloman (forthcoming) presented subjects with two scenarios. In the first, a coin standing unstably on its edge is about to fall tails. Billy and Suzy roll marbles in such a way that each will strike the coin and after impact the coin will land heads but Billy's marble strikes first. In this scenario, 74% of subjects judged that Billy's marble caused the coin to land heads.

In the second scenario, we have an unstable coin about to land heads. A third party rolls a marble in such a way that if it strikes the coin, it will land tails. Both Frank and Jane reach out to stop the marble. Frank reaches it first, stops it, and the coin lands heads; Jane does not reach the coin but she would have if Frank had not. In this case, only 18% judged that Frank caused the coin to land heads.

Note that both scenarios have a very similar counterfactual or difference-making structure[12]: (a) it is *not* the case that if Billy's marble had not struck the coin, the coin would not have landed heads (since Suzy's would have struck it); (b) it *is* the case that holding fixed the fact that Suzy's marble does not strike the coin, the coin's landing heads is counterfactually dependent on the impact of Billy's marble. The judgment that Billy's marble caused the coin to land heads is made despite (a) and (some[13] would claim) on the basis of (b). In the second scenario, (a′) it is not the case that if Frank had not reached the coin, it would have landed heads (because Jane would have stopped it) but (b′) given that Jane does not stop the coin, the coins landing heads is counterfactually dependent on whether Frank reaches it. Nonetheless, far fewer (although a non-negligible proportion of) subjects judge that Frank's action caused the coin to land heads than the proportion who make the corresponding judgment in the Billy scenario.

It is a natural thought that the difference in judgments about the two cases reflects the different role that geometrical/mechanical information plays in them. In the first scenario, there is spatio-temporal contact and the transmission of energy from Billy's marble to the coin that we readily interpret as causal. In the second scenario, there is no spatio-temporal contact or connecting process between Frank's interception of the marble and the coin's landing heads. Although a more sophisticated version of a DM theory might judge otherwise, a simple version diverges in its judgments from those recommended by GM theories, with the latter seeing a difference between the two scenarios that the former does not recognize. Moreover, the latter seems closer (in this particular case) to the judgments that the majority of subjects make. The example illustrates how in some cases GM-based considerations seem to operate independently of DM-based considerations in influencing causal judgment.

---

[12] This is noted by Pinker (2007) although he describes simpler versions of the scenarios.
[13] See Hitchcock (2001).

5 Two concepts of causation?

One possible reaction to the differences between geometrical/mechanical and difference-making accounts of causation is that this shows that we operate with two distinct
"concepts" or "senses" of causation. Something like this position is adopted by Ned
Hall (2004), whose candidates for the two concepts, which he calls dependence and
production, coincide in significant measure, although not entirely, with the distinctions that I have drawn. However, there are at least two reasons why this reaction does
not seem entirely satisfactory. First, as Hall recognizes (p. 255), it isn't clear why we
should describe the situation in terms of there being two concepts rather than in some
other way—e.g., in terms of their being two different ways that one event can be a
cause of another, or (for yet another alternative) in terms of their being different
accounts of a single concept of causation that focus on different strands or elements
in that concept.[14]

A more fundamental reason why it seems unilluminating simply to rest content with a
"two concepts" diagnosis is this: both conceptually and as matter of empirical psychology, the two concepts (or whatever) seem interconnected or interrelated in all sorts of
ways. As we have noted, adults bring together both information about difference-
making and information deriving from geometrical/mechanical cues in arriving at causal
judgments, and often move relatively seamlessly from geometrical/mechanical information to conclusions about difference-making and conversely. Seeing that one object
supports another, we often readily make the difference-making judgment that the
second object will fall if we remove the first and use this information to guide planning
and action. It thus seems that in addition to appreciating the differences between the
geometrical/mechanical and difference-making approaches, we also need to better
understand how adult causal judgment combines elements of both.

6 Causal perception in launching experiments

I turn now to a more detailed look at some psychological research concerning causal
perception, with a particular focus on dissociations of various kinds between perception and contingency-based causal judgment. This will illustrate some of the ideas and
contrasts described in previous sections.

The general contours of the collision or "launching" phenomena studied by
Michotte (1963) and subsequently by many (e.g. Leslie, Scholl) others are probably
known to the reader. In a typical experiment subjects view an object A which moves in
such a way that it appears to collide with or closely approach a second object B. After
the collision A stops and very shortly afterwards B begins to move in the same direction

---

[14] It also seems relevant that people generally do not seem to be confused by a systematic ambiguity in the
meaning of causal claims, do not seem to feel a need to distinguish which of two possible meanings they have
in mind when they use causal claims etc.—all of which one might think they would do if there were two
sharply distinct senses of causation.

as A's previous movement. Depending in various delicate ways on the spatio-temporal parameters characterizing the collision, most (or at least many) subjects will report either a strong perceptual impression of causality or no such impression. The impression of causation persists even though subjects are aware that they are viewing two dimensional shapes on a computer screen (or in Michotte's case film images projected on a screen)—that is, even though subjects know that they are looking at illusory causal interactions rather than the real thing.

Although the launching effect has been extensively studied, it is certainly not the only case involving interactions among moving objects in which there is perception of causation. For example, when shapes are lined up in a column on a screen and exhibit staggered motion, the first shape to move is perceived as pulling the others, even if no spatial contact is present. Simultaneous motion of the shapes does not give rise to this impression. Other stimuli giving rise to perceptual impressions of causation involve "disintegration" and "bursting" (cf. Scholl and Tremoulet, 2000). Although spatio-temporal contiguity is not required for causal perception in such cases, it is still true it is the appearance of a characteristic spatio-temporal pattern that seems to guide causal perception.

7 Causal perception and contingency-based causal judgment

In a fascinating series of experiments, Schlottmann and Shanks (1992) investigated the relationship between what they called "judged" (this being causal judgment influenced by contingency information) causality and "perceived" causality, finding evidence for a dissociation. In their first experiment, subjects viewed launching-like events in which the temporal delay between A and B was varied in such a way that impact of A did not predict (was not correlated with) when B would move. However, in half of the viewings, a color change in A reliably predicted when B would move. The motivation for this experiment was that verbal judgments of the strength of causal relatedness are known to track the contingency or covariation between potential causes and the effect. In particular, even when there is spatio-temporal contiguity between events A and B, if A is not a reliable predictor of B, but some third event C is, judgments of causal strength between C and B should increase over the course of the trials and judgments for the relation between A and B should drop—A is said in this case to be "discounted" (or overshadowed by C) as a cause of B. The color change = C was chosen because it was known on the basis of other evidence that subjects do not report a perception of causation when a color change in A precedes movement in B, although the color change is sufficiently perceptually salient that subjects will notice its association with B's motion.

Subjects were asked to "rate" the relationship between A and B along a scale, one end of which was labeled "A caused B to move," and the other end, "A did not cause B to move." The rating task was introduced with the following words:

Your task in this experiment will be to judge how confident you are that A caused B to move or that A did not cause B to move. In other words, you will judge just how "good" or "bad" a collision looks to you.

Subjects were also prompted in this task by such questions as, "Did it look to you as though A hit B and caused it to move?" (p. 328). Schlottmann and Shanks take these ratings to be measures of perceived causality and find, strikingly, that the color changes had no effect on these ratings at the various temporal delays between A and B, although the temporal delay itself did of course influence these ratings. Schlottmann and Shanks interpret this as evidence for a "dissociation" between perceived and judged causality—the alternative candidate C for the cause of B has no effect on the perceived causality between A and B (that is, as far as perceived causation goes, there is no discounting of A as a cause of B) even though (at least in other circumstances) the presence of such an alternative is known to affect causal judgment.[15]

In a second, more direct experiment, subjects viewed launching events in which the color change not only predicted when B would move but whether it would move at all. In *contingent* trials, subjects saw launch events with a color change at the point of impact, on half of the trials. For the other half, object A remained in its starting position and B changed color and did not move. Thus the probability of movement in B given launching by A was 1.0 and the probability of movement of B in the absence of launching was 0. In the non-contingent trials, the subjects saw the same number of launch events with color changes as in the contingent trials. On the other half of trials, subjects saw A remaining in its starting position and a color change in B preceding its movement. Thus, while B would move whenever there was a collision, it would also move whenever there was a color change, even without a collision. There was thus no contingency between collision with A and B's movement.

As before, subjects were asked to rate perceived causality in single launch events. They were also asked to judge how "necessary" collisions with A were for making B move. Ratings of perceived causality "show[ed] a substantial contiguity effect but no contingency effect whatsoever" (1992, p. 337)—that is ratings fell with increased

---

[15] An important issue raised by this interpretation has to do with how subjects interpret the verbal probe for perceptual causality. Consider the following analogy: subjects are shown the Muller-Lyer illusion and then asked (a) whether it "looks to them" as though one of the lines is shorter than the other. They are also asked (b) whether they would judge that one of the lines is shorter than the other (or something equivalent.) If subjects answer "yes" to the first question and "no" to the second, it would be (at least) problematic to interpret this as a "dissociation" between perceived and judged length and even more problematic to take it as evidence that "different mechanisms" (in the non-trivial sense of "different mechanisms" that Schlottmann and Shanks have in mind) were responsible for reports of perceived and judged length. I take it that Schlottman and Shanks are assuming that their experimental task is not (and is not interpreted by their subjects as) like this. That is, subjects do not think of the relationship between perceptual ratings of causation and judged causation as like the relationship between a visual illusion of X and X itself. I think that this assumption is justified, but regret that I cannot for reasons of space address it in the kind of detail it deserves. It would be relevant to see what subject's ratings/judgments are when other sorts of probes are used that do not suggest an appearance/reality distinction—e.g., they might simply be asked if A caused B to move. I am grateful to Chris Hitchcock for raising this issue in characteristically persuasive way.

temporal delay but were uninfluenced by the contingency between collision with A and subsequent movement of B. On the other hand, judgments of causal necessity showed a "large contingency effect and a much smaller contiguity effect." (p. 337). Subjects' spontaneous comments reflected this dissociation; several commented that on contingent problems with delay, they were aware that collision was necessary for A to move but that "it just did not look as if it should be." On non-contingent problems with no temporal delay, they commented that "they knew the collision was not necessary for B to move but it looked as if it should be" (328).

As Schlottmann and Shanks interpret these experiments, they involve situations in which subjects reported perceiving that collision with A caused B's movement (because the appropriate spatio-temporal relationship between A and B's motion was present), but also claimed that collision with A was not necessary for B to move, which sounds like the claim that A was not a difference-making cause of B. The authors take this to show that distinct "mechanisms" underlie perceived and judged causality. If this interpretation is accepted, it does not seem farfetched also to take the experiments to illustrate a dissociation between two kinds of causal *judgment*, resulting from different psychological mechanisms, one based on perceived causality and reflecting elements of a geometrical/mechanical conception of causation and the other reflecting a difference-making conception.[16]

More recent neuro-imaging data shows that causal perception and contingency-based causal judgment involves distinct neural regions or mechanisms and hence supports the conclusion that the brain processes underlying these are in principle dissociable. In particular causal perception of collisions involves visual area V5/MT (middle temporal), STS (superior temporal sulcus), and left IPS (intra-parietal sulcus) (Blakemore et al., 2003). V5/MT is a higher visual area known to be involved in motion processing, and STS is known to be involved in the processing and recognition of complex visual stimuli, including those having to do with facial movements, hand actions, and movements suggesting animacy. Finding activation in MT/V5 is not in itself surprising (the region is sensitive to relative motion) but the greater activation in this area when causal events (as opposed to non-causal events) are perceived may suggest that causal events are perceived as more complex or that they trigger more processing than non-causal events. The other two regions (STS and IPS) are also often involved in the higher-level interpretation of visual events, although not part of occipital cortex.

By contrast, contingency influenced causal judgment, including such judgments concerning mechanical interactions like collisions, is believed to involve more frontal areas, in particular dorsolateral prefrontal cortex (DLPFC) and, especially when motor action and planning are involved (as in tool use), also portions of the parietal cortex. To

---

[16] Schlottman and Shanks do not describe reports of perceptual causality as judgments but rather as "ratings." The proposed connection with DM and GM conceptions is not suggested by Schlottman and Shanks but is rather my own addition.

my knowledge, it is not known what neural areas are involved in causal perception associated with other contact/mechanical phenomena such as support.

At this point, it is worth pausing and relating these observations explicitly to some of the claims made in section 4. I noted there that it seemed to be part of our common-sense picture of collisions that we can tell whether one object has caused another to move just by noting that a collision with the right spatio-temporal parameters occurred; it appears that the contingency information on which difference-making accounts focus (how the second ball would have moved in the absence of a collision with the first) is not required for this assessment. The experimental results from Schlottmann and Shanks seem consistent with this common-sense picture, since they seem to imply that perception-based causal judgments or assessments based on individual collisions are independent of and can even be inconsistent with what contingency information suggests about causal relationships. Of course ordinary subjects will not be aware of the Schlottmann and Shanks experiment, but it is a natural conjecture that the partial independence or dissociability of causal assessments based on geometrical/mechanical cues and those based on contingency information underlies and motivates (at least in part) some of the causal intuitions that both ordinary people and philosophers have about cases involving both geometrical/mechanical and contingency information. In other words, the thought that one can tell, just on the basis of information about the local spatio-temporal parameters governing the relationship between two objects, and in the absence of supporting contingency information, that a collision with the first has caused the second to move is one source of the intuitions that underlie causal process accounts of causation. (I should perhaps add that of course I do *not* mean that mere possession of causal perception abilities also means one will possess a worked-out GM account of causation; my suggestion is rather that reflection on certain judgments associated with causal perception helps to make GM accounts seem plausible and that the dissociation in the Schlottmann/Shanks experiments mirrors the way in which GM-based and DM-based judgments can come apart in particular cases.)

Now consider a thought experiment. Imagine a creature who possesses just one but not both of the capacities for causal learning and judgment exhibited in the Schlottmann/Shanks experiment or alternatively, possesses both capacities but is unable to integrate them—that is, a creature who either (i) is able to make the kinds of perceptual discriminations that we associate with causal perception (discriminates causal-looking launching events from events that do not look causal), but does not make causal judgments based on contingency information or (ii) has the opposite profile or (iii) has both capacities but does not connect or integrate them. The possibility envisioned under (iii) is that in the Schlottmann/Shanks experiment the subject would make both the same perceptual causal judgments that normal subjects do and the same contingency-based judgments but would not be puzzled or surprised by any inconsistency between the two classes of judgments, as the subjects in the Schlottmann/Shanks experiment are. That is, the subject would not be surprised to see an interaction between A and B that "looks causal" in individual cases, but is not accompanied by any contingency between A and B. We might think of such a subject as possessing two entirely distinct and unconnected concepts of causation, corresponding respectively to aspects of the geometrical/mechanical conception and the difference-making conception.

Are the subjects described under (i)–(iii) a "conceptual" possibility? The term in quotes of course is vague, but given the apparent conceptual distinctness of the geometrical/mechanical and the difference-making views of causation and the empirical results about dissociability described above, there is an obvious case for answering "yes" for each of (i)–(iii). Now let us ask whether such a subject possesses the full range of capacities for causal cognition that adult humans possess. I take it that there are obvious reasons to answer "no" to these questions. Normal adult capacities for causal cognition involve capacities for both sorts of causal judgment or assessment exhibited in the Schlottmann/Shanks experiment as well as the ability to appreciate the interconnections between the two.

I draw several conclusions from this thought experiment. First, it reinforces the claim that a simple "two distinct concepts" diagnosis of the relationship between the geometrical/mechanical and difference-making conceptions is incomplete and unsatisfying—if what we are interested in understanding is adult human causal concepts and causal thinking, we need to understand how these two ways of thinking about causation (or of assessing causal relationships) are interconnected, both psychologically and conceptually. Second, it appears that there is nothing inevitable or logically required about the eventual integration of these two sets of abilities and two ways of thinking with which they are apparently associated. This means that the issue of how they eventually come to be integrated in normal adult human causal thinking and whether there might be a stage in human development (or among some non-human animals) in which they are not fully integrated should be regarded as live questions. Third, although we shall return to this issue below, even at this point it is hard to see how one might develop a difference-making conception of causation *just* out of a geometrical/mechanical conception that does not in any way incorporate difference-making considerations. Both conceptually and (it would appear from the Schottman/Shanks experiment) empirically, it appears there is nothing about the capacity to discriminate whether individual token events are joined by a connecting process that automatically carries with it the idea of those events standing in a difference-making relationship. So to the extent that human adult concepts of causation incorporate difference-making commitments, it is hard to see how these can emerge just from a generalization or extension of experiences involving causal perception, unless these are already sensitive to or in some way incorporate difference-making considerations. Thus, contrary to what is sometimes suggested, it looks as though causal perception (at least insofar as this is insensitive to difference-making) or the representations that underlie causal perception cannot be the foundation for all other forms of causal thinking.

This last observation suggests another possibility that may have already occurred to the reader—instead of taking causal perception or geometrical/mechanical connectedness to be the foundation for causal thinking generally, why not turn things around and take difference-making to be the fundamental notion? In other words, when subjects perceive episodes involving collisions, support, etc. as causal, we should think of them as engaging in perceptual judgments or perceptual recognition (or at least judgment/recognition that is based on perception) that certain features of those episodes are difference-makers: the subject who perceives that the collision with the first ball caused the second to move judges or recognizes that the collision was a difference-maker for the motion of the second ball, the subject who sees that the table supports the plate recognizes that the presence of the table is a difference-maker for the position of the plate and so on. If this idea could be made to work, it would seem to suggest that the opposition we initially set up between difference-making and the geometrical/mechanical (as well as the way philosophers formulate the geometrical/mechanical) is misconceived—the geometrical/mechanical approach is just a particular version of the difference-making approach, in which mechanical properties are taken to be the difference-makers.

Some apparent empirical support for this idea can be found in the observation that in some cases (e.g., development of an appreciation of support) causal perception seems to involve learning which features are difference-makers (Cf. Baillargeon et al., 1995[17]). On the other hand, this idea doesn't seem to do full justice to all of the features of causal perception. In particular, if causal perception just involves perceptual recognition of contingency relations among mechanical properties, it is not easy to see how to account for dissociation results like those reported by Schlottmann and Shanks, in which subjects report causal perception that is not just unsupported by but actually inconsistent with contingency information.[18]

I shall return to these questions below, but I want first to take a brief look at some related issues involving causal perception and understanding in infancy.

8 Causal perception in infancy

An important question that has long intrigued developmental psychologists concerns the origins of the capacity for causal perception in launching events. Is this capacity "innate," as Michotte himself thought, (whatever "innate" might mean) or is it

---

[17] Baillergeon shows that infants' looking-time behavior suggests that they initially regard any form of spatio-temporal contact as sufficient for support; only gradually do they come to appreciate that the supported object must be on top of the support, that in normal circumstances the former must overlap considerably with the latter and so on. This is naturally interpreted as a matter of learning which specific features of support are difference-makers.

[18] One might argue that the subjects have learned on the basis of previous experience with ecologically natural collisions that spatio-temporal contact is a difference-maker and are unable to quickly unlearn (or correct for) this when presented with inconsistent difference-making information in the Schlottmann/Shanks experiment. But this seems adhoc in the absence of independent evidence.

acquired or learned and if so, when? In a frequently cited experiment, Leslie and Keeble (1987) presented evidence, based on a looking time or dishabituation paradigm, that this capacity is present at an early age—that, as the title of their paper claims, six month old infants "perceive causality." Since the dishabitutation paradigm will figure importantly in some aspects of what follows, a brief summary is in order.

In a simple version of this paradigm, the infant is exposed repeatedly to a stimulus until her duration of looking at the stimulus falls back to some baseline. A novel stimulus is then presented and if this results in a significant increase in looking time (dishabitutation), this is taken to show (at least) that the infant can discriminate between the novel stimulus and the stimulus to which she has been previously habituated. This conclusion seems relatively uncontroversial; controversy arises, however, when infant differences in looking time are given richer interpretations, involving more sophisti-cated forms of representation and cogniton/information processing, as they frequently are in the developmental literature.

Here, it will be useful to distinguish two possibilities, which I shall call the "violation of expectations interpretation" and the "causal knowledge and reasoning interpreta-tion." As a matter of empirical fact, infants will often look longer at events that adults consider physically or causally impossible, such as the apparent passage of one solid object through another, discontinuous object trajectories and so on. This is often taken to show that the infant is "surprised" by such events or that the events "violate the infant's expectations"—that is, the infant has expectations regarding the usual or expected behavior of physical objects and responds to behavior that is inconsistent with these. Under some suitable construal, this interpretation also strikes me as often warranted. Note, though, that by itself this interpretation commits us to nothing very specific about the nature or content of the violated expectations—for all that has been said, the expectations in question might be merely implicit or procedural, perhaps reflecting in part features of visual or attentional processing that influence looking behavior, but that are not "explicitly" represented and not available for abstract reasoning or inference or naturally described as knowledge that certain principles hold. Nor should we necessarily assume that the expectations are *causal* in character (on any reasonable understanding of "causal"). After all, even adults have many expectations that various patterns will persist that do not take the form of causal beliefs about those patterns—think of expectations about the seasons (violations of which are readily noticed) but which often do not take the form of any causal understanding of why summer follows spring. Association is not causation and expectations based on experience with associations need not involve causal beliefs, still less correct causal beliefs.

By contrast, the "causal knowledge and reasoning interpretation" does make much more specific claims about the nature of the infant's expectations that are revealed in looking-time studies—it is claimed that these encode distinctively causal *knowledge* of principles governing the behavior and interaction of bodies, that in virtue of possessing these the infant is able to reason about or make inferences regarding elementary features of physical causation, as exhibited in launching events etc. and that this in turn explains features of infant looking-time behavior. Both the violations of expectations and the causal knowledge interpretations thus go beyond the mere observation that infants will distinguish in looking behavior among certain events, and offer explanations about why this behavior occurs (or of the processing that lies behind it) but the causal knowledge interpretation offers a much more specific and cognitively richer explanation. To support the causal knowledge interpretation, one would need to provide evidence that discriminates in favor of that interpretation and against the violation of expectations interpretation. For the moment, I want to postpone considering what evidence might play this role and whether (and when) this richer interpretation is justified; I shall return to this issue below.

Earlier experiments by Leslie, using looking-time methods, had shown that young infants are sensitive to the difference between launching type events in which there is a spatio-temporal gap (and which of course are not perceived as causal by adults) and those in which there is no such gap. However, this does not rule out the possibility that the infants respond differently simply because they perceive the difference in the spatio-temporal parameters that characterize the two sets of events, and not because they perceive the first interaction as causal and the second as not. Leslie and Keeble (1987) attempted to address this possibility by means of an experimental design that compared the responses of infants to two sequences of events and their "time reverses". In the "causal" sequence, infants first saw moving A strike stationary B and B begin to move with a temporal delay that leads adults to perceive the interaction as causal; they also saw a reverse of this sequence in which B moved and struck A, which was stationary. The second "non-causal" sequence and its reverse were just like the first except that there was a noticeable temporal gap between the impact and subsequent movement, so that adults did not perceive the interaction as causal. Infants looked longer at the reversed sequence in the causal case than in the non-causal case. Leslie and Keeble interpreted this as showing that the infants were responding to the distinctively causal features of the interaction in the first sequence; their reasoning was that in the case of the causal sequence, the reverse sequence involved a causal change in the roles of A and B—the motion of A went from being the cause to being the effect. The second sequence and its reverse involved no such change in causal role but merely a change in spatio-temporal properties. According to Leslie and Keeble, infants looked longer at the first change because they saw it as a causal change rather than just a change in spatio-temporal properties. The authors conclude from this and other experimental results that infants can perceive causation in collisions in essentially the same way as adults do and that this capacity is innate, since it appears early in development.

Subsequent studies have challenged the claim of innateness, presenting instead a picture in which the capacity for causal perception develops over time, as the result of learning (Cohen et al., 1998). Nonetheless, there seems to be general agreement that the capacity to discriminate collision type events that look causal to adults from those that do not emerges relatively early.

Looking-time experiments have been used to probe many other phenomena in which infants seem visually sensitive to causal features of objects and their interactions and to "violations" of normal causal and physical behavior. These include experiments showing sensitivity to violations of object permanence (e.g. an object moving behind a screen fails to appear at gaps in the screen (Baillergon et al., 1995)), object cohesion (objects whose parts fail to move together as cohesive wholes) (Spelke et al., 1995), impenetrability (a solid object moving behind a screen appears to pass through another solid object) and support (showing, e.g., that infants look longer at an event in which an object appears to be suspended in mid-air without support than at an otherwise similar event in which the object is supported by a platform in a normal fashion). Like the Leslie and Keeble experiment, these results are often interpreted as showing not just that infants make certain perceptual discriminations but that they have *knowledge* of or are capable of *reasoning* with basic physical ideas concerning mechanical or contact causation, impenetrability, support, and so on and that they possess adult-like *concepts* of physical causation.

One reason for skepticism about these last claims has already been alluded to—it is not obvious that the expectations the infants possess are distinctively causal. Another relevant consideration has to do with the distinction between, on the one hand, the ability to make perceptual discriminations based on membership (or not) in some category X, and, on the other hand, possession of the (or "a") concept of X or the capacity to reason about X. Of course the notion of "possessing a concept" is notoriously murky. I assume, however, that if this notion has any utility at all, we cannot automatically conclude just from the fact that a subject has the capacity to perceptually distinguish between instances and non-instances of category X that the subject possesses adult human understanding of the concept of X or adult-like appreciation of the principles governing X. A cat may be able to perceptually distinguish dogs from non-dogs, but this does not necessarily mean the cat possesses a human-like concept of "dog" (loyal, man's best friend, related to wolves, etc.). Similarly, it does not follow just from the fact that a subject is able to distinguish interactions that "look" causal from those that are not that the subject possesses a full-fledged adult-like concept of causation that is available for other forms of reasoning or that the subject has abilities to generalize, conceptualize, theorize, and reason about causation that are similar to those of adult humans—it is always a further, empirical question whether subjects with the former, perceptual abilities also possess the latter abilities. This is so both for the concept of causation associated with causal process or geometrical/mechanical accounts, and even more obviously so (in view of the dissociation results above) for the concept of a cause as difference-maker.

What evidence might be relevant to establishing that pre-verbal infants and non-verbal animals possess something like a concept of causation rather than just capacities for causal perception? Let me suggest two *relevant* considerations, which draw on my discussion in earlier sections. (I do not claim that either consideration or their conjunction is sufficient and am not sure whether either is strictly necessary.)

Both considerations have to do with the extent to which the discriminations based on causal perception are connected to or integrated with an appreciation of the causal significance of difference-making considerations. In section 7, we considered a thought experiment involving a subject who failed to integrate the results of causal perception with information involving observed contingencies ("observed" as opposed to generated by the subject's own actions or manipulations). To the extent that pre-verbal infants or non-verbal animals with a capacity for causal perception fail to exhibit such integration, it seems to me that this would be some evidence that their causal perception abilities did not provide them anything like a full adult-like concept of causation.

Since I am a philosopher, I hesitate to suggest a specific experimental design, but one possibility might be a sort of an analogue to the Schlottmann/Shanks experiment in which infants or non-human animals are shown displays involving both opportunities for causal perception (e.g. launching events involving X and Y) and contingency information involving the same events X and Y. In the first condition the contingency information is consistent with the launching relationships—that is, the interactions between X and Y look causal and there is contingency between X and Y. In the second condition, there is inconsistency between launching and contingency; there is again launching, but now no contingency between X and Y. The question would be whether the subjects look longer at the displays in the second condition, showing that they have the expectations about the relationship between geometrical/mechanical contact and contingency that human adults have.

9 Dissociations between seeing and acting

A second relevant set of considerations bearing on the possession of an adult-like concept of causation and capacity for causal cognition has to do with the extent to which there is integration between causal perception abilities and the appropriate use of difference-making information in action. Consider a normal adult given a choice between (i) rolling a ball down a ramp in such a way that it will move via an unobstructed path to collide with a second ball and cause it to move and (ii) rolling a ball down a ramp along which there is a visible barrier that will prevent the first ball from striking the second. The adult will be able to see at a glance that the impact of the first ball will cause the second to move in case (i) but not in case (ii). Moreover, if for some reason the adult wants to make the second ball move, she will choose to roll the ball down the first ramp rather than the second. In other words, the adult will be able to use causal information obtained perceptually on the basis of geometrical/mechanical clues to guide her choice of action and manipulative activities. Ordinarily, we would think that an adult who had normal capacities for manipulation, but who behaved as though she failed to recognize that the choice of (i) rather than (ii) was superior from the point of view of manipulating the second ball had less than full causal understanding of the structures corresponding to (i) and (ii), even if other measures indicated perceptual sensitivity to the difference between (i) and (ii).[19]

Although there is empirical disagreement about how extensive such dissociations are,[20] there is certainly evidence that in some situations, both infants and non-human animals fail to exploit in their behavior the geometrical/mechanical causal knowledge that they are claimed to possess on the basis of looking-time results—that is, they do not behave like the "normal adult" described above.

As one illustration, consider an experiment by Spelke et al. (1992) in which four-month-old infants are exposed to one of two test events. In the first, the infants are shown an apparently solid table which is then placed behind an occluder. A ball is then dropped toward the surface of the table. In the first test condition, the screen is removed to show the ball resting on the table—the outcome that respects ordinary physical or contact mechanical constraints. In the second condition, the dropped ball is shown under the table, a violation of these constraints. The infants look longer at the second outcome, suggesting (to a number of psychologists, including Spelke) that the infants "understand" that the ball could not pass through a solid object. However when a similar display is used and much older children (two years old) are given the opportunity to search for the ball, they tend to search under the table rather than on top of it, suggesting that they are unable to make use of the physical knowledge attributed to them on the basis of the looking-time experiments in conducting their search. Interestingly, a similar dissociation is found in several species of *adult* monkeys (rhesus and cotton-top tamarins)—they also will look longer at a display in which removal of an occluder seems to suggest that a dropped object has fallen through a solid surface but will search for the object under the surface (Hauser, 2001). A number of other experiments reveal similar patterns of dissociation (Santos and Hauser, 2002).

In the experiment just described, the dissociation is between the causal or physical understanding (allegedly) revealed in looking-time experiments and the causal under-standing revealed in actions involving searching. From the point of view of an

---

[19] Another, perhaps more demanding test would be to ask whether the subject places a movable barrier appropriately depending on whether she wants one ball to strike another.

[20] Perception/action dissociations do not show up in all tasks. For example, Hespos and Baillargeon (2008) report evidence that changes in infants' understanding of support, as assessed by looking-time measures is closely tracked by the changes in the infants' performance in an action task involving support. In a similar vein, Sommerville (2007) reports evidence that infants' understanding of the contact between a toy and a blanket (as revealed by looking-time measures) required if pulling on the latter is to bring the former is influenced by the infants' own experience with the action of pulling on the blanket.

If such dissociations are rarer or less extensive than I have supposed above, this suggests another possibility—perhaps the ability to recognize causal relationships based on perceptual cues and the ability to exploit such relationships in action develop together, with each influencing the other, but with there never being a stage in which one exists without the other or in which the abilities are entirely unintegrated. This would make some of the apparent dissociations described above (including the Schlottman/Shanks results and the way in which GM and DM considerations apparently pull in different directions in connection with particular examples) harder to understand, but it would leave intact many of the other claims of this paper—in particular, the claim that it is implausible that the adult capacities for causal cognition develop just from capacities and representations associated with causal perception.

interventionist framework for thinking about causation, it would be even more revealing to look for dissociations between apparent perceptual sensitivity to causal relationships (as assessed by looking-time measures) and sensitivity to causal relationships as revealed in action tasks involving opportunities for manipulation. From an interventionist viewpoint an appreciation of the implications of causal information for manipulation and intervention plays a particularly central role in causal thinking and in the possession of full-fledged causal concepts—it is particularly diagnostic of whether the subject has causal beliefs rather than just expectations based on associations.[21] The hypothetical experiment described at the beginning of this section is one such "intervention" experiment.

10 Consequences and conclusion

Suppose, for the sake of argument, that the causal perception/action dissociation just described is (at least to some extent) "real." What would follow from this about the role of causal perception in causal understanding and in the achievement of adult like capacities for causal cognition?

We may distinguish several different possibilities:

10.1 Causal perception as expressed in sensitivity to geometrical/mechanical clues reveals possession of adult-like causal concepts and capacities for causal cognition even if it is not integrated into action.

This position is advocated by Spelke (e.g., 1994) among others. It is claimed that infant failure to act successfully on the causal knowledge that (it is supposed) they can be shown to possess on the basis of looking-time studies can be attributed to performance failures rather than limitations in competence in causal understanding. In other words, according to this position, looking-time experiments show that infants have adult-like competence in terms of their grasp of basic causal concepts and principles. However, because of various performance limitations, they are not always able to reflect this understanding in their actions—this is what accounts for seeing/acting dissociations. A number of possible candidates for these performance limitations have been proposed: limitations on manual dexterity and motor control, failures to inhibit or control pre-potent responses that lead to normatively incorrect behavior in searching and reaching tasks, and more general limitations in planning, short-term memory and/or executive control. I take it to be is crucial to this position that these limitations are conceived of as "external" to the infant's causal knowledge—that is, they may affect the expression of that knowledge in action, but do not indicate that the knowledge in question is limited or underdeveloped in comparison with adults.

---

[21] Prima facie, a subject who is aware of a correlation between X and Y, but does not behave as though she believes that manipulating X is a way of changing Y (even though she has the capacity to do so etc.) does not interpret X as a cause of Y.

A natural further extension of this line of thought is that to the extent that infants have causal knowledge in the absence of the ability to exploit it in successful manipulation, this shows that the infants' capacities to intervene and manipulate are not fundamental to the acquisition/development of causal knowledge (perhaps Spelke et al., 1992). Indeed, it follows that there is no fundamental link between causal knowledge and knowledge relevant to manipulation at all. Instead, at a fundamental level causal understanding is about the appreciation of the significance of geometrical/ mechanical relationships of the sort associated with action by contact. Infants' perceptual behavior (with respect to looking-time etc.) is more reflective of their causal knowledge than their capacities for (non-perceptual) action involving searching, grasping, manipulating, etc. Following this line of thought, it might be argued that, at least when construed as a psychological/developmental theory about the origins and character of causal knowledge, interventionist accounts are mistaken—they assign too central a role to the connection between causation and action. To the extent there also exist dissociations between the causal information revealed by perception and appreciation of the significance of difference-making information more generally (whether this results from action or passive observation), one might argue for a similar negative assessment of difference-making treatments of causation generally, at least when construed as psychological theories.

10.2. Infant causal perception does not require adult-like causal concepts and understanding although it may play a role in the development of these.

According to this second position, adult causal concepts and reasoning involve abilities that genuinely develop over time and that are not fully present in infants with capacities for various forms of causal perception. Causal perception involving geometrical/ mechanical cues may (in fact, probably does—see below) play an important boot-strapping role in facilitating the learning and development of full-fledged adult causal concepts and capacities for causal cognition, but the latter go well beyond the abilities that are deployed in causal perception tasks—the content of what is learned is not just a generalization of whatever is at work in the perception of launching, or a concept/ representation corresponding to the output of a "Michottean" module that is activated in causal perception. In particular, adult causal cognition requires some appreciation of the role of covariational information and some appreciation of the implications of causal knowledge for action and planning.

There are a number of reasons why this second position (10.2) seems more plausible than the first position (10.1). In what follows I briefly review some new considerations and then return to some that have already been introduced.

As I have already argued, the results from looking-time experiments do not seem to require an interpretation in terms of infant possession of rich causal knowledge— weaker, "violations of expectations" interpretations often seem at least as plausible. Moreover, prima facie, the case for such weaker interpretations seems strengthened to the extent that infant causal perception abilities do not carry with them the kind of appreciation of the significance of causal information for action and planning that are characteristic of adult causal cognition—this is exactly what we would expect if infant causal perception did not really show the possession of adult-like causal concepts and understanding. In other words, the apparent failure of the looking-time results, taken in themselves, to discriminate between a rich causal interpretation and a weaker violation of expectations interpretation, coupled with apparent perception/action dissociations seems to provide a prima facie case against the rich causal interpretation. Thus, in order to defend (10.1), the evidence that perception/action dissociations merely reflect performance limitations needs to be strong.[22]

However, many of the empirical arguments for these limitations seem problematic.[23] Some perception/action dissociations persist for human two year olds even though they do not have the manual dexterity limitations of infants. Moreover, as noted, such dissociations are also present in adult rhesus and cotton-top tamerin monkeys who appear to have no problems with manual dexterity at all. In addition, two-year-old human children and adult monkeys succeed on many standard tests of inhibition, suggesting that something more specific than a general failure of inhibitory mechanisms underlies the dissociation. More fundamentally, many of the proposed performance limitations do not successfully explain a striking feature of the dissociations, which is that they seem to occur much more frequently in connection with failures to exploit causal or mechanical information in action than in connection with spatio-temporal or numerical information. For example, Santos (2004) shows that adult rhesus monkeys perform successfully in searches for hidden objects when these can be located just by using spatio-temporal information but fail on otherwise similar search tasks requiring use of causal mechanical information. This pattern of failure suggests that there is some specific problem about the integration of geometrical/mechanical based causal information (as opposed to numerical or spatio-temporal information) into action, despite the fact subjects seem to exhibit sensitivity to this causal information in looking-time studies.

We noted earlier that perception of causation in collisions seems to activate structures in the occipital (MT/V5) and temporal areas (STS), although it does also activate the IPS. By contrast, planning, and the organization/carrying out of complex actions (as well as inhibition of prepotent responses) involves parietal and prefrontal areas, including DLPFC (dorsolateral prefrontal cortex). As we have seen, DLPFC is also differentially activated in contingency sensitive causal judgments of various sorts (as opposed to causal perception). Various aspects of tool use and recognition also activate parietal areas. A natural although admittedly speculative conjecture is that some of the causal perception/action dissociations described above involve a failure in infants and

---

[22] If there is systematic evidence of dissociations in infancy between causal perception and casual assessments based on observational (non-action based) contingency information this would also be problematic for 10.1 and for some of the claims about performance-based limitations.

[23] See, e.g., Moore and Meltzoff (2008) and the references therein.

non-human primates to integrate processing in visual and temporal areas involved in causal perception with processing in parietal and frontal areas—either because the former develop somewhat before the latter or because their full integration and coordinated use only occurs several years or more after birth in humans and may not occur at all in non-human primates. (cf. Johnson, 2005).

Whether or not these neurobiological speculations are correct, it seems plausible that (as I have argued) mature human causal understanding involves the successful integration of systems involved in causal perception and systems involved in planning, action, and successful manipulation and that the action/causal perception dissociations described above suggest failures to achieve this kind of integration. To the extent this is so, it seems question-begging to describe subjects exhibiting the dissociations as possessing human adult-like causal knowledge and abilities and merely facing performance limitations on its expression in action, especially if the source of those performance limitations is immaturity in or lack of integration with neural areas involved in planning of action. The monkeys and human infants described above do not suffer from "performance limitations" merely in the sense that, say, they know that (1) C causes E, recognize that (2) if C causes E, then if it is possible to manipulate C, this is a way of manipulating E, but (3) face obstacles to their ability to manipulate C, such as limitations in manual dexterity. Rather they act as though their alleged causal understanding does not incorporate the link represented by (2). Or at least their causal understanding is such that recognition of (2) does not get integrated into their action and planning in the way that it would in a normal human adult—again not because of an inability to perform the relevant action but because the relevance of the causal information they possess for action and planning does not seem to be recognized. This seems more like a limitation on the subject's causal understanding than an extrinsic obstacle to its expression in action. To put the point in terms of the neurobiological speculations described above, my suggestion is that immature development of prefrontal and parietal structures or their lack of integration with temporal and occipital structures involved in causal perception is not a mere performance limitation on the expression of causal competence—instead the involvement of the former structures is essential to human adult causal understanding.

A number of considerations discussed in earlier sections seem to reinforce the judgment that possession of causal perception abilities by themselves does not automatically yield adult-like capacities for causal learning and judgment. The Schlottmann/Shanks dissociation results show that the deliverances of causal perception are relatively insensitive to contingency or difference-making information, at least under appropriate conditions. This suggests that it is not just logically but also psychologically possible for subjects to have the experiences and to make the discriminations associated with causal perception, while failing to integrate this perceptual ability (and whatever representations underlie it) with an appreciation of the role of contingency information in causal judgment. The fact that within the philosophical literature the development of the ideas associated with causal perception (continuity of trajectories, the role of spatial contact, etc.) seem to yield a way of thinking about causation that is conceptually distinct from the difference-making conception (with respect to do-main-specificity, the role of comparative information and so on) reinforces this point.

I suggested above that although causal perception abilities do not necessarily require the presence of adult-like capacities for causal cognition, the former may well play an important role in the development of the latter. I conclude by sketching one possible way in which this might occur, which draws on observations from section 4.4.[24] Suppose that we have a primitive (either innate or very early emerging) mechanism (the *GM* mechanism) that notes or keeps track of spatio-temporal coincidences and Michottean-type interactions, and perhaps certain other types of mechanical interac-tions that have distinctive spatio-temporal signatures as well. As a matter of empirical fact, in ecologically normal situations, these interactions will also exhibit contingency relations—the second ball tends to move when and only when the first ball strikes it and so on. Although young infants are sensitive to and learn from contingency information (e.g., they learn from classical and operant conditioning) they do not necessarily or automatically integrate such information with the information to which the *GM* mechanism is sensitive—instead this integration has to be achieved or learned. That is, it is only gradually that the infant comes to learn that there is a correlation or connection between whether the first ball exhibits a Michottean interaction with the second and whether the motion of the second is contingent on the movement of the first. The infant comes to learn which specific features of the first ball and its motion are difference-makers for the motion of the second even later. (Recall from section 4.4 that perceptual awareness of a causal connection between the balls does not require or necessarily present us with fine-grained information about difference-making). More generally, the infant comes to learn which spatio-temporal relations (to which it may be previously sensitive) are clues to the existence of a difference-making relation and which are not. For example, as we have seen, the infant gradually learns that not just any spatial contact is sufficient for support (the wrong sort of spatial contact makes no difference for whether there will be support), that more substantial spatial overlap will often make a difference for whether there is support and so on. Initial focus on these spatio-temporal relationships in mechanical interactions thus allows the infant to begin to extract or appreciate a more general category of difference-making, of which difference-making relationships mediated by mechanical interactions are just one type. Thus the broader category of difference-making is taken to involve something that can be present even in the absence of obvious spatio-temporal connectedness.[25]

---

[24] The remarks which follow have been greatly influenced by a conversation with David Danks.

[25] Another speculation: Consider the so-called perception of animacy. This may be regarded as a kind of causal perception which is different from the causal perception prompted by collisions and similar launching-type stimuli, which involve spatial contact. Perception of animacy may be another route by which infants learn a general category of difference-making which transcends association with the particular kind of spatial connectedness which is characteristic of collisions and similar interactions. When the infant perceives one agent chase another and similar phenomena, the infant observes a systematic covariational or difference-

Young causal learners may then conjecture that at least sometimes when difference-making is present and there is no obvious mediating mechanism, that a hidden mechanism or connecting process is present—a conjecture that often turns out to be empirically correct and heuristically fruitful.

11 Conclusion

Since this is a lengthy paper, it may be helpful to conclude by briefly summarizing some of the main claims advanced above. I have suggested that ordinary adult human causal thinking as well as a great deal of philosophical and psychological theorizing about such thinking is influenced by two different conceptions of causation, one (the DM conception) associated with the idea that causes make a difference for their effects and the other (the GM conception) associated with idea that causes must be appropriately "connected" to their effects. It seems plausible that part of the motivation for the GM conception can be found in phenomena involving causal perception, not in the sense that adherents of the GM conception self-consciously or explicitly appeal to such phenomena, but in the sense that the GM approach captures or reproduces salient features of the phenomenology of causal perception. The DM and GM conceptions differ both conceptually and, as an empirical matter, can lead to different judgments. Nonetheless the two conceptions seem ordinarily to be well integrated in adult causal judgment, which raises the question of how such integration is achieved in the course of development. The answer to this last question requires further empirical investigation, but (contrary to what some psychologists have claimed), it seems unlikely that the full range of adult capacities for causal reasoning can be derived just from the representations that underlie causal perception.

References

Armstrong, D. (2004) "Going Through the Open Door Again: Counterfactual versus Singularist Theories of Causation," in J. Collins, N. Hall, and L. Paul (eds.), *Causation and Counterfactuals* (Cambridge, Mass.: MIT Press).

Baillargeon, R., Kotovsky, L., and Needham A. (1995) "The Acquisition of Physical Knowledge in Infancy," in D. Sperber, D. Premack, and A. Premack (eds.), *Causal Cognition: A Multidisciplinary Debate* (Oxford: Clarendon Press).

Beebee, H. (2003, published online) "Seeing Causing," *Proceedings of the Aristotelian Society* 103: 257–280.

Bechtel, B. (2006) *Discovering Cell Mechanisms* (Cambridge: Cambridge University Press.

making relationship between the movements of the two agents, even though there is no spatial contact. (Other sorts of spatio-temporal patterns in which one of the agents changes its movements in response to the other agent will of course be present.) So there is perception of the movement of one agent causing the movement of the other, even though literal spatio-temporal connectedness is usually not present. A more general notion of difference-making may be extracted from such experiences.

Blakemore, S., Boyer, P., Pachot-Clouard, M., Meltzoff, A., Segebarth, C., and Decety, J. (2003) "The Detection of Contingency and Animacy from Simple Animations in the Human Brain," *Cerebral Cortex* 13: 837–844.

Butterfill, S. (forthcoming) "Seeing Causes and Hearing Gestures," *Philosophical Quarterly*.

Cohen, L. B., Amsel, G., Redford, M. A., and Casasola, M. (1998) "The Development of Infant Causal Perception," in A. Slater (ed.), *Perceptual Development: Visual, Auditory, and Speech Perception in Infancy* (East Sussex, UK: Psychology Press Ltd).

Dowe, P. (2000) *Physical Causality* (Cambridge: Cambridge University Press).

Eells, E. (1991) *Probabilistic Causality* (Cambridge: Cambridge University Press).

Eells, E. and Sober, E. (1983) "Probabilistic Causality and the Question of Transitivity," *Philosophy of Science* 50: 35–57.

Hall, N. (2004) "Two Concepts of Causation," in J. Collins, N. Hall, and L. Paul (eds.), *Causation and Counterfactuals* (Cambridge, Mass.: MIT Press).

Hauser, M. (2001) "Searching for Food in the Wild: A Nonhuman Primate's Expectations about Invisible Displacement," *Developmental Science* 4: 84–93.

Hespos, S. and Baillargeon, R. (2008) "Young Infants' Actions Reveal their Developing Knowledge of Support Variables: Converging Evidence for Violation-of-Expectation Findings," *Cognition*, 107: 304–316.

Hitchcock, C. (1995) "Discussion: Salmon on Causal Relevance," *Philosophy of Science* 62: 304–320.

—— (2001) "The Intransitivity of Causation Revealed in Equations and Graphs," *Journal of Philosophy* 98: 273–299.

Johnson, M. (2005) *Developmental Cognitive Neuroscience*, 2nd edn (Malden, Mass.: Blackwell).

Leslie, A. (1995) "A Theory of Agency," in D. Sperber, D. Premack, and A. Premack (eds.), *Causal Cognition: A Multidisciplinary Debate* (Oxford: Clarendon Press).

Leslie, A. and Keeble, S. (1987) "Do Six-Month Old Infants Perceive Causality?," *Cognition* 25: 265–288.

Lewis, D. (1973) "Causation," *Journal of Philosophy* 70: 556–567.

Machamer, P., Darden, L., and Craver, C. (2000) "Thinking About Mechanisms," *Philosophy of Science* 57: 1–25.

Mackie, J. (1974) *The Cement of the Universe* (Oxford: Oxford University Press).

Menzies, P. (1998) "How Justified are the Human Doubts about Intrinsic Causal Links?," *Communication and Cognition* 31: 339–364.

Michotte, A. E. (1963) *The Perception of Causality*, trans. T. R. Miles and E. Miles. (London: Methuen; original publication 1946).

Moore, M. and Meltzoff, A. (2008) "Factors Affecting Infants' Manual Search for Occluded Objects and the Genesis of Object Permanence," *Infant Behavior & Development* 31: 168–180.

Pinker, S. (2007) *The Stuff of Thought: Language as a Window on Human Nature* (New York, New York: Penguin Group).

Salmon, W. (1984) *Scientific Explanation and the Causal Structure of the World* (Princeton, New Jersey: Princeton University Press).

Santos, L. (2004) "'Core Knowledges': A Dissociation between Spatiotemporal Knowledge and Contact-Mechanics in a Non-Human Primate?," *Developmental Science* 7: 167–174.

Santos, L. and Hauser, M. (2002) "A Non-Human Primate's Understanding of Solidity: Dissociations between Seeing and Acting," *Developmental Science* 5: F1–F7.

Schlottmann, A. and Shanks D. (2002) "Evidence for a Distinction between Judged and Perceived Causality," *The Quarterly Journal of Experimental Psychology* 44A: 321–342.

Scholl, B., and Leslie, A. (1999) "Explaining the Infant's Object Concept: beyond the Perception/Cognition Dichotomy," in E. Lepore and Z. Pylyshyn (eds.), *What is Cognitive Science?* (Oxford: Blackwell).

Scholl, B. and Nakayama, K. (2001) "Causal Capture: Contextual Effects on the Perception of Collision Events," *Journal of Vision* 1: 476.

Scholl, B. and Tremoulet P. (2000) "Perceptual Causality and Animacy," *Trends in Cognitive Science* 4: 299–309.

Sommerville, J. (2000) "Detecting Structure in Action: Infants as Causal Agents," in A. Gopnik and L. E. Schulz (eds.), *Causal Learning: Psychology, Philosophy and Computation* (New York, New York: Oxford University Press).

Spelke, E. S. (1994) "Initial Knowledge: Six Suggestions," *Cognition* 50: 431–445.

Spelke, E. S., Breinlinger, K., Macomber, J., and Jacobson, K. (1992) "Origins of Knowledge," *Psychological Review* 99: 605–632.

Spelke, E. S., Phillips, A., and Woodward, A. L. (1995) "Infants' Knowledge of Object Motion and Human Action," in D. Sperber, D. Premack, and A. Premack (eds.), *Causal Cognition: A Multidisciplinary Debate* (Oxford: Clarendon Press).

Walsh, C. and Sloman, S. (forthcoming) "The Meaning of Cause and Prevent: The Role of Causal Mechanism."

Wolff, P. (2007) "Representing Causation," *Journal of Experimental Psychology: General* 136: 82–111.

Woodward, J. (2003) *Making Things Happen: A Theory of Causal Explanation* (New York, New York: Oxford University Press).

15

Children's Understanding of Perceptual Appearances

Matthew Nudds★

Introduction

The development of children's understanding of perception has been tested using a number of experimental paradigms. These suggest that from around two-and-a-half to three years old children begin to understand perception as such, and can show a sensitivity to whether other people can perceive things and to the factors that affect whether something is perceivable. At around this age children are able to perform so-called level-1 perspective-taking tasks. In these tasks a child is asked whether or not another person—typically the experimenter—can see an object—usually a toy—as it is moved relative to occluding objects so that sometimes the experimenter can see it, and sometimes she cannot. Children who succeed at the task understand, for example, that the experimenter cannot see the toy if something is blocking her line of sight (Flavell, Shipstead, and Croft 1978). Children's understanding of whether something is perceivable is not limited to visual perception; they understand the different conditions associated with the different sensory modalities (Yaniv and Shatz 1988).

From around four or four-and-a-half years children can successfully perform so-called level-2 perspective-taking tasks in which they are, for example, shown a white object that another person views through a red-coloured filter, and then are asked what colour the object looks to them and what colour it looks to the other person. Children who answer correctly understand not just that the other person can see the object, but how that object looks to them. At around the same age as they are able to successfully perform level-2 perspective-taking tasks, children are able to demonstrate an understanding of the difference between perceptual appearances and reality—that something

★ Ancestors of this chapter were presented at the University of Warwick, at the ESPP conference in Utrecht, and more recently at the Institute Jean Nicod. Thanks to the audiences on those occasions for comments, and to Steve Butterfill, Henrike Moll, Josef Perner, Liz Robinson, and the editors of this volume for many helpful suggestions.

that is really one thing can look like something else. When shown an object—a sponge, say—that looks like something else—a piece of rock—and asked what the object looks like and what it is really, they answer correctly. Both level-2 perspective-taking tasks and appearance–reality tasks seem to require a similar kind of understanding that an object may appear differently in different contexts of perceiving it: in perspective-taking tasks they are contexts in which the child and another person perceive the object; in appearance–reality tasks, the different contexts are different contexts in which the child perceives the object. Younger children who succeed at level-1 perspective-taking tasks fail at level-2 perspective-taking tasks and at appearance–reality tasks.

According to what I will call the 'standard interpretation' we can explain this development of children's understanding in terms of their gradual acquisition of a rudimentary theory of perception. According to this theory of perception, someone perceives an object as being some way if and only if the object causes them to have a perceptual experience that represents that object as being that way. For example (and simplifying) a subject S sees object O as F if and only if:

S has a visual experience E that represents O as F
O causes S's experience E
O is F

The way object O looks to S is explained in terms of the way S's experience represents that object to be. The object's looking F to S is a matter of S's experience representing O as F. The theory can be generalized to other sense modalities by substituting experiences associated with the other senses for visual experience. An experience is misleading or illusory if it misrepresents an object; when that happens, the object will look to S to be some way that it is not. According to the standard interpretation, children's success at level-1 perspective-taking tasks can be explained in terms of their understanding that someone perceives an object only if they have an experience of it, and knowing the conditions that must be satisfied for that to happen. Children's success at level-2 perspective-taking and appearance–reality tasks can be explained by their coming to understand, in addition, that perceptual experience represents objects or situations as being a certain way and that the way an object looks to someone is a matter of how their experience represents it to be. In what follows I argue that this standard interpretation is not supported by the evidence provided by the experiments, and that the developmental changes probed by the experiments are better explained in terms of children's developing understanding of objects (and their ability to understand and make claims about them).

Two uses of 'looks'-statements

'Looks'-statements are sometimes used *evidentially* to makes claims about objects, and sometimes used *comparatively* to make claims about the looks (or appearances) of objects.[1] When used evidentially a 'looks'-statement puts forward a proposition and indicates that there is visual evidence or grounds for doing so.[2] For example, in saying 'Richard looks ill' a speaker puts forward the proposition that Richard *is* ill and that there is visual evidence for thinking so.[3] The speaker's use of the evidential 'looks' may indicate some attenuation of their commitment to the truth of the proposition put forward, and so in using 'looks' evidentially speakers do not necessarily commit themselves to an outright assertion of the proposition put forward.[4] Nevertheless, it is likely to be a consequence of making the statement that the audience takes the speaker to be committed in some degree to the truth of the proposition put forward, and so it follows that it is inappropriate to make this kind of 'looks'-statement in a context in which the proposition is known to be false.[5]

When used evidentially, the focus of the statement 'Richard looks ill' is on whether the adjectival phrase 'is ill' applies to the object in question (and on the truth of the associated proposition). Such evidential uses of 'looks'-statements contrast with 'looks'-statements used with what Chisholm calls the 'comparative' sense, where the purpose of making the statement is not to put forward a proposition, but to characterise the appearance of an object. If, for example, a speaker says of a man with a large beer-belly that he looks pregnant, or of a man with a hunched back that he looks like a camel, she will not be taken as putting forward the proposition that the man *is* pregnant, or that he *is* a camel, but rather that the man has a certain appearance or look. In these cases the adjective characterises or describes a way of looking, rather than the object directly, and the statement is true just in case the object looks that way. The contrast between the two uses of 'looks'-statements is between cases in which the complement predicates something of the object and the focus is on the object and whether it really is that way or not, and cases in which the complement qualifies the verb 'looks' and the focus is on the look of the object and on whether it does look that way or not.

---

[1] It is a matter for debate whether the difference in uses reflects a semantic difference or merely a pragmatic one.

[2] Note that this is not the same as what philosophers sometimes call the 'epistemic' sense of 'looks'. According to Jackson (1977, ch. 2), 'the sun looks as if it's sinking into the sea' uses 'looks' in an epistemic sense: it says that there is visual evidence for the proposition. Since we know that the sun is not sinking into the sea, we are not putting forward the claim that it is.

[3] In some cases, the 'looks'-statement involves an explicit propositional complement—e.g., 'it looks as if *p*'—in most of the cases I discuss—of the form 'o looks F'—the proposition put forward is that formed by applying the adjective or adjectival phrase F to the subject of the verb o: *o is F*. In talking of the propositional put forward by a 'looks'-statement I mean either the explicit propositional complement, *p*, or the proposition formed in this way, *o is F*.

[4] Quinton talks of using looks in this sense to 'tentatively assert a conclusion' (Quinton 1955, 33), Chisholm that it expresses the speaker's 'inclination to believe' the proposition (Chisholm 1957, 44).

[5] Martin suggests that it is only appropriate to make this kind of 'looks'-statement in a situation in which the proposition put forward is epistemically possible, i.e. 'that its truth is not inconsistent with what is common knowledge . . . in the conversational context' (Martin 2010, 7).

What is it for an object to look a certain way? Two objects look the same just in case it is not possible to tell them apart simply by looking. Only some properties determine whether two objects can be told apart simply by looking; the properties that do so are *visible* properties. For example, two objects look the same only if they have the same colour and shape properties, so colour and shape are visible properties; two objects can look the same whether or not they have the same weight and density, so weight and density are not visible properties. In characterising the look of an object we are characterising the way it is in virtue of its visible properties: the look of an object—the way it looks—is that aspect of the object which, in virtue of the object's visible properties, resembles or fails to resemble any other object. Two objects that look the same or similar may differ substantially in their non-visible properties. That means that objects that are grouped together in virtue of having the same or similar look, will not necessarily be objects of the same kind.[6]

When used comparatively a 'looks'-statement characterises the look of an object by inviting a comparison between the object in question and another object; that is, by saying that the object in question has a look which is similar to the look of something else. For example, when we say of something that it looks like a rock, we are saying that it has a look which is similar to the look of rocks; or when we say of something that it looks red, we are saying that it has a look which is similar to the look of red things. Used this way, a 'looks'-statement makes a claim that is true just in case the object has the look in question. Something looks the way a rock looks just in case it is visually similar to characteristic rocks, and that is something that will be determined by the object's visible properties. Since what visible properties an object has is an objective matter, the fact that an object looks like a rock is also an objective matter, and so independent of anyone actually perceiving it.

Understanding this kind of 'looks'-statement requires understanding the relevant comparison: that means both knowing what is characteristic of the look of the object to which the comparison is being made, and understanding which dimensions of similarity between two objects are relevant to the claim that they look similar. Only some visual similarities will be relevant to the claim that two objects look similar, and which similarities are relevant will vary according to the kind of object in question and the context in which the question is being asked. In some cases—e.g., looking like a car—having the same colour is likely to be irrelevant to their looking the same, in other cases—e.g., looking red—it will be essential. Similarly, knowing what the characteristic look of an object is will require different things in different contexts. To understand, for example, the claim that a sponge looks like a rock requires knowing that there is a range of characteristic looks that rocks can have, and that the sponge is being said to have a look similar to one of that range. To understand the claim that an object looks red may simply require knowing that it looks similar to the look of red things. But what

---

[6] This conception of an object's way of looking is developed and defended by Martin (Martin 2010).

is characteristic of the look of something red may vary with context: the colour a car must have when we say that a car looks red is different from the colour hair must have when we say that someone's hair looks red.[7] The context sensitivity of this knowledge means that someone might understand comparative 'looks'-statements in general without knowing (because they are ignorant of the look characteristic of the object in question, say) what claim is being made by the use of a 'looks'-statement on a particular occasion.

It's difficult to imagine a context in which 'he looks like a camel' or 'he looks pregnant' could be used evidentially. In both these examples it is clear from the fact that the adjective could not be true of its object that we should understand the 'looks'-statement as making a comparative claim. Things are not always so clear-cut. In many cases it's possible that the adjective is true of the object, and so may be known to be true of it. In such cases what the 'looks'-statement can be used to say—whether it is used evidentially or comparatively—will vary according to what is assumed to be common knowledge between the speaker and audience; and that is something that can vary according to the context of a conversation, and even during the course of a conversation. This can be illustrated with a simple example.

Suppose that you are looking at a number of objects on the table in front of you: a mixture of sweets and pencil erasers some of which have been made to look like sweets. You are told that your task is to pick out one of the sweets. Having looked at the objects, you might say (indicating one): 'that one looks like a sweet'. In doing so you are making the claim, perhaps not outright, that that one *is* a sweet. This is evident from the fact that if what you pointed to was not a sweet, it would be perfectly appropriate for your interlocutor to reply: 'No: that's an eraser', and to do so even if the thing you pointed to had the appearance of—had the look of—a sweet. If, having just been told that it is not a sweet, you said again 'it looks like a sweet' then you would not normally (on the assumption that you are being conversationally cooperative) be taken to be making the claim that it *is* a sweet. That is, you would not normally be taken to be making the same claim as the one you made with your initial utterance of 'that looks like a sweet'. If you are not saying the same thing then what could your repeated utterance be used to convey?

Before answering that question, consider a variation on the task. Suppose you are looking at the same objects, but rather than picking out a sweet you are asked to group the objects into those that look like sweets and those that do not, irrespective of whether they are in fact sweets. In carrying out this task your interest is simply in whether the items share a certain look or appearance. If, having examined them, you say 'that one looks like a sweet' then you will not be taken to be claiming, even tentatively, that that one *is* a sweet, but rather that it has a certain look, namely a look that is similar to the look characteristic of sweets (whatever exactly that look is).

---

[7] Cf. Travis's discussion of the colour of leaves in Travis 1997.

Now, to go back to the first task, what might your repeated utterance of 'that one looks like a sweet' be used to convey? You might be making a comment directly about the look of the object, and so convey the same as you convey in the second task: that it has a look which is like the look of sweets. Perhaps, having been told that it is not a sweet, you want to express your surprise at how sweet-like it is in appearance: 'It's very realistic: it looks just the way sweets look'. Or, alternatively, you might be making a comment on the grounds or basis for your original claim that it is a sweet: that the way it looks is such that it would reasonably lead someone to judge that it is a sweet. Perhaps, having been told that it is not a sweet, you want to explain your mistake: 'Going by the way it looks, I would have said that's a sweet'. These two comments do not convey the same thing. The look of the object you picked out might be such that one would reasonably judge (in the context) that it was a sweet even if it did not have a look which is like that of typical sweets (perhaps, for example, it has 'eat me' written on it and you think that no one would write that on an eraser). But both comments make claims about the way the object looks.

It should be noted that using 'looks' to comment on the grounds or basis for a claim in this way involves characterising the way the object looks rather than characterising the object directly, and so is not an evidential use of 'looks'. The difference between this way of using 'looks' and the comparative use is that in this case the object's way of looking is being characterised in terms of what one might reasonably judge on its basis rather than in terms of a comparison with the look of another object. Martin (2010, section 2) suggests that we might, nonetheless, treat this kind of case as a special case of the comparative use of 'looks': the object has a look similar to the look characteristic of things that one would reasonably judge to be such and such. But a case could be made that this is a way of characterising the look of an object that does not involve any comparison: it is possible to imagine a context in which it is reasonable to judge that this is such and such only because it does not look similar to anything else. Understanding that objects have looks that can be characterised is one thing, understanding comparative statements another. Both kinds of understanding are required for understanding the comparative uses of 'looks'-statements.

What the discussion of these examples makes clear is that what a particular 'looks'-sentence can be used to say varies according to the conversational context. That matters when it comes to interpreting the results of the various experimental tasks involving 'looks'-statements. In particular, it means that in interpreting children's responses to 'looks'-questions, we need to pay careful attention to the conversational context, and to what *they* might take the conversational context to be. It is to these experimental tasks that I now turn.

Interpreting appearance–reality tasks

In the prototypical appearance–reality task children are shown a sponge that looks like a piece of rock. When they are first shown the sponge they are asked what it is, and they generally answer that it is a rock. The experimenter then lets them examine it more closely, holding and squeezing it, before asking them two questions, the reality question: 'What is this really really? Is it really really a rock, or is it really really a piece of sponge?' and the appearance question: 'When you look at this with your eyes right now, does it look like a rock or does it look like a sponge?' Most three-year-olds fail to answer both questions correctly. Instead, they tend to give 'realist' answers, namely, that it really is a sponge, and that it looks like a sponge. Most four-year-olds answer correctly. They say that it looks like a rock, but that it's really a sponge. Children show a similar pattern of development when tested with alternative versions of the task. Why is it that three-year-olds get one of the questions wrong, but four-year-olds get both right?

Although children show a similar pattern of development with alternative versions of the appearance–reality task, young children make different kinds of errors in different tasks. In Flavell et al.'s (1986) 'is-task', for example, children aged three-and-a-half to four years were asked about the colour and identity of objects in different circumstances. The colour task involved a red-coloured car that could be placed behind a green filter to make it look black. Children were shown how the appearance of the car changed when placed behind the filter, and were then asked, both with the car in front and behind the filter, 'What colour is the car, is it red or black?' Only half answered the question correctly when the car was behind the filter. The identity task involved a pencil eraser that could be wrapped in a sweet wrapper to make it look like a sweet. Children were shown the eraser and the eraser wrapped in the sweet wrapper. With the eraser in the wrapper they were asked 'What is this, is it an eraser or a sweet?'. Almost all answered correctly that it was an eraser. Older children answered correctly for both colour and identity questions.

It seems that when they are questioned about object identities—as they are in the sponge–rock task and the pencil–eraser task—young children tend to make 'realist' errors, that is they answer the appearance question with the object's actual identity rather than its apparent identity. When questioned about the properties of objects—as they are, e.g., in tasks that involve the changing the apparent colour of an object—they tend to make 'phenomenist' errors, that is they take the property that an object appears to have to be the property it actually has and answer the reality question accordingly (Flavell, Flavell, and Green 1983).

This suggests that children's pattern of errors in the appearance–reality tasks reflects a difference in their understanding of the nature of objects and their properties. It may be that young children think that the colour of an object is the simply the colour it looks to have, so that changing the way an object looks just is changing its colour. For them, placing an object behind a coloured filter is the same as colouring an object. Since the identity of a colour is tied closely to its appearance and since, in many cases, the colour of an object just is the colour it appears to have, it may take longer for children to learn that we favour some colour appearances over others as the *real* colour of an object (i.e. they must learn that we favour the stable colour appearances that are maintained through changes in lighting conditions, and so on). For many objects, the identity of the object—what makes it the kind of object it is—is not tied to its appearance, but to its function. For these objects, understanding what kind of object it is at least partly involves understanding its function. Children who understand what kind of object it is can presumably understand that an object can retain its function—and so its identity— even when its appearance is changed by, e.g., being wrapped in a sweet wrapper. It is plausible, then, that they would come to understand that changing the appearance of an object does not change its identity before understanding that changing the appearance of a colour does not necessarily change the colour. We might speculate that children are more likely to make 'realist errors' with objects whose identity is clearly functional than with objects whose identity is less clearly functional, and more likely to make 'phenomenist' errors with objects or properties whose identity is closely tied to their appearance. This means that we might expect them to have more difficulty with a doll wearing a mask than with the pencil eraser. The identity of a doll may be closely tied to the appearance of its face, and so changing the appearance of its face may, for the children, be changing its identity.

Although the pattern of errors made by children in the appearance–reality task varies, what is significant—and so what needs to be explained—is not just that young children make one kind of error rather than the other, but that they give the *same* answer to both the appearance and the reality questions. It is this that is supposed to show that they have failed to understand the distinction between appearance and reality. How does it show that?

According to the 'standard' interpretation of the appearance–reality task,[8] older children understand that their experience is representational, and so understand that it can *misrepresent* an object; in virtue of this understanding they are able to distinguish the appearance of the object—the way their experience represents it to be—from the object itself. Younger children lack this understanding and so cannot conceive of the appearance of an object as distinct from the object itself. Three-year-olds 'lack the *metarepresentational* ability of understanding [perception's] representational nature— they cannot conceive of perception as *misrepresenting* and therefore cannot distinguish appearance from reality' (Perner 1991, 93). Because they do not understand that visual experience can misrepresent an object, they do not understand that when they are asked what the object looks like they are being asked about the appearance of the object—about the way their experience represents it to be—and so they answer the 'looks'-question by simply saying what the object is. Once children 'have a notion of misrepresentation, they can understand "look like" as referring to how vision . . . misspecifies the looked-at sponge *as* a rock . . . [They] can understand that visual input has a representational *content* that, in the case of deceptive appearances, makes

[8] See, for example, Flavell (1986); Flavell et al. (1986); Perner (1991), ch.4; Gopnik and Astington (1988).

its *sense* deviate from its *referent*.' (*ibid*.) Hence four-year-olds understand that the object is a sponge, but appears to be a rock, and so are able to answer the appearance question correctly. The difference between children who answer the questions correctly and those who do not is that those who answer correctly understand representation and the representational nature of experience. They have acquired the same metarepresentational ability that explains a typical four-year-old's success at the false belief task.[9]

Is the standard interpretation correct? In the appearance–reality task the focus of the conversation is the object and whether it is a rock or a sponge. When presented with the object, the children initially say that it's a rock and then, after feeling it, they say that it's a sponge. When asked what it is really, they say that it is a sponge (children of all ages answer this question correctly so apparently are not confused about what the object is); they are then asked to say what it *looks* like. How do children understand this question: what do they think they are being asked? Given that the conversation concerns the nature of the object—and the question of whether it is a rock or a sponge—it might seem plausible that the children interpret the 'looks'-question evidentially, that is, as asking them to make an evidential claim about the object. But we saw, in the example above, that it is inappropriate to make an evidential claim in a context in which one knows the claim to be false. So when the children are asked whether it looks like a rock or a sponge they ought to be reluctant to make the evidential claim 'it looks like a rock', which carries with it the commitment to the truth of the proposition that it is a rock, given that they know that it is not a rock.

Although it seems plausible that the children should interpret the 'looks'-question in an evidential way, there is clearly something conversationally inappropriate or odd about asking someone an evidential 'looks'-question who has just said what the object *really* is. Such a question about the look of an object, if it is understood evidentially, is in effect asking a question that has just been answered: is it a rock or a sponge? Since the children have just answered this question, we might expect them to find the repetition of the question odd. Most adults would take the oddness of being asked the evidential 'looks'-question, given that they have just said what the object is, to indicate a change in the conversational context. An explicit reconstruction of how we might expect them to reason would be as follows:[10] 'Since speakers generally do not repeat a question that has just been answered, the speaker cannot be using the "looks"-question evidentially to ask what the object is, they must instead be using the "looks"-question

---

[9] I think it is a failing of the standard interpretation that it does not really explain why, if children do not understand that their experience can misrepresent, they ignore the fact that the object looks to be a rock in answering the reality question. In the case of a sponge that looks like a rock, what the children are confronted with is a conflict between what the object feels to be, and what it looks to be. Why do they not answer both reality and appearance question by saying that it is a rock? If the answer is that they stick with the first answer they give, then why does changing the order of the questions not matter?

[10] This is a reconstruction of the reasoning involved; I take it that most people do not *explicitly* reason in this way.

to ask something else'. That should lead an adult audience to seek an alternative interpretation of the 'looks'-question, one that would make sense of what the speaker is asking.

There are, I think, two alternative interpretations of the question both of which involve shifting from talking about the object—and the question of whether it is a rock or a sponge—to talking about the look or the appearance of the object. The question might be interpreted simply as asking for a characterisation of the way the object looks. In that case, it could be answered with a 'looks'-statement used to make a comparative claim: 'it looks like a rock', i.e. it has a look which is similar to the look characteristic of rocks. Alternatively, the question could be taken to be asking the audience to reflect on or evaluate the evidential basis for making different claims about the object. That is, the question might be interpreted as asking what, on the basis of *the way it looks*, one would judge the object to be: 'Although it is a sponge, what would you say it was if you were to judge what it was going by the way it looks alone?' In this case, the question is not asking the audience to make a claim about the object, but about the connection between the way the object looks and the judgement that would be made on that basis. If this is how the question is understood, then a relevant contrast would be between the way it looks and the way it feels, and we could ask the question more explicitly: Going by the way it looks, what would you say it was? Going by the way it feels, what would you say it was? Interpreting the question in either way will lead to a 'correct' answer in the task.

In order to answer the 'looks'-question in the appearance–reality task correctly, a speaker needs both to recognise that the context of the conversation has changed and to be able to reinterpret the question in an appropriate way. So an initial question to ask is whether young children *do* understand that the focus of the conversation has changed. Are they able to engage in the kind of pragmatic reasoning required? If not, then they are likely either to find the 'looks'-question confusing and so answer inappropriately and randomly, or to interpret it as asking again about the object (rather than about the look of the object) and so to answer by repeating the answer they gave to the previous question.[11]

Even if they do recognise that the focus of the conversation has changed, young children may simply be unable to reinterpret the question in a way appropriate to the new context. The two alternative ways of interpreting the question that I described make different cognitive demands of the speaker. Interpreting it in the first way requires understanding what features of the object determine the way it looks, and that the way an object looks can be characterised comparatively, which in turn requires the ability to understand comparative claims. Even children who understand

---

[11] Deák describes evidence that suggests that children have difficulty with the unfamiliar discourse format in appearance–reality tasks and says the questions are 'pragmatically odd . . . [but the] oddness is hard to define' (Deák 2006, 548).

the comparative use of 'looks'-statements in general may have a problem in assessing the truth of the particular comparative claim. Assessing its truth requires bringing to mind the look of the object to which the comparison is being made. In many cases the children are asked to make a comparison with an object that is not actually present; they are asked, for example, 'Does this sponge look like a rock?' when there is no rock for them to compare it to. In order to answer the question they need to imagine or otherwise bring to mind a characteristic rock and compare the look of the sponge to the look of the (imagined) rock. A child may understand how to make the comparison—how to compare the looks of two objects—and yet be unable to answer the question because they are incapable of bringing to mind the look of a characteristic rock that is not actually present.

It is more difficult to compare the look of an object that is actually in front of you to the look of an imaginary object than it is to compare the look of two objects that are both in front of you. So one way to make the appearance–reality task easier would be to ask the participants to respond by making an explicit comparison, rather than asking them a 'looks'-question. For example, rather than asking them whether the rock-looking sponge looks like a rock or a sponge they could be shown a characteristic sponge and a characteristic piece of rock and then asked whether the rock-looking sponge looks the same as this (the paradigmatic sponge) or this (the piece of rock). Because the question makes explicit the need to make a comparison, asking the question in this way might also ameliorate any difficulties the children have with appropriately reinterpreting the 'looks'-question.[12]

Interpreting the question in the second way again requires understanding what features of an object determine the way it looks, but in addition it requires an explicit understanding of the connection between the way an object looks and the kind of judgement that might be reasonably made on the basis of the way it looks. The evidence suggests that this understanding develops at a much later stage than the understanding of the distinction between appearance and reality, so the barrier to children's understanding of the appearance–reality distinction cannot be their under-standing of this connection.[13]

---

[12] In many appearance-reality experimental tasks, children are given pre-training to facilitate their comprehension of the task and improve their performance. This pre-training often consists in showing them the object and pointing out how its appearance changes. 'Really this is a sponge, but it looks like a rock'. The problem with this is that, if I am right that children interpret the looks claim evidentially, they are unlikely to be able to understand what they are being told during the training in the way intended. The consequence would then be that the pre-training confuses rather than enlightens them. If I am right, then to be helpful the pre-training needs to involve an explicit comparison between two objects.

[13] See chapter 18, this volume. This is related to children's ability to understand the source of their knowledge. There's no reason to think that children will acquire the cognitive capacities required to make these different interpretations simultaneously, so it may well be that they are able to interpret the question in one way before they are able to interpret it in the other way (I discuss this in more detail below).

Understanding the distinction between appearance and reality

Failing to answer the questions in the appearance–reality task correctly does not show that children do not understand the distinction between appearance and reality. They may fail because they cannot keep track of the change in focus of the conversation, or because they cannot appropriately interpret what they are being asked. It might be suggested, however, that such an explanation of children's failure at the appearance–reality task is consistent with the claim that success at the task requires understanding experiences as representational: after all, in order to answer the questions correctly children need to be able to make the distinction between appearance and reality, and in order to do that they must understand experiences as representational.

Such a suggestion assumes that the look of an object is a matter of how it is experienced to be, so that to understand the distinction between appearance and reality requires understanding the relation between the way an object is experienced to be and the way it is in reality, which in turn requires a conception of experience as representational. However, according to the account of appearances I have been drawing on, the appearance of an object is not a matter of how the object is experienced to be; it is that aspect of the object that determines a certain kind of its perceptual similarity with other objects (Martin 2010, section 2). In the case of looks, it is that aspect of the object that determines its visual similarity with other objects. To understand the distinction between appearance and reality is to understand that two objects may appear the same—may have the same look, for example—and yet be different kinds of objects. That requires understanding (visual) appearances in general as a certain aspect of objects, and understanding the connection between that aspect of an object and the kind of object it is. It does not require understanding the relation between the way an object is experienced to be and the way it is in reality.

Understanding visual appearances does not require conceiving of the appearance of an object *as* that aspect of it that determines its perceptual similarity with other objects. Someone who is simply capable of understanding that objects look similar if they are grouped together by looking at them—grouped using a particular method of grouping—would have enough of an understanding of visual appearances to be able to make the distinction between appearance and reality. They would be in a position to understand that objects that are grouped by looking at them—using that method— may nonetheless be different kinds of objects.[14] Understanding looking, or touching, as

---

[14] In fact, many of the appearance–reality tasks do not contrast looking with any other sense modality, so success at these tasks may not require understanding visual appearances per se, rather than appearances in a more general sense; that is, they may not require that children understand looking vs touching as a method of grouping rather than simply grouping similar objects. There is some evidence that children have quite a poor understanding of what can be discovered by looking vs what can be discovered by touching, so one might doubt that even four-year-old children have an understanding that objects can be grouped as similar by looking (see chapter 18, this volume).

a method of grouping together objects need not involve any explicit understanding of perception, or of perceptual experiences; and, in particular, it does not require thinking that objects look the same because they produce experiences of the same kind. I might simply know that looking is something I do with my eyes, and so know that two objects look similar if I find out that they are similar using my eyes; that touching is something I do with my hands, so two objects feel similar if I find out that they are similar using my hands; and so on. This basic understanding of appearances does not imply the ability to characterise appearances comparatively. Someone might be able to group together visually similar objects—that is, be able to group together objects that look the same—and yet be unable, when presented with a particular object, to characterise its look in terms of a comparison between it and a characteristic kind of object with which it is visually similar and with which it could be grouped. That means we cannot test this basic understanding of appearances by asking questions about the way objects look.

What is involved in understanding the connection between the appearance of an object and what the object really is? In many cases the visual appearance of an object is closely connected to its identity—to the kind of object it is. Something that looks *like* a cube when viewed from different angles *is* a cube; normally, something that looks *like* a tomato *is* a tomato. But it is not always the case that objects are what they look like: in some circumstances, the look of an object is not a good guide to its identity. Although (arguably at least) something could not look like a cube when viewed from different angles and not be a cube, something could look like a tomato and not be a tomato (something can look like a tomato—look the same way that a typical tomato looks—and yet be made of wax). So there are circumstances in which the fact that something looks like a tomato is not a good guide to its being a tomato. In such circumstances, there is a gap between the way something appears and the way it really is, between appearance and reality.

The extent to which the look of an object is a good guide to its identity varies with the kind of object in question—there is a close connection between the property of being a cube and the property of looking cubic; there is not between the property of being a tomato and the property of looking like a tomato—and is therefore something that needs to be learnt from case to case. It may involve learning that what we mean when we say that something is a tomato, for example, is that it is a certain kind of fruit, and not just something with a tomato-like appearance.[15] Someone might learn this about tomatoes, and yet not know in general what the connection is between an object's appearance and its identity. They might not know, for example, whether something that looks like a pencil, but which does not make marks on paper, is really a

[15] Suppose artificially manufactured tomatoes that are difficult to tell apart from real tomatoes without specialised equipment became widespread. In such a situation, what we now regard as sufficient to determine that something really is a tomato—that it looks, tastes, and smells like a tomato—would no longer be sufficient.

pencil. Furthermore, claims about what something *really* is can vary with context: perhaps it really is a pencil, just not a very good one, or perhaps it is not really a pencil. If it was intended to be decorative, for use in a window display, we might say that it is not really a pencil; if the pencil in the display serves, at a pinch, for noting down a number, then we might say it really is a pencil, just not a very good one. The same thing might in one context be said to really be a pencil, and in another to not really be a pencil. What something can be said to be *really* varies with context in which the question arises. Again, this is something that must be learnt from case to case. Someone might have a basic understanding of appearances, and know that something that looks like a tomato is not really a tomato (it is made of wax), and yet be unsure, in the case of another kind of object, whether it really is what it looks like. What they lack is not an understanding of experience, but of the object or what in the context it can be said to really be.

A number of conclusions can be drawn from all this. One is that understanding the distinction between appearance and reality may be domain specific: children may learn about the connection between the identity and appearances of one kind of object before they do another.[16] A second is that children may have a basic understanding of appearances before they are able to use 'looks'-statements comparatively to characterise and report appearances. It may be, too, that children understand appearances in general before they understand visual appearances, tactile appearances, and so on; because most tasks fix the method by which perceptual similarities are to be judged they do not tell us that the understanding of appearances involved is modality specific. Thirdly, and finally, if what I have been arguing is correct, success at the prototypical appearance–reality task does not tell us that children understand experience as representational, and understand a representational theory of perception, or even that they are able to meta-represent (though it doesn't, of course, rule that out). It does tell us that they understand the connection between appearance (understood as an aspect of the object) and 'reality' for the kind of object in question, that they are sensitive to the changing conversational context in the relevant experimental task, and that they are able to understand the comparative use of 'looks'-statements to report the (visual) appearances of objects.

Interpreting perspective–taking tasks

In a prototypical perspective-taking task a child sits facing an experimenter across a small table on which there is a vertical blue filter. The child is shown a pink-coloured cut-out of a seal, which is placed in front of or behind the blue filter so that it either looks pink to the child and blue to the experimenter, or vice versa (Flavell et al. 1986). The child is then asked two questions, the 'appearance' question: 'Does the seal look

---

[16] This may be exactly what the results of Flavell's 'is-task' shows.

blue to you or does it look pink?', and the 'appearance-for-other' question: 'I'm looking at the seal now, does it look blue to me or does it look pink?'[17] In another version of the task, a child sits facing an experimenter across a table on which there is a picture of a turtle arranged to look to the child like it is lying on its back and to the experimenter like it is standing on its feet, or vice versa. The child is asked 'Does the turtle look to you like it is standing on its feet or does it look like it is upside-down?' and 'I am looking at the turtle now, does it look like it is upside-down to me or standing on its feet?' Children below about four-and-a-half years old answer the appearance question correctly, but answer the appearance-for-other question incorrectly; they tend either to give 'egocentric' answers to both questions, or to answer the second question randomly. Most five-year-old children can answer both questions correctly. Children show a similar pattern of development when tested with any one of the many variations on this kind of perspective-taking task. Why is it that young children get one of the questions wrong, but older children get both right?

According to the standard interpretation, older children understand that experience is representational and so understand that one and the same object may appear—and so may be described or characterised—in different ways, depending on the perceiver's perspective on it. A turtle may look upside-down to one person and right-side-up to another; from one perspective a dog might look like it is in front of a hut, and from another perspective look like it is behind the hut; the turtle cannot be simultaneously upside-down *and* right-side-up; the dog cannot be simultaneously in front of *and* behind the hut. The object or situation could not actually be the ways it appears. Younger children lack the understanding of representation required to conceive that an object can appear to someone else to be a way that is incompatible with the way it appears to them, and so answer the 'appearance-for-other' question incorrectly. Older children are able to think about different representations of the same situation and not just about the situation itself, and so answer the 'appearance-for-other' question correctly (Perner 1991, 119–20). Because they understand representation, older children understand that the way an object appears from a particular perspective depends on how the perceiver's experience represents it to be from that perspective, and that different experiences can represent one and the same object in different—incompatible—ways. According to the standard interpretation, there is a connection between perspective-taking tasks and appearance–reality tasks. Younger children fail perspective-taking tasks because they lack the meta-representational ability required for thinking about different representations of the same situation; younger children fail the appearance–reality tasks because they lack the meta-representational ability required for understanding that an object may appear other than it really is. Older children succeed at both tasks because, between the ages of three and five, they have

---

[17] Experiments using these tasks usually involve a training phase during which the experimenter shows the child how the appearance of the target object changes and explains, e.g., that 'The seal looks blue to you because you are looking through this thing', and 'I'm looking at the seal too, but it looks pink to me'.

acquired the necessary meta-representational ability. There is some evidence that success at the two tasks is correlated, and this correlation is explained on the assumption that they both involve meta-representation.[18]

Is the standard interpretation correct? In the perspective-taking task the child is asked a question about how the object actually looks, and how it looks from another perspective: 'Does the seal look blue to you or does it look pink?' and 'I'm looking at the seal now, does it look blue to me or does it look pink?' The focus of the conversation here is not the object and whether it *is* blue or pink, but the *look* of the object and whether the object *looks* blue or pink. To answer correctly requires that the 'looks'-questions be understood comparatively.

If young children do not understand the comparative use of 'looks'-statements and so do not interpret the questions comparatively, then we might expect them to interpret them evidentially, as asking about the nature rather than the look of the object. In that case, their answer to the question 'Does the seal look blue to you or does it look pink?' will express their commitment to the claim that the seal actually is blue or pink. Suppose that they are then asked 'Does the seal look blue to me or does it look pink?' Understood evidentially, this is asking the very same question as the one that they just answered: is the seal actually blue or pink? On the assumption that they take the object to be the way it looks, we might expect them to get the 'appearance' question right; then to give the same answer to the 'appearance-for-other' question (or to answer it randomly because they find it confusing to be asked a question they have just answered), even if they know what the seal looks like from the experimenter's perspective.[19] This is just the pattern of response typically seen with younger children.

We saw above that understanding the comparative use of 'looks'-statements requires understanding both that objects look a certain way—that they are similar or different in virtue of the way they look—and knowing how to characterise the way they look using a comparative statement. In discussing the appearance–reality task, I suggested that these two aspects of understanding might develop independently: that children might understand the way objects look before they understand how to use comparative statements to characterise the way they look. The way the questions are asked in the perspective-taking task does not distinguish these different aspects of understanding. Children who do not understand that objects look a certain way will not know what an object looks like from *any* perspective. Children who understand that objects look a certain way and are able to work out how an object looks from another perspective—by, for example, imagining (or remembering)[20] the way the object looks from that

---

[18]   See Moll and Meltzoff (2011) for sceptics.

[19]   We will see the same pattern of errors as we do in the appearance–reality task. That we can explain the pattern of errors in some versions of the perspective-taking tasks in the same way as in the appearance–reality task would seem sufficient to explain what evidence there is that success and failure at both tasks is correlated.

[20]   In some cases the child has actually seen the object from the other perspective, so they can come to know how it looks from that perspective by remembering how it looked; when they have not seen the object from that perspective they will have to imagine how it looks.

perspective—but who do not understand the comparative use of 'looks'-statements will not be able to report what the object looks like and so will not be able to answer the 'appearance-for-other' question correctly.

Even children who understand the comparative use of 'looks'-statements in general may have difficulty assessing the truth of the particular looks claims in the perspective-taking task. To assess their truth they need to bring to mind the look of the object to which the comparison is being made, which in most versions of the task is not actually present. For example, in order to answer the question 'Does the seal look blue to you or does it look pink?' the child must imagine or bring to mind the look that is typical of something blue and the look that is typical of something pink, and compare the look of the seal in front of them to this imagined look. To answer the question 'Does the seal look blue to me or does it look pink to me?' correctly they need first to imagine how the seal looks from my perspective; then imagine or bring to mind the look that is typical of something blue and the look that is typical of something pink; and then compare this imagined look to the (imagined) look of the seal from the experimenter's perspective.[21] It is more difficult to compare the look of an object in front of you to the look of an object that is brought to mind or imagined, than it is to the look of an object that is actually in front of you. So one way to make the perspective-taking easier would be to ask the children to respond to the questions by making an explicit comparison. For example, rather than asking them whether the object looks pink or blue, they could be shown a piece of pink card and a piece of blue card and asked whether the object looks like one or other card.

Even if children are unable to understand the comparative use of 'looks'-statements, it may be possible to elicit the apparently correct answer to the 'appearance-for-other question' by getting them to make an evidential 'looks'-statement. Suppose that the child has been shown, and can remember, an object as looking blue from the experimenter's perspective, but has not considered (or has ignored) its colour from their own perspective; they may take the object to be blue and so be willing to *claim* that the object is blue, even if now it does not actually look blue to them. If they are then asked 'Does the seal look blue to me or pink?' they may reply by making the evidential claim 'it looks blue' to express the claim that the object is blue.[22] Although

---

[21] In the task involving a picture of a turtle, the question asks whether the turtle has a look that is similar to the look of a right-side-up turtle, or an upside-down turtle; the child must imagine or bring to mind the look that is typical of an upside-down turtle and the look typical of a right-side-up turtle, and then compare the look of the turtle in front of them or the experimenter to this imagined look.

[22] Moll and Meltzoff (2011) have used a version of the task in which children were presented with a white object that was seen through a blue-coloured filter by the experimenter, or a blue-coloured object that was seen through a yellow filter (so that it looked green) by the experimenter. In the demonstration phase a picture of a blue dog was moved from behind the clear part of the screen to behind the yellow part of the screen so that it looked green; the experimenter held up a cut-out of a green flower and said 'Now it looks like this'. Each time the object changed colour the experimenter said 'Now it looks like this' and held up the flower of matching colour. In the test phase the experimenter says 'That one looks blue/green from here, can you put it in the bag for me?' The child had to determine which of the two identically coloured objects (e.g. the two blue-coloured dogs) in front of her the experimenter was talking about. Younger children

this task might elicit a 'correct' response, it is not clear that it requires the child to understand that objects look a certain way; therefore, it is not clear that success at this kind of task would be sufficient to show that the child understood that the way an object looks can be different from different perspectives.

Young children's failure to answer the questions in the perspective-taking task does not show that they lack a meta-representational ability. Nor does their failure necessarily show that they do not know how an object looks from a perspective other than their own. They *might* fail because they do not know what an object looks like—because they do not understand that objects look a certain way or because they cannot work out what the object looks like from the other perspective—or they might fail because they cannot use a comparative 'looks'-statement to describe the way the object looks. Either way, what they lack is not a representational understanding of perceptual experience, but a certain kind of understanding of objects, their looks, and how to describe them.

Understanding other perspectives

The questions in the perspective-taking task are intended to test whether children can understand that an object that looks a certain way to them may look different to someone else viewing it from a different perspective. The best explanation of children's *failure* to answer both questions correctly might be in terms of their failure to understand comparative use of 'looks'-statements. It might be objected, however, that since the same object cannot be both pink and blue, or upside-down and right-side-up, in order to understand that an object can both look blue (from my perspective) *and* pink (from your perspective), or look both upside-down *and* right-side-up, and so to answer both questions correctly and *succeed* at the task, they must be able to think of experiences as representational.

We have seen that, when used comparatively, a 'looks'-statement characterises an object's way of looking. Comparative 'looks'-statements are true in virtue of the visible properties of objects: the comparative claim 'that (object) looks blue' does not entail that the object is blue, but that it has a blue look (i.e. has a look which is like that of blue things); so, prima facie, it does not entail that the object is some way that is inconsistent with its being (or looking) pink. How must an object be to have a look which is

---

perform better in this task than in the standard perspective-taking task; Moll suggests that this is because they have only to consider the experimenter's perspective and do not have to 'confront' a perspective that's different from their own. In completing the task they can ignore their own perspective (see general discussion). If that is the correct interpretation, then it is not clear that children in this task understand the 'appearance-for-other' question comparatively, nor that they understand that objects look a certain way. The task is set up in such a way that they will respond correctly if they interpret the 'looks'-statement evidentially, as asking them to pick the object that *is* blue or *is* green. The challenge is for them to track the colour of the objects. Since they have seen the objects from the experimenter's perspective, the object that is green is the one that is green from that perspective. Their success at the task may manifest their ability to remember what colour the object is from that perspective, rather than any understanding of the way the object looks.

like that of blue things? An obvious way it could be is to be coloured blue (objects which are coloured blue normally have a look which is like that of blue-coloured things); but an object's colour can look different in different contexts, so that is not the only way it could be. It could be coloured pink and be illuminated with a blue light; pink objects in blue light have a look which is similar to the look of objects which are coloured blue. Similarly, it could be coloured pink and have a sheet of blue glass placed over it; pink objects viewed through blue glass have a look which is similar to the look of blue objects. Looking blue is not inconsistent with being pink nor, *a fortiori*, with looking pink. Therefore an object can be correctly characterised using two different 'looks'-statements, both of which are true in virtue of the same visible properties of the object.[23]

What is true of colour is true more generally. When used comparatively, the statement 'the dog looks like it is in front of the hut' does not entail that the dog is in front of the hut; and 'the dog looks like it is behind the hut' does not entail that the dog is behind the hut. They describe the way the situation looks, rather than the way it is and, therefore, both statements can be simultaneously true of the same situation. In general, the same objective situation can look like one thing from one perspective and something different from another perspective. To understand how both 'looks'-statements can be true of the same situation does not require being able to think about the way experience represents the situation, it just requires thinking about the situation itself, and how what it looks like—i.e. what it looks similar to—can change with your perspective on it.

One way to think of a perspective on an object is in terms of the perceptual experience of someone viewing the object from that perspective; to think of the way an object looks from a perspective would then be to think about the way the object looks to the person occupying that perspective. Nothing about the way of understanding looks that I have been discussing requires understanding a perspective in this *subjective* way: we can understand a perspective as simply the *objective* circumstances or context in which an object is seen. Viewing an object from different perspectives is a way of discovering what it looks like, given the particular visible properties it has, from those perspectives. Likewise, perspective-taking is a way of discovering what something looks like from different perspectives, but one that involves imagining (or remembering) the object and its visible properties rather than actually viewing it.

Suppose, for example, that you are standing facing a statue that you cannot walk behind, and you wonder what it looks like when viewed from behind. To answer that, you could imagine what that statue would look like if you could walk behind it and view it from that perspective, or you could imagine what it would look like if you simply turned it around on the plinth in front of you. Imagining rotating the statue involves imagining a change in the arrangement of things in the world; to answer the

---

[23] See Kalderon (forthcoming) for a discussion of reasons for doubting that there are any cases of something's being some way that is inconsistent with its looking F-coloured.

question you would need to imagine what the statue would look like, given its visible properties, if you made those changes. Imagining that does not involve thinking about experiences, so imagining what the statue would look like if rotated does not require any conception of experience as representational. Imagining walking around the statue to view it from another perspective is another way of imagining a change in the arrangement of things in the world. Just as imagining what the statue would look like if rotated does not involve thinking about experience, neither does imagining what the statue would look like if viewed from another perspective. In neither case do you need to think about the *experience* you would have, you just need to think about the statue and its visible properties, and what it would look like, if things in the world were rearranged in the way imagined.

Success at the perspective-taking task requires the ability to imagine what an object looks like, given its actual properties, from different perspectives or in different contexts of viewing, and the ability to understand and use comparative-'looks' statements to characterise what an object looks like. That requires understanding that objects look a certain way, but it does not require the ability to think about perceptual experiences, and so does not require the ability to think of experiences as representational.

The standard interpretation is wrong, therefore, to view success at perspective-taking tasks as depending on the ability to think of perceptual experiences as representational. Children can succeed at perspective-taking without having that ability, and may fail because they do not understand that objects look a certain way, because they cannot imagine how an object looks from a perspective other than their own, or because they cannot understand the comparative use of 'looks'-statements required to characterise the way an object looks.

Conclusion

In this chapter I have argued that a correct account of the use of 'looks'-statements suggests that the standard interpretation of appearance–reality and level-2 perspective-taking tasks is incorrect. Since children's failure at those tasks can be explained by their failure to understand how to use 'looks'-statements to report the way things look, their failure does not imply that they do not understand either the distinction between appearance and reality or how things look from another perspective. The account of 'looks'-statements goes together with an account of perceptual appearances as aspects of objects. I have argued that it follows from that account of perceptual appearances that children who succeed at both tasks can do so without having a conception of experience as representational. That means we do not have any reason to explain children's developing understanding of perception in terms of their acquisition of the rudimentary representational theory of perception favoured by the standard interpretation.

Although the representational theory of perception has attained the status of orthodoxy within philosophy and, perhaps, within psychology, it is not obviously the correct account of our commonsense understanding of perception. According to the alternative—relational—view of perception, perceptual experiences have their objects as constituents and are therefore essentially relational; we perceive an object in virtue of being perceptually related to it.

On a Relational View . . . your experience, as you look around the room, is constituted by the actual layout of the room itself: which particular objects are there, their intrinsic properties, such as colour and shape, and how they are arranged in relation to one another and to you. (Campbell, *Reference and Consciousness*, p.116)

According to this view, how things appear to someone is a matter of what objects and properties they are perceptually related to. For an object to look a certain way to someone is not for them to have an experience that represents the object as being that way, it is for them to be perceptually related to an object with that look. To understand how things look to someone does not require an understanding of the nature of certain kinds of psychological states—visual experiences—that determine how things look, it requires knowing the look of the objects to which they are perceptually related.

One of my aims, in arguing against the standard interpretation of the appearance– reality and perspective-taking tasks, is to allow for the possibility that children acquire, and adults have, a conception of perception and perceptual experience that is better characterised by the relational than by the representational theory of perception.

References

Campbell, John. 2002. *Reference and Consciousness*. Oxford: Oxford University Press.

Chisholm, Roderick M. 1957. *Perceiving: A Philosophical Study*. Ithaca: Cornell University Press.

Deák, Gedeon O. 2006. 'Do Children Really Confuse Appearance and Reality?' *Trends in Cognitive Sciences*, 10 (12) (December): 546–550.

Deák, Gedeon O., Ray, Shanna D., and Brenneman, Kimberly. 2003. 'Children's Perseverative Appearance–Reality Errors Are Related to Emerging Language Skills'. *Child Development* 74 (3) (June): 944–964.

Flavell, J. H. 1978. 'The Development of Knowledge about Visual Perception'. In C. B. Keasey (ed.) *Nebraska Symposium on Motivation*. Lincoln: University of Nebraska Press.

Flavell, J. H. 1986. 'The Development of Children's Knowledge about the Appearance–Reality Distinction'. *American Psychologist*, 41(4), 418–425.

Flavell, John H., Everett, Barabara A, Karen Croft, and Eleanor R. Flavell. 1981. 'Young Children's Knowledge about Visual Perception: Further Evidence for the level 1-level 2 Distinction'. *Developmental Psychology*, 17 (1): 99–103.

Flavell, John H., Flavell, Eleanor R., and Green, Frances L. 1983. 'Development of the Appearance–Reality Distinction'. *Cognitive Psychology*, 15 (1) (January): 95–120.

Flavell, John H., Green, Frances L., and Flavell, Eleanor R. 1989. 'Young Children's Ability to Differentiate Appearance-Reality and Level 2 Perspectives in the Tactile Modality'. *Child Development*, 60 (1) (February): 201–213.

Flavell, John H., Green, Frances L., Flavell, Eleanor R., Watson, Malcolm W., and Campione, Joseph C. 1986. 'Development of Knowledge about the Appearance-Reality Distinction'. *Monographs of the Society for Research in Child Development*, 51 (1): i–87.

Flavell, John H., Shipstead, Susan G., and Croft, Karen. 1978. 'Young Children's Knowledge about Visual Perception: Hiding Objects from Others'. *Child Development*, 49 (4) (December): 1208–1211.

Gopnik, A. and Astington, J. W. 1988. 'Children's Understanding of Representational Change and its Relation to the Understanding of False Belief and the Appearance–Reality Distinction'. *Child Development*, 59 (1): 26–37.

Jackson, Frank. 1977. *Perception: A Representative Theory*. Cambridge: Cambridge University Press.

Kalderon, Mark E. forthcoming. 'Color Illusion'. *Nous*.

Martin, M. G. F. 2010. 'What's In a Look?'. In *Perceiving the World*, ed. Bence Nanay. New York: Oxford University Press.

Moll, H. and Meltzoff, A. N. in press. 'How Does It Look? Level 2. Visual Perspective-Taking at 36 Months of age'. *Child Development*, 82(2).

O'Neill, D. K. and Chong, C. F. 2001. 'Preschool Children's Difficulty Understanding the Types of Information Obtained through the Five Senses'. *Child Development*, 72 (3): 803–815.

Perner, Josef. 1991. *Understanding the Representational Mind*. Learning, development, and conceptual change. Cambridge, Mass: MIT Press.

Pillow, Bradford H. and Flavell, John H. 1986. 'Young Children's Knowledge about Visual Perception: Projective Size and Shape'. *Child Development*, 57 (1) (February): 125–135.

Pillow, B. H. 1993. 'Preschool Children's Understanding of the Relationship between Modality of Perceptual Access and Knowledge of Perceptual Properties'. *British Journal of Developmental Psychology*, 11: 371–389.

Quinton, A. M. 1955. 'The Problem of Perception'. *Mind*, n.s. 64 (253). (January): 28–55.

Travis, Charles. 1997. 'Pragmatics'. In Hale and Wright, eds., *A Companion to Philosophy of Language*. Oxford: Blackwell. 87–107.

Yaniv, I., & Shatz, M. (1988). 'Children's Understanding of Perceptibility'. In J. Astington, P. Harris, and D. Olson (eds.) *Developing Theories of Mind*. London: Cambridge University Press. 93–108.

16

Perspective-Taking and its Foundation in Joint Attention

Henrike Moll and Andrew N. Meltzoff

Unlike any other species, humans can think about perspectives that are not currently their own. They can put themselves in the "mental shoes" of others and imagine how they perceive, think, or feel about an object or event. Perspectivity in its mature, adult form even goes beyond the ability to determine a specific person's point of view at a certain moment in time. It entails the general comprehension that one and the same thing or event can be viewed or construed differently depending on one's standpoint—whether this is a visuo-spatial, epistemic, conceptual, or affective standpoint (Perner, Brandl, and Garnham, 2003). From a developmental perspective, the question arises when and how children acquire this knowledge.

We offer a new look at the early ontogeny of understanding visual perception and experiences—with a major emphasis on the ability to take and understand the perspectives of others. The central claim we aim to develop is that human children first learn about perspectives within the context of joint attentional engagement. Infants' ability and motivation to jointly attend to objects and events with others allows them to share perceptions and experiences from very early on in life (Tomasello, Call, Carpenter, Behne, and Moll, 2005). This sharing sets the ground for later perspective-taking.

Developmental inquiries of joint attention and perspective-taking have mostly been conducted in separation: The term "joint visual attention" is often used as a synonym for the specific case of gaze following, which is rarely looked at in terms of its relation to later perspective-taking; and models of perspective-taking have failed to recognize early joint attentional skills as a foundational first step towards perspectivity (but see Martin, Sokol, and Elvers, 2008).

We want to bring these two strands together and argue that joint attention is a necessary condition for appreciating perspectives. Perspectival differences, however distinct and incompatible they may be—in the sense that they cannot consistently be held by one person at the same time—necessarily converge on one and the same object (where "object" can refer to a thing, an event, a state of affairs etc.). They thus have at their basis a common ground, and this common ground is constituted by the joint attention devoted to the object by two or more individuals.

We propose a series of social-cognitive steps taken by infants and young children on their way to a mature understanding of perspectives.[1] Our model overlaps in some respects with previous stage models, such as that by Flavell and colleagues (see Flavell 1978, 1992, for overviews) or Selman (1980). But it differs from these accounts in important ways. First and foremost, we acknowledge the joint attentional abilities demonstrated by infants at around one year of age as a staging post for the emergence of perspectivity. At this stage, infants are at "level 0 perspective-taking": they do not yet know anything about perspectives, but they can share them in joint attention or joint engagement with others—as evidenced by such behaviors as gaze following, alternating gaze between object and co-attender, holding up and showing, or pointing to objects or events. This sharing of attention is qualitatively and structurally different from the tempo-spatial co-ordination of behavior that is found in primates (see Moll and Tomasello, 2007a) and it lays the grounds for the more complex forms of taking and understanding perspectives that follow during the next months and years in young childhood. About a year later, at around 2 years, children reach "level 1 visual perspective-taking": they know *what*, e.g. which objects in a room, others can and cannot see from their current visuo-spatial viewpoint (at least when the spatial requirements, e.g. projective geometry, are minimal). We will compare this skill with infants' knowledge about what someone is or is not familiar with from past experience—which may analogously be called "level 1 experiential perspective-taking." Counterintuitively, the latter seems to develop significantly earlier than level 1 visual perspective-taking. We think that this puzzling developmental order may reflect something about infants' early engagement with others and the world, and about a particular challenge tied specifically to the understanding of visual perception as opposed to more holistic ways of engaging with or experiencing objects in the world. At level 2, children know what but also *how* others see things. They understand the specific way in which something is seen, construed, or (re)presented. However, in the light of new data, we argue for a division of this level in two distinct sublevels: At level 2A, which seems to be reached by 3 years, a child is able to recognize how another sees something, even when this differs from how the child sees at that moment. Yet, this does not entail the ability to "confront" perspectives and comprehend that one object, event etc. can be seen in multiple ways depending on one's viewpoint. This, as is evidenced by many theory of mind studies, seems to emerge at around 4.5 years of age, when preschoolers gain an explicit knowledge about perspectives in the various domains, including perception and knowledge. This full-blown acknowledgement of perspectives is achieved at level 2B.

---

[1] We limit our analysis to the first 4 to 5 years of life, thereby not taking account of any higher-order understanding of perspectives that may follow, for example, in adolescence.

1 Level 0 perspective-taking: Sharing attention

As early as in the first year, human children can share their visual attention with others. This ability manifests itself in two chief ways, both of which emerge at around the same time between 9 and 12 months of age. At this age, infants begin to *follow into* another person's already established focus of attention and *direct* another person's attentional focus by pointing to or showing the person excitedly an object of their interest (see, e.g. Carpenter, Nagell, and Tomasello, 1998). Before producing linguistic utterances to direct others' attention to things verbally, infants thus know how to use a variety of non-linguistic means to achieve a "meeting of minds" with others (Bruner, 1995). We chose to focus on the cases of gaze following (as one way of participating in joint attention) and pointing (as one way of initiating joint attention) as these have been subjected to numerous experimental investigations.

1.1 Gaze following

Gaze following is probably the most widely investigated behavior that often marks the beginning of a joint attentional sequence. In the first half of their first year of life, human infants look in the general direction another person is looking (e.g. D'Entremont, Hains, and Muir, 1997; Scaife and Bruner, 1975). However, at this young age they only follow gaze to a target when it is inside their visual field and the first object on their scan path, suggesting the possibility that infants are simply orienting in the same direction in which another's head is oriented (Butterworth, 1983). By around 12 months, however, gaze following is flexible and robust and seems to reflect an understanding that people do not just look in some direction, but rather, that they see things where they look. This may also be evidenced by the fact that infants' gaze following is not limited to their immediate visual fields: they locomote behind barriers to see what others have just seen there (Moll and Tomasello, 2004) and follow gaze to the space behind their own bodies (Deák, Flom, and Pick, 2000). Other clever variations of the classic gaze following have established that shortly after their first birthdays, infants have implicit knowledge that the eyes play a critical role in seeing, i.e. they need to be oriented towards the object, open (Brooks and Meltzoff, 2002; Meltzoff and Brooks, 2008), and that opaque barriers on the visual scan path to objects prevent people from seeing these objects (Caron, Kiel, Dayton, Butler, 2002).

However, humans are not the only species that align their regard with that of a conspecific or human. Not only non-human primates follow gaze to where another has just looked (even behind barriers, Tomasello, Hare, and Agnetta, 1999), but also dolphins (Pack and Herman, 2004), goats (Kaminski, Riedel, Call, and Tomasello, 2005), and ravens (Schloegl, Kotrschal, and Bugnyar, 2007). The mere behavior of "looking where someone else is looking" (Butterworth, 1991, p. 223) then does not necessarily indicate a sharing of attention or experiences—unless one wanted to attribute joint attention to all these species. We think it is important to broaden the scope and take into account the social context in which gaze following behavior occurs in human infants, its distinct phenomenal quality, and the alternative ways in which infants not only participate in, but also actively establish joint attention by gesturally inviting others to share experiences with them.

Having followed an adult's gaze, infants frequently point to the object, vocalize (Brooks and Meltzoff, 2002), or look back to the adult (Carpenter et al., 1998). These "checking looks" to the other person close the circuit of the triangulation by providing the arrow that connects the two co-attenders with each other. Additionally, infants often show a "knowing smile" as they look to the other's face—thereby demonstrating an awareness of the mutuality of the experience. More so, this may be a manifestation of the infants' feeling of "interpersonal connectedness" and identification with the other. It certainly means that there is not just an identical target attended to separately by two individuals at the same time, but that we have here an instance of two people sharing an orientation or attitude towards an object (Hobson, 2005). Furthermore, gaze following in humans usually initiates or continues an extended joint attentional episode or "format" (Bruner, 1983). These are the mundane, simple cooperative activities shared by caregiver and infant such as sharing a meal, taking a bath, playing, engaging in simple problem-solving tasks (see Heal, 2005). A lot of these activities have a structure of reciprocal role- and turn-taking (give–take, hide–seek, etc.). Roles and perspectives can be thought of as equivalent constituents in the action and the perceptual domain: just as role-taking is learned within the context of simple cooperative activities, so is perspective-taking acquired within joint attentional sequences. In any case, gaze following is just a snapshot extracted from a longer scene in which infant and adult alternate gaze, vocally "comment" on the object and engage in shared experiences and explorations.

1.2 Pointing

At around the same time as infants follow into others' attentional focus, they also direct others' attention by pointing. While non-human primates seem to point only imperatively, using others as "social tools" (Bates, Camaioni, and Volterra, 1975) to get them what they want (Tomasello, 2006; but see Racine, Leavens, Susswein, and Wehera, 2008), human infants point for a variety of motives. They often point not to request things, but simply to share their experience of something with another person—what has been called declarative pointing (see Bates et al., 1975). This may be most obvious when "requesting" cannot be what the child attempts to do, for example because what she points to is i) well within her own reach, so that no help retrieving it would be required, or ii) far outside of hers as well as the adult's reach (e.g. a plane in the sky), such that no such help can be expected, or iii) not a thing, but an event or a state of the world.

One may still object that what looks like a sharing motive at first is really an imperative one—for example the desire to attract another's attention, to get the other to attend to oneself (Moore and Corkum, 1994). However, experimental data suggest that this is unlikely. In one experiment, pointing gestures were elicited in 12-month-old infants by showing them an event an adult did not attend to at first. The infants were satisfied and ceased to point for the adult only when the adult alternated gaze and truly shared the interesting sight with them. By contrast, if the adult either attended to the infant or the event alone, infants were dissatisfied and persisted to point (Liszkowksi, Carpenter, Henning, Striano, and Tomasello, 2004). Thus, infants urged the other to close the triangulation and share her orientation to the attended-to event. Just witnessing the other establish a "parallel" instead of a joint engagement with the event alone, or, witnessing the other establish *dyadic* engagement with them alone was not satisfactory. Other studies have shown that infants complement their gestures with looks to the adult's face to check if their point is received and acknowledged—with these looks changing from being "reactive" to being anticipatory over the course of the first half of the second year of life (Franco and Butterworth, 1996). It seems that a whole variety of motives to point for others are "buried" under the label of declarative pointing, so that the category is perhaps better seen as "non-imperative pointing," where non-imperative motives include: providing others with information about the presence/status of something, sharing simply for the sake of sharing, requesting information such as the name or function of the pointed-to object etc. (see also Tomasello, Carpenter, and Liszkowski, 2007; Tomasello, 2008).

1.3 Synopsis

By around one year of age, human infants establish joint visual attention by both tuning into another's pre-established focus of attention as well as inviting others to share theirs. Some of the behaviors we would call joint visual attention in human children, such as gaze and point following, are also found in non-human animals, but the social scenarios in which they are embedded, their phenomenal quality, their bi-directionality (the ability to take the role of the initiator and follower in joint attention and switch between them) and the diversity of motives are clearly distinctive in human-human-interactions. For these reasons, we feel confident to say that the infant in these situations is aware that the other shares her attentional focus—a criterion for joint attention which most philosophers and psychologists seem to agree upon (see Eilan, Hoerl, McCormack, and Roessler, 2005). However, we do not think that at this early point the sharing of attention reflects an understanding of perspectives or perspectival differences. As Barresi and Moore (1993) have put it the "sharing of perspectives precedes the understanding of these perspectives" (p. 513). In this regard, we follow a philosophical tradition that construes the early joint attentional abilities of infants as a form of "knowing how" rather than "knowing that" (e.g. Seemann, 2007). Participating and engaging in joint attention is primarily an "empractical" (Bühler, 1965; Stekeler-Weithofer, 2005) skill. The use of this skill then allows for and blossoms into the development of the more complex forms of perspective-taking and understanding gained in the next months and years of life.

2 Level 1 Perspective-taking

In level 1 perspective-taking according to Flavell (e.g. 1992) and colleagues' framework, a child not only recognizes others' attention, but also knows *what* others can and cannot visually perceive in the moment (visual perspective-taking). In other words, a child at this level knows what objects do and do not figure in another's visual perspective. There is also an analogous level of understanding that has received much attention in developmental research in the past years, namely the understanding of what others have and have not become familiar with from past perceptual experience. As will become clear in the following sections, these two abilities are quite distinct and challenge infants and young children to different degrees.

2.1 Level 1 visual perspective-taking

According to Flavell and colleagues' framework, level 1 visual perspective-taking starts with an understanding of what others can (and cannot) see from their specific viewpoint. A child who has reached "level 1 visual perspective-taking" should be able to know what objects can and cannot be seen from a certain visuo-spatial position. The gaze following procedure and its variations are informative about infants' implicit knowledge about some basic enabling and defeating conditions of seeing (e.g. that the eyes need to be open and the line of sight clear)—but are not appropriate measures when it comes to determining if a child knows what is and is not part of another person's perspective. Richer response measures are required for this. The child needs to specify somehow—verbally, gesturally, or by complying to a request with some sort of action—exactly what can or cannot be seen from a certain spatial position.

A seminal study was conducted by Masangkay, McCluskey, McIntyre, Sims-Knight, Vaughn, and Flavell (1974). In their experiment, an adult held up a card between herself and the child. The side of the card facing the child contained a picture of one animal, e.g. a dog, while the side facing the adult showed a different animal, e.g. a cat. The child was previously shown both sides of the card and so knew what each side depicted. She was then asked what she herself saw and what the adult saw. Most children at the age of 2.5 years and older could say correctly what they saw and what the adult saw.

Two other studies have provided converging evidence that level 1 perspective-taking develops at around 2.5 years—but also point at some limitations at this age. In a study by Flavell, Shipstead, and Croft (1978) a child was asked to hide an object from an adult (who sat either next to or across from the child) by either placing an object in relation to a barrier that was already on the table or by placing a barrier in relation to an object that was already on the table. The youngest age group of 2.5 year-olds successfully placed the toy on the table so that it was hidden from the adult's view, but not from themselves. However, only children 3 years and older knew how to "interrupt" an adult's already established visual engagement with an object by positioning a barrier between the object and the adult (see also McGuigan and Doherty, 2002).

In a study using a search paradigm, Moll and Tomasello (2006) found that 24-month-olds have a nascent understanding of what others can and cannot see from their viewpoint. An adult pretended to be searching for an object. There were two candidate objects in the room, both of which were well visible and equidistant from the child position. Behind (from the child's perspective) one of the objects was an opaque barrier which blocked the adult's view to it. The 24-month-olds selected this object significantly in response to the adult's searching, but had no preference for this object in a control condition in which the adult made a neutral and ambiguous request for an object. The children thus knew i) that people search for things they cannot see, and ii) which of the two objects in this situation could not be seen by the adult.

The research suggests that young children begin to appreciate that others may not see what they see at around 2 to 2.5 years of age.[2] It is not surprising that this ability comes into place significantly later than gaze following and other level 0 skills. More surprising, however, is the finding that level 1 visual perspective-taking is *preceded*, not succeeded, as will be shown in the following section, by the understanding of what others are and are not familiar with from past experience.

2.2 Level 1 experiential perspective-taking

Recent research suggests that children can understand what others know and do not know at a surprisingly young age; at least if "know" refers not to propositional knowledge, but to the type of knowledge that is conveyed by "connaître" in French, "kennen" in German, and "conocer" in Spanish—which is probably best translated with "being familiar" or "acquainted" with something from past perceptual experience. In O'Neill's (1996) well-known study, a child saw an experimenter place a desirable object in one of two containers out of the child's reach. The parent, who had the role of the child's helper, either witnessed the hiding event or missed it because she was out of the room or covered up her eyes (in which case the child was explicitly told that she cannot see). Children of 2.3 and 2.7 years of age tailored their requests for the parent according to her knowledge state. If the parent was ignorant, they made more frequent and more specific requests than when she knew where the object was placed.

A series of recent studies shows that even infants early in the second year of life can judge what others are and are not familiar with. In a study by Tomasello and Haberl (2003), 12- and 18-month-old infants and an adult jointly engaged with two novel objects in turn for one minute each. Then the adult left the room. While she was gone, the infant and a second adult played with a third novel object. Finally, all three objects were held in front of the infant, at which point the first adult returned and excitedly exclaimed "Wow! Look! Look at that one!" gazing in the direction of all three objects. She then made an ambiguous request for the infant to hand "it" to her. Both the

---

[2] Though an implicit ability for level 1 visual perspective-taking may be in place by only 14 months of age, as evidenced by looking-time measures (see Luo and Baillargeon, 2007; Sodian, Thoermer, and Metz, 2007).

12- and 18-month-olds significantly chose the third object—but not in a control condition in which the adult experienced all three objects. The infants thus knew what the adult did and did not experience, independently from their own experience.

Importantly, this understanding is not limited to the specific novelty paradigm. In other tasks, infants of 14 months and older were equally able to i) select an object that was mutually familiar, but had been shared in special ways between infant and adult prior to her making an ambiguous request for "it" (Moll, Richter, Carpenter, and Tomasello, 2008), and ii) see an adult's expression of excitement as being directed at either an entire object or a part of the object, depending on whether the adult saw it for the first time or knew it from prior experience (Moll, Koring, Carpenter, and Tomasello, 2006).

2.3 Making sense of a puzzling developmental order

The procedures that have been developed to assess level 1 visual and experiential perspective-taking seem highly similar: In addition to one or more objects that are mutually seen/known, there is another object which only the child sees/knows but the adult does not. In both cases the question is if the child can ignore her perception of/familiarity with that object and recognize the adult's ignorance of it. Yet, children are successful in the 'experiential task' almost a year before they solve the visual perception task. Intuitively, one would assume that children come to know what others can and cannot see "in the here and now" *before* they come to know what others do and do not know from previous experience—which involves keeping track of what happened in the recent past. The pressing question then is why the recognition of past experiences develops so early, and why level 1 visual perspective-taking emerges relatively late.

2.3.1 Social engagement facilitates recognizing what others experience In an attempt to reconcile these seemingly contradictory findings, Moll and Tomasello (2007b) put forth the "sharing hypothesis". They argued that what enabled infants to perform well in knowledge-ignorance studies was the "sharing" of the two known objects: being jointly engaged with the adult as she explored the familiar objects allowed them to register the adult as knowing the objects a few moments later. The unknown object stuck out as the one that the infant and adult had not shared together. To test this hypothesis, Moll and Tomasello (2007b) varied the specific way in which the adult became familiar with the two known objects. In one condition—modelled on Tomasello and Haberl's experimental condition—the adult shared her experience of the two known objects with the infant in joint engagement. In two other conditions, (1) infants observed the adult examine the two known objects individually instead of in joint engagement, or (2) the adult looked on from afar as the infant and the assistant examined the two familiar objects. As in Tomasello and Haberl's (2003) study, the adult then left the room while the assistant presented the infant with the third object.

In line with the hypothesis, 14-month-old infants knew which object was new for the adult only when they had shared the experience of the known objects together. In both other conditions in which the objects were not shared, infants failed to identify what the adult was referring to in her excited request. (By 18 months, infants knew what the adult had experienced not just through joint attentional engagement, but also by observing the adult actively manipulate the known objects.)

More empirical support for the view that infants come to understand what others experience through joint engagement stems from a study by Moll, Carpenter, and Tomasello (2007). They found that 14-month-olds failed on the test if they simply witnessed an adult jointly engaging with the familiar objects with *another* person from a third-person perspective. Instead, infants had to share the objects with the adult *directly* in order to register her as knowing them. Thus, joint engagement is at least helpful, probably even necessary for infants at 14 months to register others as having experienced objects. This is in accord with a point made by Heal (2005) about the critical importance of the second person. Children do not learn about the social world mostly and usually from third persons—"he"s and "she"s that are distantly observed from the outside. Instead, they learn from the "you"s with whom they interact and engage in collaborative activities with joint goals and shared attention. As Heal writes "the basic subjects of psychological predicates will be 'us': viz. you and me" (2005, p. 41). Only later do children learn from third parties by observing, eavesdropping, and overhearing. For example, 18-month-olds regulate their imitation of actions on an object through observing an emotional interaction between two *other* people (Repacholi and Meltzoff, 2007; Repacholi, Meltzoff, and Olsen, 2008). Likewise, infants 18 months and older learn novel words by overhearing what third persons say to each other (Floor and Akhtar, 2006). But at the beginning—and this may only be a few months prior—learning takes place strictly within the "I–thou" (Buber, 1958) relationship.

2.2.2 Social engagement compromises a recognition of what others do not experience These studies thus help to understand why or under what social conditions infants attribute experiences to others at a surprisingly young age—but they do not address the particular challenge posed by visual perspective-taking. To account for this as well, Moll, Carpenter, and Tomasello (2011) extended the "sharing hypothesis" and postulated that just as social engagement facilitates children's ability to recognize others' experiences, it might lead them to overestimate what has been shared, that is, it might hinder their ability to detect ignorance in others.

When a young child is engaged with another person, she might act on the presumption that she and the other person perceptually share the space around them—even though the other person cannot see what the child sees. Even adults can be "tricked" into falsely assuming a shared perceptual space with others in social situations (see, e.g. Epley, Morewedge, and Keysar, 2004). For example, a speaker might point to his computer screen instead of the projection on the wall behind him to show a graph to his audience—not realizing in that moment that the audience cannot see the laptop screen. The joint presence and social interaction suggests a shared perceptual access to the things in the room. It is possible then that children attribute ignorance to another person readily as long as the person is not socially engaged with them at all, which is the case in classic knowledge–ignorance tasks. In these tasks, the adult disengages entirely from the situation by leaving (e.g. O'Neill, 1996; Tomasello and Haberl, 2003) or at least turning away (Southgate, Senju, and Csibra, 2007). In contrast, in visual perspective-taking tasks the adult is necessarily physically co-present. What is experimentally manipulated is not the other's presence, but merely her visual access to the objects. In such a situation it should be much harder to detect ignorance or perceptual non-connectedness, as children would need to realize that *despite* the other's co-presence, a mutual perceptual access to the objects cannot be taken for granted.

An adult's physical co-presence in the child's visual field (close by and facing the child) may be the most obvious basis for an assumption of shared experience—especially at a very young age when the objects of joint attention are mostly physical objects in the near environment. But errors of over-attributing perception and knowledge can also occur when the other is absent, but jointly engaged via verbal communication. For instance, people sometimes provide visual gestures for others with whom they are talking on the phone, but who cannot see them. Two-year-olds, who have just begun to be language users, may also overestimate another person's perceptual access in communicative situations.

To investigate the separate and combined effects of physical co-presence and verbal communication on children's detection of ignorance, Moll et al. (2010) again modified Tomasello and Haberl's (2003) selection paradigm. In each of four conditions, 24-month-old children shared two novel objects in turn with an adult in joint engagement, making those objects mutually known. Then, in all conditions, the third object (the target) was presented to children, but the adult never saw it. What was varied across conditions was the social situation in which children experienced the target: the adult was physically co-present or not and/or communicated verbally with children or not, in a 2x2 design. The question was if children were able to register the adult as being ignorant of the third object in these different situations. In line with the extended "sharing hypothesis," the two-year-olds over-attributed experience to the adult in all these three cases: when the adult was co-present (irrespective of whether she additionally communicated or not) and when she was absent, but communicated. Only when the adult terminated the social interaction entirely by leaving and stopping to communicate did the 2-year-olds clearly register her ignorance of the object.

What this study shows is that young children's social engagement with others may sometimes lead them to overestimate what is shared. When interacting with a co-present or communicating person, they tend to erroneously assume a shared perceptual space with that person. Just as the "curse of knowledge" compromises the ability to reason about others' false beliefs (Birch, and Bloom, 2007), so can the "curse of social engagement" compromise the ability to register others' ignorance. Importantly, this study helps to explain the discrepancy between an understanding of seeing in the here and now (visual perspective-taking) on the one hand and having experienced things in the recent past (experiential perspective-taking) on the other. While visual perspective-taking inherently involves a co-present adult, the person in experiential perspective-taking tasks usually breaks the social engagement entirely, e.g. by saying goodbye and leaving. In this situation, it is much easier to register others' ignorance.

From a broader perspective, this shows that what is primary is the sharedness of the situation, the "being-in-this-together." It is likely that infants at this stage conceive of perception more holistically as someone's engagement with things. It seems that "seeing" is understood as "being engaged" or "occupied" with something (see also McGuigan and Doherty, 2002, O'Neill, 1996). Only later does the concept of seeing become refined and identified as the specific form of *visual* experience that it is, with an *explicit* understanding of the conditions for informational access and its relation to knowledge (see Wimmer, Hogrefe, and Perner, 1988). Starting at around two years, children can be brought to understand that a person may not see something despite being present and even posturally and visually oriented towards an object. But to achieve this, the other person must make very clear that there is something she cannot visually get in "contact" with—by either verbally saying that she cannot see something (as in O'Neill's, 1996, study) or by searching (as in Moll and Tomasello's, 2006, study). The impeding effect of one's co-presence can thus be counteracted by providing specific cues to one's inability to see.

3 Level 2 perspective-taking: Understanding "seeing as"

When a child comes to understand not only *what* is visible from a certain point of view, but also *how* a given object is seen or presented, she is considered to have reached "level 2 perspective-taking." In philosophical terms, the child can now specify an object's *mode of presentation* or *aspectual shape* (Perner et al., 2003; Searle, 1992). For instance, an object can only be said to be "left"/"right" or "in front of"/ "behind" another object as a function of one's visuo-spatial perspective. Perner and colleagues (Perner et al., 2003) have pointed out that this is the first level that strictly deserves to be called an understanding of perspectives: If a perspective is a way of seeing, then an understanding of perspectives necessarily entails knowledge of how people see what they see.

The most well-known level 2 perspective taking task is probably the three-mountain problem designed by Piaget and Inhelder (1956). Children sat in front of a three-dimensional model showing three mountains each with a distinctive landmark (a church etc.). A doll was placed at various positions facing the model and the child had to determine the doll's visual perspective, for example, by choosing from among a set of pictures depicting the model as seen from different viewpoints. For reasons such as the complexity of the visual array (see Borke, 1975), the use of this task has led to significant underestimations of children's capacities to imagine how an object looks from a viewpoint other than their own.

A more child-friendly task for preschoolers is that developed by Masangkay et al. (1974). They presented children a picture of a turtle placed on the table in front of them. The children correctly identified the turtle as "right-side up" when the turtle's feet were facing them, and as "upside down" when the picture was turned so that the turtle's feet were facing away from them. However, children below 4.5 years of age did not understand that while they saw the turtle right-side up, an adult sitting across the table saw it upside-down. Replacing the word pair "upside down" and "right-side up" with the potentially more child-friendly expressions "standing on its feet" and "lying on its back" failed to improve 3-year-olds performance (Flavell, Everett, Croft, and Flavell, 1981). Other studies have looked at children's understanding of how an observer's distance from an object affects its perceived clarity and size (Flavell, Flavell, Green, and Wilcox, 1980; Pillow and Flavell, 1986). Taken together, level 2 research has consistently shown that 4.5-year-olds are mostly successful in judging how an object looks from perspectives other than their own, whereas 3-year-olds are not.

This is in line with the idea of a strong ontogenetic tie among the classic theory-of-mind abilities. Reasoning about beliefs (epistemic perspective-taking), distinguishing between appearance and reality (conceptual perspective-taking) accepting alternative names for a given object (e.g. "bunny" and "rabbit" for the same animal, see below), and level 2 visual perspective-taking all emerge in synchrony. They co-emerge not per coincidence, but because of conceptual relatedness: they all require an understanding that one and the same object or event can be looked at, conceptualized or interpreted in multiple ways depending on one's point of view (Perner, 2000; Perner, Stummer, Sprung, and Doherty, 2002).

Some recent studies prima facie seem to challenge this "unitary view," including a series of experiments coming from our laboratory. We re-examined the development of level 2 visual perspective-taking using a color filter technique (Moll and Meltzoff, in press). An advantage of this approach may be that children at this age know the basic color terms, whereas perspectival word-pairs such as "left/right," "in front of/behind" are not yet well understood by children this young (Wanska, 1984). In one experiment, 36-month-old children were presented with an ambiguous verbal request for an object and had to take an adult's visual perspective in order to disambiguate it. There were two candidate objects both of which the children saw in their true, same color: either white (Color Task) or blue (Color Mix Task). However, an adult saw one of them through a tinted filter—resulting in a perception of a different color for this object. Despite the fact that the children themselves saw two identically-colored objects, they systematically chose the object that the adult requested. For example, in the Color Mix Task, when the adult requested a green object, the children chose that one of the two blue objects that looked green to the adult. Moreover, children succeeded in the opposite case: they correctly chose that one of the two blue objects that the adult saw as blue (through the clear side of the screen, when the adult requested "the blue one" (Moll and Meltzoff, 2011).[3]

In a second experiment, children of the same age could also take an adult's perspective in a production version. The children sat next to the adult (90 degrees to her left or right) who faced a screen containing a yellow filter. The children were then requested to make a blue object look green for the adult by placing it on either side of the filter. In this production task, 36-month-old children correctly placed the object relative to the screen such that the adult saw it green—even though the children still saw the object in its true, blue color. This result together with the previous one again suggests that 36-month-olds understand how another person sees something when this differs from how they themselves see it.

A pressing question then is why the children in the present studies performed so well. One possibility is that 3-year-olds' understanding of visual perspectives has previously been underestimated due to extraneous task demands, such as the verbal ability to use perspectival word pairs. The new task may simply be a more sensitive measure for the same competence tested with the classic tasks. On this view, level 2 visual perspective-taking has been brought down by about 1.5 years, to 36 months of age.

This would have profound theoretical implications. Most importantly, it would undermine the idea of a common cognitive denominator shared by perceptual, conceptual, epistemic perspective-taking and so forth. One theoretical response might be to draw a distinction between different kinds of mental states such as perception and belief. Maybe visual perspectives are understood prior to epistemic ones and the challenge of classic theory-of-mind is limited to belief reasoning. In line with this view, many have argued that perception and desire are grasped by children well before epistemic states (e.g. Astington and Gopnik, 1991; Rakoczy, Warneken, and Tomasello, 2007). However, perceiving, along with believing and knowing, is considered a "cognitive attitude" with a mind-to-world direction of fit and is thus in this regard more similar to these mental states than to desires and other "conative attitudes" (which have a "world-to-mind direction of fit", see, e.g. Gopnik, Slaughter, Meltzoff, 1994).

3.1 Level 2: Taking (2A) versus confronting (2B) perspectives

We would like to take a route that accommodates our findings with the unitary view. Our study may not capture perspectives at the same level that is required for an understanding of false belief, the distinction between appearance and reality, alternative

---

[3] It may seem surprising that children solved the Color Mix Task equally well as the Color Task—even though the former involved subtractive color mixing, which 3-year-olds may not know about. But note that prior to the test, children were exposed to the color filters and experienced the color change of the objects themselves (a white object was held behind a blue filter and a blue object behind a yellow filter).

naming, and level 2 visual perspective-taking as measured by the turtle task. In these tasks children have to simultaneously "confront", to borrow Perner et al.'s (2002) term, two different perspectives on the same thing. In the false belief task, the child needs to understand that another's false epistemic perspective (on an object's location or the content of a box) clashes with what she herself knows to be true. In appearance–reality tasks, two conceptual perspectives have to be confronted: the self-same object can be construed as, e.g. a rock from the "phenomenological perspective" and as a sponge from the "reality perspective." Similarly in the alternative naming task, it needs to be acknowledged that one and the same object, e.g. a rabbit, can be conceptualized and labeled both as a "rabbit" and as a "bunny" (Doherty and Perner, 1998). Likewise in Masangkay et al.'s (1974) turtle task children have to understand that the turtle looks "upside-down" from one visual perspective but "right side-up" from another. In other words, what is put to a test is the understanding that there can be two different judgments, construals, or (re)presentations of one and the same thing held by two people at the same time.

Such a simultaneous confrontation of perspectives, however, is not necessary in the color filter tasks (Moll and Meltzoff, 2011). To succeed in these tasks, the child needs to recognize how the adult sees an object but not how that compares to their own perception of it. They can ignore the fact that what looks, for example, green to the adult looks blue to them—because they are not asked to contrast or confront the others' perspective with their own at that time.

The difference is the following: children as young as 36 months can take another's visual perspective of something even when the visual input of the same object is different for the child at that moment. In this sense, 3-year-olds engage in a form of perspective-taking that fulfills the classic definition of level 2 (e.g., Masangkay et al., 1974). However, level 2 perspective-taking has also been described as the understanding that two people may "have different perspectives or views of the same display" (Flavell, 1992, p. 119) or that an object can be seen in multiple ways. It has been taken for granted that this knowledge comes for free once a child engages in perspective-taking—the clash with the child's own perspective was simply presupposed as being registered by the child. But it seems that the 3-year-olds can just ignore the fact that they see the object differently from the way the adult sees it. The ability to register and reflect on perspectival differences must be seen as a distinct capacity. Two things that have been subsumed under "level 2 visual perspective-taking" thus need to be differentiated in two sublevels: the ability to take another's perspective on an object (2A) and the ability to confront two perspectives on the same object (2B). While 2A is well in place by 3 years of age, 2B emerges at around 4.5 years, as has been established and replicated in numerous false belief and similar theory of mind tasks (see e.g., Wellman, Cross, and Watson, 2001). The child has come to understand that people's relations to objects are perspectival— they understand their own perspective *as* their own and that of another *as* that of the other. They know that an object can be viewed as one thing or another— for example as a sponge or a rock in the appearance–reality test or as a duck or a rabbit in the famous duck–rabbit figure (see Doherty and Wimmer, 2005). What our color filter tasks have surprisingly shown, *ex negativo*, is that to capture this full-blown understanding of perspectives experimentally, children have to confront two perspectives at the same time.

Summary

Past stage models of perspective-taking have started with the ability of children to put themselves in perspectives that are different from their own. The ability of infants to share perspectives in joint attention was not seen as relevant in these accounts. In the present chapter, we argued that this early sharing of experiences in joint attention (level 0 perspective-taking) needs to be acknowledged as a staging post in the development of perspectivity, as it permits the later emergence of taking and understanding perspectives. When first taking others' perspectives, young children surprisingly find it easier to grasp what another has and has not experienced in the recent past (level 1 experiential perspective-taking) than to judge what another can and cannot see here and now (level 1 visual perspective-taking). To explain this counterintuitive order, we have again drawn on social engagement: while social engagement helps young children to register others' experiences with things, it sometimes leads them to overestimate the shared perceptual space and thus hinders their recognition of others' ignorance. Finally, we have urged for a distinction between two separate abilities that have so far been subsumed under level 2 (Flavell, 1992): the ability to *take* another's perspective that differs from one's own view of an object and the ability to *confront* perspectives with another (be these actual perspectives held by concrete individuals or possible perspectives that "one" could hold). New data suggest that 3-year-olds have no problems taking another's perspective (and leaving behind their own), but they still lack the ability to confront perspectives and understand the perspectival nature of people's construals of objects and events.

References

Astington, J. W., and Gopnik, A. (1991). Theoretical explanations of children's understanding of the mind. *British Journal of Developmental Psychology*, 9, 7–31.

Barresi, J., and Moore, C. (1993). Sharing a perspective precedes the understanding of that perspective. *Behavioral and Brain Sciences*, 16, 513–514.

Bates, E., Camaioni, L., and Volterra, V. (1975). The acquisition of performatives prior to speech. *Merril-Palmer Quarterly*, 21(3), 205–226.

Birch, S. A. J., and Bloom, P. (2007). The curse of knowledge in reasoning about false beliefs. *Psychological Science*, 18(5), 382–386.

Borke, H. (1975). Piaget's mountains revisited: Changes in the egocentric landscape. *Developmental Psychology*, 11, 240–243.

Brooks, R., and Meltzoff, A. N. (2002). The importance of eyes: How infants interpret adult looking behavior. *Developmental Psychology*, 38(6), 958–966.

Bruner, J. (1983). *Child's talk: Learning to use language*. New York: Norton.

Bruner, J. (1995). From joint attention to the meeting of minds: An introduction. In C. Moore and P. J. Dunham (eds.), *Joint attention: Its origins and role in development* (pp. 1–14). Hillsdale, NJ: Erlbaum.

Buber, M. (1958). *I and thou* (R. G. Smith, trans.). New York: Charles Scribner's Sons.

Bühler, K. (1934): *Sprachtheorie. Die Darstellungsfunktion der Sprache*. Jena: Fischer.

Butterworth, G. (1983). Structure of the mind in human infancy. *Advances in Infancy Research*, (Vol. 2, pp. 1–29). Norwood, NJ: Ablex.

Butterworth, G. (1991). The ontogeny and phylogeny of joint visual attention. In A. Whiten (ed.), *Natural theories of mind: Evolution, development, and simulation of everyday mindreading* (pp. 223–232). Oxford: Blackwell.

Caron, A. J., Kiel, E. J., Dayton, M., and Butler, S. C. (2002). Comprehension of the referential intent of looking and pointing between 12 and 15 months. *Journal of Cognition and Development*, 3(4), 445–464.

Carpenter, M., Nagell, K., and Tomasello, M. (1998). Social cognition, joint attention, and communicative competence from 9 to 15 months of age. *Monographs of the Society for Research in Child Development*, 63 (4, Serial No. 255).

D'Entremont, B., Hains, S. M. J., and Muir, D. W. (1997). A demonstration of gaze following in 3- to 6-month-olds. *Infant Behavior and Development*, 20(4), 569–572.

Deák, G. O., Flom, R. A., and Pick, A. D. (2000). Effects of gesture and target on 12- and 18-month-olds' joint visual attention to objects in front of or behind them. *Developmental Psychology*, 36(4), 511–523.

Doherty, M., and Perner, J. (1998). Metalinguistic awareness and theory of mind: Just two words for the same thing? *Cognitive Development*, 13, 279–305.

Doherty, M. J., and Wimmer, M. C. (2005). Children's understanding of ambiguous figures: Which cognitive developments are necessary to experience reversal? *Cognitive Development*, 20, 407–421.

Eilan, N., Hoerl, C., McCormack, T., and Roessler, J. (eds.) (2005). *Joint attention: Communication and other minds*. Oxford: Oxford University Press.

Epley, N., Morewedge, C. K., and Keysar, B. (2004). Perspective taking in children and adults: Equivalent egocentrism but differential correction. *Journal of Experimental Social Psychology*, 40, 760–768.

Flavell, J. H. (1978). The development of knowledge about visual perception. In C. B. Keasey (ed.), *The Nebraska Symposium on Motivation:* Vol. 25. *Social cognitive development* (pp. 43–76). Lincoln: University of Nebraska Press.

Flavell, J. H. (1992). Perspectives on perspective taking. In H. Beilin and P. B. Pufall (eds.) *The Jean Piaget symposium series*. Vol. 14: *Piaget's theory: prospects and possibilities* (pp. 107–139). Hillsdale, NJ: Erlbaum.

Flavell, J. H., Everett, B. A., Croft, K., and Flavell, E. R. (1981). Young children's knowledge about visual perception: Further evidence for the level 1–level 2 distinction. *Developmental Psychology*, 17, 99–103.

Flavell, J. H., Flavell, E. R., Green, F. L., and Wilcox, S. A. (1980). Young children's knowledge about visual perception. Effect of observer's distance from target on perceptual clarity of target. *Developmental Psychology,* 16, 10–12.

Flavell, J. H., Shipstead, S. G., and Croft, K. (1978). Young children's knowledge about visual perception: Hiding objects from others. *Child Development,* 49, 1208–1211.

Floor, P., and Akhtar, N. (2006). Can 18-month-old infants learn words by listening in on conversations? *Infancy,* 9, 327–339.

Franco, F., and Butterworth, G. (1996). Pointing and social awareness: Declaring and requesting in the second year. *Journal of Child Language,* 23, 307–336.

Gopnik, A., Slaughter, V., and Meltzoff, A. N. (1994). Changing your views: How understanding visual perception can lead to a new theory of the mind. In C. Lewis, and P. Mitchell (eds.), *Children's early understanding of mind: Origins and development* (pp. 157–181). Hillsdale, NJ: Erlbaum.

Heal, J. (2005). Joint attention and understanding the mind. In N. Eilan, C. Hoerl, T. McCormack, and J. Roessler (eds.), *Joint attention: Communication and other minds* (34–44). Oxford: Oxford University Press.

Hobson, P. (2005). What puts the jointness into joint attention? In N. Eilan, C. Hoerl, T. McCormack, and J. Roessler (eds.), *Joint attention: Communication and other minds* (185–204). Oxford: Oxford University Press.

Kaminski, J., Riedel, J., Call, J., and Tomasello, M. (2005). Domestic goats, *Capra hircus,* follow gaze direction and use social cues in an object choice task. *Animal Behaviour,* 69(1), 11–18.

Keysar, B., Lin, S., and Barr, D. J. (2003). Limits on theory of mind use in adults. *Cognition,* 89, 25–41.

Liszkowski, U., Carpenter, M., Henning, A., Striano, T., and Tomasello, M. (2004). Twelve-month-olds point to share attention and interest. *Developmental Science,* 7(3), 297–307.

Luo, Y., and Baillargeon, R. (2007). Do 12.5-month-old infants consider what objects others can see when interpreting their actions? *Cognition,* 105, 489–512.

Martin, J., Sokol, B. W., and Elfers, T. (2008). Taking and coordinating perspectives: From prereflective interactivity, through reflective intersubjectivity, to metareflective sociality. *Human Development,* 51, 294–317.

Masangkay, Z. S., McCluskey, K. A., McIntyre, C. W., Sims-Knight, J., Vaughn, B. E., and Flavell, J. H. (1974). The early development of inferences about the visual percepts of others. *Child Development,* 45, 357–366.

McGuigan, N., and Doherty, M. J. (2002). The relation between hiding skill and judgment of eye direction in preschool children. *Developmental Psychology,* 38(3), 418–427.

Meltzoff, A. N., and Brooks, R. (2008). Self-experience as a mechanism for learning about others: a training study in social cognition. *Developmental Psychology,* 44(5), 1257–1265.

Moll, H., Carpenter, M., and Tomasello, M. (2007). Fourteen-month-olds know what others experience only in joint engagement. *Developmental Science,* 10(6), 826–835.

Moll, H., Carpenter, M., and Tomasello, M. (2010). Social engagement leads 2-year-olds to overestimate others. *Infancy,* no. doi: 10.111/j.1532-7078.210.00044.x.

Moll, H., Koring, C., Carpenter, M., and Tomasello, M. (2006). Infants determine others' focus of attention by pragmatics and exclusion. *Journal of Cognition and Development,* 7(3), 411–430.

Moll, H., and Meltzoff, A. N. (2011). How does it look? Level 2 perspective-taking at 36 months of age. *Child Development,* 82(2).

Moll, H., Richter, N., Carpenter, M., and Tomasello, M. (2008). Fourteen-month-olds know what "we" have shared in a special way. *Infancy*, 13(1), 90–101.

Moll, H., and Tomasello, M. (2004). 12- and 18-month-old infants follow gaze to spaces behind barriers. *Developmental Science*, 7(1), F1–F9.

Moll, H., and Tomasello, M. (2006). Level 1 perspective-taking at 24 months of age. *British Journal of Developmental Psychology*, 24, 603–613.

Moll, H., and Tomasello, M. (2007a). Cooperation and human cognition: The Vygotskian intelligence hypothesis. *Philosophical Transactions of the Royal Society B*, 362(1480), 639–648.

Moll, H., and Tomasello, M. (2007b). How 14- and 18-month-olds know what others have experienced. *Developmental Psychology*, 43(2), 309–317.

Moore, C., and Corkum, V. (1994). Social understanding at the end of the first year of life. *Developmental Review*, 14, 349–372.

O'Neill, D. K. (1996). Two-year-old children's sensitivity to a parent's knowledge state when making requests. *Child Development*, 67, 659–677.

Pack, A. A., and Herman, L. M. (2004). Bottlenosed dolphins (*Tursiops truncatus*) comprehend the referent of both static and dynamic human gazing and pointing in an object-choice task. *Journal of Comparative Psychology*, 118, 160–171.

Perner, J. (2000). RUM, PUM, and the perspectival relativity of sortals. In J. W. Astington (ed.), *Minds in the making: Essays in honour of David R Olson* (pp. 212–232). Malden, MA: Blackwell Publishers.

Perner, J., Brandl, J. L., and Garnham, A. (2003). What is a perspective problem? Developmental issues in belief ascription and dual identity. *Facta Philosophica*, 5, 355–378.

Perner, J., Stummer, S., Sprung, M., and Doherty, M. (2002). Theory of mind finds its Piagetian *perspective*: Why alternative naming comes with understanding belief. *Cognitive Development*, 17, 1451–1472.

Piaget, J., and Inhelder, B. (1956). *The child's conception of space*. London: Routledge.

Pillow, B. H., and Flavell, J. H. (1986). Young children's knowledge about visual perception: Projective size and shape. *Child Development*, 57(1), 125–135.

Racine, T. P., Leavens, D. A., Susswein, N., and Wereha, T. J. (2008). Conceptual and methodological issuses in the investigation of primate intersubjectivity. In F. Morganti, A. Carassa, and G. Riva (eds.), *Enacting intersubjectivity: A cognitive and social perspective to the study of interactions* (pp. 65–79). Amsterdam: IOS Press.

Rakoczy, H., Warneken, F., and Tomasello, M. (2007). "This way!", "No! That way!"—3-year-olds know that two people can have mutually incompatible desires. *Cognitive Development*, 22, 47–68.

Repacholi, B. M., and Meltzoff, A. N. (2007). Emotional eavesdropping: Infants selectively respond to indirect emotional signals. *Child Development*, 78, 503–521.

Repacholi, B. M., Meltzoff, A. N., and Olsen, B. (2008). Infants' understanding of the link between visual perception and emotion: "If she can't see me doing it, she won't get angry." *Developmental Psychology*, 44, 561–574.

Scaife, M., and Bruner, J. S. (1975). The capacity for joint visual attention in the infant. *Nature*, 253, 265–266.

Schloegl, C., Kotrschal, K., and Bugnyar, T. (2007). Gaze following in common ravens, *Corvus corax*: Ontogeny and habituation. *Animal Behaviour*, 74, 769–778.

Searle, J. R. (1992). *The rediscovery of the mind*. Cambridge, MA: MIT Press.

Seemann, A. (2007). Joint attention, collective knowledge, and the "we" perspective. *Social Epistemology*, 21(3), 217–230.

Selman, R. L. (1980). The growth of interpersonal understanding: Developmental and clinical analyses. New York: Academic Press.

Sodian, B., Thoermer, C., and Metz, U. (2007). Now I see it but you don't: 14-month-olds can represent another person's visual perspective. *Developmental Science*, 10(2), 199–204.

Southgate, V., Senju, A., and Csibra, G. (2007). Action anticipation through attribution of false belief by two-year-olds. *Psychological Science*, 18, 587–592.

Stekeler-Weithofer, P. (2005). *Philosophie des Selbstbewußtseins: Hegels System als Formanalyse von Wissen und Autonomie*. Frankfurt: Suhrkamp.

Tomasello, M. (2006). Why don't apes point? In N. Enfield and S. C. Levinson (eds.), *Roots of human sociality: Culture, cognition, and interaction* (pp. 506–524). Oxford: Berg.

Tomasello, M., Carpenter, M., Call, J., Behne, T., and Moll, H. (2005). Understanding and sharing intentions: The origins of cultural cognition. *Behavioral and Brain Sciences*, 28, 675–735.

Tomasello, M., Carpenter, M., and Liszkowski, U. (2007). A new look at infant pointing. *Child Development*, 78(3), 705–722.

Tomasello, M., and Haberl, K. (2003). Understanding attention: 12- and 18-month-olds know what is new for other persons. *Developmental Psychology*, 39, 906–912.

Tomasello, M., Hare, B., and Agnetta, B. (1999). Chimpanzees, *Pan troglodytes*, follow gaze direction geometrically. *Animal Behaviour*, 769–777.

Wanska, S. (1984). The relationship of spatial concept development to the acquisition of locative understanding. *The Journal of Genetic Psychology*, 145, 11–21.

Wellman, H. M., Cross, D., and Watson, J. (2001). Meta-analysis of theory-of-mind development: The truth about false belief. *Child Development*, 72, 655–684.

Wimmer, H., Hogrefe, G. J., Perner, J. (1988). Children's understanding of informational access as a source of knowledge. *Child Development*, 59, 386–396.

17

A Two-Systems Theory of Social Cognition

Engagement and Theory of Mind

Martin Doherty

Introduction

Two sets of findings stand out in theory of mind research. Children fail tests of belief reasoning until the age of roughly 4 years (Wellman, Cross, and Watson, 2001). Infants show sensitivity to others' beliefs and other mental states from 1 year old onwards (Surian, Caldi, and Sperber, 2007; Onishi and Baillargeon, 2005; Southgate, Senju, and Csibra, 2007). There are several ways to explain these discrepant findings, but currently little relevant evidence. The aim of the present chapter is to examine similarly discrepant findings in gaze understanding, and derive a more general way of accounting for both sets of findings.

Infants show very good gaze following abilities from about the age at which they start to pass implicit belief tasks (Corkum and Moore, 1995), if not earlier (D'Entremont, Hains, and Muir, 1997). Nevertheless, children are unable to make judgements of eye-direction until about the age at which they start to pass other explicit mental state tasks. This can only be adequately explained in terms of 2 developmentally distinct gaze understanding systems (Doherty, 2006) and considerable data exist on each set of findings and intermediate phenomena. Here I characterise the two systems, using existing data and drawing the minimum necessary conclusions. The performance of the earlier system can be explained using a relatively simple conception of relationships between people and objects, that nevertheless has considerable explanatory power. The later system is motivated by interest in internally represented mental states, and is part of explicit theory of mind developments around 3 to 4 years. I close by showing how younger children's theory of mind skills can be accounted for using the early system.

The development of gaze processing

The special detectability of the human eye

There are claims that humans have evolved specialised gaze processing brain mechanisms. Whether or not this is true, it is clear that human eyes have evolved to be easy to detect. In marked contrast to other primates, humans have 'whites of the eyes'. The sclera of other primates is pigmented, typically to match the iris and the surrounding face. This helps disguise direct gaze, which is perceived by others as aggressive. This camouflage can make predators uncertain about whether the primate has seen them; survival chances are higher if a predator thinks it has been spotted (Kobayashi and Kohshima, 2001). Human's extensive white sclera strongly contrasts with the iris and pupil. This makes it easier to detect eyes, and also to assess their deviation from forward, thus making gaze direction detection easier. Our most fundamental evolutionary adaptation for gaze detection seems to have been an adaptation of the stimulus itself.

Direct gaze

The earliest developing and most fundamental gaze detection ability is the detection of direct gaze. This may be present from birth. Farroni, Csibra, Simion, and Johnson (2002) showed newborn infants pairs of pictures of faces, one with direct and one with averted gaze. Infants looked significantly longer and more often at the direct gaze picture, suggesting that even in their first 5 days children can distinguish direct and averted gaze. Other studies have found this skill does not appear until 4 months of age (Samuels, 1985; Vecera and Johnson, 1995). Either way, this ability appears early in infancy. At around this age, infant chimpanzees also prefer human faces with open eyes and direct gaze (Myowa-Yamakoshi, Tomonaga, Tanaka, and Matsuzawa, 2003).

Gaze following

Most research on the subject has concerned gaze following. Several factors affect the difficulty of this. In particular, whether the head also turns and whether the viewer and target are simultaneously in the child's field of view are important. Scaife and Bruner (1975) initiated joint attention research with the finding that when an adult broke off eye-contact with an infant and looked elsewhere, infants as young as 3 months looked in approximately the same direction. Recent research suggests this ability does not arise until later. In early research, the measure used was typically whether the infant looked to the same side as the experimenter. This neglects the number of times infants look to the opposite side. If they looked to the opposite side equally often, previous joint attention research might simply indicate infants' increasing tendency to look around. Corkum and Moore (1995) corrected for looks to the opposite direction, and found that children could only follow head turns from 15–16 months onwards.

Younger children may follow head turns to objects if the head and the object are simultaneously visible. D'Entremont, Hains, and Muir (1997), for example, had targets

(2 puppets) either side of the experimenter's head, which she periodically looked at by turning her head through 90° (and talked to the puppets too, which is perhaps more natural). In this case, even 3-month-old infants looked more often to the puppet she was looking at rather than the other one.

This early cuing may be caused more by motion cues than the final configuration of head and eyes. For example, Hood, Willen, and Driver (1998) presented children with a computer monitor on which a face made an eye turn to one side. Shortly afterwards, a target appeared to one side of the face, either in the direction looked in or in the opposite direction. Four-month-old infants looked at the target more quickly if it appeared to the side looked at.[1] Although this appears to be gaze following, Farroni, Johnson, Brockbank, and Simion (2000) produced a similar effect by moving the image of the face to one side, while the pupils of the eyes remained stationary; the final configuration of eyes and face was identical to the original condition, the only difference being in what moved. This produced as big a cueing effect, but in the opposite direction, i.e. in the direction the face had moved.

Farroni et al. (2000) also showed that if the original stimuli were used but the eye movement was masked by a long blink, there was no cuing effect. Thus, infants were cued in the direction of whatever moved, eyes or face; when there was no apparent motion, they were not cued by the eyes. Gaze following within the visual field may therefore be entirely a result of motion, and therefore not involve computation of eye direction. Interestingly, Downing, Dodds, and Bray (2004) conclude that for adults too the cueing effect of gaze shifts is entirely due to the motion of the stimulus.

Using gaze outside of the infant's immediate visual field, Corkum and Moore (1995) found that infants could not follow eye turns by 18–19 months, the oldest age group in the study. However, this group were sensitive to eye movements; they were significantly more likely to follow a head turn accompanied by a corresponding eye movement than one without. Younger children did not distinguish between the two types of cue. In a later study, Moore and Corkum (1998) showed that 18–19-month-old infants do have a fragile ability to follow eye-turns. Infants were only presented with trials in which the head remained stationary while the eyes moved, thus isolating the stimulus of interest. The objects were particularly interesting toys, which animated if the infant looked to the same toy as the experimenter. The improvement with age was sudden: over 80% of 18–19-month-old infants reached criterion, compared to about 15% of 15–16-month-olds.

What gaze following entails

Infants' early gaze detection skills can be characterised as the ability to use others' gaze cues to orient the child's own attention. Very early gaze following probably largely relies on the properties of the stimulus. The high contrast between the sclera and the

---

[1] Note that this result is only obtained if the face disappeared before the target appeared. This rarely happens with real faces.

iris and pupil draws attention to the eyes, and the motion of the head is sufficient to direct children's attention towards objects already visible. By the second year of life however, children are clearly representing a spatial relationship between the other's head direction and the object gazed at. For example, Woodward (2003) used a habituation paradigm, in which an experimenter turned her head to look at one of two objects, both simultaneously visible to the child. Once children were habituated to this, the position of the two toys was reversed and one of two novel trials was presented. The experimenter either looked at the old toy in its new position, or looked to the original position at the new toy. Twelve-month-old infants looked longer when the actor looked at the novel toy, suggesting that they were more sensitive to the change in the gaze relationship than to the surface characteristics of the events. Younger children did not distinguish between the two trials, despite following the experimenter's head direction as often as older children.

Further evidence that 1-year-olds represent a relationship between gazers and objects comes from experiments involving occlusion. For example, Butler, Caron, and Brooks (2000) adapted a standard joint attention procedure by adding conditions with occluding screens that blocked the experimenter's line of sight. The experimenter turned her head as usual, but was not able to see either target. In a window condition, a large conspicuous aperture was cut into the screens, allowing the experimenter to see the targets. Eighteen-month-old infants responded appropriately to the experimenter's gaze, following her head turn when there was no barrier or a barrier with a window, but tending not to follow it otherwise. Fourteen-month-olds also looked less often when there was a barrier, but looked less often still when the barrier had a window, perhaps indicating that they did not yet fully understand occlusion. Over a third of the older children leaned forward to try to see what was behind the barrier, compared to only one 14-month-old.

These results imply that children represent gaze as a spatial relationship between a person and an object. They understand that this relationship can be impeded by barriers, and they seem to view gaze roughly as a straight line between the head and the object. Children expect gaze to terminate at an object, which is why they investigate further if they cannot see an object from their vantage point. This may also be why children start to track others' gaze to the space behind them around this time (Butterworth and Cochran, 1980; Butterworth and Jarrett, 1991; see Deák, Flom, and Pick, 2000, for evidence that this ability may emerge earlier).

It is natural to give these findings a rich interpretation. Clearly, children understand something about others' attention. Attention is properly understood in terms of representational mental states. Further, it is a critical feature of perception, and what is attended to influences other mental states such as belief, knowledge, and desire. It is therefore very plausible that understanding of attention is a relatively early-developing feature of theory of mind. Gomez (1996: 334) makes the claim for a connection between following gaze and understanding mind in this way: 'this ability to follow the gaze of others with the expectation of finding an object . . . can also be considered to be an early and simple way to know what is in the other's mind, because the contents of the other's mind—the object looked at—is in front of the beholder's eyes'.

Almost all theorists give a rich interpretation to infants' abilities. Some argue that young infants' sensitivity to direct gaze shows sophisticated mentalistic understanding (e.g., Baron-Cohen, 1995; Vecera and Johnson, 1995). Others limit this kind of judgement to infants from 18 months onwards (e.g., Moore, 1999; Butler et al., 2000). Butler et al. argue that by 18 months, infants understand that gaze is *referential*. Referentiality is defined as 'understanding that all mental states are about or directed to some content (perceptible or representational)' (p. 360). This is a rich mentalistic interpretation of what infant gaze following entails, which most theorists accept by the end of infancy. I shall refer to this characterisation as mentalistic understanding of gaze.

Although plausible, this is more than needs to be concluded from existing data. It is based on the fact that infants clearly represent a relationship between the object and the gazer, and the assumption that infants therefore represent the relationship in the same way adults do, in mentalistic terms. In fact, there are strong reasons for thinking that infants do not do this. A mentalistic understanding of gaze relationships should allow certain kinds of judgements. Children cannot make these until they are 3 years old.

Research demonstrating this is discussed below. First, however, chimpanzee gaze understanding is discussed. Like human infants, chimpanzees also clearly represent relationships between people and objects based on head direction and eye direction. Also like human infants, chimpanzees show a marked inability to make simple judgements on the basis of gaze cues. Unlike human infants, however, it is accepted that chimpanzee understanding of gaze differs from that of human adults. The uncontroversial conclusions concerning chimpanzee understanding are based on much the same data as the more controversial conclusion that will be made for human infants.

Gaze understanding

Chimpanzees

Human-reared chimpanzees appear to have exactly the same gaze following abilities as 2-year-old children. They will turn to follow an experimenter's head turn, and even turn when the experimenter only moves his eyes. However, they will not do so if an occluder intersects the experimenter's line of sight; in this case the chimp will try to see what the experimenter might be looking at on the other side of the screen (Povinelli and Eddy, 1996a).

This facility following gaze is in marked contrast with poor ability to use others' visual signals for anything other than orienting the chimpanzee's own attention. In a well-known series of experiments, Povinelli and Eddy (1996b) looked at chimpanzees' choice of whom to beg from. Chimpanzees have a species-specific begging gesture, which much like ours, involves holding out the hand in the hope of having a piece of fruit put into it. If this gesture is not noticed, chimps sometimes reach out further, or slap their palms against the wall or cage. It is tempting to conclude from this that chimpanzees are trying to attract the experimenter's attention, and therefore that they have some notion of attention and perhaps of seeing. Povinelli and Eddy presented chimps with pairs of experimenters, one of whom could not see them for one of several reasons: she was covering her eyes, or was blindfold, or had a bucket over her head, or had her back turned. Even a very rudimentary understanding of visual attention should incline the chimpanzee to beg selectively from the experimenter who could see him or her. In fact, chimpanzees showed no preference. The only cue that reliably caused them to choose was when one experimenter had her whole body facing away from the chimp. Chimpanzees may be very good at using others' gaze cues to orient their own attention towards objects, but they do not appear to be able to use gaze cues for other purposes, even the important matter of begging for fruit.

Preschool children

The example of chimpanzees serves to show that it is possible to have sophisticated gaze following abilities, yet still clearly not have a proper understanding of visual attention. The same is true for human 2-year-olds. Toddlers' enthusiasm for pieces of fruit is less marked than that of chimpanzees, so the begging experiment has not been carried out (making children beg is probably unethical). Happily, human children offer one source of information about their gaze understanding that chimpanzees do not: you can ask them. If children properly understood gaze by the time they are 2 years old, they should be able to answer questions about what a person is looking at. Successfully doing this may not necessarily require a sophisticated or mentalistic conception of gaze, but inability to do so would certainly make a sophisticated conception implausible.

Research shows convincingly that judgements of eye direction are hard for 2-year-olds. In an early study by Masangkay et al. (1974), the experimenter kept her head facing forward and stared at one of several objects positioned around the child. Most 3-year-olds, but only about a third of 2-year-olds could say what she was looking at. Recent studies confirm this finding. For example, Doherty and Anderson (1999) found that most 3- and 4-year-olds, but no 2-year-olds could say which of four objects a schematic drawing face was looking at. Performance was no better with a real person (Doherty and Anderson, 1999, Experiment 2; Doherty, Anderson, and Howieson, 2009). When a congruent head turn was included, however, even 2-year-olds performed almost perfectly. This shows that the difficulty of the task is specific to judging eye direction, and not attributable to other factors such as failure to understand the test question (including the word 'looking') or the ability to extrapolate from a central cue to a peripheral target.

Children have equal difficulty judging whether gaze is direct. As discussed, detection of direct gaze may be present from birth, and predates the ability to follow gaze to an object. However, *judging* whether one is being looked at is as hard as judging which object another person is looking at, and is strongly associated with it (Doherty and Anderson, 1999; Doherty et al., 2009).

What infants understand about gaze

Both 2-year-old children and chimpanzees have excellent gaze following abilities. The data strongly suggest that both can represent a relationship between a person and an object on the basis of their gaze cues. Nevertheless both toddlers and chimps fail to make some simple inferences or judgements that could be made on the basis of this represented relationship. Instead they use other cues, such as head or body direction, on tasks where human adults and older children rely on eye direction as the critical cue. If children had a mentalistic understanding of gaze, they should realise the critical importance of eye direction in indicating moment-to-moment attention. Since younger children lack this realisation, they may lack a mentalistic understanding of gaze.

Characterising early understanding: engagement

One reason why this conclusion is hard to accept is that, if children do not understand gaze in a similar way to adults, they do a good job of faking it. This means that to understand how children conceive of attention, it is also necessary to look at tasks which they perform well at. For example, O'Neill (1996) showed that 2-year-olds are sensitive to whether their parents have attended to a particular event. When requesting parents' help to retrieve a desired object, 2-year-olds significantly more often named the object and its location, and gestured towards it when their parents had not witnessed the object being placed there. This indicates considerable sensitivity to the parent's attentional experience.

It could also indicate sensitivity to the parent's knowledge state, and thus demonstrate early theory of mind abilities: if someone has not seen something put somewhere, they will not know where it is, and have to be informed more about it if they are to get it. O'Neill herself gives a more parsimonious explanation in terms of 'disengagement + updating'. She argues that the results do not 'imply that the child recognizes that one or more of the parent's specific sensory capabilities has been (negatively) affected' (O'Neill, 1996, p. 674). In other words, it is not about perception. Instead, children are sensitive to adults' general involvement in their activities. Even young infants increase communication when adults do not seem to be involved in current activities (Ross and Lollis, 1987). By the time they are 2 years old, O'Neill suggests, children can also take into account past disengagement and increase their communication about events that took place during that period. This communication is a way of updating the adult about those events. How children conceive of updating is not described, but it is easy to cast it in terms of engagement—children simply want to engage their parents with the relevant aspects of the situation. Talking about it and gesturing towards it are effective ways of doing this.[2]

---

[2] It is interesting to note that there was an increase in naming the location and gesturing towards it, but also an increase in naming the toy. Information about the object's location is relevant to the adult's task, but information about the identity of the (currently invisible) toy is not. Toddlers are not differentiating between useful and irrelevant information.

Chimpanzees have also had one conspicuous and similar success involving appreciating what another is attending to, and to a lesser extent, has attended to. Hare, Call, Agnetta and Tomasello (2000) allowed a dominant and a subordinate chimpanzee to look into a room through opposite doors. Two pieces of food were placed in the room, one in open view and the other obscured by an opaque barrier, such that it was visible only to the subordinate chimpanzee. The doors then opened, with the subordinate chimpanzee getting a slight head start. Subordinates were significantly more likely to go for the hidden food (roughly 75% of times). Subordinates did not prefer the hidden food in non-competitive situations.

In a later experiment, Hare, Call, and Tomasello (2001) used a similar set-up in which the subordinate had to remember whether the dominant chimpanzee had witnessed an event. If the dominant chimpanzee had witnessed a piece of fruit hidden, subordinates only approached the food about 80% of the time, compared to 90% when the dominant had not witnessed it being placed, a small but significant difference. These findings are similar to O'Neill's. Chimpanzees are sensitive to what conspecifics are currently involved with and show some sensitivity to their past state of engagement too.

Defining engagement

Understanding of engagement seems to capture the abilities of toddlers and chimpanzees to take account of others' attention. It is a very simple conception, which nevertheless has considerable explanatory power. It first needs clearer description and definition. The minimum that has to be concluded from both gaze following research and studies of engagement is that children conceive of a relationship between people and objects or situations. O'Neill's findings indicate that the location of an object must also be taken into account: the important factor appears to be that the parent has not been involved with the target object at its current location. Thus engagement at minimum must be a relationship between a person and an object at its present location. The significance of the relationship is that another is likely to act on an object she is engaged with, and unlikely to act on an object she is not engaged with.

Further, this relationship appears to persist over time, in the absence of a change in location. When the parent returns to the room, children only consider her disengagement with the object which has changed location. Plausibly she is assumed to have remained engaged or to have re-engaged with the unchanged aspects of the situation.

Disengagement occurs when one aspect of the situation is changed in the person's absence. When an object is moved in someone's absence, for example, the person is disengaged from this aspect of the situation.

A distinction should be made between immediate involvement with the current object of attention and a general persistent potential for involvement with other aspects of the situation. In order to keep terminology to a minimum, these could be termed focal and peripheral engagement. However, this particular distinction is not necessary for the present chapter.

Cues

The nature of engagement is strongly tied to the cues used to infer it. Children could view this connection in a very general way, either as amodal or indicated by one or more of a number of cues. O'Neill suggests as possible cues to engagement: whether the parent is present, has his or her eyes shut, is talking to someone else, or appears distracted. Body posture, head direction, and eye direction can be added to these. Clearly children can represent a relationship between the head or the eyes and an object by the end of infancy. Importantly for the present topic, eye direction is one of the least valid and most hard to detect of the potential cues to engagement. It changes rapidly and constantly independently of head direction (Kobayashi and Kohshima, 2001), the eyes are not always visible, and when visible are a small and subtle cue relative to posture and head direction.

When presented with a number of cues to engagement, it is plausible that children habitually attend to cues other than eye direction. When these other cues are uninformative, as in the gaze judgement experiments discussed, children respond incorrectly. A similar claim can be made for chimpanzees, although in their case they seem to favour body direction over both head direction and eye direction.

In sum, young children conceive of people's interactions with objects in terms of engagement. Engagement is a relationship between a person and an object in its current position, or a situation in its current form. If engaged, a person is likely to act appropriately on an object or situation. If not engaged, they are unlikely to do so. Children rely on a number of attentional cues to infer engagement. It is assumed that no particular cue is diagnostic of engagement. For practical reasons, broad, stable, and easily perceived cues are probably relied upon.

Development: the two systems account

The research on gaze understanding suggests that there are two ways of understanding others' attention. One develops in infancy and is part of a system[3] that allows children to represent relationships between people, objects, and locations. This system employs a number of relational cues, depending on context of use. Gaze cues, including eye direction, are used to direct the child's attention to interesting objects and events. When the task is to determine adults' ongoing involvement with events, eye direction is not employed because it is unstable over time and difficult to detect. This is why children can follow eye direction but do not use it in judgements of attention.

The second way of understanding attention develops around three years, and is responsible for explicit eye direction judgement. The primary evidence for this is that children become able to make such judgements from this age. The abilities to explicitly

---

[3] 'System' is intended in a neutral sense as a means of understanding social stimuli. No particular instantiation of the knowledge and concepts is implied.

judge what object someone is looking at, which of two people are looking at the viewer, and which of two people are looking at an object, arise at the same time. Why they arise at this particular age remains a matter for conjecture. Notably, this is roughly the age that other explicit theory of mind abilities are arising. Doherty and Anderson (1999) found that gaze judgement ability was significantly associated with performance on a standard false belief task. Although the association was no longer significant when age was partialled out, the two tasks were of roughly equal difficulty. This is suggestive of a relationship, but so far we have not examined this further.[4]

A key theoretical issue here is why eye direction detection would relate to theory of mind reasoning. The idea that they are related is far from original, but only one direction of relation has been considered. Most theorists have cast gaze understanding as a precursor to mental state reasoning. However, this is based on the assumption that gaze following in infancy constitutes a relatively sophisticated understanding of gaze. The research discussed here calls this into doubt. The timing of the development of explicit eye direction understanding would mean that at most it is a very immediate precursor. It seems more likely that it is a concurrent development, suggesting a different relation between theory of mind and gaze understanding. As Gomez noted, 'the contents of the other's mind—the object looked at—is in front of the beholder's eyes' (1996, p. 334). Children with a developing theory of the other's mind should become increasingly interested in its contents, and the ways in which those contents get there in the first place. Eye direction determines the current content of visual attention, and plays a key role in belief formation. Thus children may become interested in the direction of the eyes because of this. Rather than gaze understanding being a precursor to theory of mind development, the relationship may be the other way around.

Relationship between the two systems

The two hypothesised gaze understanding systems could be related in 3 general ways. First, they could be entirely separate. They would embody some of the same knowledge because they relate to the same phenomena, but the later system would not acquire this knowledge from the former. Second, the later system could build on or extend the earlier system. Third, the later system could embody exactly the same knowledge as the earlier system, but be able to employ it more flexibly. In this case, gaze understanding could be said to start as implicit and finish as explicit. This could occur through the knowledge becoming available to the wider cognitive system, or through a transformation of the knowledge into an explicit format.

---

[4] The false belief task is not the most appropriate comparison task. Tasks assessing understanding of knowledge versus ignorance based on perceptual exposure are more relevant to the gaze tasks (and follow on developmentally from engagement tasks). These tasks appear to be easier than standard false belief tasks (Pratt and Bryant, 1990; Pillow, 1989).)

The two-systems theory introduced here is consistent with the first two possibilities. Theories which assume mentalistic gaze understanding in infancy are only consistent with the third possibility, of early understanding in an implicit form. The issue is potentially difficult to resolve empirically, but existing data support the first possibility. If explicit gaze judgement ability is new at 3 years, it may be inaccurate at first and undergo a subsequent extended increase in precision. If it is based on a long-standing implicit ability that becomes available to explicit judgement, there would be no need for protracted relearning.[5]

The few studies of fine-grained gaze judgements in older children suggest that development continues beyond 4 years. Leekam, Baron-Cohen, Perrett, Milders, and Brown (1997) found that only 45% of normal 4-year-olds passed a fine-grained gaze task requiring judgement of which of three rods was being fixated. Doherty, Anderson, and Howieson (2009) used a similar procedure in which the three targets were all to one side of the experimenter, so she had to move her eyes 15°, 30°, or 45°. Three-year-olds were at chance at this task. Performance improved in a roughly linear fashion over the next 3 years, and six-year-old children had still not reached the adult level. These results suggest that gaze judgement is a novel skill. At 3 years children can judge which of four quadrants a person is looking to, but cannot distinguish between, say, 30° to the left and 45° to the left. This fine-grained ability undergoes protracted development over the next few years. In turn this suggests that the new system is not drawing on knowledge held by the earlier developing gaze following system; it is learning to follow gaze from first principles.

It appears that the preschool gaze judgement system is not drawing information directly from the infant gaze following system. However, this does not necessarily mean there is no developmental connection between earlier and later gaze understanding systems. Moore (2006) has suggested that an important intervening step between gaze following and gaze judgement is to understand gaze as subjective. Once children can represent a relationship between people and objects, they have two quite different sources of information about gaze: information about the relationship between others' attentional cues and objects, and the child's own first-person experience of seeing. Episodes of joint attention between the child, an adult, and an object bring these two types of information together. From this experience, children may be able to learn a common way of encoding the two manifestations of 'seeing'. An important thing that can be learned is that what can and cannot be seen varies from person to person. Until this is realised, there is no need to postulate representational states intervening between the viewer and the object.

---

[5] It should however be noted that the accuracy with which infants and toddlers can follow eye direction is assumed to be good but is actually unknown. Typical experiments have one target on each side or no targets at all. Some joint attention studies have included more than one target to the correct side (e.g. Butterworth and Jarrett, 1991), but involved head turns and large gaze deviations (60°). Poor accuracy in later judgement might therefore reflect poor accuracy in gaze following.

Children appear to understand the subjective nature of visual attention from perhaps two years of age. For example, Moll and Tomasello (2006) examined infants' reactions to an adult's apparent inability to find a desired object. Children could see two objects, one of which was clearly occluded from the adult's view. By 24 months, children were handing over the occluded object more often than would be expected by chance, whereas 18-month-old children were below chance. By this age, children have not yet completely mastered occlusion, however, as a curious finding by Flavell, Shipstead, and Croft (1978) shows. They placed a small opaque screen on a table, gave children a toy, and asked them to hide it from the experimenter. Almost all children from the age of 2½ years were able to hide the toy behind the screen. However, in another condition the toy was placed on the table and children were asked to use the screen to conceal it from the experimenter. Younger children performed surprisingly poorly at this move-screen task despite the fact that it seems to require exactly the same understanding as the first task.

This finding supports the engagement theory (and so far no other explanation has been offered). Children at this age understand something about occlusion: occlusion prevents a person becoming engaged with an object, or makes it less likely. When young children hear the word 'see' in the test question, they interpret it roughly as 'be engaged with'. Putting the object behind the screen prevents the establishment of engagement, and also prevents the adult from seeing it. Thus adult and child understandings intersect for this condition.

The move-screen task is different in a subtle but important way. The trial begins with the experimenter sitting, facing towards and looking at the object (not to mention referring to it and gesturing towards it while asking the test question); the experimenter therefore sees the object and is already fully engaged with it. Even from the adult point of view, placing the screen appropriately will not alter this engagement. The experimenter remains aware of the location of the object, is still oriented toward it, and could easily reach around the small card screen used. The effect of placing the screen is more specific: to stop the experimenter from seeing the object. To successfully perform the move-screen task, then, children have to be able to distinguish between being engaged with an object and seeing it. The reason why younger children fail the task is because they cannot yet make this distinction.

If this is correct, the ability to pass the move-screen task marks passing from an engagement-based understanding of visual attention to a more mentalistic understanding. Confirming this idea, McGuigan and Doherty (2002) replicated Flavell et al.'s findings, and found a significant correlation between performance on the move-screen task and the ability to judge gaze direction. This suggests that performance on either task required children to go beyond an understanding of attention in terms of engagement.

Discussion

The motivation for proposing a two-systems theory of gaze understanding is to account for the discrepancy between infants' good gaze following and toddlers' poor gaze judgement. Both findings are well-established. The minimal reasonable conclusions from these findings are: infants must be able to represent some kind of relationship between people and the objects of their attention; and toddlers do not have an adult-like understanding of eye direction. Thus children do not have a mentalistic under-standing of attention until they are 3 years old. Mentalistic is used here to mean understanding attention in terms of representational mental states. Before the age of three years, children understand attention in terms of relationships between people and objects, but do not conceive of these relationships as representational or internal. Instead, it is claimed that children conceive of them in terms of involvement, drawing on O'Neill's concept of engagement.

Two different contexts in which children make use of these relationships have been considered. One is gaze following, in which another person's attention is directed elsewhere. Children use others' gaze cues to identify or locate the objects of their attention. In this case children can use head direction and/or eye direction (although head direction remains the primary cue). The other context is interaction between another person and the child, typically with objects. Children use the other's atten-tional cues to monitor their involvement with the situation. In this case, the most informative cues are demeanour, posture, and head direction. Objectively, eye-direction is not a good cue to involvement because it changes from moment to moment and is relatively difficult to detect. This is why children do not use eye direction cues in judgements of what someone is attending to (which they interpret in terms of the broader concept of what someone is engaged with).

Broader explanatory power

Although the account is presented as a two-systems theory, there is clear scope for the development of these to be more nuanced than a simple emergence of two monolithic systems. There is clearly a very gradual development of sensitivity to eye direction over the first 20 months of life. It is not clear at which point children can be said to represent relationships between people and objects on the basis of gaze cues. It may be as late as 16 months, when children begin to follow head turns to locations outside of their immediate visual field (Corkum and Moore, 1995). Even at this point, children are not able to follow eye turns when the head does not move congruently. Understanding of occlusion is also beginning around this time. It appears to develop first in the context of gaze following, at around 18 months. By 24 months, infants show some understanding of occlusion in interactions with objects (Moll and Tomasello, 2006). The typical measure in virtually all the studies discussed is whether infants perform better than would be expected through chance. Thus the ages listed give a lower limit beyond which children's abilities may improve for some time.

The theory has been developed in the context of gaze research, and thus far consideration has been restricted to how the two hypothesised systems deal with attention. Engagement was introduced as a concept to explain toddlers' sensitivity to knowledge (O'Neill, 1996). The idea as developed here has considerable scope for explaining early theory of mind phenomena.

Understanding of engagement can also be used to gain information about the environment. The form already considered is gaze following, which can allow children to locate interesting objects or events. There are other forms. For example, if an infant is in an ambiguous situation, he may look to his mother. If she is looking on with a happy expression, the infant will probably relax and continue to explore. If she appears anxious, the infant may stop or retreat (Sorce, Emde, Campos and Klinnert, 1985). This is one form of *social referencing*. Research shows that infants take into account what the other is attending to when using emotional signals to determine their own reaction to objects (e.g., Moses, Baldwin, Rosicky, and Tidball, 2001). To do this, the infant needs to be able to determine that the adult is connected to the ambiguous situation, and make an inference about the situation based on the adult's emotional expression. Thus social referencing requires an assessment of engagement plus a simple inference. Virtually the same argument can be made for infants' flexible ability to infer the referent of a novel word, by checking what the speaker is connected with when uttering the word (e.g., Baldwin, 1991).

By perhaps as young as 18 months old, infants understand that other people can have discrepant desires. Repacholi and Gopnik (1997) conducted an experiment in which the experimenter ostentatiously expressed pleasure at eating a piece of broccoli, and disgust at eating a cracker. This was naturally the opposite of the child's own prefer-ence. Some 18-month-old children were able to use this information to give the experimenter the broccoli when invited to give her something. Repacholi and Gopnik argue that children understand desire as a subjective internal state. This can be explained in simpler terms using engagement. Thus far, action has only been consid-ered in terms of its appropriateness. The parent can be assumed to be cooperative if the child can engage him or her with the object; the dominant chimpanzee can be assumed to retrieve forcefully the hidden fruit if he becomes engaged with it. With discrepant desires, as well as representing a relationship between a person and an object, one must understand that the relationship is different for different people. This difference only needs to be distinguished in terms of the action tendencies involved. In the case of objectively desirable objects (such as chocolate) one simply has to understand one set of action tendencies (approach, acquisition, ingestion, and so on). Similar but opposite tendencies hold for undesirable objects. In the case of discrepant desires, different action tendencies must be attributed to different people (inferred from their previous behaviour). This clearly adds complexity to the task, which may explain why even 18-month-olds struggle with it. Nevertheless, this understanding is based on representa-tion of a relationship between a person and an object. Additionally children must understand something about the quality of the relationship, and what kinds of action it affords. There is no need to conceive of any of this in terms of internal or mental states.

Recent demonstrations of infant sensitivity to mental states can also be accounted for in terms of engagement. Two plausible assumptions need to be made: that children are sensitive to episodes of disengagement and subsequent behaviour, and that the aspect of a scene an agent is disengaged from remains salient.

For example, Surian, Caldi, and Sperber (2007) showed 13-month-old children videos of two opaque screens with food behind them. In familiarisation trials, a caterpillar consistently went to chew food behind one screen, thus indicating a preference. In experimental trials the positions of the two foods were reversed. The caterpillar could either see the food (the screens were replaced by very low ones) or could not. Children looked longer when the caterpillar could see but approached the unpreferred type of food. When the caterpillar could not see, looking time did not differ significantly according to which food it approached.

In the seeing condition, the caterpillar is engaged with both objects; in the not-seeing condition it is not (there is only lack of engagement rather than disengagement in this study). When engaged the caterpillar is able to act on its usual preferences, so children look longer if it does not. No particular action is expected of an unengaged person, so looking time does not differ. (There was a trend towards longer looking when the caterpillar went to the preferred food, suggesting increased interest in effective action without engagement.)

Onishi and Baillargeon's (2005) well-known implicit false belief task can also be explained in terms of engagement. In this experiment, infants were familiarised with a woman reaching into one of two boxes. The one reached into had an object inside. In the true belief condition, the object moved while the woman watched. She then reached, either to the original or new box. Infants looked longer if she reached to the empty box. In the false belief condition, the woman was absent when the object moved. Infants looked longer if she reached to the box containing the object.

In the true belief condition, the woman is engaged with the object, so it is odd for her to act inappropriately. Thus children look longer. The false belief condition involves a clear episode of disengagement, which should cause infants to be more interested (and looking times in all false belief conditions were higher than in the corresponding true belief conditions). Infants do not expect effective unhesitating action following disengagement, and find this interesting. This explains the observed pattern of looking times.

The two studies discussed measured looking time differences when observing action. Southgate, Senju, and Csibra (2007) found that 25-month-old children also looked in anticipation of action following an actor's belief becoming false. The actor watched as an object was placed in a location. While she was turned away, the object was removed entirely. Thus, the actor was now disengaged from this part of the situation. Assuming children are sensitive to episodes of disengagement, the changed part of the situation will be particularly salient. This was the location children looked towards when anticipating the actor's reach. The anticipatory looking could be explained either in terms of sensitivity to the actor's false belief. However, it could also be due to toddlers' sensitivity to the disengagement that gave rise to the false belief.

This paradigm was based on an implicit false belief task introduced by Clements and Perner (1994). Their original findings were that implicit sensitivity to false belief arose just before children turned 3 years, but a majority of children did not pass the typical explicit question until they were 4 years old. Both studies reveal an implicit sensitivity to false belief, but it apparently arises at quite different ages. This is an unresolved puzzle. The main differences between studies were that in the original the object was moved to a second location in scene, whereas in the later study, it was removed entirely, and that in the original there was a verbal prompt. Southgate et al. (2007) suggest that when children heard the verbal prompt, 'I wonder where he's going to look?', they prematurely interpreted the 'where' as referring to the location of the object rather than the behaviour of the protagonist.

With no independent reasons to think that younger children are more likely to make this kind of impulsive interpretation, this suggestion is at best arbitrary. A more plausible reason is that the object remained in the scene, and the child knew where it was. In terms of engagement, this means that the actor was disengaged from two locations, the old and new location of the object. The engagement hypothesis does not predict either of these locations should be more salient than the other. However, this would plausibly be one with the object of interest rather than the empty one. The child's knowledge of the true location of the object may add to the salience of this location. Thus the engagement hypothesis predicts the early success on Southgate et al.'s procedure, and can also account for the typical failure of 2-year-old children on Clements and Perner's version of the task. The two competing explanations could readily be resolved by a version of Southgate et al.'s procedure with no verbal prompt where the object is moved to the other location in the scene. Engagement would predict this version to be as difficult as Clements and Perner's version, whereas if the verbal prompt explanation is correct, this version should be no harder than Southgate et al.'s.

Conclusion

A challenge of theory of mind research is how to square infant and toddlers' competence with some theory of mind tasks with their inability to perform other kinds. It is a challenge shared with research on gaze understanding. Here I present a theory that can account for the discrepancies in both fields. The theory was developed on the basis of gaze research, to explain how children can be very good at following gaze and using attentional cues, yet are unable to make explicit judgements of eye direction until the age of 3 years. The two systems theory extends readily to explain many early theory of mind abilities, including recent demonstrations of 'implicit' theory of mind.

The main focus has been the early system. Data show that 2-year-olds must be able to represent a relationship between people and objects, on the basis of a variety of attentional cues. Further, they can track this relationship over time. Children must be able to understand how the presence or absence of a relationship affects the likely behaviour of the person concerned. That is sufficient to explain the existing data reviewed here. The relationship does not need to be viewed as representational, or in terms of internal mental states. It is simply a relationship that affords certain kinds of actions on the part of the agent. The relationship is characterised as one of *engagement*, a development of the term introduced by O'Neill (1996).

The minimalist approach adopted here contrasts with that of many researchers in this area. Demonstrations of social sensitivity are typically attributed to a representational theory of mind (in a rudimentary and implicit form). This possibility is consistent with the data but by no means required. The data can adequately be accounted for by the much simpler system sketched out here.

References

Baldwin, D. A. (1991). Infant's contribution to the achievement of joint reference. *Child Development*, 62: 875–890.

Baron-Cohen, S. (1995). *Mindblindness*. Cambridge, MA: MIT Press/Bradford.

Butler, S. C., Caron, A. J., and Brooks, R. (2000). Infant understanding of the referential nature of looking. *Journal of Cognition and Development*, 1: 359–377.

Butterworth, G., and Cochran, E. (1980). Towards a mechanism of joint visual attention in human infancy. *International Journal of Behavioral Development*, 3: 253–272.

Butterworth, G., and Jarrett, N. (1991). What minds have in common is space: spacial mechanisms serving joint visual attention in infancy. *British Journal of Developmental Psychology*, 9: 55–72.

Clements, W. A., and Perner, J. (1994). Implicit understanding of belief. *Cognitive Development*, 9: 377–395.

Corkum, V., and Moore, C. (1995). Development of joint visual attention in infants. In C. Moore and P. Dunham (eds.) *Joint attention: Its origins and role in development* (pp. 61–84). Hove, UK: Lawrence Erlbaum Associates.

Deák, G. O., Flom, R. A., and Pick, A. D. (2000). Effects of gesture and target on 12- and 18-month-olds' joint visual attention to objects in front of or behind them. *Developmental Psychology*, 36: 511–523.

D'Entremont, B., Hains, S. M. J., and Muir, D. W. (1997). A demonstration of gaze following in 3- to 6-month-olds. *Infant Behavior and Development*, 20: 569–572.

Doherty, M. J. (2006). The development of mentalistic gaze understanding. *Infant and Child Development*, 15: 179–186.

Doherty, M. J., and Anderson, J. R. (1999) A new look at gaze: preschool children's understanding of eye-direction. *Cognitive Development*, 14: 549–571.

Doherty, M. J., Anderson, J. R., and Howieson, L. (2009) The rapid development of explicit gaze judgment ability at 3 years. *Journal of Experimental Child Psychology*, 104: 296–312.

Downing, P. E., Dodds, C. M., and Bray, D. (2004). Why does the gaze of others direct visual attention? *Visual Cognition*, 11: 71–79.

Farroni, T., Csibra, G., Simion, F., and Johnson, M. H. (2002). Eye contact detection in humans from birth. *Proceedings of the National Academy of Sciences*, 99: 9602–9605.

Farroni, T., Johnson, M. H., Brockbank, M., and Simion, F. (2000). Infants' use of gaze direction to cue attention: The importance of perceived motion. *Visual Cognition*, 7: 705–718.

Flavell, J. H., Shipstead, S. G., and Croft, K. (1978). Young children's knowledge about visual perception: Hiding objects from others. *Child Development*, 49: 1208–1211.

Goméz, J. C. (1996). Non-human primate theories of (non-human primate) minds: some issues concerning the origins of mind-reading. In: P. Carruthers and P. Smith (eds.) *Theories of theories of mind* (pp. 330–343). Cambridge, Cambridge University Press.

Hare, B., Call, J., Agnetta, M., and Tomasello, M. (2000). Chimpanzees know what conspecifics do and do not see. *Animal Behaviour*, 59: 771–78.

Hare, B., Call, J., and Tomasello, M. (2001). Do chimpanzees know what conspecifics know? *Animal Behaviour*, 61: 139–151.

Hood, B. M., Willen, J. D., and Driver, J. (1998). Adult's eyes trigger shifts of visual attention in human infants. *Psychological Science*, 9: 131–134.

Kobayashi, H., and Kohshima, S. (2001). Unique morphology of the human eye and its adaptive meaning: Comparative studies on external morphology of the primate eye. *Journal of Human Evolution*, 40: 419–453.

Leekam, S., Baron-Cohen, S., Perrett, D., Milders, M., and Brown, S. (1997). Eye-direction detection: A dissociation between geometric and joint attention skills in autism. *British Journal of Developmental Psychology*, 15: 77–95.

McGuigan, N., and Doherty, M. J,. (2002). The relation between hiding skill and judgment of eye-direction in preschool children. *Developmental Psychology*, 38:: 418–427.

Moore C., and Corkum, V. (1998). The origins of joint visual attention in infants. *Developmental Psychology*, 34: 28–38.

Masangkay, Z. S., McCluskey, K. A., McIntyre, C. W., Sims-Knight, J., Vaughn, B. E., and Flavell, J. H. (1974). The early development of inferences about the visual percepts of others. *Child Development*, 45: 349–372.

Moll, H., and Tomasello, M. (2006). Level 1 perspective-taking at 24 months of age. *British Journal of Developmental Psychology*, 24: 603–613.

Moore, C. (1999). Gaze following and the control of attention. In P. Rochat (ed.), *Early social cognition: Understanding others in the first months of life* (pp. 241–256). Mahwah, NJ: Lawrence Erlbaum Associates.

Moore, C. (2006). Commentary on The Development of Mentalistic Gaze Understanding. Understanding the directedness of gaze: three ways of doing it. *Infant and Child Development*, 15: 191–193.

Moses, L. J., Baldwin, D. A., Rosicky, J. G., and Tidball, G. (2001). Evidence for referential understanding in the emotions domain at twelve and eighteen months. *Child Development*, 72: 718–735.

Myowa-Yamakoshi, M., Tomonaga, M., Tanaka, M., and Matsuzawa, T. (2003). Preference for human direct gaze in infant chimpanzees (*Pan trogolodytes*). *Cognition*, 89: B53-B64.

O'Neill, D. K. (1996). Two-year-old children's sensitivity to a parent's knowledge state when making requests. *Child Development*, 67: 659–677.

Onishi, K. H., and Baillargeon, R. (2005). Do 15-month-old infants understand false beliefs? *Science*, 308: 255–258.

Pillow, B. H. (1989). Early understanding of perception as a source of knowledge. *Journal of Experimental Child Psychology*, 47: 116–129.

Povinelli, D. J., and Eddy, T. J. (1996a). Chimpanzees: joint visual attention. *Psychological Science*, 7: 129–135.

Povinelli, D. J., and Eddy, T. J. (1996b). What young chimpanzees know about seeing. *Monographs of the Society for Research in Child Development*, 61: no. 3.

Pratt, C., and Bryant, P. (1990). Young children understand that looking leads to knowing (so long as they are looking into a single barrel). *Child Development*, 61: 973–982.

Repacholi, B. M., and Gopnik, A. (1997). Early reasoning about desires: Evidence from 14- and 18-month-olds. *Developmental Psychology*, 33: 12–21.

Ross, H. S., and Lollis, S. P. (1987). Communication within infant social games. *Developmental Psychology*, 23: 241–248.

Samuels, C. (1985). Attention to eye contact opportunity and facial motion by 3 month old infants. *Journal of Experimental Child Psychology*, 40: 105–114.

Scaife, M., and Bruner, J. S. (1975). The capacity for joint visual attention in the infant. *Nature*, 253: 265–266.

Sorce, J., Emde, R. N., Campos, J. J., and Klinnert, M. (1985). Maternal emotional signaling: Its effect on the visual cliff behavior of 1-year-olds. *Developmental Psychology*, 21: 195–200.

Southgate, V., Senju, A., and Csibra, G. (2007). Action anticipation through attribution of false belief by 2-year-olds. *Psychological Science*, 18: 587–592.

Surian, L., Caldi, S., and Sperber, D. (2007). Attribution of Beliefs by 13-Month-Old Infants, *Psychological Science*, 18: 580–586.

Vecera, S. P., and Johnson, M. H. (1995). Gaze detection and the cortical processing of faces: Evidence from infants and adults. *Visual Cognition*, 2: 59–87.

Wellman, H. M., Cross, D., and Watson, J. (2001). Meta-analysis of theory-of-mind development: The truth about false belief. *Child Development*, 72: 655–684.

Woodward, A. L. (2003). Infants' developing understanding of the link between looker and object. *Developmental Science*, 6: 297–311.

18

Development of Understanding of the Causal Connection between Perceptual Access and Knowledge State

Elizabeth J. Robinson

1 Introduction

When an infant shows familiarity with faces or places, adult observers assume she must have had previous experience of them. That is, as adults we assume a causal connection between perceptual access and knowledge state. Yet we do not impute the infant with understanding of that causal connection. Rather, we assume that she cannot help but gain knowledge as a result of her perceptual experiences, without realising that she is so doing, and without understanding how she is so doing. At some point in development, we assume, she will come to realise and understand. When? How? Answering even the first question is not easy, and most of the research summarised in this chapter focuses on that, aiming to identify the course of development. We know virtually nothing about 'how'—what underlying processes lead to advances in understanding—but the chapter finishes with brief speculation about how we might begin to find out.

One difficulty associated with answering the question 'when?' is deciding what the child must do for the observing researcher to impute understanding of the causal connection between perceptual access and knowledge state. There have been two broad approaches to this. With the first approach, the child is expected to reflect upon the knowing process and, usually, make an oral report. For example, children are asked whether somebody who has seen or not seen inside a box, knows what it contains; are asked whether they need to see or feel a hidden toy to identify its colour or hardness; or are asked how they found out about the toy's properties having just seen or felt it. These studies follow the classic approach taken in research into children's developing understanding about the mind, in which the child usually makes her understanding verbally explicit (e.g. research presented in Astington, Harris, and Olson, 1988). The next section of this chapter reports work that follows this approach.

The second broad approach, summarised in the third section of this chapter, examines children's patterns of knowledge-gaining behaviour. For example, researchers examine whether children's pattern of behaviour is consistent with treating a well-informed person as more knowledgeable than a poorly informed one. Similarly, we can find out whether children spontaneously access the informative modality (e.g. seeing or feeling) in order to identify an object's properties. We can find out whether they behave as if they realise that their knowledge derived from a particular source (e.g. seeing or feeling the object, or being told by someone). The child's understanding is implicit in her pattern of behaviour, but she is not required to make it verbally explicit.

The two broad approaches differ in the balance of reflection demanded from the child and from the observing researcher. With the first approach, the child is expected to reveal more or less directly what she understands by verbalising it. Suppose a child gains knowledge by seeing or feeling an object and is then asked 'How do you know it's the red cat?' or 'How do you know it's the soft bear?' If she answers 'Because I saw it' in the first case but not the second, then it takes rather little interpretive work on the part of the observing researcher to conclude that the child understands about seeing as a source of her knowledge. In contrast, with the second approach, the child's task is merely to gain knowledge, for example to find out whether a cat hidden inside a box is red or blue. Suppose she looks rather than feels, but feels rather than looks when the hidden bear is hard or soft. The child may not reflect on the knowing process at all, but the observing researcher can infer from the pattern of behaviour that the child understands, at least on some level, what knowledge can be gained from a particular modality of access.

It is of interest to consider to what extent conclusions drawn from these contrasting empirical approaches are consistent with each other, and what the implications are if they are inconsistent. It could be, for example, that children show the pattern of finding out behaviour consistent with understanding a particular aspect of the process of gaining knowledge from perceptual experience, only when they can also reflect and report on it explicitly. Another possibility is that finding out behaviour seems to be in advance of reflective, explicit understanding, and if so this would raise the question of what is to be gained by achieving the latter. Finally, should it turn out that children could report explicitly on an aspect of the knowing process, without equivalent understanding being evident in their finding out behaviour, then the researcher might suspect that something was amiss with one or other of the assessments.

Each of the next two sections in the chapter is broken into three matching sub-sections, dealing with 'Evaluating other people's knowledge on the basis of their perceptual access', 'Knowing how to gain knowledge oneself', and 'Knowing how knowledge was gained'. Both the reflective and the behavioural approaches have examined children's understanding of each of these aspects of understanding about the knowing process. The research summarised in this chapter focuses on children aged between around three and five years, since both approaches reveal interesting developments in understanding about the process of gaining knowledge that occur over this age range.

2   Children's reflections on the knowing process

2.1   Evaluating other people's knowledge on the basis of their perceptual access

What reflective understanding of the knowing process seems already to be in place amongst three-year-olds? Several studies suggest children this young are not completely unaware of the relationship between perceptual access and knowledge state. For example in Pillow's (1989) study, one of a set of differently coloured dinosaurs was hidden in a box. The child watched two puppets, one of whom looked inside a box and the other of whom pushed the closed box (so that both puppets had interacted with the box in some way). Children were asked 'Who can tell you what colour the dinosaur is?' Note that in this study children did not need to understand the meaning of 'know' to answer this question correctly. Each child played this game several times. Both three- and four-year-olds performed well, being much more likely to attribute knowledge to the puppet who had seen than to the one who had not. The conclusion was that they 'understood perceptual exposure to the external world as a determinant of mental states . . .' (p. 125). A similar conclusion arises from other studies in which the word 'know' was used in the test question. Note however that children might just associate knowing with seeing, without necessarily interpreting the relationship as causal. Several authors have argued that young children make the crude association 'seeing = knowing' (e.g. Perner, 1991).

Incidentally, puppets or dolls are commonly used in this research. The reason is that puppets and dolls are easier to manage than having children in pairs, cheaper and more convenient than using two adult experimenters, and importantly, are less likely to over-awe the young child. Yet this seems to add an unwanted layer of complexity since the child has to treat the dolls as if they gain knowledge in the same way as real people. However, although the occasional five-year-old makes comments such as 'It's only a puppet, it can't see anything,' younger children's judgments appear to be no less accurate with these procedures, and so most researchers generally assume that they do not produce misleading results.

At around three years of age, then, children may make at least a gross distinction between epistemic and non-epistemic access (Pillow, 1993). They still have a good deal to learn, however, before we can impute to them adult-like understanding of the causal connection between perceptual access and knowledge state. One limitation is that three-year-olds, as well as four-year-olds, tend to over-estimate the knowledge to be gained from limited perceptual access. In the dinosaur experiment described above, looking inside the box was sufficient to find out the dinosaur's colour, and pushing the box provided no knowledge of its content. But suppose, instead of finding out the dinosaur's colour, the puppet was trying to find out whether it was the large or the small brontosaurus in the box, and the puppet only peeped through a tiny window that provided insufficient information. The evidence suggests that children would have still attributed knowledge to the puppet who looked, wrongly in this case (Robinson and Robinson, 1982; Robinson, Thomas, Parton, and Nye, 1997; Taylor, 1988).

Furthermore, three- and four-year-olds cannot yet judge what knowledge is gained from different kinds of perceptual access such as seeing, feeling, smelling, or tasting (O'Neill, Astington, and Flavell, 1992; Pillow, 1993). For example, in one of O'Neill et al.'s studies, children watched two puppets, one of whom saw a hidden toy, and the other of whom felt it. On each trial, only one modality of access was informative, since the hidden toy was identified by colour or hardness. Children were asked which puppet was knowledgeable, for example 'Who knows the pig inside is squishy?' Children aged three, four and even five years were biased to judge that the puppet who had seen the toy was knowledgeable. Although the older children performed better than the younger ones, even the five-year-olds made errors.

Summary Many three-year-olds' explicit judgments about others' knowledge are consistent with their differentiating epistemic from non-epistemic access (whether or not the word 'know' is used), but three- and four-year olds commonly make errors when judging what knowledge others gain from particular modalities of access such as seeing or feeling an object. These children may simply associate seeing with knowing.

2.2 Knowing how to gain knowledge oneself

This difficulty understanding what kind of knowledge is gained from particular modalities was apparent in another of O'Neill et al.'s (1992) studies in which children made predictions about what knowledge they themselves would gain by seeing or feeling a toy hidden inside a tunnel. Children could either raise a curtain to look inside, or put their arm in to feel the hidden toy. The hidden toy was identified by colour or hardness. Children were asked, for example 'To find out for sure what colour the football inside the tunnel is, what would you have to do?' In response, children selected a card depicting an eye or a card depicting a hand, to indicate whether they would need to see or feel the toy. Many three- and four-year-olds chose the same mode of access on every occasion, whereas five-year-olds performed well. Difficulties remain when three- and four-year-olds do not have to predict the informative modality of access, but merely have to re-enact what they have just done (under the Experimenter's guidance) to identify, for example, whether water was warm or cold (O'Neill and Chong, 2001). In this study, the Experimenter showed children how find out a certain property, for example to smell a bubble bath to find out whether it was strawberry or lemon. Then children were asked 'Show me how you found out...?' All they had to do was repeat the action they had just performed, yet 3-year-olds were correct only 60 % of the time.

Summary When asked how to find out an object's properties, three- and four-year-olds again reveal limits in their understanding of what knowledge can be gained from particular modalities of access. They seem not yet to construe knowledge as arising from, or caused by, particular kinds of perceptual experience. It remains unclear whether children make a causal interpretation but remain ignorant of the details of what knowledge arises from particular experiences (and so make errors in their specific predictions), or whether they see no causal connection between experience and knowledge state.

2.3 Knowing how one's knowledge was gained

Perhaps the most obvious way to find out if someone understands the causal connection between having seen inside a box and knowing its content is to ask them directly, and this is what many researchers have done with young children. In a typical task, a novel object is hidden inside a container, and the child is invited to have a look or have a feel to identify it. Immediately after, she is asked 'What is it?' and 'How do you know?' Each child plays the game several times with different target objects. Most five-year-olds can answer both questions correctly, but some four-year-olds and many three-year-olds are correct on the first question only: They can report what they know ('There's an elephant in the box'), but not how they know it ('Because I saw it').

When asked 'How do you know there's an elephant in there?' the answer 'Because I saw it' might convince us that causal understanding is in place. On the other hand, failure to give that answer is not necessarily sufficient grounds for concluding absence of causal understanding. Even adults sometimes make errors about how their knowledge was gained (e.g. Johnson, Hashtroudi, and Lindsay, 1993). For example, on feeling familiar with the content of a particular book, I might believe I have read it, whereas in fact I only read a review. Mistakes such as these are interpreted as performance errors. With adults, they generally occur when there is considerable delay between experience and recall, or when there has been an intervening event such as misleading questioning ('You had the book at the airport, didn't you?') Children, with their less secure grasp of the knowing process, may be particularly prone to such errors, and might make them even with short delays between experience and recall. The conditions under which children make such errors, and how to minimise the risks of their occurring, are examined in the literatures on suggestibility and eye witness testimony (e.g. Roberts and Blades, 2000).

How then can we be sure when children's errors answering 'How do you know?' arise from failures to understand how they gained knowledge, rather than just being performance errors? Researchers try to make the child's task as simple as possible, and to ask the child to report her source immediately after she has gained the knowledge. If children repeatedly make errors answering 'How do you know?' under these conditions, then it seems unlikely that they are just making the kinds of performance errors described above. On the other hand, they might misunderstand the question. In an attempt to deal with this, Gopnik and Graf (1988), and O'Neill and Gopnik (1991) gave children in their sample a short training session before the experiment proper began, with the aim of drawing children's attention to the source of their knowledge and clarifying the intended meaning of the test question. On the training trials, children experienced seeing or feeling an object, and were asked for example 'What did you see?' followed by 'How do you know that's what's inside?' They were then told what the correct answer was. One or two practices of this kind would not be sufficient to teach the child something she did not already understand, but could serve to clarify the purpose of the Experimenter's questions. This may be particularly important given the social peculiarity of showing a child a picture, for example, and then asking 'How do you know...?' Perhaps by four years, with nursery experience, children have become more used to the idea that adults test them in strange ways. Although training led to no significant improvement in the accuracy of children's answers on subsequent trials (Gopnik and Graf, 1988), some kind of training has commonly been included in subsequent research as a precaution. Checks are also made on failure to understand what behaviours 'seeing' and 'feeling' refer to (e.g. Gopnik and Graf, 1988; O'Neill and Gopnik, 1991; Wimmer, Hogrefe, and Perner, 1988).

Another way of ensuring children understand the intended meaning of the question 'How do you know?' is to offer alternative answers such as 'Is it because you saw it, or because you felt it?' but even with such prompts, three-year-olds typically perform poorly. Yet children who fail to answer correctly how they know, can nevertheless report what their perceptual experience was. Haigh and Robinson (2009) gave children two modes of access to the identity of a hidden toy, one of which was informative (for example seeing a toy identified by colour) and the other of which was uninformative (for example being told the toy's colour by the Experimenter who had only felt it). Children were able to report accurately who saw and who felt the hidden toy, without necessarily being able to report how they knew its identity. That is, children apparently failed to make the causal connection between perceptual access and knowledge state, despite being able to report both what they knew (the hidden toy's identity) and what their access had been (for example, that they had seen it).

Children's failure to report how they gained knowledge leads to the conclusion that around three years of age they '...do not seem to be able to understand how their beliefs...are causally related to the world itself through perceptual...processes' (Gopnik and Graf, 1988, p.1370). Wimmer, Hogrefe, and Perner (1988) conclude similarly that 'most three- and some four-year-olds seemed completely ignorant about the causal connection between access to an informational source and resulting knowledge' (p. 386).

Summary The most direct way of finding out whether children understand the causal connection between perceptual access and knowledge state is to ask 'How do you know?' immediately after they have acquired knowledge. Even with precautions in place to minimise the risk of children misunderstanding the question in some way, three- and four-year-olds often cannot report how they know (for example 'I know because I felt it'). Despite being unable to report how they know, children may report accurately what their perceptual experience was (for example, that they felt the toy), and also, of course, what the content of their knowledge is (for example, the soft bear). This pinpoints children's problem: They seem to fail to make a causal connection between perceptual experience and knowledge state.

2.4 Conclusions from the work on explicit, reflective understanding

By around five or six years of age, children can demonstrate adult-like understanding of the connection between perceptual access and knowledge state, although errors are still made in particular cases. In contrast, three- and four-year-olds are often poor at reporting what another person knows on the basis of their particular experience, poor at predicting what perceptual experience would lead them to gain particular knowledge, and poor at reporting the source of knowledge they have only just gained. The broad conclusion on the basis of the evidence summarised so far, then, is that many three- and four-year-olds have quite severe limitations in their understanding of the process of acquiring knowledge as a result of perceptual experiences.

It is important to bear in mind that these ages provide only a very rough estimate of when children come to understand the causal connection between perceptual experience and knowledge state. In some tasks, some four-year-olds and even some three-year-olds, answer correctly. Some five-year-olds make errors. None of the tasks described in the preceding (or following) sections have been given to large, representative samples of children of different ages in the way that reading tests, for example, are standardised. Researchers aim not to identify a particular age at which we can say children achieve causal understanding, but rather to identify the developmental course and how it relates to other aspects of development.

During the early years when children apparently lack explicit understanding of the knowing process, children have of course been gaining knowledge as a result of their perceptual experiences. The next section reports studies that examine how they go about gaining such knowledge, and discusses what this in turn tells us about children's understanding of the causal connection between perceptual access and knowledge state.

3 Children's finding out behaviour

3.1 Behaviour consistent with evaluating other people's knowledge on the basis of their perceptual access

Suppose you observe somebody looking inside a coffee jar, who then tells you it contains teabags. You are likely to believe this informant because he appears to have had access to the necessary information. You are less likely to believe a second person who now enters the room and announces, without looking inside, that the coffee jar contains sugar. This pattern of belief and disbelief of what we are told, based on the informant's access to information, relies on understanding the connection between perceptual access and knowledge state, and so offers a way of assessing children's understanding. A child who shows the predicted pattern of belief and disbelief, behaves in a manner consistent with such understanding.

On the other hand, failure to show the predicted pattern might not indicate failure to understand the relation between perceptual access and knowledge state. The child might understand the causal connection between experience and consequent internal knowledge state, but fail to understand the connection between internal knowledge state and consequent output (in this case, what the person says).

In addition, other factors might influence children's readiness to believe what they are told, such as the status of the informant, presence of cues that the person is joking or teasing, or knowledge of the person's past history of reliability (Harris, 2007; Koenig and Harris, 2005; Nurmsoo and Robinson, 2008a; 2008b; Robinson and Nurmsoo, 2008). Hence a child who fully understands the causal connection between input, knowledge state, and output might nevertheless disbelieve what she is told for other reasons. As highlighted in section 2.3, negative results might be hard to interpret in terms of absence of causal understanding, although positive results provide evidence of such understanding.

To find out whether children behave as if they take into account another person's perceptual access when deciding whether or not to believe what they say, Robinson, Champion, and Mitchell (1999) devised a game in which children aimed to identify the content of a container. Three- and four-year-olds were shown that two identical dustbins contained different toys: One contained a teddy bear and the other a toy snowman. The two dustbins were mixed up and one was chosen. Was it the one with the teddy bear, or the one with the snowman? A monkey puppet operated by the Experimenter asked the child what she thought, and the child made a guess, for example 'Snowman'. Next, the monkey asked the Experimenter what she thought, and the Experimenter always contradicted what the child had said, for example, 'Teddy'. Crucially, on half the trials the child observed that Experimenter had looked inside the dustbin before answering, and on the other half she, like the child, simply guessed. Finally, Monkey, puzzled by the contradictory suggestions, asked the child again: 'So which one is it, the snowman or the teddy?' If children understood the likely truth of the Experimenter's suggestion when she had seen inside, and its unreliability when she had not, then as a group they should repeat the Experimenter's suggestion more frequently when the Experimenter had seen than when she had not. This is the pattern of results obtained. The conclusion was that children as a group understood the connection between perceptual access and knowledge state, and took that into account when deciding whether or not to believe what they were told.

In contrast, when the children were asked to make an explicit knowledge judgment such as 'Who knows best what's inside?' they performed much more poorly. Although their readiness to believe what the Experimenter told them was influenced by the

Experimenter's access to relevant information, children often seemed not to be able to reflect on knowledge states directly. Children this age are familiar with the word 'know', but they do not yet apply the word in an adult-like manner.

The fine details of the procedure used in games such as this are crucial. For example, it is important that a poorly informed adult does not appear to be untrustworthy due to the mere fact that she offers a suggestion about the content of a container she has not looked inside. By having Monkey ask each player 'What do you think it is?' the Experimenter can reply with a guess such as 'Snowman' without seeming to be irresponsible, but equally can reply in the same way when she has seen inside the dustbin without implying uncertainty.

In the experiment just described, the child had only to differentiate occasions when the Experimenter was fully informed, having seen inside the dustbin, from occasions when she was completely ignorant, having not seen inside. In subsequent experiments the child listener's task was made more difficult (Haigh and Robinson, 2009; Whitcombe and Robinson, 2000; Robinson and Whitcombe, 2003): on trials when the Experimenter was only guessing, she took uninformative access to the target toy, such as feeling it to find out its colour. This variant of the game used pairs of toys that either looked the same but felt different, one hard and one soft, or felt the same but differed in colour, for example one red and one blue. One toy from a pair was placed in a box in secret, and the child's task was to identify it. On each trial, both child and Experimenter made a suggestion as to which toy was in the box, with the child having a second (final) opportunity to say what she thought having heard the Experimenter's suggestion. For example, on some trials the child was invited to feel a hidden toy identified by colour, said which one she thought it was (for example, 'Red cat'), then the Experimenter had a look, contradicted the child ('Blue cat'), and the child made a final judgment which was then checked by taking the toy out of the box. On other trials it was the Experimenter who had uninformative access, and the child who then had informative access. On yet other trials, both child and Experimenter had the same uninformative access.

As in the dustbin task described above, the pattern of results suggested that three- and four-year-olds understood when the Experimenter was better informed than they were: Children were much more inclined to change their mind and make a final judgment consistent with the Experimenter's suggestion when the Experimenter was the one who had informative access, for example having seen a toy identified by colour. When both child and Experimenter had the same uninformative access, for example when both felt a toy identified by colour, children were much less likely to make a final suggestion consistent with the Experimenter's. And when the child had informative access (for example, she saw the red cat) and the Experimenter only felt it, children more rarely gave a final judgment in line with the Experimenter's suggestion.

The conclusion is that as a group, children aged three to four years, as well as four- to five-year-olds, revealed that they understood the causal connection between the Experimenter's access to information and the likely truth of her suggestion.

Yet when these children were asked, for example, 'How do you know it's the red bug, because you saw it or because I said so?' the three- to four-year-olds performed no better than they would if they were guessing the answer to that question (Robinson and Whitcombe, 2003).

An obvious interpretation of these results is that children's decisions to believe or ignore the Experimenter drew on implicit or working understanding about the knowing process, whereas to answer 'How do you know…?' children needed to have achieved explicit, reflective understanding. By differentiating different levels of understanding that are more or less explicit, we can allow children to understand at a lower, more implicit, level but not at a higher, more explicit level (e.g. Dienes and Perner, 1999; Karmiloff-Smith, 1992). This approach, and problems with it (in this context) are discussed further in section 4.

Summary Three- and four-year-olds' tendency to believe what they are told by the Experimenter when she is well informed, but to disregard what they are told by the Experimenter when she is ignorant, suggests that on some level they do understand the causal connection between perceptual access and knowledge state, even if their verbally explicit comments do not yet reveal such understanding. It is important to note that what is identified in this research is a pattern of behaviour within groups of children: the results show that children are more likely as a group to believe what the Experimenter tells them when she is well informed rather than poorly informed. It is not the case that every individual child shows this pattern. In any case, individual children's responses cannot be interpreted. Whereas an individual child's responses to the explicit questions described in sections 2.1 to 2.3 are either correct or incorrect, this is not the case with the behavioural measures used in this section. It is not wrong to follow the Experimenter's guess on any particular trial, although in general we would expect to find that someone who understands how knowledge is gained will be more likely to believe the Experimenter when she is well informed.

3.2 Behaviour consistent with knowing how your knowledge was gained

In section 3.1, children's decisions to believe or ignore the Experimenter's suggestion about the hidden toy provided a behavioural parallel to the explicit question used in section 2.1: 'Does the Experimenter know what's in the box?' We can take the finding out game a step further to examine a behavioural parallel to 'How do you know?' If the child believed what the Experimenter told her *because* she thought the Experimenter was well informed, but then it turns out that the Experimenter might not have been well informed after all, then the knowledge gained from the Experimenter might not be reliable. Haigh and Robinson (2009) and Robinson, Haigh, and Nurmsoo (2008) examined whether children realised the implications of their informant's expressed doubt about the adequacy of his information access to the target toy. The game was a modification of the one described above: the Experimenter had either informative or uninformative access to the target toy, said which toy she thought it was, then the child had uninformative or informative access and said which toy she thought it was, appropriately relying on the Experimenter's suggestion more frequently when the Experimenter was the better informed. There was a further stage just after the child had said which toy she thought it was: the Experimenter then said 'I'm not sure I felt it properly that time. Could it be the other one?' Children simply answered 'Yes' or 'No'. If the child's judgment had been based on the suggestion made by the apparently well-informed Experimenter (for example if she had felt a toy that was hard or soft, and the child had only seen it), then the correct answer was 'Yes' (it could be the other one, because the child was reliant on the Experimenter's feeling). On the other hand, if the child's final judgment was based on her own informative access (for example if she had seen a toy identified by colour but the Experimenter had only felt it), then the correct answer was 'No' (it could not be the other one, and it is completely irrelevant whether or not the Experimenter felt properly). This pattern was indeed found amongst children aged between three and five years.

It could, however, be over-interpreting to treat this as evidence that children realised the implications of the Experimenter's doubt about his perceptual access. Various further checks are needed. Perhaps children are simply less confident in knowledge gained indirectly from what somebody tells them, than in knowledge gained by their own direct access (in this case, seeing the toy's colour or feeling its hardness). If so, then any expression of uncertainty from the informant (the Experimenter in this case) might be sufficient to make them accept 'It could be the other one', without any suggestion that the Experimenter's access to relevant information was in doubt. Checks on this showed that general lack of confidence in knowledge gained indirectly from another person, compared with knowledge gained directly, was not sufficient to explain the results. Children did indeed appear to understand the specific implications of the Experimenters' doubt about the reliability of her access to the hidden toy.

As in section 3.1, it is of interest to examine the relationship between the understanding revealed by children's responses to the Experimenter's doubt about this access, and their ability to report explicitly how they gained their knowledge. Robinson, Haigh, and Nurmsoo (2008), instead of asking children 'How do you know . . . ?', used an explicit source question that was better matched to the doubt question (which was 'Could it be the other one, yes or no?'), so that in both cases the correct answer was either 'Yes' or 'No'. The new source reporting question was, for example 'So, you found out it was the hard one. Did you find out it was the hard one because I told you, yes or no?' (Importantly, sometimes the correct answer was 'Yes' and sometimes 'No', so children who were biased always to say 'Yes' were not mis-diagnosed as understanding about their knowledge sources.) There was a significant relationship between children's answers to these two questions, suggesting that as children came to realise the implications of the Experimenter's doubt about his access, they also became more aware of how they had found out the toy's identity. In addition, there was weak evidence that some children who failed the explicit source question, nevertheless realised the implications of the Experimenter's doubt about his access (thereby behaving as if they understood implicitly that he was the source of their knowledge). That is, there was an indication, but not strong evidence, that children's finding out behaviour was in advance of their ability to reflect on and report explicitly how they got to know.

Summary Children aged three to five years who appropriately believed what the apparently well-informed Experimenter told them, appropriately revised their belief in the light of doubts about the Experimenter's perceptual access. This implies that on some level they understood the source of their knowledge. Children may reveal source understanding in this way without yet being able to report explicitly how they knew, although further research is needed to check on whether that is the case.

3.3 *Behaviour consistent with knowing how to gain knowledge*

The final set of experiments to be reported was the behavioural equivalent of the work reported in section 2.3, in which children reported how they would gain knowledge of a hidden object's properties. In the studies below, children were simply asked to identify the hidden object by its colour or shape, and the researchers observed how they set about it: did they spontaneously take the informative modality of access? Full details of the experiments appear in Robinson, Haigh, and Pendle (2008).

In the first experiment we tested three- and four-year-olds. Half the children had the task of identifying which one of a pair of toys the Experimenter had placed on the table in front of them. For some pairs, both toys felt the same but differed in colour, for example a red and a blue cat. For other pairs, both toys looked identical, but they felt different, for example a hard and a soft worm. At the beginning of each trial, the child saw and felt both toys in a pair and agreed on their properties, for example that they felt the same but looked different. Then the Experimenter held them both behind his back, mixed them up, and placed one on the table just out of the child's reach, saying 'Which one is it?' We were interested in whether children answered before or after touching the toy. One possibility was that children would always grab the toy before answering, even though this was unnecessary when the toy was identified by colour. Another possibility was that children would always answer without feeling the toy, even though feeling was necessary when the toy was either hard or soft.

In practice, children showed neither of these patterns. Instead, they were more likely to touch the toy before answering when it was either hard or soft, and to answer without touching it when it was identified by colour. Furthermore, children were no more or less likely to do nothing when that was sufficient, than to touch the toy when that was necessary. That is, as a group, children behaved as if they understood when feeling was necessary, and when looking was sufficient.

A second group of children played a similar game, but instead of placing the toy on the table, the Experimenter handed it to the child so that the child saw and felt it more or less simultaneously. Children in this group were asked 'Which one is it?' and 'How did you know it was the (hard) one?' Prompts were given if necessary, for example 'Do you know because you saw it or because you felt it?' Children in this group had already received training trials in which they were told explicitly, for example, 'You knew it was the hard one because you felt it'. As expected, children always identified the toy correctly. However, despite their training trials, they often were unable to report how they knew which toy it was.

In this experiment, then, children in the first group deliberately took the perceptual access that was necessary to identify the toy, yet those in the second group, who had both seen and felt the toy, appeared not to realise which was the informative modality of access. We cannot be too quick to interpret this as further evidence that children's finding out behaviour reveals causal understanding not evident in their verbally explicit judgments. Children in the first, behavioural, group merely had to recognise whether or not they could identify the toy on seeing it, and act to gain further information if they could not. There was really only one way of gaining further information, and that was to touch the toy. Children may not have realised *touching* in particular was necessary to find out if the toy was hard or soft; we can infer only that they realised seeing was insufficient. In contrast, children in the second, explicit reporting, group had to identify which of their two modes of access to the toy (seeing and feeling) was the informative one. For example, they had to understand that touching in particular was the source of their knowledge about the toy's hardness. That is, the behavioural and explicit tasks were not tapping the same causal understanding.

We therefore devised a behavioural (finding out) task that demanded the more complex understanding that seems to be assessed in the explicit task ('How do you know . . .?') This experiment involved three-, four- and five-year-olds. The target toy was hidden in a box, similar to the task devised by O'Neill et al., (1992) and described in section 2.2. Whereas in O'Neill et al.'s experiment, children had to indicate how they would identify the toy, in this experiment children were simply asked to find out which toy it was (for example, the hard or the soft dog). Children could either see or feel it, since the apparatus did not allow them to do both at once. Would they choose the informative mode of access? Children performed poorly in this behavioural task, compared with their performance when they could already see the target toy and only had to decide whether or not to feel it. They were no better at the more complex task than they were at answering 'How do you know?' after they had both seen and felt the hidden toy.

In further studies we confirmed the conclusion from the experiments described in this section so far: children acted to gain knowledge efficiently when they had only to recognise whether or not they already had sufficient information to identify the target toy, and there was only one additional modality of access to take when they had insufficient information. They were much less efficient when they had a choice of modes of access. Then, they seemed just to explore further to gain more information without being able to predict the best way of finding out what they needed to know. That is, children who recognised that they needed more information did not necessarily know what kind of information they needed. Those who did know, were generally able also to report explicitly how they knew.

Summary In contrast to the findings reported in sections 3.1 and 3.2, in which three- and four-year-olds 'finding out behaviour was consistent with understanding the causal connection between perceptual access and knowledge state, the tasks in this section reveal weaknesses as well as strengths in children's finding out behaviour. Under simple conditions with limited choices (for example, 'Having seen the toy, do I also need to feel it [when that is the only other option]?'), three- and four-year-olds were efficient at finding out more when that was necessary to identify the hidden toy. On the other hand, when children that age had to choose between different modalities of access ('Do I need to see the toy or feel it?'), their finding out behaviour was not efficient. They seemed simply to explore without predicting the best way of finding out what they needed to know. Furthermore, there was no evidence that their finding out behaviour revealed understanding not evident in their verbally explicit responses.

3.4 Conclusions from work on children's finding out behaviour

In section 2.4, the conclusion concerning children's explicit, reflective understanding about the knowing process was that by five to six years of age, causal understanding is often clearly in evidence, in that children can report who knows what on the basis of what access, while many 3- and 4-year-olds demonstrate at best limited understanding. (Remember the proviso in that section that the ages offer only a rough guide.)

In contrast, the behavioural tasks discussed in sections 3.1, 3.2, and 3.3. summarise convincing evidence of understanding the causal connection between perceptual experience and knowledge amongst three- and four-year-olds. In section 3.1, children's evaluations of the reliability of what they were told were consistent with understanding about the knowledge gained by the Experimenter on the basis of her perceptual access. Their behaviour seemed to be in advance of their explicit judgments of the Experimenter's knowledge, and in advance of their explicit reports of the source of their own knowledge. In section 3.2, children revised their evaluations of the reliability of the Experimenter's suggestion when doubts were expressed about the Experimenter's access, consistent with understanding about knowledge sources. Here there was only weak evidence that this behaviour was in advance of children's explicit reports of how they knew. Finally, in section 3.3, in which children aimed to identify a hidden toy for themselves rather than in interaction with the Experimenter, three- and four-year-olds efficiently took additional information access when it was necessary, and generally did not do so when they already had sufficient information to identify the hidden toy.

However, in the most demanding behavioural tasks in section 3.3, when behavioural and explicit judgment tasks drew on equivalent understanding of precisely what knowledge is acquired from what perceptual experience, there was no evidence of finding out behaviour being in advance of explicit judgments.

In general, by examining children's finding out behaviour, rather than just their ability to reflect and comment on the process of gaining knowledge, we might create a more fine-grained picture of the course of development of understanding of the causal connection between information access and knowledge state. However it is not simply the case that children's behaviour is in advance of their explicit, reflective understanding. This is discussed further in the next section.

4   Children's causal understanding of the knowing process: When and how?

As pointed out in the opening section, one difficulty associated with answering the question 'when?' is deciding what the child must do for the observing researcher to impute understanding of the causal connection between perceptual access and knowledge state. It is now clear that there is no single criterion, and no single point at which we would deem a child to have achieved understanding. Rather, between the ages of around three and six years, children show increasing mastery of the process of gaining knowledge from perceptual experience, mastery that relies on their making a causal connection between experience and knowledge state, and that includes being able to reflect on how knowledge was gained or predict how to gain particular knowledge.

In the opening section, two plausible patterns of results (and one implausible one) were specified: (i) children might show a pattern of finding out behaviour consistent with understanding a particular aspect of the knowing process, only when they can also reflect and report on it explicitly; (ii) finding out behaviour might be in advance of reflective, explicit understanding. Results in line with pattern (i) would raise the question of the nature of the relationship between the ability to reflect on the process of gaining knowledge, and strategic behaviour: does the former cause the latter? Results in line with pattern (ii) raise the question of the advantage of being able to reflect on the process of gaining knowledge if children behave efficiently and gain knowledge effectively without being able to do so.

As it turns out, both patterns appear in the results summarised in sections 2 and 3. Pattern (i) was found in section 3.3: children's finding out behaviour was exploratory rather than strategic before they could report explicitly the source of the knowledge they had gained. Pattern (ii) was found in section 3.1: children appropriately believed or disbelieved what the well- or poorly-informed Experimenter told them despite being unable to report on sources of knowledge explicitly.

How should we resolve the finding that causal understanding as assessed by behavioural measures is sometimes in advance of explicit understanding, but sometimes is not? The mixed results seem to cast doubt on the usefulness of the suggestion offered in section 3.1, that the behavioural tasks could be seen as revealing implicit as opposed to explicit understanding, implicit understanding being seen as a lower level. Perhaps some more difficult finding out tasks, despite not requiring the child to comment explicitly on the process of gaining knowledge, nevertheless demand a similar level of reflective understanding. If so, how would we decide independently which of the finding out tasks fall into that category? Children's spontaneous responses to 'Which one is it?' when one of two toys was placed on the table in front of them (section 3.3: they felt the toy when that was necessary, but answered on the basis of looking when that was sufficient), seem uncontroversially to assess implicit rather than explicit understanding. On the other hand, when children were asked 'Which one is it?' of a target toy hidden inside a box (section 3.3), perhaps reflective understanding was required—children found it just as difficult to select the informative modality of access as they did to report how they had found out. Robinson, Haigh, and Pendle (2008) describe a sequence of finding out tasks which move in small steps from uncontroversially assessing only implicit understanding, to uncontroversially assessing explicit, reflective understanding, but in which it is hard to see where a step change takes place from assessing only implicit to assessing reflective understanding. One challenge for the future is to characterise the various measures of causal understanding in terms of their cognitive demands, and to develop an account of the relationship between children's finding out behaviour and their ability to reflect and comment on the process of gaining knowledge.

Such an account would also move us forward in understanding how development in causal understanding takes place. As mentioned in the opening section, at present we know virtually nothing about the underlying processes responsible for the increases in strategic, efficient finding out behaviour, or the increases in reflective awareness of how particular perceptual experiences lead to knowledge. One possibility is that advances occur simply as a result of experience exploring the world. If we gave a two-year-old concentrated experience of different modalities of access, separated rather than combined as they usually are in everyday life, would this be sufficient to allow her to show the kinds of strategic finding out typical of five-year-olds without having developed the more general cognitive skills typical of the older child? Some children in nurseries play games intended to raise their awareness of the different modalities of access, but we do not know how effective these are. Neither do we know what underlying conceptual and general cognitive developments are necessary for children to advance in their causal understanding.

One thing that does seem clear, however, is that young children whose causal understanding about the process of gaining knowledge is still limited, are not seriously hampered by their lack of understanding. By the age of three years, most children have gained a large stock of knowledge as a result of their perceptual experiences. Incorrect expectations about what knowledge can be gained from a particular experience can be corrected with further exploration. For example, in the task described in section 3.3, with the target toy hidden in a box, most of the children who initially felt it to identify its colour, realised their mistake and went on to have a look. Similarly, most of the children who initially looked at the toy to find out if it was hard or soft, realised their mistake and went on to have a feel. They continued to explore until they gained the knowledge they needed. Children who gain knowledge without knowing how they do so may not behave as efficiently as those with more advanced understanding, but that understanding seems not to be critical for learning about the physical world.

References

Astington, J. W., Harris, P. L., and Olson, D. R. (1988). (Eds) *Developing Theories of Mind* Cambridge: Cambridge University Press.

Dienes, Z., and Perner, J. (1999). A theory of implicit knowledge. *Behavioural and Brain Sciences*, 22: 735–808.

Gopnik, A. and Graf, P. (1988). Knowing how you know: young children's ability to identify and remember the sources of their beliefs. *Child Development*, 59: 1366–1371.

Haigh, S. N. and Robinson, E. J. (2009). What children know about the source of their knowledge without reporting it as the source. *European Journal of Developmental Psychology*, 6: 318–336.

Harris, P. L. (2007). Trust. *Developmental Science*, 10: 135–138.

Johnson, M. K., Hashtroudi, S., and Lindsay, S. D. (1993). Source monitoring. *Psychological Bulletin*, 114, 3–28.

Karmiloff-Smith, A. (1992). *Beyond Modularity*. Cambridge: MIT Press.

Koenig, M. A., and Harris, P. L. (2005). Preschoolers mistrust ignorant and inaccurate speakers. *Child Development*, 76, 1261–1277.

Nurmsoo, E., and Robinson, E. J. (2009a). Identifying unreliable informants: Do children excuse past inaccuracies? *Developmental Science*, 11, 905–911.

Nurmsoo, E. and Robinson, E. J. (2009b). Children's trust in previously inaccurate informants who were well or poorly-informed: When past errors can be excused. *Child Development*, 80: 23–27.

O'Neill, D. K., Astington, J. W., and Flavell, J. H. (1992). Young children's understanding of the role that sensory experience plays in knowledge acquisition. *Child Development*, 63: 474–490.

O'Neill, D. K. and Chong, C. F. (2001). Pre-school children's difficulty understanding the types of information obtained through the five senses. *Child Development*, 72 (3): 803–815.

O'Neill, D. K. and Gopnik, A. (1991). Young children's ability to identify the sources of their beliefs. *Developmental Psychology*, 27: 390–397.

Perner, J. (1991). *Understanding the Representational Mind*. Cambridge: MIT Press.

Pillow, B. H. (1989). Early understanding of perception as a source of knowledge. *Journal of Experimental Child Psychology*, 47: 116–129.

Pillow, B. H. (1993). Pre-school children's understanding of the relationship between modality of perceptual access and knowledge of perceptual properties. *British Journal of Developmental Psychology*, 11: 371–389.

Roberts, K. P. and Blades, M. (2000). *Children's Source Monitoring*. Mahwah, New Jersey: Erlbaum.

Robinson, E. J., Champion, H., and Mitchell, P. (1999). Children's ability to infer utterance veracity from speaker informedness. *Developmental Psychology*, 35: 535–546.

Robinson, E. J., Haigh, S. J., and Nurmsoo, E. (2008). Children's working understanding of knowledge sources: Confidence in knowledge gained from testimony. *Cognitive Development*, 23: 105–118.

Robinson, E. J., Haigh, S. N., and Pendle, J. E. C. (2008). Children's working understanding of the knowledge gained from seeing and feeling. *Developmental Science,* 11: 299–305.

Robinson, E. J. and Nurmsoo, E. (2009). When do children learn from unreliable speakers? *Cognitive Development*, 24: 16–22.

Robinson, E. J. and Robinson, W. P. (1982). Knowing when you don't know enough: children's judgements about ambiguous information. *Cognition*, 12, 267–280.

Robinson, E. J., Thomas, G. V., Parton, A., and Nye, R. (1997). Children's overestimation of the knowledge to be gained from seeing. *British Journal of Developmental Psychology*, 15: 257–273.

Robinson, E. J. and Whitcombe, E. L. (2003). Children's suggestibility in relation to their understanding about sources of knowledge. *Child Development*, 74: 48–62.

Taylor, M (1988). The development of children's ability to distinguish what they know from what they see. *Child Development*, 58: 424–433.

Whitcombe, E. L. and Robinson, E. J. (2000). Children's decisions about what to believe and the ability to report the source of their beliefs. *Cognitive Development*, 15: 329–346.

Wimmer, H., Hogrefe, G. J., and Perner, J. (1988). Children's understanding of information access as a source of knowledge. *Child Development*, 59: 386–396.

19

Social and Physical Reasoning in Human-reared Chimpanzees
Preliminary Studies

Jennifer Vonk and Daniel J. Povinelli[*]

A challenging issue in the comparative and developmental literature concerns the effort to define and describe the underlying nature of concepts and representations. This volume represents an attempt to define perception, and what it might mean for an organism to have a "theory of perception." Typically, if an organism is able to differentiate between different objects, making operational choices between them, that organism is said to have an understanding of the objects' different properties, or at least to have discriminated between them in a meaningful way. If the organism can predict that different objects will have differential effects on the world that organism may be said to have some limited causal understanding. Adding complexity to the study of such topics is the issue of implicit versus explicit levels of understanding. To act on objects in the world in meaningfully different ways is not necessarily functionally equivalent to reflecting on those objects, or one's own actions, in a conscious or metacognitive manner.

As evolutionary psychologists, our focus has been to understand how our closest living relatives may be both similar to and different from humans in their approach to solving social and physical problems. We have previously proposed that one critical way in which non-humans, even the other apes, may differ from humans, is in their ability to represent and reason about unobservables (Povinelli, 2004; Vonk and Povinelli, 2006). We posit that to have a true "theory" of objects or other organisms (whether it be a theory of perception or a theory of mind), an organism must represent

[*] This work was supported by a Centennial Fellowship to DJP from the James S. McDonnell Foundation, funded from the State of Louisiana. The participation of the chimpanzees and their caretakers is gratefully acknowledged. These studies could not have taken place without the hard work and dedication of several individuals including James Reaux, Conni Castille, Anthony Rideaux, John Sharp, Jo Lynn Bergeron, Beth De Blanc, Amy Roberthon, and Anne Hoops.

properties of objects as being inherently tied to that object, whether that organism is currently perceiving that object and its effects or not, and whether those properties are available to the senses or are unobservable but inferred properties. Thus, in our work, we have chosen to explore chimpanzees' understanding of the mental state of seeing in the social realm, and physical states such as weight (which is tied to objects but not perceived when objects are not currently being lifted) in the physical realm. In what follows, we discuss the effects of rearing environment on chimpanzees' abilities to form causal "theories" in these domains.

Theorists from multiple disciplines have become increasingly interested in the question of how uniquely human rearing practices affect a child's cognitive development (Astington, 1996; Bard and Gardner, 1996; Brown, Collins, and Duguid, 1989; Harlow and Harlow, 1965; Lave and Wenger, 1991; Lewis and Rosenblum, 1975; Russon, 1990; Tomasello, 1999). Social constructivists, such as Vygotsky (1962, 1978), argued that a child's (specifically human) intellectual development depends upon immersion in human culture, a fundamental component of which is engagement in social learning practices and verbal communication with other beings. More recently, Call and Tomasello (1994, 1996) have argued that the experience of being engaged in triadic social interactions, in which the human child is treated as an intentional being by other humans, is critical for the development of particular cognitive abilities, such as the ability to represent and reason about mental states (i.e., theory of mind; see also Tomasello, 1995, 1999; Tomasello, Kruger, and Ratner, 1993; Tomasello, Savage-Rumbaugh, and Kruger, 1993). Of course, a range of views on the plasticity of human cognition exist, including strong nativism (Fodor, 1986), starting state nativism (Gopnik and Meltzoff, 1997), and representational re-description (Karmiloff-Smith, 1992).

For Vygotsky (1978), the human social and cultural environment fostered an expansion of cognitive abilities in human children, which was possible only by virtue of the uniquely human biological prepotency for such abilities. Later social constructivists, in contrast, have argued that these same rearing experiences, when directed toward our closest living relatives (the great apes), can lead to the development (or extensive elaboration) of at least certain aspects of what were previously thought to be uniquely human abilities, such as theory of mind (Call and Tomasello, 1994; 1996). Of course, the ability to represent mental states is only one among several psychological capacities that may turn out to be uniquely human, and that may be affected by the human rearing environment (see Povinelli, 2000; Bering, Bjorklund, and Ragan, 2000). Determining whether these abilities can be fostered in other species, and to what extent, is an important avenue for exploring the plasticity of psychological development in both humans and other species. It is also a vital method for setting limits on the nature of the uniqueness of human psychological specializations.

A range of more specific hypotheses regarding the role of human-rearing on cognitive development in non-human apes have been proposed (Bering et al., 2000; Call and Tomasello, 1994, 1996; Carpenter, Tomasello, and Savage-Rumbaugh, 1995; Donald, 2000; Gardner and Gardner, 1971; Hayes and Hayes, 1951; Leavens and Hopkins, 1998; Miles, 1990; Russon and Galdikas, 1993; Savage-Rumbaugh, McDonald, Sevcik, Hopkins, and Rubert, 1986; Tomasello, 2000; Tomasello, Kruger, and Ratner, 1993; Whiten, 1993). Perhaps the strongest of these claims, labeled the "enculturation hypothesis," is an extension of social constructivist theory to other species. In this analysis, human rearing substantially alters the cognitive systems of young apes such that they develop psychological abilities never expressed in their wild counterparts, or other apes who, although they interact with humans on a daily basis, are primarily reared with each other (Bering et al., 2000; Tomasello, Savage-Rumbaugh, and Kruger, 1993b). Human rearing practices directed toward these apes are seen as leading to the development of psychological abilities otherwise uniquely human (Call and Tomasello, 1996; Donald, 2000; Premack, 1983; Tomasello, Kruger and Ratner, 1993). Conversely, Suddendorf and Whiten (2001) argue that, although rearing environment guides the ape's cognitive development, human rearing practices may merely function to restore the species-typical pattern of development normally disrupted with more typical captive rearing environments. They have suggested that the "special" abilities sometimes attributed to only human-reared apes may in fact be shared with apes reared by their natural mothers in the wild.

A more moderate version of the "enculturation hypothesis" posits that human-reared apes will differ only in certain specific domains or abilities, such as the ability to reason about mental states (for example, the intentions of another; Bjorklund and Pellegrini, 2002; Call, Agnetta, and Tomasello, 2000; Call and Tomasello, 1996; Miles, 1990; Tomasello, 1999; Tomasello and Call, 2004; Tomasello and Camaioni, 1997, or communicative abilities; Lyn, Russell, and Hopkins, 2010). Proponents of this moderate hypothesis predict that the effects of the environment have a more narrowly focused impact. They share with modularity theorists at least the idea that certain abilities can develop independently from other cognitive structures or domains (cf. Baron-Cohen and Swettenham, 1996; Fodor, 1986; Leslie, 1994; Scholl and Leslie, 1999; Segal, 1996).

A third hypothesis suggests that the core cognitive systems of human-reared apes do not differ at all from other chimpanzees, but that they develop a greater breadth of skill sets for coping with human social and material culture (Bering, 2004; Bjorklund, Yunger, Bering, and Ragan, 2002; Call and Carpenter, 2003; Call and Tomasello, 1996; Povinelli, 2000). In other words, the human rearing experience would not lead to any fundamental change in their conceptual systems, but instead would lead to the accretion of a different skill set. This general hypothesis has also been instantiated in both broadly and narrowly focused forms. For instance, Bering (2004) focused on the human-reared apes' extensive experience with the manipulation of objects, whereas Tomasello and Call (2004) point to the human-reared apes' social skills, namely the ability to represent the intentions of other beings.

All of these and other more specific hypotheses concerning the effects of early experience on psychological development in apes can be tested by comparing apes reared under various environmental conditions. Researchers have not yet taken full advantage of such opportunities. Chimpanzees are the ideal participants for such studies. First, they are arguably the closest living relatives of modern humans (Jensen-Seaman, Deinard, and Kidd, 2001; Pennisi, 2002; Ruvolo, Zehr, Goldberg, Disotell, and von Dornum, 1994). Second, they are perhaps the best-studied of all great apes, with a reasonable corpus of data dating back to the turn of the previous century. Finally, large numbers of socially enriched chimpanzees, reared in a variety of ways, currently exist in the United States and elsewhere. The range of such early experiences is impressive, and includes (a) chimpanzees who have been (or are currently being) reared in human homes as "foster children" (for examples, see Appendix), (b) chimpanzees reared with chimpanzee peers with extensive human contact, (c) chimpanzees reared by chimpanzee mothers in sanctuaries in African countries such as Liberia, and (d) chimpanzees reared in captivity by their chimpanzee mothers. This range of early rearing histories allows for a large-scale test of the hypothesis that human-rearing leads to fundamental changes in cognitive development in this species. Properly conducted, such a long-term study could address historical questions concerning the malleability of chimpanzee cognitive development, and the biological disposition for human cognition (see also Bering, 2004; Lyn et al., 2010; Povinelli, 1996b, 2000; Suddendorf and Whiten, 2001).

The studies reported here were conducted as part of a feasibility project to determine whether one critical group of participants (human-reared chimpanzees) could be suitably adapted to the study procedures necessary for the comparisons described above, as well as to obtain some preliminary data on social and physical reasoning in these participants. These feasibility studies were conducted as a prelude to a large-scale project that could be developed. A critical component of this larger project is the ability to compare chimpanzees from various rearing backgrounds in an identical testing environment using identical procedures. We report the results of four studies that explored the ability of three human-reared chimpanzees to reason about the visual perspective of others (one well-studied component of the human theory-of-mind system), as well as their understanding of certain physical interactions in the context of simple tool-using problems. These studies were designed to carefully match the general procedures of previous studies involving peer-raised chimpanzees (see Povinelli, 2000; Povinelli and Eddy, 1996a, 1996b; Reaux, Theall, and Povinelli. 1999).

Study 1: Understanding of Visual Attention I

In Study 1, we assessed three human-reared chimpanzees' understanding of visual attention using procedures developed in our laboratory (and replicated elsewhere) with peer-reared chimpanzees (Kaminsky, Call, and Tomasello, 2004; Povinelli and Eddy, 1996a; Reaux et al., 1999), to determine whether human-reared chimpanzees exhibit a heightened sensitivity to more subtle indicators of visual attention. The participants were required to use a species-typical, visual gesture to request a treat from one of two human experimenters, one of whom could see them and another who could not.

Method

Participants Participants were three juvenile chimpanzees who had been raised by human surrogate parents from about six weeks of age. Two of the participants (03 and 02) were females (41 and 62 months, respectively) and one (04) was male (73 months). The participants were selected after documenting their extensive history of human-rearing and immersion in human social and material culture (see Appendix for details). All applicable federal and State regulations were followed in the testing of the participants, and the research protocols were approved by the University of Louisiana Institutional Animal Care and Use Committee (approval numbers: 2003-8717-015). The participants and their surrogate parents traveled to Lafayette, Louisiana, and during the day, were guests of the University and were accommodated in a 4,000 square ft residence dedicated for this purpose. At night, they provided their own accommodations or stayed at the guest house. They participated in the study over a period ranging from four to nine days.

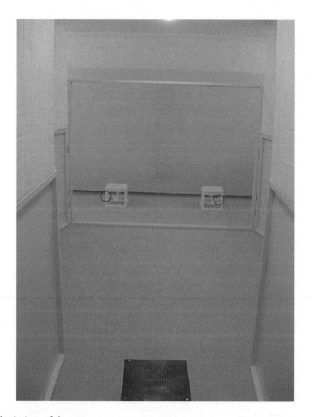

Figure 1. A depiction of the test arena.

Procedure General Orientation. Several rooms of the residence were dedicated to the testing of the participants (a suite of warm-up rooms, a study room, and a video control room). For a period of one to three days, the participants were adapted in the context of free play to the warm-up and study room as well as to the materials to be used in various studies. The study room contained a spacious testing arena, enclosed in front by a large, transparent partition, containing two large response holes through which the participants could reach (see Figure 1). Once the participants were comfortable in these environments, they began training.

Training. Participants underwent a training phase in which they were acclimated to the test arena and encouraged to gesture to a single experimenter through the holes in the partition for a food reward before testing began. Before each trial, a single experimenter was seated approximately 100 cm in front of one of the two response holes, at a height designed to be close to eye-level with the participants. The left/right position of the experimenter was randomized in blocks of four trials, with the constraint that an experimenter was not seated on the same side for more than two consecutive trials. Within a block of four trials, two different individuals served as experimenter twice each, once on each side of the test arena (in a random order). On all trials, the experimenter fixed their gaze on a pre-determined location directly above the response hole in front of her, so as to be looking where the chimpanzee would gesture, without making direct eye contact. The trainer then brought the chimpanzee to the rear entrance of the test arena, to a point equidistant between the two response holes. The trainer released the participant into the testing arena, thus allowing the participant to approach the partition and gesture. If the participant gestured through the correct hole, the experimenter praised the participant, and handed him or her a food reward. The food reward was originally held out to the participants, subsequently placed within view of the participants, and ultimately placed out-of-sight behind the experimenter's back. A gesture was considered to have been made as soon as the participant's wrist broke the plane of one of the two response holes. If the participant gestured through the wrong hole, or did not respond within 30 seconds, the trainer was signaled (via an earpiece) from the video control room to call the participant back to the starting position, and the participant did not receive a reward. In order to advance to testing, the participants were required to execute 6 consecutive correct trials without any prompting from the trainer.

Testing. For participant 02, testing consisted of seven 12-trial sessions (always beginning with a standard trial) in which standard and test trials alternated. Standard trials were identical to those used in training. Within each session, each of two experimenters participated in 3 standard trials in random order, with one experimenter seated on the left twice and on the right once, and the other seated on the right twice and on the left once. Each session included one test trial of each of the six experimental conditions depicted in Figure 2, with the trials occurring in random order. For the test trials, each experimenter served as the correct experimenter three times and as the incorrect

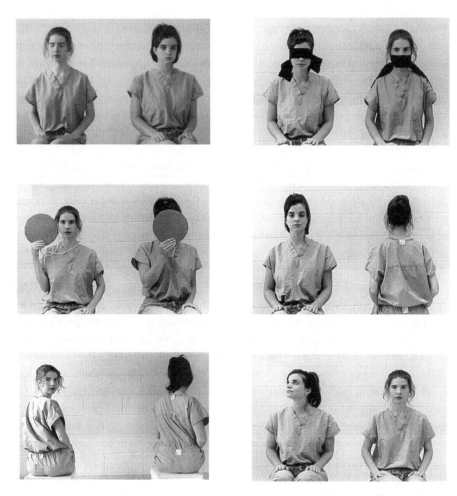

Figure 2. A depiction of the conditions presented to the chimpanzees in the test trials of Study 1. From top left to bottom right; "eyes open/closed," "blindfolds," "screens," "front/back," "looking over shoulder," "attending/distracted"

experimenter three times, with the left/right position of the correct and incorrect experimenter counterbalanced within each session. The identity of the correct and incorrect experimenters and their left/right positions were also counterbalanced across the experiment within each type of test trial.

For participants 03 and 04, testing initially consisted of 12-trial sessions in which each session consisted of four standard trials (trials 1, 4, 7, and 10) and eight test trials (trials 2, 3, 5, 6, 8, 9, 11, and 12). After two sessions of testing for 04, and one testing session for 03, a decision was made to increase the ratio of standard trials to test trials to maintain motivation. From that point forward, sessions consisted of six trials. Trials 1, 2, 4, and 6 were standard trials and trials 3 and 5 were test trials. Each experimenter participated in two standard trials per session, once on the left and once on the right, in random order. The six test conditions were presented in random order across sessions with side location and identity of the correct experimenter counterbalanced within each test trial type across sessions. Each condition occurred once before any repeated. Each condition was presented a total of six times for a total of 36 test trials for each participant.

Data Coding

For all of the studies reported here (Studies 1–4), two coders independently viewed all trials from the video records, and scored whether the participants' first choices were correct. Inter-rater reliability was perfect for all measures in all studies (Cohen's kappa's = 1).

Results and Discussion

The participants adapted rapidly to the environment, and were easily trained to gesture to the experimenters through the response holes. They required only 9 to 14 trials to meet criterion, in contrast to the lengthy training required by the previously tested peer-reared chimpanzees (see Povinelli and Eddy, 1996a).

In testing, the participants maintained a high level of performance on the standard trials (which were identical to those used in training). Participant 02 gestured correctly on 39/42 (92.8%) of the standard trials, and participants 03 and 04 gestured correctly on all 64 and 68, respectively, (100%) of their standard trials (binomial tests, $p < .001$ in all cases). These results are important, because they demonstrate that the participants were highly motivated and were attending across the entire testing phase.

The critical results of the testing phase concern the participants' performances on the embedded test trials, and these results are presented in Table 1. The results reveal that none of the participants performed at levels exceeding chance in their first session (although Participant 02 did perform 5/6 (83%) of her test trials accurately), nor did their overall responses (within any of the individual conditions) exceed chance. Participant 02's performance in the "looking-over-shoulder" and "front/back" conditions approached significance ($p = .06$, binomial test). Finally, there was no evidence of learning across sessions (see Table 1).

The chimpanzees in this study were juveniles (3–6 years), but their ages are comparable to that of the peer-reared apes who participated in the studies that the present work replicates (those chimpanzees were 4–5 years when training began, and 5–6 years when testing ended; see Povinelli and Eddy, 1996a). Those peer-reared chimpanzees performed at levels exceeding chance from trial one forward in the "front/back" condition, but not the other conditions used here (although they did learn to do so across 8 to 20 trials, depending on participant and condition; see Povinelli and Eddy, 1996a). Interestingly, in the present study, for two of the participants (02 and 03), body orientation (i.e., "front-versus-back") appeared to be more

Table 1. Trial by trial performance on test trials of Study 1 by participant and experimental condition. A "+" indicates that the participant chose the correct experimenter on that trial.

Participant	Age (months)	Trial	A/D	Eyes	L/O/S	B/Fold	F/B	Screens	Mean
03	41	1	+	−	−	+	+	−	50.0
		2	+	+	−	−	−	+	50.0
		3	−	−	+	+	+	+	66.7
		4	−	+	+	−	−	−	33.3
		5	−	−	−	+	+	+	50.0
		6	−	+	+	−	+	−	50.0
		Mean	33.3	50.0	50.0	50.0	66.7	50.0	
02	62	1	+	+	+	+	+	−	83.0
		2	+	−	+	−	+	+	66.7
		3	−	+	+	+	+	−	66.7
		4	−	+	+	+	+	+	83.0
		5	−	+	+	+	−	−	50.0
		6	−	−	−	−	+	+	33.3
		7	−	−	+	+	+	+	66.7
		Mean	28.6	57.1	85.7	71.4	85.7	57.1	
04	73	1	+	−	+	+	−	+	66.7
		2	+	−	+	+	−	−	50.0
		3	−	+	−	−	+	+	50.0
		4	+	−	+	−	+	−	50.0
		5	+	+	+	−	+	−	66.7
		6	−	+	−	+	−	+	50.0
		Mean	66.7	50.0	66.7	50.0	50.0	50.0	

Note. A/D = attending versus distracted, Eyes = eyes open versus closed, L/O/S = looking over shoulder, B/Fold = Blindfolds, F/B = front/back. See Figure 2 for a depiction of the test conditions.

salient than presence of the face (i.e., "screens") or the presence or absence of the eyes ("eyes open/closed" and "blindfolds"). Thus, the results from these human-reared chimpanzees appears similar to those from the peer-reared chimpanzees in that body orientation was the most salient feature in determining to whom they directed their visually based gesture. Longitudinal studies of the peer-reared chimpanzees revealed no evidence of improved performance in experiments as they matured, and in fact they failed to retain much of what they learned in the early studies (see Reaux et al., 1999). It is possible that the human-reared apes might show an improvement in performance with age that the peer-reared group did not. Certainly this limited sample suggests that, before the age of six, human-reared chimpanzees do not have a greater understanding of the observable features of "seeing" compared to similarly aged peer-reared chimpanzees. Importantly, the results of the current study demonstrate the feasibility of acclimating home-reared chimpanzees to novel testing environments and completing data collecting within a short time period.

Study 2: Understanding Visual Attention II

In Study 1, there were salient visual cues (e.g. body orientation, presence of the eyes), as to the attentional states of the experimenters, and the chimpanzees were highly familiar with the significance of such cues in social interactions. In contrast, Study 2 created a context in which the participants, after having had extensive first-person experience wearing two buckets over their heads, could later infer, in the absence of behavioral cues, which of two humans (each wearing one of the buckets) would respond to their visual gestures (see Povinelli and Vonk, 2003; 2004). The important feature of the buckets was that, although the first person experiences when wearing the buckets were radically different (being able to see versus not being able to see out of the bucket), when viewed from a third-person perspective, they looked identical except for their color. The participants experienced the buckets from only a first person perspective prior to testing.

Method

Participants The three chimpanzees described in Study 1 also participated in this study. However, only Participants 02 and 04 took part in testing. Participant 03 was not tested because she did not spend the criterial amount of time experiencing the critical properties of both buckets during familiarization sessions (see below).

Materials Both buckets contained visors that appeared opaque from the outside; that is, an observer could not see the face of the wearer. However, one visor allowed the wearer to see out of the bucket (the blue bucket), and the other did not (yellow bucket).

Procedure Familiarization. Participants took part in three (for Participant 02) and seven (for Participant 04) free play sessions in which they interacted with the trainer and the buckets in the test arena for a minimum of five minutes per session. One session was conducted per day. The trainer encouraged participants to look inside of the buckets and placed the buckets over their heads but did not wear the buckets himself. It was critical that the participants obtained the first-person experience of wearing both buckets but did not observe another individual wearing the buckets prior to testing. Sessions continued until the investigators deemed that the participants had met a criterial amount of time interacting with the buckets.

Testing. The general procedure was identical to that described for Study 1. Testing sessions consisted of standard and test trials. Standard trials were the same as those described in Study 1. On test trials, before the participant entered the testing arena, two experimenters positioned themselves as in Study 1, and then placed the buckets over their heads (and kept them in place until after the trial was over and the participant had exited the testing arena). Participant 02 participated in four 12-trial sessions in which standard and test trials alternated, always beginning with a standard trial, for a total of 24 test trials. On the test trials within each session, each experimenter wore each bucket an equal number of times, and each bucket appeared on each side an equal number of times. Within a session, one experimenter sat on the left four times during test trials and two times on the right, and the other sat on the right four times and on the left two times. Each experimenter participated in three standard trials, one experimenter sitting on the left twice and on the right once and the other sitting on the right twice and on the left once. This positioning of experimenters was counterbalanced across sessions. Participant 04 participated in eight 6-trial sessions, which followed the exact same counterbalancing procedure as in Study 1, for a total of 16 test trials. Side location and identity of the correct experimenter were counterbalanced within the first and last half of the total number of test trials.

Results and Discussion

The participants were extremely interested in the buckets and placed their heads inside them repeatedly (with occasional prompting from the trainer). They ambled about the testing arena with the buckets on their heads and when wearing the see-through bucket, looked through the visor at the environment and at the trainer, who made waving motions in front of their faces. When wearing the opaque bucket they moved about the test arena gingerly and examined the inside and outside of the buckets with their hands.

On the standard trials of testing, participants 02 and 04 correctly gestured on 24/24 (100%) and 32/32 (100%) trials, respectively (binomial tests, $p < .001$ in both cases). Again, these results demonstrate that the participants were attending and motivated throughout the testing phase.

The critical data from the test trials are presented in Table 2. Across testing, neither participant performed at levels exceeding chance (binomial tests, $p =$ ns in both cases). Participant 03-002 performed at chance on her first session, and 66.7% correct on the following three sessions. Although this constitutes some weak evidence for learning by this participant, it would not uniquely implicate a first/third-person mapping given that after the initial trials, participants could learn to gesture to the experimenter wearing the blue bucket, without making the attribution that only that experimenter could see their gesture. In contrast, participant 04 exhibited no evidence of learning across trials, and instead demonstrated a strong person preference, selecting the same individual, regardless of which bucket she wore on 14/16 (87.5%) trials (binomial tests, $p = .002$).

In summary, Studies 1 and 2 demonstrated the feasibility of quickly adapting home-raised chimpanzees to an environment in which their social cognition could be explored. At the same time, they provided some preliminary evidence that the performances of

Table 2. Trial by trial performance on test trials of Study 2 by participant. A "+" indicates that the participant chose the correct experimenter on that trial.

Participant	Age (months)	Trial	Session 1	2	3	4	5	6	7	8
02	62	1	−	−	+	+				
		2	−	+	+	+				
		3	−	+	−	+				
		4	+	−	+	−				
		5	+	+	+	+				
		6	+	+	−	−				
		Mean	50	66.7	66.7	66.7				
										+
04	73	1	+	+	+	−	−	−	−	−
		2	−	−	−	+	+	+	−	+
		Mean	50	50	50	50	50	50	0	50

such chimpanzees may not differ substantially from peer-reared chimpanzees (although this conclusion must be strongly tempered given the extremely small sample). In addition, this work demonstrates that more diagnostic procedures for testing the attribution of mental states (e.g., Study 2) can be conducted using these participants.

Study 3: Trap Table

Next, we report two studies exploring whether human-reared chimpanzees might perform differently from peer-reared chimpanzees on tasks related to an understanding of physical causality. Study 3 tested whether they understood that an object dragged across a surface interrupted by a large open space would fall into the open space, whereas an object dragged across a smooth, uninterrupted surface would travel across the surface to within reach. The procedures of this study were carefully designed to match those used previously with our peer-reared chimpanzees (see Povinelli, 2000, Chapter 5, Experiment 3).

Method

Participants and Materials Participants 03 and 04 participated in this study.

The two rake tools and table apparatus (94 × 85 × 46 cm) depicted in Figure 3 were constructed. The table apparatus was constructed so that it had two removable surfaces (each 92 × 41 cm), allowing for surfaces with different properties to be inserted. On familiarization and standard trials, two identical, solid surfaces were used. On testing trials, one of the testing surfaces had a large, rectangular hole (10 × 30.5 cm) cut into its center, hereafter described as "the trap," through which food rewards would fall if the tool placed behind the food was pulled forward. The other testing surface possessed a painted blue rectangle of the same dimensions in the same relative position.

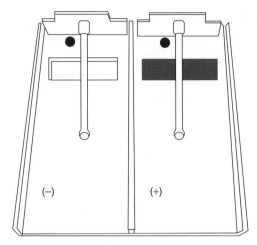

Figure 3. A depiction of the trap table apparatus used in the test trials of Study 3. (+) indicates the side of the table containing the tool that the chimpanzee must choose in order to retrieve the food reward.

Procedure Familiarization. For two sessions, the participants were released into the test arena and an experimenter demonstrated how to pull the tool so that the food reward would slide to within the chimpanzees' reach.

Criterion. Participants entered the test arena to find a tool on one side of the table with a food reward placed directly in front of it. Each side of the table was aligned with one of the response holes cut into the partition so that the participant could reach through only one hole at a time to reach a tool. The side of the table on which the tool was placed varied randomly across trials, with the constraint that the tool appeared on the left twice and on the right twice within each block of 4 trials. Participants were given one minute from the time they entered the test arena to retrieve the reward. Trials continued until the participants successfully used the tool to obtain the food reward on four consecutive trials.

Testing. Testing consisted of a single 14-trial session. Eight of these trials were standard trials and were exactly the same as criterion trials. For 03, standard trials occurred as trials 2, 4, 5, 6, 8, 9, 11, and 14. For 04, standard trials occurred as trials 1, 2, 3, 6, 8, 9, 11, and 14. The left/right location of the tool on these trials was randomized within the constraint that it occurred equally often on each side. The remaining six trials were test trials, in which one side of the table contained the trap and the other side contained the painted rectangle. The left/right location of the two surfaces was determined randomly within the constraint that each occurred equally often on both sides. Identical tools and food rewards were placed directly behind the trap and painted rectangle on each side of the table before the participants entered the test arena. The handles of the tools were positioned so that the participants could not pull both handles simultaneously. Participants were given one minute to respond from the time they entered the test unit. A choice was defined as grabbing the handle of one of the two tools. A trial was ended when the participant pulled on the tool in front of the "trap," by the trainer remotely covering the response holes and calling the participant to exit the test arena. If the participant pulled on the correct tool, the trial was ended as soon as he or she had retrieved the reward and before they could make a second choice. However, on the first test trial for both participants, they initially chose the correct tool and retrieved a reward, but subsequently pulled in the incorrect tool and saw the reward fall into the trap before the response holes were covered.

Results and Discussion

Across the familiarization and criterion phases, participants 03 and 04 received 8 and 19 trials, respectively, before reaching criterion.

In testing, both participants successfully retrieved the food reward on all standard trials (again indicating a high degree of attention and motivation). The critical data concerns their performance on the test trials, and these are presented in Table 3. Participant 03 was correct on only 2/6 (33.3%) test trials, and participant 04 was correct on 4/6 (66.7 %) test trials (binomial tests, p = ns). Neither participants' choices were the clear result of a side bias, nor was there any evidence of learning across trials.

These results again revealed rapid acquisition to the testing procedures and little in the way of differences from the peer-reared chimpanzees previously tested (Povinelli, 2000, Chapter 5, Exp. 3). Indeed, one of the peer-reared chimpanzees from the previous investigations, performed at levels exceeding chance from Trial 1 forward (see Povinelli, 2000, Chapter 5, Exp. 3). The experience of human rearing thus did not seem to engender any special skills in these animals with respect to their abilities to anticipate the consequences of pulling the food reward toward the trap.

Girndt, Meier, and Call (2008) have suggested that it is easier for apes to succeed in the trap-table problem when presented with only a single tool, which they are allowed to position themselves, rather than being asked to choose between two tools—one being positioned in front of the trap and the other not. However, their series of experiments presented various other confounds concurrently along with the manipulation of number of tools presented, and the apes accumulated experience in the task as the experiments went along so it is difficult to ascertain precisely what component of

Table 3. Trial by trial performance of participants in the test trials of Study 3. A "+" indicates a correct choice. A "−" indicates an incorrect choice.

Participant	Age (months)	Trial						Mean %
		1	2	3	4	5	6	
03	41	+	−	+	−	−	−	33.3
04	73	+	+	−	+	+	−	66.7

the task engendered success. What their experiments did show is that apes may be very limited by particular task constraints and thus, their problem-solving may not be flexible. Similarly, Seed, Call, Emery, and Clayton (2009) found that chimpanzees had greater success solving the trap-tube problem when the tool was not inserted in the tube at the onset of the problem. Thus far, our limited sample size does not suggest that enculturation confers any greater flexibility in problem-solving with regards to tool use.

Study 4: Rigid versus Flimsy Tool

Study 4 also examined the participants' understanding of physical interactions using previously developed procedures (Povinelli, 2000, Chapter 7, Experiment 9). In this experiment, they were required to reason about the affordances of two tools made out of visually similar but tactilely distinct materials. One tool was made of rigid material (wood) and the other was made of malleable (flimsy) material (rubber). Only the rigid tool could be used as a rake to drag a food reward to within reach across the surface of a table.

Method

Participants and Materials The two chimpanzees who participated in Study 3 also participated here. The table apparatus from Study 3 was also used, but exclusively with the solid surfaces from standard trials installed. Three rake-tools, with identical handles as those used in Study 3 were constructed. Two of the tools contained a wooden, rigid base (4 × 41 cm); the base of one of these tools was painted red and was used in the familiarization and criterion phases and standard trials during testing; the base of the other tool was painted grey, and was used in test trials during testing. The remaining tool was also used in test trials during testing. It was of identical dimensions as the others, but its base was constructed from a highly pliant strip of rubber. The testing tools are depicted in Figure 4.

Procedure

Familiarization. In order to familiarize them with the properties of the specific materials to be used (outside of the experimental context), the participants were given three free play sessions in the test arena (ranging from 5 to 20 minutes each) in which they interacted with the tools in the presence of the trainer. The trainer encouraged them to pick up and manipulate the tools, which they did, using their hands and mouths.

Criterion. Before the participant entered the test arena, the experimenter entered and seated herself on a crate behind the table. Once the chimpanzee entered the test arena, the experimenter held the training tool upright, and then positioned it on one side of the table with the handle of the tool placed just within reach of the chimpanzee. The side location of the tool was randomized across trials with the constraint that, within every block of four trials, the tool appeared on the left twice and on the right twice.

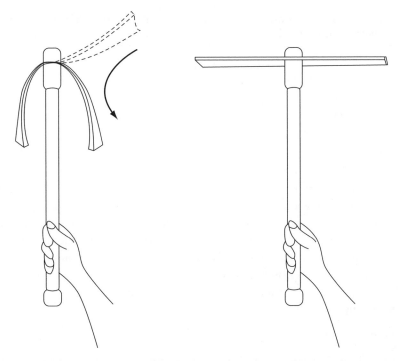

Figure 4. Tools used in test trials of testing, Study 4. The "flimsy tool" is on the left. The "rigid tool" is on the right.

The tool did not appear on the same side for more than two consecutive trials. After positioning the tool, the experimenter held up the food reward and placed it inside the left corner of the tool. She then exited the test arena. Five seconds after her exit, a transparent barrier was lowered exposing the holes in the partition through which the chimpanzee could reach to gain access to the tool. The chimpanzee was given one minute from the time the barrier was lowered to reach through the response hole aligned with the tool in order to pull it in to retrieve the food reward. Trials continued until the participants successfully received a food reward on four consecutive trials.

Testing. Testing consisted of three 6-trial sessions. Four of these trials (trials 1, 2, 4, and 6) were standard trials, and were identical to the criterion trials. The left/right location of the tool on these trials was randomized within the constraint that it appeared on the left twice and on the right twice within a session. The remaining two trials were test trials. On test trials, once the ape was in the arena and attending, the experimenter demonstrated the properties of each of the tools by holding the tool upright and tapping three times on each side of the base of each tool, before placing it on the table, always beginning with the tool on her left and demonstrating with each tool for an equivalent amount of time (three seconds). The experimenter then simultaneously placed the food rewards inside the left-hand corner of each tool, and

Table 4. Trial by trial performance of participants in the test trials of Studies 4 and 4a.
A "+" indicates a correct choice. A "−" indicates an incorrect choice.

Participant	Age(months)	Study	Trial						Mean %
			1	2	3	4	5	6	
03	41	4	+	−	+	−	−	+	50.0
04	73	4	−	+	+	+	+	+	83.3
		4a	−	+	−	+	+	+	66.7

after doing so, left the room. Following a five-second count and a signal from the video control room, the trainer then remotely opened the response holes, allowing the chimpanzee to choose a tool. A choice was defined as grabbing one of the tools. A trial ended with the barrier being raised to cover the response holes and the participant being called by the trainer, as soon as he or she pulled in the incorrect tool or pulled in the correct tool to retrieve a reward. The chimpanzees always responded before the one minute time limit expired. The left/right location of the tools on test trials was randomized across sessions within the constraint that the correct tool appeared on each side three times.

Results and Discussion

Both participants required nine trials to reach criterion and, as in the previous studies, both successfully retrieved a food reward on all standard trials during testing.

The results from the critical test trials are presented in Table 4. Participant 03 was correct on only 3/6 trials (50% correct, binomial tests, p = ns). In contrast, participant 04 made only a single mistake (5/6 or 83.3% correct, binomial tests, p = ns), which occurred on the first test trial of his first test session. It appeared that this participant either entered the study with an appreciation of the functional affordances of the tools given their distinct properties, or demonstrated single-trial learning after observing the flimsy tool fail to bring in the food reward on the first test trial. We had encountered a similarly impressive performance on this task by one of our seven peer-reared chimpanzees (see Povinelli, 2000, Chapter 7, Experiment 9). However, in follow-up tests designed to probe that chimpanzee's understanding of the affordances of the different tool materials (Povinelli, 2000, Chapter 7, Experiment 10) she performed at chance. Therefore, we decided to administer the same follow-up test (see below) to Participant 04 to further probe his understanding of the relation between the tool's properties and their affordances in this task.

Study 4a: Flimsy versus Rigid Tool Follow-Up

To explore whether Participant 04 understood that it was the rigid nature of the correct tool that assisted him in pushing a food reward forward across a smooth table surface, we constructed two tools identical to that used in Experiment 4 except that, on one side of the handle, the tool portion was constructed out of wood and, on the other side of the handle, the tool portion was constructed out of pliable rubber (i.e a "hybrid tool"). Both sides of the tools were colored grey as before. Test trials involved a choice between two of these identical tools oriented differently. If the participant understood that it was the properties of the material the tool was constructed from that either aided or impeded his performance in Experiment 4 he should correctly choose a tool that was oriented in such a way that the food reward was placed in front of the rigid portion of the tool.

Method

Participant and Materials Participant 04 was the sole participant of this study. The table apparatus used in Studies 3 and 4 was used with identical solid inserts installed. Two "hybrid" flimsy-rigid tools described above were constructed for use on test trials. The tool used in the standard trials of testing for Study 4, was used in the standard trials of this study as well.

Procedure

The participant was given a single 5-minute session of free play in the test arena with the trainer, in order to introduce him to the new "hybrid" tool to be used in testing. The experimenter manipulated both sides of the base of the tool when the participant was attending, and encouraged the participant to manipulate the tool himself. Given his performance in Study 4, a criterion phase to establish competence with the standard (rigid) tool was deemed unnecessary.

The testing procedure was identical to that of Study 4, with the following exceptions. On test trials, the two identical "hybrid" tools were used, one placed on each side of the table. A food reward was placed directly in front of the left-side base of each tool. The orientation of the tools was varied, however, so that either the flimsy, rubber side of the tool or the rigid, wooden side of the tool was in front of the food reward (see Figure 5). Thus, on each trial, there was an option of pulling a tool which could retrieve the reward (food against rigid base) versus one that could not (food against flimsy base), even though the tools were the same. The left/right location of the tool orientations were randomized within the constraint that each orientation occurred equally often on each side of the table.

Results and Discussion

The participant successfully retrieved the food reward on all standard trials during testing, suggesting the same level of motivation and interest as in Study 4. In contrast, he was correct on 4/6 (66.7%, binomial tests, p = ns) of the critical test trials. He was incorrect on the first probe trial. The data indicate an intriguing intermediate-level performance (see Table 4), but additional testing with this and other participants are clearly needed. The only previously tested peer-reared participant who succeeded on a version of the flimsy versus rigid tool task had performed at chance when presented

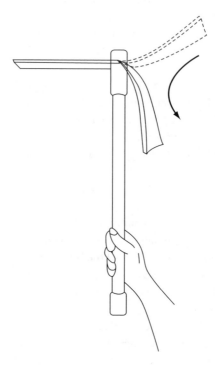

Figure 5. "Hybrid" tool used in testing trials of Study 4a. One side of the base of the tool is wooden and "rigid." The other side is rubber and "flimsy."

with the "hybrid" tool (see above). One possible explanation for both apes' performances is that they chose correctly in the initial experiment because they had some aversion to the flimsy tool, not because they appreciated the properties of the object that allowed for successful retrieval of the food reward.

Our results stand in contrast to the conclusions of Furlong, Boose, and Boysen (2008), who replicated Povinelli's experiments with a group of what they described as "enculturated" and "semi-enculturated" chimpanzees. These researchers suggested that enculturated apes succeeded in choosing the rigid rather than the floppy tool, while semi-enculturated apes showed an "intermediate" level of performance. However, they did not report first trial performance, so learning could not be ruled out. Although three of the enculturated chimpanzees were perfect on this task, the authors themselves acknowledge that only the rigid tool appeared similar to the training tool and so they may have simply continued to use the tool that they had been "primed" and reinforced for using previously. In addition, the researchers conducted a follow-up study to rule-out the use of perceptual features that differed between the tools and there was a significant drop in performance for all but one of the apes tested (Sheba). This decline in performance suggests the apes were not reasoning about the functional properties of the materials but instead were basing their choices on some visual cue linked to training. Moreover, it should be noted that the enculturated apes in the Furlong et al. studies were not only human-reared but also experienced laboratory subjects, so perhaps the combined experience with human objects and experimental testing led to their high levels of performance on this task.

Furlong et al. (2008) also conducted the hybrid tool task with mixed results. One of the enculturated apes performed perfectly on this task but none of the other apes were above 75 % correct (only 3 of 14 apes tested performed at 75%). Again it is not possible to evaluate any effects of learning based on the information presented. So, while it appears that one enculturated chimpanzee evidenced an understanding of the properties of the tool used to rake in food rewards, this result could just as easily be attributed to individual differences as to any particular rearing history.

General Discussion

These preliminary studies can provide only limited insight on the question of whether the cognitive abilities of human-reared chimpanzees might differ in some important and previously undetermined ways from those of mother or peer-reared chimpanzees. Although the studies reported here were constructed to closely approximate past research conducted on peer-reared chimpanzees in our laboratory (Povinelli, 2000; Povinelli and Eddy, 1996a; Reaux et al., 1999), the sample of apes is too small, and the breadth of procedures too narrow, to draw any firm conclusions regarding the effects of various rearing environments on chimpanzee cognitive development. Our preliminary findings do not suggest any overt differences in their approach to the tasks presented here. Future research will determine whether differences do exist in cognitive domains not yet explored, or may emerge later in development than we could ascertain within this sample.

In fact, although there are a few very interesting and suggestive experimental reports comparing the abilities of human-reared to peer-reared chimpanzees (Call et al., 2000; Call and Tomasello, 1994; Furlong et al., 2008; Tomasello et al., 1993b), and orang-utans (Call and Tomasello, 1995, 1998; Tomasello, Call, and Gluckman, 1997), those studies have always been constrained to very small sample sizes (1–9 apes from each rearing background) and have typically involved subjects from single laboratories, tested on a single task. Furthermore, the conclusions from these studies have been mixed and open to interpretation (see critique by Bering, 2004). Early support for the enculturation hypothesis rested predominantly on the finding that human-reared chimpanzees might show a superior capacity for imitation relative to their peers (Tomasello, Savage-Rumbaugh, and Kruger, 1993) and that one human-reared orang-utan demonstrated a better understanding regarding human pointing behaviors compared to one of his peers (Call and Tomasello, 1994). Importantly, the enculturated orang-utan had also undergone more explicit training to comprehend and produce such gestures (Miles, 1990). Thus, it is difficult to determine whether it is more than a different training regime that leads to the differential performances of apes with varying experimental histories. In support of this supposition, a related study by Tomasello et al. (1997) revealed that the same enculturated orang-utan responded more appropriately to human gestures he was already familiar with, but did not show a superior ability to learn novel signs relative to his non-enculturated peers (see also Call and Tomasello, 1998). He also passed certain control tasks more readily than non-enculturated orangutans and chimpanzees, but fared no better than them on the critical false belief tasks (Call and Tomasello, 1999). Call et al. (2000) concluded that enculturated apes might understand communicative intentions better than their peers but they still fail to demonstrate any appreciation of different knowledge states in other individuals. Notably, Tomasello and Call (2004) have recently come to believe that non-enculturated chimpanzees might display greater social-cognitive abilities than previously attributed to them, (although this conclusion is debatable; Povinelli and Vonk, 2003; 2004), thus diminishing their emphasis on the importance of human culture in altering the cognitive development of apes. Recently, Buttelmann and colleagues (Buttelmann, Carpenter, Call, and Tomasello, 2007) have suggested that enculturated chimpanzees can imitate rationally, implying an ability to infer the goals of the demonstrator, whereas non-enculturated apes are likely to emulate rather than imitate, further suggesting important differences in mental state attribution based on rearing histories. Obviously, any conclusions drawn from the existing data base must be tempered by its paucity.

The primary contribution of the current studies is their value as a tool to assess the feasibility of developing a large-scale, long-term project that could involve a much expanded number of participants with a greater diversity of backgrounds than have ever been tested before. The studies reported here were conducted with the goal of assessing the feasibility of undertaking such a project to investigate the cognitive development of an existing population of chimpanzees—those who are currently being, or have been, reared in human homes with human "foster parents." Based on our own preliminary surveys, we estimate that more than 150 such animals currently exist in the United States alone and, of these chimpanzees, upwards of 75 are currently residing in human households. The existence of this very special population permits comparative psychologists to envision the possibility of designing an extensive, longitudinal research program that would investigate and track the development of cognitive abilities in a large number of individual chimpanzees. These studies show that they could in principle be recruited. Also, survey instruments could be carefully developed to provide a detailed assessment of their rearing environments, their participation in a large-scale project would be invaluable. One of the benefits of any such project is that chimpanzees with various rearing histories could travel to a single test facility, allowing for direct comparison with the performances of chimpanzees from other rearing backgrounds tested in a comparable environment using highly standardized experimental procedures. In addition, testing of the chimpanzees could be carefully coordinated to provide a longitudinal assessment of the development of their cognitive abilities. Although, the task of implementing such a large-scale and long-term project is obvious, the three chimpanzees who participated in these initial studies encourage us by providing practical demonstrations of the project's feasibility. These chimpanzees adapted rapidly to the novel environment, objects, and tasks, evidencing that they could be tested on multiple, diverse, experimental tasks within the time frame of approximately one week.

If conducted properly, this project could make an invaluable contribution to the understanding of the plasticity of psychological development in both our own species and other closely related species. The types of tasks presented to the participants in this project should not be limited to those investigating their social and physical reasoning abilities, but should tap into the broadest range of domains, drawing on the expertise of a range of scholars. The results of such an extensive series of studies are unlikely to provide a uniform answer to the question of whether the cognitive capacities of another species can be molded by the human rearing experience in such a way as to fundamentally re-sculpt their cognitive architecture (in the vein of social constructivist theory), or whether fundamental changes occur only in very specific components of the cognitive system, or whether the cognitive capacities of these specially enriched chimpanzees might undergo no substantial changes at all (regardless of whether they develop an atypical skill set relative to their peers raised outside of human culture). Even glimpses of answers to such historically profound questions concerning the plasticity of development can provide insight into the identification of unique aspects of human cognition, and the degree to which such unique traits are constrained by our biological endowment, and our unique cultural practices.

References

Astington, J. (1996). What is theoretical about the child's theory of mind? A Vygotskian view of its development. In P. Carruthers and P. K. Smith (eds.) *Theories of Theories of Mind*, Cambridge UK: Cambridge University Press. pp 184–199.

Bard, K. A. and Gardner, K. H. (1996). Influences on development in infant chimpanzees: Enculturation, temperament, and cognition. In A. E. Russon, K. A. Bard, and S. T. Parker (eds.) *Reaching Into Thought: The Minds of the Great Apes*, Cambridge UK: Cambridge University Press.

Baron-Cohen, S. and Swettenham, J. (1996). The relationship between SAM and ToMM: two hypotheses. In P. Carruthers and P. K. Smith (eds.) *Theories of Theories of Mind*, Cambridge UK: Cambridge University Press, pp. 158–168.

Bering, J. M. (2004). A Critical review of the "enculturation hypothesis": The effects of human rearing on great ape social cognition. *Animal Cognition*, 7: 201–212.

Bering, J. M., Bjorklund, D. F., and Ragan, P. (2000). Deferred imitation of object-related actions in human-reared juvenile chimpanzees and orangutans. *Developmental Psychobiology*, 36: 218–232.

Bjorklund, D. F. and Pellegrini, A. D. (2002). The origins of human nature: Evolutionary developmental psychology. *American Psychological Association*, Washington, DC.

Bjorklund, D. F., Yunger, J. L., Bering, J. M., and Ragan, P. (2002). The generalization of deferred imitation in enculturated chimpanzees (Pan troglodytes). *Animal Cognition*, 5: 49–58.

Brown, J. S., Collins, A., and Duguid, S. (1989). Situated cognition and the culture of learning. *Educational Researcher*, 18: 32–42.

Buttelmann, D., Carpenter, M., Call, J., and Tomasello, M. (2007). Enculturated chimpanzees imitate rationally. *Developmental Science*, 10: F31–F38.

Call, J., Agnetta, B., and Tomasello, M. (2000). Cues that chimpanzees do and do not use to find hidden objects, *Animal Cognition*, 3: 23–34.

Call, J. and Carpenter, M. (2003). On Imitation in apes and children. *Infancia Aprendizaje*, 26: 325–349.

Call, J. and Tomasello, M. (1994). Production and comprehension of referential pointing by orangutans (Pongo pygmaeus). *Journal of Comparative Psychology*, 108: 107–117.

Call, J. and Tomasello, M. (1995). Use of social information in the problem-solving of orang-utans (*Pongo pygmaeus*) and human children (*Homo sapiens*). *Journal of Comparative Psychology*, 109: 309–320.

Call, J. and Tomasello, M. (1996). The effects of humans on the cognitive development of apes. In A. E. Russon, K. A. Bard, and S. T. Parker (eds.) *Reaching Into Thought: The Minds of the Great Apes*. Cambridge: Cambridge University Press.

Call, J. and Tomasello, M. (1998). Distinguishing intentional from accidental actions in orang-utans (*Pongo pygmaeus*), chimpanzees (*Pan troglodytes*) and humanchildren (*Homo sapiens*). *Journal of Comparative Psychology*, 112: 192–206.

Call, J. and Tomasello, M. (1999). A nonverbal false belief task: The performance of children and great apes. *Child Development*, 70: 381–395.

Carpenter, M., Tomasello, M., and Savage-Rumbaugh, S. (1995). Joint attention and imitative learning in children, chimpanzees, and enculturated chimpanzees. *Social Development*, 4: 217–237.

Donald, M. (2000). The Central rose of culture in cognitive evolution: A Reflection on the myth of the "isolated mind." In Nucci, L. P., Saxe, G. B., and Turiel, E. (eds.) *Culture, Thought and Development*. Mahwah, NJ: Erlbaum. pp. 19–38.

Fodor, J. (1986). Modularity of the mind. In Z. W. Pylyshyn, W. Demopoulos, and C. T. Westport, (eds.) *Meaning and Cognitive Structures: Issues in the omputational theory of mind*. Ablex Publishing, pp. 3–18.

Furlong, E. E., Boose, K. J., and Boysen, S. T. (2008). Raking it in: The impact of enculturation on chimpanzee tool use. *Animal Cognition*, 11: 83–97.

Gardner, B. T. and Gardner, R. A. (1971). Two-way communication with an infant chimpanzee. In A. M. Schrier and F. Stollnitz (eds.) *Behavior of Nonhuman primates*. New York, Academic Press. vol. iv, pp. 117–184.

Girndt, A., Meier, T., and Call, J. (2008). Task constraints mask great apes' ability to solve the trap-table task. *Journal of Experimental Psychology: Animal Behavior Processes*, 34: 54–62.

Gopnik, A. and Meltzoff, A. N. (1997). *Words, Thought and Theories*. Cambridge, MA: MIT Press.

Harlow, H. F. and Harlow, M. K. (1965). The affectional systems. In A. Schrier, H. Harlow, and F. Stollnitz (eds.) *Behavior of Nonhuman Primates*. New York: Academic Press. vol. ii, pp. 287–334.

Hayes, K. J. and Hayes, C. (1951). The intellectual development of a home-raised chimpanzee. *Proceedings of the American Philosophical Society*, 95: 105–109.

Jensen-Seaman, M. I., Deinard, A. S., and Kidd, K. K. (2001). Modern African ape populations as genetic and demographic models of the last common ancestor of humans, chimpanzees and gorillas. *Journal of Heredity*, 92: 474–480.

Kaminski, J., Call, J., and Tomasello, M. (2004). Body orientation and face orientation: Two factors controlling apes' begging behavior from humans. *Animal Cognition*, 7: 216–223.

Karmiloff-Smith, A. (1992). *Beyond Modularity: A Developmental Perspective on Cognitive Science*. Cambridge, MA: MIT Press.

Lave, J. and Wenger, E. (1991). *Situated Learning: Legitimate Peripheral Participation*. Cambridge UK: Cambridge University Press.

Leavens, D..A. and Hopkins, W. D. (1998). Intentional communication by chimpanzees: A Cross-sectional study of the use of referential gestures. *Developmental Psychology*, 34: 813–822.

Leslie, Alan M. (1994). ToMM, ToBy, and Agency: Core architecture and domain specificity. In Lawrence A. Hirschfeld and Susan A. Gelman (eds.) *Mapping the mind: Domain specificity in cognition and culture*. New York: Cambridge University Press, pp. 119–148.

Lewis, M. and Rosenblum, L. A. (1975). *Friendship and Peer Relations*. New York: Wiley.

Lyn, H., Russell, J. L., and Hopkins, W. D. (2010). The impact of environment on the comprehension of declarative communication in apes. *Psychological Science*, 21: 360–365.

Miles, H. L. W. (1990). The cognitive foundations for reference in a signing orangutan. In S. T. Parker and K. R. Gibson (eds.) *Language and Intelligence in Monkeys and Apes: Comparative Developmental Perspectives*. New York: Cambridge University Press, pp. 511–539.

Pennisi, E. (2002). Jumbled DNA separates chimps and humans. *Science*, 298: 719–721.

Povinelli, D. J. (1996). Chimpanzee theory of mind? The long road to strong inference. In P. Carruthers and P. Smith (eds.) *Theories of Theories of Mind*. Cambridge: Cambridge University Press, pp. 293–329.

Povinelli, D. J. (1996). Growing up ape. *Monographs for the Society of Research in Child Development*, 61 Serial # 247: 174–189.

Povinelli, D. J. (2000). *Folk Physics for Apes: The Chimpanzee's Theory of How the World Works*. Oxford: Oxford University Press [Reprinted with revisions, 2003].

Povinelli, D. J. (2004, Winter). Behind the ape's appearance: Escaping anthropocentrism in the study of other minds, *Daedalus*, 29–41.

Povinelli, D. J. and Eddy, T. (1996a). *What Young Chimpanzees Know about Seeing*. Monographs of the Society for Research in Child Development, 61, (Serial No. 247).

Povinelli, D. J. and Eddy, T. J. (1996b). Factors influencing young chimpanzees' (*Pantroglodytes*) recognition of attention. *Journal of Comparative Psychology*, 110: 336–345.

Povinelli, D. J. and Vonk, J. (2003). Chimpanzee minds: Suspiciously human? *Trends in Cognitive Science*, 7: 157–160.

Povinelli, D. J. and Vonk, J. (2004). We don't need a microscope to explore the Chimpanzee mind. *Mind and Language*, 19: 1–28.

Premack, D. (1983). The codes of man and beasts. *Behavioral and Brain Sciences*, 6: 125–167.

Reaux, J. E., Theall, L. A., and Povinelli, D. J. (1999). A longitudinal investigation of chimpanzees' understanding of visual perception. *Child Development*, 70: 275–290.

Russon, A. E. (1990). The Development of peer social interactions in infant chimpanzees: Comparative social, Piagetian, and brain perspectives. In S. T. Parker and K. R. Gibson (eds.) *Language and Intelligence in Monkeys and Apes: Comparative Developmental Perspectives*. New York: Cambridge University Press, pp. 511–539.

Russon, A. E. and Galdikas, B. M. (1993). Imitation in free-ranging rehabilitant orangutans (Pongo pygmaeus). *Journal of Comparative Psychology*, 107: 147–161.

Ruvolo, M., Pan, D., Zehr, S., Goldberg, T., Disotell, T. R., and von Dornum M. (1994). Gene trees and hominoid phylogeny. *Proceedings of the National Academy of Science*, 91 (19), 8900–8904.

Savage-Rumbaugh, E. S., McDonald, K., Sevcik, R. A., Hopkins, W. D., and Rubert, E. (1986). Spontaneous symbol acquisition and communication use by pygmy chimpanzees (Pan paniscus). *Journal of Experimental Psychology: General*, 115: 211–235.

Scholl, B. J. and Leslie, A. M. (1999). Modularity, development and "theory of mind." *Mind and Language*, 14: 131–153.

Seed, A. M., Call, J., Emery, N. J., and Clayton, N. S. (2009). Chimpanzees solve the trap problem when the confound of tool-use is removed. *Journal of Experimental Psychology: Animal Behavior Processes*, 35: 23–34.

Segal, G. (1996). The modularity of theory of mind. In P. Carruthers and P. K. Smith (eds.) *Theories of Theories of Mind*. Cambridge UK: Cambridge University Press, pp. 141–157.

Suddendorf, T. and Whiten, A. (2001). Mental evolution and development: Evidence for secondary representation in children, great apes and other animals. *Psychological Bulletin*, 127: 629–650.

Tomasello, M. (1995). Joint attention as social cognition. In C. Moore and P. Dunhman (eds.) *Joint Attention: Its Origins and Role in Development*. Hillsdale, NJ: Lawrence Erlbaum, pp. 103–130.

Tomasello, M. (1999). The human adaptation for culture. *Annual Review of Anthropology*, 28: 509–529.

Tomasello, M. (2000). Culture and cognitive development. *Current Directions in Psychological Science*, 9: 37–40.

Tomasello, M. and Call, J. (2004). The Role of humans in the cognitive development of apes revisited. *Animal Cognition*, 7: 213–215.

Tomasello, M., Call, J., and Gluckman, A. (1997). Comprehension of novel communicative signs by apes and human children. *Child Development*, 68: 1067–1080.

Tomasello, M. and Camaioni, L. (1997). A Comparison of the gestural communication of apes and human infants. *Human Development*, 40: 7–24.

Tomasello, M., Kruger, A. C., and Ratner, H. H. (1993). Cultural learning. *Behavioral and Brain Sciences*, 16: 495–552.

Tomasello, M., Savage-Rumbaugh, S., and Kruger, A. C. (1993). Imitative learning of actions on objects by children, chimpanzees, and enculturated chimpanzees. *Child Development*, 64: 1688–1705.

Vonk, J. and Povinelli, D. J. (2006). Similarity and difference in the conceptual systems of primates: The unobservability hypothesis. In E. Wasserman and T. Zentall (eds.) *Comparative Cognition: Experimental Explorations of Animal Intelligence*. Oxford: Oxford University Press, pp. 363–387.

Vygotsky, L. S. (1962). *Thought and Language*. Cambridge, MA: MIT Press.

Vygotsky, L. S. (1978). *Mind in Society: The Development of Higher Psychological Processes*. Cambridge, MA: Harvard University Press.

Whiten, A. (1993). Human enculturation, chimpanzee enculturation and the nature of imitation. Commentary on cultural learning. In M. Tomasello et al. *Behavioral and Brain Sciences*, 16: 538–539.

Appendix

Chimpanzee Rearing Environments

All three participants came from private breeders and were kept with their natural mothers until about a week before they were received by their human families (at the approximate age of 6 weeks). From this point on, they were considered members of the human family. Until roughly one-year of age, they were hand-bottle-fed, slept in cribs in the caregiver's room, and remained in the main house and outdoor yard. The chimpanzees were engaged with toys and activities that are typical of human children; for example, stuffed animals, balls, plastic interactive toys, blocks, pull-toys, mechanical toys, colors, paints, blankets, peek-a-boo-type games, books, televisions etc. At around 3-years-old, the chimpanzees began spending more time in their outdoor enclosures during the day. At night, one of the participants (03-002) maintained sleeping in the main house, while the other two resided mainly in enclosures detached from the main house. All participants wore diapers daily, and clothing frequently, ate with feeding utensils in high chairs, rode in cars and strollers, ate out in restaurants, and interacted with human children occasionally, and human adults daily. Of the three participants, two had other chimpanzees living with them from infancy, and one (03-004) was about the age of three when integrated with another chimpanzee. All animals were bathed weekly until about 4-years-old. All families had dogs and cats as part of the household.

All participants were recruited to the project through in-person interviews between the chimpanzee caregivers and the research staff. Caregivers were contacted through personal contacts and recommendations and their participation in this project was entirely voluntary.

Index

action 125
  dissociations between perception and, *see*
    perception, dissociations between action
    and
  simple theory of 222–6
Agnetta, M. 312
Allais, L. 86, 90
analysis, conceptual 8, 123, 125, 162, 209
  criticism and alternatives to 105n., 168–74
Anderson, J. R. 310, 314, 315
Anscombe, G. E. M. 121–3
appearance-reality tasks 264–5, 269–77, 299
  'standard' interpretation of 271–2, 278–9
Armstrong, D. M. 87, 239
attention
  children's sensitivity to attentional cues, *see*
    gaze; attention, joint
  children's understanding of others' 308–9,
    311–17
  joint 286, 288–9, 306–12
  non-human primates' sensitivity to attentional
    cues 306, 309–10, 345–53
  to regions of space, *see* perception, of regions
    of space
auditory field 195–9, 202–5
Austin, J. L. 110–11
Ayer, A. J. 53, 62–3

Baillargeon, R. 250, 319
Baldwin, T. 143
Berkeley, G. 2, 18–23, 30, 32, 35–8, 41–2, 47,
    69, 76
blindsight 56–8, 60–1
Block, N. 57–8
Boose, K. J. 360–1
Boysen, S. T. 360–1
Brandom, R. 113
Brewer, B. 14, 60
Burge, T. 52–6, 59, 62–3, 65–7
Butler, S. C. 309
Buttelmann, D. 362

Call, J. 222–4, 312, 343, 344, 355, 362
Campbell, J. 2–3, 4, 7, 11–15, 18–33, 61, 95,
    110, 113, 118, 212, 219n., 284
Carey S. 175–9
Carpenter, M. 294
Cassam, Q. 14, 35–7, 41–7, 49, 116–17

causal explanations 8, 110–11, 115–16, 147–8,
    174, 218–20, 224 *see also* causal reasoning;
    perception, simple theory of
causal powers as extrinsic properties 86
causal reasoning 172–4, 251 *see also* perception,
    simple theory of
causal relevance 115, 150–1, 154, 157–8, 187–9,
    199–200, 239, 241
causal structuralism 85–9
causal understanding, *see also* causation, concept
    of *and* common-sense concept of
  and concept possession 221–6, 253–4
  development 175–9, 230–2, 249, 258–61
  implicit/purely practical/limited vs. explicit/
    theoretical/reflective 216–7, 251–2, 342–3
    see also causal understanding, and concept
    possession; knowledge, children's
    understanding of perceptual access to
  and understanding of action/agency 221–6,
    254, 256–9 *see also* action, simple theory of;
    perception, dissociations between action
    and
causality, *see* causation
causation, *see also* causal reasoning, and possession
    of a concept of causation
  common-sense/naïve concept of 208–9
  concept of 7, 152, 155, 158, 173, 212, 215–7,
    220, 222–3, 225, 226, 230–2, 244, 248–9,
    253–4 *see also* causation, common-sense
    concept of *and* concept of, possession by
    children
  concept of, possession by children 253–4,
    256–62 *see also* causal understanding, and
    concept possession
  contingency based judgements about 230,
    231, 235, 245–50
  counterfactual theories of 208 *see also*
    causation, difference-making theories of
  difference-making theories of 187–8,
    210–12, 214–15, 226, 231–5, 239–50,
    254
  geometrical/mechanical theories of 187, 226,
    230–2, 234–50
  interventionist theories of 36–7, 156, 211,
    233–4, 255–6, 257 *see also* causation,
    difference-making theories of
  negative 213–14
  ontology of 145–54

causation, (*cont.*)
  operative 187–9, 200
  perception of, *see* perception, of causation
  process theories of 207, 210–15 *see also*
    causation, geometrical/mechanical
    theories of
  regularity theories of 208 *see also* causation,
    difference-making theories of
  spatial constraints on 207–8, 214–5, 224–6
  specific vs general causal concepts 121–3,
    173–4
Champion, H. 331
Child, W. 8–10, 11, 133–8, 142, 164–6, 167,
  219–20
Clements, A. W. 320
concepts, *see also* analysis, conceptual; causation,
    concept of; perception, concept of
  unanalysable 2, 173
consciousness
  access 57, 60
  and objective perceptual import 52, 59–66
  phenomenal 56–9
Croft, K. 219, 316
Csibra, G. 319

Davidson, D. 146–7, 148–51
demonstrative thought 44–5, 54, 60–1, 63,
  118–19, 132n., 182, 183
disjunctivism 3, 8, 103, 133, 139–45, 156–9
  see also perception, relational view of
Doherty, M. J. 6, 9, 310, 314, 315, 316
Dowe, P. 208n., 213, 235–6, 237, 240

Eddy, T. J. 309–10
empiricism 68
episodic recollection 182–6
experience, perceptual, *see* perception
Evans, G. 4, 26, 31, 54, 218–9, 223

Flavell, J. H. 270, 277, 287, 291, 299, 316
Furlong, E. E. 360–1

gaze
  detectability of 306
  following 286, 288–9, 291, 306–8, 311, 313,
    317
  mentalistic understanding of 309, 311, 315, 316
  understanding of 6, 309–311, 313–6, 317
Girndt, A. 355
Gomez, J. C. 308, 314
Gopnik, A. 318, 329
Graf, P. 329
Grice, H. P. 7, 10, 161–2, 168

Haberl, K. 292
Haigh, S. J. 329, 332, 333–5, 339
Hall, N. 244

Hare, B. 312
Hawthorne, J. 88–9
Heal, J. 294
Hitchcock, C. 242, 246n.
Hogrefe, G. J. 329
Hornsby, J. 115
Hume, D. 32, 121–2,139–40, 164, 233

idealism 47, 100–2
  Berkeleyan 19–20, 36
  transcendental 51, 69
intrinsic properties 83–8

justification 11–15, 41–4, 97, 110

Kant, I. 14–15, 21–3, 29, 30–1, 32n., 33,
  35, 45–7, 50, 64, 82, 83, 86–8, 90,
  192, 201–2
Keeble, S. 251–3
Kim, J. 148–9
knowledge
  children's understanding of perceptual access
    to 326–40
  of intrinsic properties 69, 82–5
  perceptual 11–16, 92–100, 103–19, 137
Kukso, B. 187–8

Langton, R. 69, 82, 83–4, 86–7, 90
Leslie, A. 236, 237, 238, 239, 251–3
Lewis, D. 75, 90–1, 239
locality, *see* causation, spatial constraints on
  definition of 207
Locke, J. 2, 69–70
looking time paradigm 251–2
'looks'-statements, uses of 265–9

Martin, C. B. 191
Martin, M. G. F. 110, 182, 192, 266n.
  269, 275
Masangkay, Z. S. 291, 297
McDowell, H. J. 60, 73, 100–1
McGuigan, N. 316
Meier, T. 355
Mellor, D. H. 152–3
Melnick, A. 203
Meltzoff, A. N. 5–6, 180–1n., 294, 297, 299
memory 125, 138, 141–2, 312 *see also* episodic
  recollection
Menzies, P. 221, 222–3
Michotte, A. E. 236, 244, 257
Mitchell, P. 331
Moll, H. 5–6, 180–1n., 292, 293, 294, 295, 297,
  299, 316
Molnar, G. 187

Nagel, T. 13
Nurmsoo, E. 333–5

objectivity, *see* objects, concepts of mind-
    independent objects; perception, simple
    theory of *and* and grasp of mind-
    independence; realism
objects 18
    as causal mechanisms 38–41
    concepts of mind-independent 3–4, 18–33,
        36, 38, 41–4
    perception of, *see* perception, of objects
occasionalism 105, 169–71
O'Neill, D. K. 292, 295, 311, 312, 313, 317–18,
    327, 336
Onishi, K. H. 319
O'Shaughnessy, B. 189, 191

Peacocke, C. 25
perception (construed, as perceptual experience
    – i.e., a perceptual link with the
    environment, which involves consciousness
    of it)
    of absence 182–91, 193–5, 198, 199–201
    causal theory of 7–11, 103–7, 139–44, 156–9,
        161–79
    of causation 229–303, 236–9, 244–50,
        254–60
    of causation by infants 177–8, 249–54
    causal conditions for 131–3, 182, 183, 185–8,
        199–201, 217–8 *see also* perception,
        enabling conditions of *and* causal theory of
    common-sense/naïve concept of 64, 110,
        161–3
    concept of 7–11, 56, 126, 129, 130, 131, 132,
        134–7, 142–3, 161–3, 163–7, 167–71, 296
        see also perception, common-sense concept
        of
    and conceptual capacities 48, 100–1
    of darkness 199–200
    development of understanding of 5–7, 9,
        174–9 *see also* attention, joint *and*
        understanding of others'; gaze, following
        and understanding of; perspective taking;
        knowledge, children's understanding of
        perceptual access to
    disjunctivist view of, *see* disjunctivism;
        perception, relational view of
    dissociations between action and 254–9
    enabling conditions of 172–3, 193, 219–20,
        226, 291–2
    of events 195–7
    and grasp of mind-independence 218 *see also*
        perception, simple theory of
    of objects 12, 93–6, 109
    passivity/receptivity of 82, 83–5, 181, 182,
        185–6, 199
    relational view of 2–3, 7–8, 11–12, 21, 26–7, 37,
        44–50, 61–4, 95, 103, 105–7, 111–12,
        163–5, 284
    representational view of 21, 23–7, 43, 48–9,
        60–1, 283–4
    of regions of space 192–5, 199–201, 202–5
    of silence 188–91, 197–8, 199–201
    sense datum theory of 53, 59–60
    simple/primitive theory of 4–5, 8–9, 11,
        218–19
    structural features of 193–5, 197–205
    of time intervals 195–201, 202–5
perceptual demonstratives, *see* demonstrative
    thought
Perner, J. 271, 278, 296, 297, 320, 329
perspective-taking 5, 264–5, 277–83, 287,
    296–300
    and join attention 286–7, 288–90, 300
    standard interpretation of 265, 278–9, 296
    and (full) understanding of perspectives
        282–3, 297–300
phenomenalism 36
Pillow, B. H. 326
pointing 289–90
Povinelli, D. J. 309–10
Price, H. 221, 222–3
primates, non human 5–6, 222–4, 225, 255,
    258–9, 287, 306, 309–10, 312, 342–63
    sensitivity to attentional cues, *see* attention,
        non-human primates' sensitivity to
        attentional cues;
    sensitivity to causal power 353–61
primitive theory of perception *see* perception,
    simple/primitive theory of

realism 15, 68–71
    common-sense 1, 47, 51, 62–5, 103
    explanatory strategy for vindicating 75
recognitional capacities 95–7, 109, 114
Reid, T. 84, 91
Repacholi, B. M. 294, 318
Rey, G. 30–1
Robinson, E. J. 329, 331, 332, 333–5, 339

Salmon, W. 207, 213, 234, 235–6,
    237, 240
Santos, L. 258
Saxe, R. 176–9
scepticism 13, 92, 97
Schlottmann, A. 237, 245–7
Scholl, B. 235, 244
secondary qualities 71–2, 91
Senju, A. 319
Shanks D. 237, 245–7
Shipstead, S. G. 291, 316
Shoemaker, S. 85–7, 88, 89–90

simple theory of perception *see* perception, simple/primitive theory of
Smith A. D. 190–1
Snowdon, P. 8–10, 142n., 103–8, 161–2, 163–4
Sorensen, R. 186–90, 200n.
Southgate, V. 319, 320
Spelke, E. S. 255, 256–7
Steward, H. 9–10, 162, 163, 165–7
Stich, S. 115
Strawson, P. F. 7, 51–6, 59, 62–7, 103–10, 137, 140–1, 157, 161, 162, 174, 208n., 217–8
Stroud, B. 12–13, 15–16, 115–6
Surian, L. 319

theory of mind 297, 314, 317–20, 343, 344
Tomasello, M. 222–4, 292, 293, 294, 312, 316, 343, 344, 362
Tye, M. 60

vision, *see* perception
visual experience, *see* perception
visual field 192–5, 202–5

Williamson, T. 112, 115, 168–9
Wimmer, H. 329
Woodward, J. 10, 156, 211n., 211–4, 215–6, 218, 222, 225–6